50% OFF
Online NYSTCE ATAS Prep Course!

By Mometrix University

Dear Customer,

We consider it an honor and a privilege that you chose our NYSTCE ATAS Study Guide. As a way of showing our appreciation and to help us better serve you, we are offering **50% off our online NYSTCE ATAS Online Course.** Many NYSTCE courses are needlessly expensive and don't deliver enough value. With our course, you get access to the best NYSTCE ATAS prep material at **half price**.

We have structured our online course to perfectly complement your printed study guide. The NYSTCE ATAS Online Course contains **in-depth lessons** that cover all the most important topics, **140+ video reviews** that explain difficult concepts, over **500 practice questions** to ensure you feel prepared, and more than **400 digital flashcards**, so you can study while you're on the go.

Online NYSTCE ATAS Prep Course

Topics Covered:
- Reading
  - Literary Analysis
  - Theme and Plot

- Writing
  - Foundations of Grammar
  - Parts of an Essay

- Mathematics
  - Numbers and Operations
  - Proportions and Ratios

- Instructional Support
  - Evaluating Student Writing
  - Learning Environments

Course Features:
- NYSTCE ATAS Study Guide
  - Get content that complements our best-selling study guide

- Full-Length Practice Tests
  - With over 500 practice questions, you can test yourself again and again.

- Mobile Friendly
  - If you need to study on the go, the course is easily accessible from your mobile device.

- NYSTCE ATAS Flashcards
  - Our course includes a flashcards mode with over 400 content cards for you to study.

To receive this discount, visit our website at mometrix.com/university/nystce-atas or simply scan this QR code with your smartphone. At the checkout page, enter the discount code: **atas50off**

If you have any questions or concerns, please contact us at universityhelp@mometrix.com.

Sincerely,

FREE Study Skills Videos/DVD Offer

Dear Customer,

Thank you for your purchase from Mometrix! We consider it an honor and a privilege that you have purchased our product and we want to ensure your satisfaction.

As a way of showing our appreciation and to help us better serve you, we have developed Study Skills Videos that we would like to give you for FREE. These videos cover our *best practices* for getting ready for your exam, from how to use our study materials to how to best prepare for the day of the test.

All that we ask is that you email us with feedback that would describe your experience so far with our product. Good, bad, or indifferent, we want to know what you think!

To get your FREE Study Skills Videos, you can use the **QR code** below, or send us an **email** at studyvideos@mometrix.com with *FREE VIDEOS* in the subject line and the following information in the body of the email:

- The name of the product you purchased.
- Your product rating on a scale of 1-5, with 5 being the highest rating.
- Your feedback. It can be long, short, or anything in between. We just want to know your impressions and experience so far with our product. (Good feedback might include how our study material met your needs and ways we might be able to make it even better. You could highlight features that you found helpful or features that you think we should add.)

If you have any questions or concerns, please don't hesitate to contact me directly.

Thanks again!

Sincerely,

Jay Willis
Vice President
jay.willis@mometrix.com
1-800-673-8175

NYSTCE

Assessment of Teaching Assistant Skills (ATAS) (095)

Secrets Study Guide

Exam Review and NYSTCE Practice Test for the New York State Teacher Certification Examinations

Copyright © 2021 by Mometrix Media LLC

All rights reserved. This product, or parts thereof, may not be reproduced, stored in a retrieval system, or transmitted in any form or by any means—electronic, mechanical, photocopy, recording, scanning, or other—except for brief quotations in critical reviews or articles, without the prior written permission of the publisher.

Written and edited by Mometrix Test Prep

Printed in the United States of America

This paper meets the requirements of ANSI/NISO Z39.48-1992 (Permanence of Paper).

Mometrix offers volume discount pricing to institutions. For more information or a price quote, please contact our sales department at sales@mometrix.com or 888-248-1219.

Mometrix Media LLC is not affiliated with or endorsed by any official testing organization. All organizational and test names are trademarks of their respective owners.

Paperback
ISBN 13: 978-1-5167-3434-4
ISBN 10: 1-5167-3434-3

Dear Future Exam Success Story

First of all, **THANK YOU** for purchasing Mometrix study materials!

Second, congratulations! You are one of the few determined test-takers who are committed to doing whatever it takes to excel on your exam. **You have come to the right place.** We developed these study materials with one goal in mind: to deliver you the information you need in a format that's concise and easy to use.

In addition to optimizing your guide for the content of the test, we've outlined our recommended steps for breaking down the preparation process into small, attainable goals so you can make sure you stay on track.

We've also analyzed the entire test-taking process, identifying the most common pitfalls and showing how you can overcome them and be ready for any curveball the test throws you.

Standardized testing is one of the biggest obstacles on your road to success, which only increases the importance of doing well in the high-pressure, high-stakes environment of test day. Your results on this test could have a significant impact on your future, and this guide provides the information and practical advice to help you achieve your full potential on test day.

Your success is our success

We would love to hear from you! If you would like to share the story of your exam success or if you have any questions or comments in regard to our products, please contact us at **800-673-8175** or **support@mometrix.com**.

Thanks again for your business and we wish you continued success!

Sincerely,
The Mometrix Test Preparation Team

Need more help? Check out our flashcards at:
http://MometrixFlashcards.com/NYSTCE

Table of Contents

Introduction 1
Secret Key #1 – Plan Big, Study Small 2
Secret Key #2 – Make Your Studying Count 3
Secret Key #3 – Practice the Right Way 4
Secret Key #4 – Pace Yourself 6
Secret Key #5 – Have a Plan for Guessing 7
Test-Taking Strategies 10
Reading 15
    Informational Texts 15
    Persuasive Techniques 19
    Arguments and Logical Errors 22
    Vocabulary and Word Relationships 24
    Figurative Language 33
    Media 36
    Reading Comprehension 41
    Interactions with Texts 47
Writing 52
    Foundations of Grammar 52
    Agreement and Sentence Structure 60
    Punctuation 77
    Common Usage Mistakes 83
    The Writing Process 86
    Outlining and Organizing Ideas 88
    Style and Form 93
    Modes of Writing 97
    Research Writing 102
    Information Sources 105
Mathematics 110
    Numbers 110
    Operations 113
    Factoring 118
    Rational Numbers 119
    Proportions and Ratios 131
    Measurement Principles 136
    Units of Measurement 138
Instructional Support 142
NYSTCE Practice Test #1 177
Answer Key and Explanations for Test #1 194

NYSTCE Practice Test #2	204
Answer Key and Explanations for Test #2	221
NYSTCE Practice Test #3	232
Answer Key and Explanations for Test #3	249
NYSTCE Practice Test #4	260
Answer Key and Explanations for Test #4	276
NYSTCE Practice Test #5	287
Answer Key and Explanations for Test #5	303
How to Overcome Test Anxiety	314
Causes of Test Anxiety	314
Elements of Test Anxiety	315
Effects of Test Anxiety	315
Physical Steps for Beating Test Anxiety	316
Mental Steps for Beating Test Anxiety	317
Study Strategy	318
Test Tips	320
Important Qualification	321
How to Overcome Your Fear of Math	322
False Beliefs	323
Math Strategies	325
Teaching Tips	327
Self-Check	328
Tell Us Your Story	329
Additional Bonus Material	330

Introduction

Thank you for purchasing this resource! You have made the choice to prepare yourself for a test that could have a huge impact on your future, and this guide is designed to help you be fully ready for test day. Obviously, it's important to have a solid understanding of the test material, but you also need to be prepared for the unique environment and stressors of the test, so that you can perform to the best of your abilities.

For this purpose, the first section that appears in this guide is the **Secret Keys**. We've devoted countless hours to meticulously researching what works and what doesn't, and we've boiled down our findings to the five most impactful steps you can take to improve your performance on the test. We start at the beginning with study planning and move through the preparation process, all the way to the testing strategies that will help you get the most out of what you know when you're finally sitting in front of the test.

We recommend that you start preparing for your test as far in advance as possible. However, if you've bought this guide as a last-minute study resource and only have a few days before your test, we recommend that you skip over the first two Secret Keys since they address a long-term study plan.

If you struggle with **test anxiety**, we strongly encourage you to check out our recommendations for how you can overcome it. Test anxiety is a formidable foe, but it can be beaten, and we want to make sure you have the tools you need to defeat it.

Secret Key #1 – Plan Big, Study Small

There's a lot riding on your performance. If you want to ace this test, you're going to need to keep your skills sharp and the material fresh in your mind. You need a plan that lets you review everything you need to know while still fitting in your schedule. We'll break this strategy down into three categories.

Information Organization

Start with the information you already have: the official test outline. From this, you can make a complete list of all the concepts you need to cover before the test. Organize these concepts into groups that can be studied together, and create a list of any related vocabulary you need to learn so you can brush up on any difficult terms. You'll want to keep this vocabulary list handy once you actually start studying since you may need to add to it along the way.

Time Management

Once you have your set of study concepts, decide how to spread them out over the time you have left before the test. Break your study plan into small, clear goals so you have a manageable task for each day and know exactly what you're doing. Then just focus on one small step at a time. When you manage your time this way, you don't need to spend hours at a time studying. Studying a small block of content for a short period each day helps you retain information better and avoid stressing over how much you have left to do. You can relax knowing that you have a plan to cover everything in time. In order for this strategy to be effective though, you have to start studying early and stick to your schedule. Avoid the exhaustion and futility that comes from last-minute cramming!

Study Environment

The environment you study in has a big impact on your learning. Studying in a coffee shop, while probably more enjoyable, is not likely to be as fruitful as studying in a quiet room. It's important to keep distractions to a minimum. You're only planning to study for a short block of time, so make the most of it. Don't pause to check your phone or get up to find a snack. It's also important to **avoid multitasking**. Research has consistently shown that multitasking will make your studying dramatically less effective. Your study area should also be comfortable and well-lit so you don't have the distraction of straining your eyes or sitting on an uncomfortable chair.

The time of day you study is also important. You want to be rested and alert. Don't wait until just before bedtime. Study when you'll be most likely to comprehend and remember. Even better, if you know what time of day your test will be, set that time aside for study. That way your brain will be used to working on that subject at that specific time and you'll have a better chance of recalling information.

Finally, it can be helpful to team up with others who are studying for the same test. Your actual studying should be done in as isolated an environment as possible, but the work of organizing the information and setting up the study plan can be divided up. In between study sessions, you can discuss with your teammates the concepts that you're all studying and quiz each other on the details. Just be sure that your teammates are as serious about the test as you are. If you find that your study time is being replaced with social time, you might need to find a new team.

Secret Key #2 – Make Your Studying Count

You're devoting a lot of time and effort to preparing for this test, so you want to be absolutely certain it will pay off. This means doing more than just reading the content and hoping you can remember it on test day. It's important to make every minute of study count. There are two main areas you can focus on to make your studying count.

Retention

It doesn't matter how much time you study if you can't remember the material. You need to make sure you are retaining the concepts. To check your retention of the information you're learning, try recalling it at later times with minimal prompting. Try carrying around flashcards and glance at one or two from time to time or ask a friend who's also studying for the test to quiz you.

To enhance your retention, look for ways to put the information into practice so that you can apply it rather than simply recalling it. If you're using the information in practical ways, it will be much easier to remember. Similarly, it helps to solidify a concept in your mind if you're not only reading it to yourself but also explaining it to someone else. Ask a friend to let you teach them about a concept you're a little shaky on (or speak aloud to an imaginary audience if necessary). As you try to summarize, define, give examples, and answer your friend's questions, you'll understand the concepts better and they will stay with you longer. Finally, step back for a big picture view and ask yourself how each piece of information fits with the whole subject. When you link the different concepts together and see them working together as a whole, it's easier to remember the individual components.

Finally, practice showing your work on any multi-step problems, even if you're just studying. Writing out each step you take to solve a problem will help solidify the process in your mind, and you'll be more likely to remember it during the test.

Modality

Modality simply refers to the means or method by which you study. Choosing a study modality that fits your own individual learning style is crucial. No two people learn best in exactly the same way, so it's important to know your strengths and use them to your advantage.

For example, if you learn best by visualization, focus on visualizing a concept in your mind and draw an image or a diagram. Try color-coding your notes, illustrating them, or creating symbols that will trigger your mind to recall a learned concept. If you learn best by hearing or discussing information, find a study partner who learns the same way or read aloud to yourself. Think about how to put the information in your own words. Imagine that you are giving a lecture on the topic and record yourself so you can listen to it later.

For any learning style, flashcards can be helpful. Organize the information so you can take advantage of spare moments to review. Underline key words or phrases. Use different colors for different categories. Mnemonic devices (such as creating a short list in which every item starts with the same letter) can also help with retention. Find what works best for you and use it to store the information in your mind most effectively and easily.

Secret Key #3 – Practice the Right Way

Your success on test day depends not only on how many hours you put into preparing, but also on whether you prepared the right way. It's good to check along the way to see if your studying is paying off. One of the most effective ways to do this is by taking practice tests to evaluate your progress. Practice tests are useful because they show exactly where you need to improve. Every time you take a practice test, pay special attention to these three groups of questions:

- The questions you got wrong
- The questions you had to guess on, even if you guessed right
- The questions you found difficult or slow to work through

This will show you exactly what your weak areas are, and where you need to devote more study time. Ask yourself why each of these questions gave you trouble. Was it because you didn't understand the material? Was it because you didn't remember the vocabulary? Do you need more repetitions on this type of question to build speed and confidence? Dig into those questions and figure out how you can strengthen your weak areas as you go back to review the material.

Additionally, many practice tests have a section explaining the answer choices. It can be tempting to read the explanation and think that you now have a good understanding of the concept. However, an explanation likely only covers part of the question's broader context. Even if the explanation makes perfect sense, **go back and investigate** every concept related to the question until you're positive you have a thorough understanding.

As you go along, keep in mind that the practice test is just that: practice. Memorizing these questions and answers will not be very helpful on the actual test because it is unlikely to have any of the same exact questions. If you only know the right answers to the sample questions, you won't be prepared for the real thing. **Study the concepts** until you understand them fully, and then you'll be able to answer any question that shows up on the test.

It's important to wait on the practice tests until you're ready. If you take a test on your first day of study, you may be overwhelmed by the amount of material covered and how much you need to learn. Work up to it gradually.

On test day, you'll need to be prepared for answering questions, managing your time, and using the test-taking strategies you've learned. It's a lot to balance, like a mental marathon that will have a big impact on your future. Like training for a marathon, you'll need to start slowly and work your way up. When test day arrives, you'll be ready.

Start with the strategies you've read in the first two Secret Keys—plan your course and study in the way that works best for you. If you have time, consider using multiple study resources to get different approaches to the same concepts. It can be helpful to see difficult concepts from more than one angle. Then find a good source for practice tests. Many times, the test website will suggest potential study resources or provide sample tests.

Practice Test Strategy

If you're able to find at least three practice tests, we recommend this strategy:

UNTIMED AND OPEN-BOOK PRACTICE

Take the first test with no time constraints and with your notes and study guide handy. Take your time and focus on applying the strategies you've learned.

TIMED AND OPEN-BOOK PRACTICE

Take the second practice test open-book as well, but set a timer and practice pacing yourself to finish in time.

TIMED AND CLOSED-BOOK PRACTICE

Take any other practice tests as if it were test day. Set a timer and put away your study materials. Sit at a table or desk in a quiet room, imagine yourself at the testing center, and answer questions as quickly and accurately as possible.

Keep repeating timed and closed-book tests on a regular basis until you run out of practice tests or it's time for the actual test. Your mind will be ready for the schedule and stress of test day, and you'll be able to focus on recalling the material you've learned.

Secret Key #4 – Pace Yourself

Once you're fully prepared for the material on the test, your biggest challenge on test day will be managing your time. Just knowing that the clock is ticking can make you panic even if you have plenty of time left. Work on pacing yourself so you can build confidence against the time constraints of the exam. Pacing is a difficult skill to master, especially in a high-pressure environment, so **practice is vital**.

Set time expectations for your pace based on how much time is available. For example, if a section has 60 questions and the time limit is 30 minutes, you know you have to average 30 seconds or less per question in order to answer them all. Although 30 seconds is the hard limit, set 25 seconds per question as your goal, so you reserve extra time to spend on harder questions. When you budget extra time for the harder questions, you no longer have any reason to stress when those questions take longer to answer.

Don't let this time expectation distract you from working through the test at a calm, steady pace, but keep it in mind so you don't spend too much time on any one question. Recognize that taking extra time on one question you don't understand may keep you from answering two that you do understand later in the test. If your time limit for a question is up and you're still not sure of the answer, mark it and move on, and come back to it later if the time and the test format allow. If the testing format doesn't allow you to return to earlier questions, just make an educated guess; then put it out of your mind and move on.

On the easier questions, be careful not to rush. It may seem wise to hurry through them so you have more time for the challenging ones, but it's not worth missing one if you know the concept and just didn't take the time to read the question fully. Work efficiently but make sure you understand the question and have looked at all of the answer choices, since more than one may seem right at first.

Even if you're paying attention to the time, you may find yourself a little behind at some point. You should speed up to get back on track, but do so wisely. Don't panic; just take a few seconds less on each question until you're caught up. Don't guess without thinking, but do look through the answer choices and eliminate any you know are wrong. If you can get down to two choices, it is often worthwhile to guess from those. Once you've chosen an answer, move on and don't dwell on any that you skipped or had to hurry through. If a question was taking too long, chances are it was one of the harder ones, so you weren't as likely to get it right anyway.

On the other hand, if you find yourself getting ahead of schedule, it may be beneficial to slow down a little. The more quickly you work, the more likely you are to make a careless mistake that will affect your score. You've budgeted time for each question, so don't be afraid to spend that time. Practice an efficient but careful pace to get the most out of the time you have.

Secret Key #5 – Have a Plan for Guessing

When you're taking the test, you may find yourself stuck on a question. Some of the answer choices seem better than others, but you don't see the one answer choice that is obviously correct. What do you do?

The scenario described above is very common, yet most test takers have not effectively prepared for it. Developing and practicing a plan for guessing may be one of the single most effective uses of your time as you get ready for the exam.

In developing your plan for guessing, there are three questions to address:

- When should you start the guessing process?
- How should you narrow down the choices?
- Which answer should you choose?

When to Start the Guessing Process

Unless your plan for guessing is to select C every time (which, despite its merits, is not what we recommend), you need to leave yourself enough time to apply your answer elimination strategies. Since you have a limited amount of time for each question, that means that if you're going to give yourself the best shot at guessing correctly, you have to decide quickly whether or not you will guess.

Of course, the best-case scenario is that you don't have to guess at all, so first, see if you can answer the question based on your knowledge of the subject and basic reasoning skills. Focus on the key words in the question and try to jog your memory of related topics. Give yourself a chance to bring the knowledge to mind, but once you realize that you don't have (or you can't access) the knowledge you need to answer the question, it's time to start the guessing process.

It's almost always better to start the guessing process too early than too late. It only takes a few seconds to remember something and answer the question from knowledge. Carefully eliminating wrong answer choices takes longer. Plus, going through the process of eliminating answer choices can actually help jog your memory.

Summary: Start the guessing process as soon as you decide that you can't answer the question based on your knowledge.

How to Narrow Down the Choices

The next chapter in this book (**Test-Taking Strategies**) includes a wide range of strategies for how to approach questions and how to look for answer choices to eliminate. You will definitely want to read those carefully, practice them, and figure out which ones work best for you. Here though, we're going to address a mindset rather than a particular strategy.

Your odds of guessing an answer correctly depend on how many options you are choosing from.

Number of options left	5	4	3	2	1
Odds of guessing correctly	20%	25%	33%	50%	100%

You can see from this chart just how valuable it is to be able to eliminate incorrect answers and make an educated guess, but there are two things that many test takers do that cause them to miss out on the benefits of guessing:

- Accidentally eliminating the correct answer
- Selecting an answer based on an impression

We'll look at the first one here, and the second one in the next section.

To avoid accidentally eliminating the correct answer, we recommend a thought exercise called **the $5 challenge**. In this challenge, you only eliminate an answer choice from contention if you are willing to bet $5 on it being wrong. Why $5? Five dollars is a small but not insignificant amount of money. It's an amount you could afford to lose but wouldn't want to throw away. And while losing

$5 once might not hurt too much, doing it twenty times will set you back $100. In the same way, each small decision you make—eliminating a choice here, guessing on a question there—won't by itself impact your score very much, but when you put them all together, they can make a big difference. By holding each answer choice elimination decision to a higher standard, you can reduce the risk of accidentally eliminating the correct answer.

The $5 challenge can also be applied in a positive sense: If you are willing to bet $5 that an answer choice *is* correct, go ahead and mark it as correct.

Summary: Only eliminate an answer choice if you are willing to bet $5 that it is wrong.

Which Answer to Choose

You're taking the test. You've run into a hard question and decided you'll have to guess. You've eliminated all the answer choices you're willing to bet $5 on. Now you have to pick an answer. Why do we even need to talk about this? Why can't you just pick whichever one you feel like when the time comes?

The answer to these questions is that if you don't come into the test with a plan, you'll rely on your impression to select an answer choice, and if you do that, you risk falling into a trap. The test writers know that everyone who takes their test will be guessing on some of the questions, so they intentionally write wrong answer choices to seem plausible. You still have to pick an answer though, and if the wrong answer choices are designed to look right, how can you ever be sure that you're not falling for their trap? The best solution we've found to this dilemma is to take the decision out of your hands entirely. Here is the process we recommend:

Once you've eliminated any choices that you are confident (willing to bet $5) are wrong, select the first remaining choice as your answer.

Whether you choose to select the first remaining choice, the second, or the last, the important thing is that you use some preselected standard. Using this approach guarantees that you will not be enticed into selecting an answer choice that looks right, because you are not basing your decision on how the answer choices look.

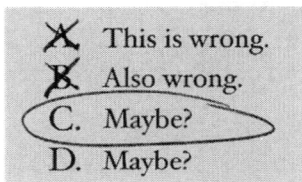

This is not meant to make you question your knowledge. Instead, it is to help you recognize the difference between your knowledge and your impressions. There's a huge difference between thinking an answer is right because of what you know, and thinking an answer is right because it looks or sounds like it should be right.

Summary: To ensure that your selection is appropriately random, make a predetermined selection from among all answer choices you have not eliminated.

Test-Taking Strategies

This section contains a list of test-taking strategies that you may find helpful as you work through the test. By taking what you know and applying logical thought, you can maximize your chances of answering any question correctly!

It is very important to realize that every question is different and every person is different: no single strategy will work on every question, and no single strategy will work for every person. That's why we've included all of them here, so you can try them out and determine which ones work best for different types of questions and which ones work best for you.

Question Strategies

⊘ READ CAREFULLY

Read the question and the answer choices carefully. Don't miss the question because you misread the terms. You have plenty of time to read each question thoroughly and make sure you understand what is being asked. Yet a happy medium must be attained, so don't waste too much time. You must read carefully and efficiently.

⊘ CONTEXTUAL CLUES

Look for contextual clues. If the question includes a word you are not familiar with, look at the immediate context for some indication of what the word might mean. Contextual clues can often give you all the information you need to decipher the meaning of an unfamiliar word. Even if you can't determine the meaning, you may be able to narrow down the possibilities enough to make a solid guess at the answer to the question.

⊘ PREFIXES

If you're having trouble with a word in the question or answer choices, try dissecting it. Take advantage of every clue that the word might include. Prefixes and suffixes can be a huge help. Usually, they allow you to determine a basic meaning. *Pre-* means before, *post-* means after, *pro-* is positive, *de-* is negative. From prefixes and suffixes, you can get an idea of the general meaning of the word and try to put it into context.

⊘ HEDGE WORDS

Watch out for critical hedge words, such as *likely, may, can, sometimes, often, almost, mostly, usually, generally, rarely*, and *sometimes*. Question writers insert these hedge phrases to cover every possibility. Often an answer choice will be wrong simply because it leaves no room for exception. Be on guard for answer choices that have definitive words such as *exactly* and *always*.

⊘ SWITCHBACK WORDS

Stay alert for *switchbacks*. These are the words and phrases frequently used to alert you to shifts in thought. The most common switchback words are *but, although*, and *however*. Others include *nevertheless, on the other hand, even though, while, in spite of, despite*, and *regardless of*. Switchback words are important to catch because they can change the direction of the question or an answer choice.

⊘ Face Value

When in doubt, use common sense. Accept the situation in the problem at face value. Don't read too much into it. These problems will not require you to make wild assumptions. If you have to go beyond creativity and warp time or space in order to have an answer choice fit the question, then you should move on and consider the other answer choices. These are normal problems rooted in reality. The applicable relationship or explanation may not be readily apparent, but it is there for you to figure out. Use your common sense to interpret anything that isn't clear.

Answer Choice Strategies

⊘ Answer Selection

The most thorough way to pick an answer choice is to identify and eliminate wrong answers until only one is left, then confirm it is the correct answer. Sometimes an answer choice may immediately seem right, but be careful. The test writers will usually put more than one reasonable answer choice on each question, so take a second to read all of them and make sure that the other choices are not equally obvious. As long as you have time left, it is better to read every answer choice than to pick the first one that looks right without checking the others.

⊘ Answer Choice Families

An answer choice family consists of two (in rare cases, three) answer choices that are very similar in construction and cannot all be true at the same time. If you see two answer choices that are direct opposites or parallels, one of them is usually the correct answer. For instance, if one answer choice says that quantity x increases and another either says that quantity x decreases (opposite) or says that quantity y increases (parallel), then those answer choices would fall into the same family. An answer choice that doesn't match the construction of the answer choice family is more likely to be incorrect. Most questions will not have answer choice families, but when they do appear, you should be prepared to recognize them.

⊘ Eliminate Answers

Eliminate answer choices as soon as you realize they are wrong, but make sure you consider all possibilities. If you are eliminating answer choices and realize that the last one you are left with is also wrong, don't panic. Start over and consider each choice again. There may be something you missed the first time that you will realize on the second pass.

⊘ Avoid Fact Traps

Don't be distracted by an answer choice that is factually true but doesn't answer the question. You are looking for the choice that answers the question. Stay focused on what the question is asking for so you don't accidentally pick an answer that is true but incorrect. Always go back to the question and make sure the answer choice you've selected actually answers the question and is not merely a true statement.

⊘ Extreme Statements

In general, you should avoid answers that put forth extreme actions as standard practice or proclaim controversial ideas as established fact. An answer choice that states the "process should be used in certain situations, if..." is much more likely to be correct than one that states the "process should be discontinued completely." The first is a calm rational statement and doesn't even make a definitive, uncompromising stance, using a hedge word *if* to provide wiggle room, whereas the second choice is far more extreme.

⊘ Benchmark

As you read through the answer choices and you come across one that seems to answer the question well, mentally select that answer choice. This is not your final answer, but it's the one that will help you evaluate the other answer choices. The one that you selected is your benchmark or standard for judging each of the other answer choices. Every other answer choice must be compared to your benchmark. That choice is correct until proven otherwise by another answer choice beating it. If you find a better answer, then that one becomes your new benchmark. Once you've decided that no other choice answers the question as well as your benchmark, you have your final answer.

⊘ Predict the Answer

Before you even start looking at the answer choices, it is often best to try to predict the answer. When you come up with the answer on your own, it is easier to avoid distractions and traps because you will know exactly what to look for. The right answer choice is unlikely to be word-for-word what you came up with, but it should be a close match. Even if you are confident that you have the right answer, you should still take the time to read each option before moving on.

General Strategies

⊘ Tough Questions

If you are stumped on a problem or it appears too hard or too difficult, don't waste time. Move on! Remember though, if you can quickly check for obviously incorrect answer choices, your chances of guessing correctly are greatly improved. Before you completely give up, at least try to knock out a couple of possible answers. Eliminate what you can and then guess at the remaining answer choices before moving on.

⊘ Check Your Work

Since you will probably not know every term listed and the answer to every question, it is important that you get credit for the ones that you do know. Don't miss any questions through careless mistakes. If at all possible, try to take a second to look back over your answer selection and make sure you've selected the correct answer choice and haven't made a costly careless mistake (such as marking an answer choice that you didn't mean to mark). This quick double check should more than pay for itself in caught mistakes for the time it costs.

⊘ Pace Yourself

It's easy to be overwhelmed when you're looking at a page full of questions; your mind is confused and full of random thoughts, and the clock is ticking down faster than you would like. Calm down and maintain the pace that you have set for yourself. Especially as you get down to the last few minutes of the test, don't let the small numbers on the clock make you panic. As long as you are on track by monitoring your pace, you are guaranteed to have time for each question.

⊘ Don't Rush

It is very easy to make errors when you are in a hurry. Maintaining a fast pace in answering questions is pointless if it makes you miss questions that you would have gotten right otherwise. Test writers like to include distracting information and wrong answers that seem right. Taking a little extra time to avoid careless mistakes can make all the difference in your test score. Find a pace that allows you to be confident in the answers that you select.

ⓧ Keep Moving

Panicking will not help you pass the test, so do your best to stay calm and keep moving. Taking deep breaths and going through the answer elimination steps you practiced can help to break through a stress barrier and keep your pace.

Final Notes

The combination of a solid foundation of content knowledge and the confidence that comes from practicing your plan for applying that knowledge is the key to maximizing your performance on test day. As your foundation of content knowledge is built up and strengthened, you'll find that the strategies included in this chapter become more and more effective in helping you quickly sift through the distractions and traps of the test to isolate the correct answer.

Now that you're preparing to move forward into the test content chapters of this book, be sure to keep your goal in mind. As you read, think about how you will be able to apply this information on the test. If you've already seen sample questions for the test and you have an idea of the question format and style, try to come up with questions of your own that you can answer based on what you're reading. This will give you valuable practice applying your knowledge in the same ways you can expect to on test day.

Good luck and good studying!

Reading

Informational Texts

TEXT FEATURES IN INFORMATIONAL TEXTS

The **title of a text** gives readers some idea of its content. The **table of contents** is a list near the beginning of a text, showing the book's sections and chapters and their coinciding page numbers. This gives readers an overview of the whole text and helps them find specific chapters easily. An **appendix**, at the back of the book or document, includes important information that is not present in the main text. Also at the back, an **index** lists the book's important topics alphabetically with their page numbers to help readers find them easily. **Glossaries**, usually found at the backs of books, list technical terms alphabetically with their definitions to aid vocabulary learning and comprehension. Boldface print is used to emphasize certain words, often identifying words included in the text's glossary where readers can look up their definitions. **Headings** separate sections of text and show the topic of each. **Subheadings** divide subject headings into smaller, more specific categories to help readers organize information. **Footnotes**, at the bottom of the page, give readers more information, such as citations or links. **Bullet points** list items separately, making facts and ideas easier to see and understand. A **sidebar** is a box of information to one side of the main text giving additional information, often on a more focused or in-depth example of a topic.

Illustrations and **photographs** are pictures that visually emphasize important points in text. The captions below the illustrations explain what those images show. Charts and tables are visual forms of information that make something easier to understand quickly. Diagrams are drawings that show relationships or explain a process. Graphs visually show the relationships among multiple sets of information plotted along vertical and horizontal axes. Maps show geographical information visually to help readers understand the relative locations of places covered in the text. Timelines are visual graphics that show historical events in chronological order to help readers see their sequence.

> **Review Video: Informative Text**
> Visit mometrix.com/academy and enter code: 924964

LANGUAGE USE

LITERAL AND FIGURATIVE LANGUAGE

As in fictional literature, informational text also uses both **literal language**, which means just what it says, and **figurative language**, which imparts more than literal meaning. For example, an informational text author might use a simile or direct comparison, such as writing that a racehorse "ran like the wind." Informational text authors also use metaphors or implied comparisons, such as "the cloud of the Great Depression." Imagery may also appear in informational texts to increase the reader's understanding of ideas and concepts discussed in the text.

> **Review Video: Figurative Language**
> Visit mometrix.com/academy and enter code: 584902

EXPLICIT AND IMPLICIT INFORMATION

When informational text states something explicitly, the reader is told by the author exactly what is meant, which can include the author's interpretation or perspective of events. For example, a professor writes, "I have seen students go into an absolute panic just because they weren't able to

complete the exam in the time they were allotted." This explicitly tells the reader that the students were afraid, and by using the words "just because," the writer indicates their fear was exaggerated out of proportion relative to what happened. However, another professor writes, "I have had students come to me, their faces drained of all color, saying 'We weren't able to finish the exam.'" This is an example of implicit meaning: the second writer did not state explicitly that the students were panicked. Instead, he wrote a description of their faces being "drained of all color." From this description, the reader can infer that the students were so frightened that their faces paled.

> **Review Video: Explicit and Implicit Information**
> Visit mometrix.com/academy and enter code: 735771

TECHNICAL LANGUAGE

Technical language is more impersonal than literary and vernacular language. Passive voice makes the tone impersonal. For example, instead of writing, "We found this a central component of protein metabolism," scientists write, "This was found a central component of protein metabolism." While science professors have traditionally instructed students to avoid active voice because it leads to first-person ("I" and "we") usage, science editors today find passive voice dull and weak. Many journal articles combine both. Tone in technical science writing should be detached, concise, and professional. While one may normally write, "This chemical has to be available for proteins to be digested," professionals write technically, "The presence of this chemical is required for the enzyme to break the covalent bonds of proteins." The use of technical language appeals to both technical and non-technical audiences by displaying the author or speaker's understanding of the subject and suggesting their credibility regarding the message they are communicating.

TECHNICAL MATERIAL FOR NON-TECHNICAL READERS

Writing about **technical subjects** for **non-technical readers** differs from writing for colleagues because authors place more importance on delivering a critical message than on imparting the maximum technical content possible. Technical authors also must assume that non-technical audiences do not have the expertise to comprehend extremely scientific or technical messages, concepts, and terminology. They must resist the temptation to impress audiences with their scientific knowledge and expertise and remember that their primary purpose is to communicate a message that non-technical readers will understand, feel, and respond to. Non-technical and technical styles include similarities. Both should formally cite any references or other authors' work utilized in the text. Both must follow intellectual property and copyright regulations. This includes the author's protecting his or her own rights, or a public domain statement, as he or she chooses.

NON-TECHNICAL AUDIENCES

Writers of technical or scientific material may need to write for many non-technical audiences. Some readers have no technical or scientific background, and those who do may not be in the same field as the authors. Government and corporate policymakers and budget managers need technical information they can understand for decision-making. Citizens affected by technology or science are a different audience. Non-governmental organizations can encompass many of the preceding groups. Elementary and secondary school programs also need non-technical language for presenting technical subject matter. Additionally, technical authors will need to use non-technical language when collecting consumer responses to surveys, presenting scientific or para-scientific material to the public, writing about the history of science, and writing about science and technology in developing countries.

Use of Everyday Language

Authors of technical information sometimes must write using non-technical language that readers outside their disciplinary fields can comprehend. They should use not only non-technical terms, but also normal, everyday language to accommodate readers whose native language is different than the language the text is written in. For example, instead of writing that "eustatic changes like thermal expansion are causing hazardous conditions in the littoral zone," an author would do better to write that "a rising sea level is threatening the coast." When technical terms cannot be avoided, authors should also define or explain them using non-technical language. Although authors must cite references and acknowledge their use of others' work, they should avoid the kinds of references or citations that they would use in scientific journals—unless they reinforce author messages. They should not use endnotes, footnotes, or any other complicated referential techniques because non-technical journal publishers usually do not accept them. Including high-resolution illustrations, photos, maps, or satellite images and incorporating multimedia into digital publications will enhance non-technical writing about technical subjects. Technical authors may publish using non-technical language in e-journals, trade journals, specialty newsletters, and daily newspapers.

Making Inferences About Informational Text

With informational text, reader comprehension depends not only on recalling important statements and details, but also on reader inferences based on examples and details. Readers add information from the text to what they already know to draw inferences about the text. These inferences help the readers to fill in the information that the text does not explicitly state, enabling them to understand the text better. When reading a nonfictional autobiography or biography, for example, the most appropriate inferences might concern the events in the book, the actions of the subject of the autobiography or biography, and the message the author means to convey. When reading a nonfictional expository (informational) text, the reader would best draw inferences about problems and their solutions, and causes and their effects. When reading a nonfictional persuasive text, the reader will want to infer ideas supporting the author's message and intent.

Structures or Organizational Patterns in Informational Texts

Informational text can be **descriptive**, appealing to the five senses and answering the questions what, who, when, where, and why. Another method of structuring informational text is sequence and order. **Chronological** texts relate events in the sequence that they occurred, from start to finish, while how-to texts organize information into a series of instructions in the sequence in which the steps should be followed. **Comparison-contrast** structures of informational text describe various ideas to their readers by pointing out how things or ideas are similar and how they are different. **Cause and effect** structures of informational text describe events that occurred and identify the causes or reasons that those events occurred. **Problem and solution** structures of informational texts introduce and describe problems and offer one or more solutions for each problem described.

> **Review Video: Organizational Methods to Structure Text**
> Visit mometrix.com/academy and enter code: 606263

Determining an Informational Author's Purpose

Informational authors' purposes are why they write texts. Readers must determine authors' motivations and goals. Readers gain greater insight into a text by considering the author's motivation. This develops critical reading skills. Readers perceive writing as a person's voice, not simply printed words. Uncovering author motivations and purposes empowers readers to know what to expect from the text, read for relevant details, evaluate authors and their work critically, and respond effectively to the motivations and persuasions of the text. The main idea of a text is what the reader is supposed to understand from reading it; the purpose of the text is why the author has written it and what the author wants readers to do with its information. Authors state some purposes clearly, while other purposes may be unstated but equally significant. When stated purposes contradict other parts of a text, the author may have a hidden agenda. Readers can better evaluate a text's effectiveness, whether they agree or disagree with it, and why they agree or disagree through identifying unstated author purposes.

IDENTIFYING AUTHOR'S POINT OF VIEW OR PURPOSE

In some informational texts, readers find it easy to identify the author's point of view and purpose, such as when the author explicitly states his or her position and reason for writing. But other texts are more difficult, either because of the content or because the authors give neutral or balanced viewpoints. This is particularly true in scientific texts, in which authors may state the purpose of their research in the report, but never state their point of view except by interpreting evidence or data.

To analyze text and identify point of view or purpose, readers should ask themselves the following four questions:

1. With what main point or idea does this author want to persuade readers to agree?
2. How does this author's word choice affect the way that readers consider this subject?
3. How do this author's choices of examples and facts affect the way that readers consider this subject?
4. What is it that this author wants to accomplish by writing this text?

> **Review Video: Purpose**
> Visit mometrix.com/academy and enter code: 511819

EVALUATING ARGUMENTS MADE BY INFORMATIONAL TEXT WRITERS

When evaluating an informational text, the first step is to identify the argument's conclusion. Then identify the author's premises that support the conclusion. Try to paraphrase premises for clarification and make the conclusion and premises fit. List all premises first, sequentially numbered, then finish with the conclusion. Identify any premises or assumptions not stated by the author but required for the stated premises to support the conclusion. Read word assumptions sympathetically, as the author might. Evaluate whether premises reasonably support the conclusion. For inductive reasoning, the reader should ask if the premises are true, if they support the conclusion, and if so, how strongly. For deductive reasoning, the reader should ask if the argument is valid or invalid. If all premises are true, then the argument is valid unless the conclusion can be false. If it can, then the argument is invalid. An invalid argument can be made valid through alterations such as the addition of needed premises.

USE OF RHETORIC IN INFORMATIONAL TEXTS

There are many ways authors can support their claims, arguments, beliefs, ideas, and reasons for writing in informational texts. For example, authors can appeal to readers' sense of **logic** by communicating their reasoning through a carefully sequenced series of logical steps to help "prove" the points made. Authors can appeal to readers' **emotions** by using descriptions and words that evoke feelings of sympathy, sadness, anger, righteous indignation, hope, happiness, or any other emotion to reinforce what they express and share with their audience. Authors may appeal to the **moral** or **ethical values** of readers by using words and descriptions that can convince readers that something is right or wrong. By relating personal anecdotes, authors can supply readers with more accessible, realistic examples of points they make, as well as appealing to their emotions. They can provide supporting evidence by reporting case studies. They can also illustrate their points by making analogies to which readers can better relate.

Persuasive Techniques

PERSUASIVE TECHNIQUES

To **appeal using reason**, writers present logical arguments, such as using "If... then... because" statements. To **appeal to emotions**, authors may ask readers how they would feel about something or to put themselves in another's place, present their argument as one that will make the audience feel good, or tell readers how they should feel. To **appeal to character**, **morality**, or **ethics**, authors present their points to readers as the right or most moral choices. Authors cite expert opinions to show readers that someone very knowledgeable about the subject or viewpoint agrees with the author's claims. **Testimonials**, usually via anecdotes or quotations regarding the author's subject, help build the audience's trust in an author's message through positive support from ordinary people. **Bandwagon appeals** claim that everybody else agrees with the author's argument and persuade readers to conform and agree, also. Authors **appeal to greed** by presenting their choice as cheaper, free, or more valuable for less cost. They **appeal to laziness** by presenting their views as more convenient, easy, or relaxing. Authors also anticipate potential objections and argue against them before audiences think of them, thereby depicting those objections as weak.

Authors can use **comparisons** like analogies, similes, and metaphors to persuade audiences. For example, a writer might represent excessive expenses as "hemorrhaging" money, which the author's recommended solution will stop. Authors can use negative word connotations to make some choices unappealing to readers, and positive word connotations to make others more appealing. Using **humor** can relax readers and garner their agreement. However, writers must take care: ridiculing opponents can be a successful strategy for appealing to readers who already agree with the author, but can backfire by angering other readers. **Rhetorical questions** need no answer, but create effect that can force agreement, such as asking the question, "Wouldn't you rather be paid more than less?" **Generalizations** persuade readers by being impossible to disagree with. Writers can easily make generalizations that appear to support their viewpoints, like saying, "We all want peace, not war" regarding more specific political arguments. **Transfer** and **association** persuade by example: if advertisements show attractive actors enjoying their products, audiences imagine they will experience the same. **Repetition** can also sometimes effectively persuade audiences.

> **Review Video: Using Rhetorical Strategies for Persuasion**
> Visit mometrix.com/academy and enter code: 302658

CLASSICAL AUTHOR APPEALS

In his *On Rhetoric,* ancient Greek philosopher Aristotle defined three basic types of appeal used in writing, which he called *pathos*, *ethos*, and *logos*. **Pathos** means suffering or experience and refers to appeals to the emotions (the English word *pathetic* comes from this root). Writing that is meant to entertain audiences, by making them either happy, as with comedy, or sad, as with tragedy, uses *pathos*. Aristotle's *Poetics* states that evoking the emotions of terror and pity is one of the criteria for writing tragedy. **Ethos** means character and connotes ideology (the English word *ethics* comes from this root). Writing that appeals to credibility, based on academic, professional, or personal merit, uses *ethos*. **Logos** means "I say" and refers to a plea, opinion, expectation, word or speech, account, opinion, or reason (the English word *logic* comes from this root.) Aristotle used it to mean persuasion that appeals to the audience through reasoning and logic to influence their opinions.

CRITICAL EVALUATION OF EFFECTIVENESS OF PERSUASIVE METHODS

First, readers should identify the author's **thesis**—what he or she argues for or against. They should consider the argument's content and the author's reason for presenting it. Does the author offer **solutions** to problems raised? If so, are they realistic? Note all central ideas and evidence supporting the author's thesis. Research any unfamiliar subjects or vocabulary. Readers should then outline or summarize the work in their own words. Identify which types of appeals the author uses. Readers should evaluate how well the author communicated meaning from the reader's perspective: Did they respond to emotional appeals with anger, concern, happiness, etc.? If so, why? Decide if the author's reasoning sufficed for changing the reader's mind. Determine whether the content and presentation were accurate, cohesive, and clear. Readers should also ask themselves whether they found the author believable or not, and why or why not.

EVALUATING AN ARGUMENT

Argumentative and persuasive passages take a stand on a debatable issue, seek to explore all sides of the issue, and find the best possible solution. Argumentative and persuasive passages should not be combative or abusive. The word *argument* may remind you of two or more people shouting at each other and walking away in anger. However, an argumentative or persuasive passage should be a calm and reasonable presentation of an author's ideas for others to consider. When an author writes reasonable arguments, his or her goal is not to win or have the last word. Instead, authors want to reveal current understanding of the question at hand and suggest a solution to a problem. The purpose of argument and persuasion in a free society is to reach the best solution.

EVIDENCE

The term **text evidence** refers to information that supports a main point or minor points and can help lead the reader to a conclusion about the text's credibility. Information used as text evidence is precise, descriptive, and factual. A main point is often followed by supporting details that provide evidence to back up a claim. For example, a passage may include the claim that winter occurs during opposite months in the Northern and Southern hemispheres. Text evidence for this claim may include examples of countries where winter occurs in opposite months. Stating that the tilt of the Earth as it rotates around the sun causes winter to occur at different times in separate hemispheres is another example of text evidence. Text evidence can come from common knowledge, but it is also valuable to include text evidence from credible, relevant outside sources.

> **Review Video: Text Evidence**
> Visit mometrix.com/academy and enter code: 486236

Evidence that supports the thesis and additional arguments needs to be provided. Most arguments must be supported by facts or statistics. A fact is something that is known with certainty, has been verified by several independent individuals, and can be proven to be true. In addition to facts, examples and illustrations can support an argument by adding an emotional component. With this component, you persuade readers in ways that facts and statistics cannot. The emotional component is effective when used alongside objective information that can be confirmed.

CREDIBILITY

The text used to support an argument can be the argument's downfall if the text is not credible. A text is **credible**, or believable, when its author is knowledgeable and objective, or unbiased. The author's motivations for writing the text play a critical role in determining the credibility of the text and must be evaluated when assessing that credibility. Reports written about the ozone layer by an environmental scientist and a hairdresser will have a different level of credibility.

> **Review Video: Credible**
> Visit mometrix.com/academy and enter code: 827257

APPEAL TO EMOTION

Sometimes, authors will appeal to the reader's emotion in an attempt to persuade or to distract the reader from the weakness of the argument. For instance, the author may try to inspire the pity of the reader by delivering a heart-rending story. An author also might use the bandwagon approach, in which he suggests that his opinion is correct because it is held by the majority. Some authors resort to name-calling, in which insults and harsh words are delivered to the opponent in an attempt to distract. In advertising, a common appeal is the celebrity testimonial, in which a famous person endorses a product. Of course, the fact that a famous person likes something should not really mean anything to the reader. These and other emotional appeals are usually evidence of poor reasoning and a weak argument.

COUNTER ARGUMENTS

When authors give both sides to the argument, they build trust with their readers. As a reader, you should start with an undecided or neutral position. If an author presents only his or her side to the argument, then they are not exhibiting credibility and are weakening their argument.

Building common ground with readers can be effective for persuading neutral, skeptical, or opposed readers. Sharing values with undecided readers can allow people to switch positions without giving up what they feel is important. People who may oppose a position need to feel that they can change their minds without betraying who they are as a person. This appeal to having an open mind can be a powerful tool in arguing a position without antagonizing other views. Objections can be countered on a point-by-point basis or in a summary paragraph. Be mindful of how an author points out flaws in counter arguments. If they are unfair to the other side of the argument, then you should lose trust with the author.

RHETORICAL DEVICES

- An **anecdote** is a brief story authors may relate to their argument, which can illustrate their points in a more real and relatable way.
- **Aphorisms** concisely state common beliefs and may rhyme. For example, Benjamin Franklin's "Early to bed and early to rise / Makes a man healthy, wealthy, and wise" is an aphorism.
- **Allusions** refer to literary or historical figures to impart symbolism to a thing or person and to create reader resonance. In John Steinbeck's *Of Mice and Men*, protagonist George's last name is Milton. This alludes to John Milton, who wrote *Paradise Lost*, and symbolizes George's eventual loss of his dream.
- **Satire** exaggerates, ridicules, or pokes fun at human flaws or ideas, as in the works of Jonathan Swift and Mark Twain.
- A **parody** is a form of satire that imitates another work to ridicule its topic or style.
- A **paradox** is a statement that is true despite appearing contradictory.
- **Hyperbole** is overstatement using exaggerated language.
- An **oxymoron** combines seeming contradictions, such as "deafening silence."
- **Analogies** compare two things that share common elements.
- **Similes** (stated comparisons using the words *like* or *as*) and **metaphors** (stated comparisons that do not use *like* or *as*) are considered forms of analogy.

- When using logic to reason with audiences, **syllogism** refers either to deductive reasoning or a deceptive, very sophisticated, or subtle argument.
- **Deductive reasoning** moves from general to specific, **inductive reasoning** from specific to general.
- **Diction** is author word choice that establishes tone and effect.
- **Understatement** achieves effects like contrast or irony by downplaying or describing something more subtly than warranted.
- **Chiasmus** uses parallel clauses, the second reversing the order of the first. Examples include T. S. Eliot's "Has the Church failed mankind, or has mankind failed the Church?" and John F. Kennedy's "Ask not what your country can do for you; ask what you can do for your country."
- **Anaphora** regularly repeats a word or phrase at the beginnings of consecutive clauses or phrases to add emphasis to an idea. A classic example of anaphora was Winston Churchill's emphasis of determination: "We shall fight in the trenches. We shall fight on the oceans. We shall fight in the sky."

Arguments and Logical Errors

AUTHOR'S ARGUMENT IN ARGUMENTATIVE WRITING

In argumentative writing, the argument is a belief, position, or opinion that the author wants to convince readers to believe as well. For the first step, readers should identify the **issue**. Some issues are controversial, meaning people disagree about them. Gun control, foreign policy, and the death penalty are all controversial issues. The next step is to determine the **author's position** on the issue. That position or viewpoint constitutes the author's argument. Readers should then identify the **author's assumptions**: things he or she accepts, believes, or takes for granted without needing proof. Inaccurate or illogical assumptions produce flawed arguments and can mislead readers. Readers should identify what kinds of **supporting evidence** the author offers, such as research results, personal observations or experiences, case studies, facts, examples, expert testimony and opinions, and comparisons. Readers should decide how relevant this support is to the argument.

> **Review Video: Argumentative Writing**
> Visit mometrix.com/academy and enter code: 561544

EVALUATING AN AUTHOR'S ARGUMENT

The first three reader steps to **evaluate an author's argument** are to identify the **author's assumptions**, identify the **supporting evidence**, and decide **whether the evidence is relevant**. For example, if an author is not an expert on a particular topic, then that author's personal experience or opinion might not be relevant. The fourth step is to assess the **author's objectivity**. For example, consider whether the author introduces clear, understandable supporting evidence and facts to support the argument. The fifth step is evaluating whether the author's **argument is complete**. When authors give sufficient support for their arguments and also anticipate and respond effectively to opposing arguments or objections to their points, their arguments are complete. However, some authors omit information that could detract from their arguments. If instead they stated this information and refuted it, it would strengthen their arguments. The sixth step in evaluating an author's argumentative writing is to assess whether the **argument is valid**. Providing clear, logical reasoning makes an author's argument valid. Readers should ask themselves whether the author's points follow a sequence that makes sense, and whether each point leads to the next. The seventh step is to determine whether the author's **argument is credible**, meaning that it is convincing and believable. Arguments that are not valid are not credible, so step seven depends on step six. Readers should be mindful of their own biases as they evaluate and should not expect authors to conclusively prove their arguments, but rather to provide effective support and reason.

Evaluating an Author's Method of Appeal

To evaluate the effectiveness of an appeal, it is important to consider the author's purpose for writing. Any appeals an author uses in their argument must be relevant to the argument's goal. For example, a writer that argues for the reclassification of Pluto, but primarily uses appeals to emotion, will not have an effective argument. This writer should focus on using appeals to logic and support their argument with provable facts. While most arguments should include appeals to logic, emotion, and credibility, some arguments only call for one or two of these types of appeal. Evidence can support an appeal, but the evidence must be relevant to truly strengthen the appeal's effectiveness. If the writer arguing for Pluto's reclassification uses the reasons for Jupiter's classification as evidence, their argument would be weak. This information may seem relevant because it is related to the classification of planets. However, this classification is highly dependent on the size of the celestial object, and Jupiter is significantly bigger than Pluto. This use of evidence is illogical and does not support the appeal. Even when appropriate evidence and appeals are used, appeals and arguments lose their effectiveness when they create logical fallacies.

Opinions, Facts, and Fallacies

Critical thinking skills are mastered through understanding various types of writing and the different purposes of authors can have for writing different passages. Every author writes for a purpose. When you understand their purpose and how they accomplish their goal, you will be able to analyze their writing and determine whether or not you agree with their conclusions.

Readers must always be aware of the difference between fact and opinion. A **fact** can be subjected to analysis and proven to be true. An **opinion**, on the other hand, is the author's personal thoughts or feelings and may not be altered by research or evidence. If the author writes that the distance from New York City to Boston is about two hundred miles, then he or she is stating a fact. If the author writes that New York City is too crowded, then he or she is giving an opinion because there is no objective standard for overpopulation. Opinions are often supported by facts. For instance, an author might use a comparison between the population density of New York City and that of other major American cities as evidence of an overcrowded population. An opinion supported by facts tends to be more convincing. On the other hand, when authors support their opinions with other opinions, readers should employ critical thinking and approach the argument with skepticism.

> **Review Video: Fact or Opinion**
> Visit mometrix.com/academy and enter code: 870899

Reliable Sources

When you have an argumentative passage, you need to be sure that facts are presented to the reader from **reliable sources**. An opinion is what the author thinks about a given topic. An opinion is not common knowledge or proven by expert sources, instead the information is the personal beliefs and thoughts of the author. To distinguish between fact and opinion, a reader needs to consider the type of source that is presenting information, the information that backs-up a claim, and the author's motivation to have a certain point-of-view on a given topic. For example, if a panel of scientists has conducted multiple studies on the effectiveness of taking a certain vitamin, then the results are more likely to be factual than those of a company that is selling a vitamin and simply claims that taking the vitamin can produce positive effects. The company is motivated to sell their product, and the scientists are using the scientific method to prove a theory. Remember, if you find sentences that contain phrases such as "I think...", then the statement is an opinion.

BIASES

In their attempts to persuade, writers often make mistakes in their thought processes and writing choices. These processes and choices are important to understand so you can make an informed decision about the author's credibility. Every author has a point of view, but authors demonstrate a **bias** when they ignore reasonable counterarguments or distort opposing viewpoints. A bias is evident whenever the author's claims are presented in a way that is unfair or inaccurate. Bias can be intentional or unintentional, but readers should be skeptical of the author's argument in either case. Remember that a biased author may still be correct. However, the author will be correct in spite of, not because of, his or her bias.

A **stereotype** is a bias applied specifically to a group of people or a place. Stereotyping is considered to be particularly abhorrent because it promotes negative, misleading generalizations about people. Readers should be very cautious of authors who use stereotypes in their writing. These faulty assumptions typically reveal the author's ignorance and lack of curiosity.

> **Review Video: Bias and Stereotype**
> Visit mometrix.com/academy and enter code: 644829

Vocabulary and Word Relationships

SYNONYMS AND ANTONYMS

When you understand how words relate to each other, you will discover more in a passage. This is explained by understanding **synonyms** (e.g., words that mean the same thing) and **antonyms** (e.g., words that mean the opposite of one another). As an example, *dry* and *arid* are synonyms, and *dry* and *wet* are antonyms.

There are many pairs of words in English that can be considered synonyms, despite having slightly different definitions. For instance, the words *friendly* and *collegial* can both be used to describe a warm interpersonal relationship, and one would be correct to call them synonyms. However, *collegial* (kin to *colleague*) is often used in reference to professional or academic relationships, and *friendly* has no such connotation.

If the difference between the two words is too great, then they should not be called synonyms. *Hot* and *warm* are not synonyms because their meanings are too distinct. A good way to determine whether two words are synonyms is to substitute one word for the other word and verify that the meaning of the sentence has not changed. Substituting *warm* for *hot* in a sentence would convey a different meaning. Although warm and hot may seem close in meaning, warm generally means that the temperature is moderate, and hot generally means that the temperature is excessively high.

Antonyms are words with opposite meanings. *Light* and *dark*, *up* and *down*, *right* and *left*, *good* and *bad*: these are all sets of antonyms. Be careful to distinguish between antonyms and pairs of words that are simply different. *Black* and *gray*, for instance, are not antonyms because gray is not the opposite of black. *Black* and *white*, on the other hand, are antonyms.

Not every word has an antonym. For instance, many nouns do not. What would be the antonym of *chair*? During your exam, the questions related to antonyms are more likely to concern adjectives. You will recall that adjectives are words that describe a noun. Some common adjectives include *purple, fast, skinny,* and *sweet.* From those four adjectives, *purple* is the item that lacks a group of obvious antonyms.

> **Review Video: Synonyms and Antonyms**
> Visit mometrix.com/academy and enter code: 105612

AFFIXES

Affixes in the English language are morphemes that are added to words to create related but different words. Derivational affixes form new words based on and related to the original words. For example, the affix *–ness* added to the end of the adjective *happy* forms the noun *happiness.* Inflectional affixes form different grammatical versions of words. For example, the plural affix *–s* changes the singular noun *book* to the plural noun *books,* and the past tense affix *–ed* changes the present tense verb *look* to the past tense *looked.* Prefixes are affixes placed in front of words. For example, *heat* means to make hot; *preheat* means to heat in advance. Suffixes are affixes placed at the ends of words. The *happiness* example above contains the suffix *–ness.* Circumfixes add parts both before and after words, such as how *light* becomes *enlighten* with the prefix *en-* and the suffix *–en.* Interfixes create compound words via central affixes: *speed* and *meter* become *speedometer* via the interfix *–o–.*

> **Review Video: Affixes**
> Visit mometrix.com/academy and enter code: 782422

WORD ROOTS, PREFIXES, AND SUFFIXES TO HELP DETERMINE MEANINGS OF WORDS

Many English words were formed from combining multiple sources. For example, the Latin *habēre* means "to have," and the prefixes *in-* and *im-* mean a lack or prevention of something, as in *insufficient* and *imperfect.* Latin combined *in-* with *habēre* to form *inhibēre,* whose past participle was *inhibitus.* This is the origin of the English word *inhibit,* meaning to prevent from having. Hence by knowing the meanings of both the prefix and the root, one can decipher the word meaning. In Greek, the root *enkephalo-* refers to the brain. Many medical terms are based on this root, such as encephalitis and hydrocephalus. Understanding the prefix and suffix meanings (*-itis* means inflammation; *hydro-* means water) allows a person to deduce that encephalitis refers to brain inflammation and hydrocephalus refers to water (or other fluid) in the brain.

> **Review Video: Determining Word Meanings**
> Visit mometrix.com/academy and enter code: 894894

PREFIXES

While knowing prefix meanings helps ESL and beginning readers learn new words, other readers take for granted the meanings of known words. However, prefix knowledge will also benefit them for determining meanings or definitions of unfamiliar words. For example, native English speakers and readers familiar with recipes know what *preheat* means. Knowing that *pre-* means in advance can also inform them that *presume* means to assume in advance, that *prejudice* means advance judgment, and that this understanding can be applied to many other words beginning with *pre-*. Knowing that the prefix *dis-* indicates opposition informs the meanings of words like *disbar, disagree, disestablish,* and many more. Knowing *dys-* means bad, impaired, abnormal, or difficult informs *dyslogistic, dysfunctional, dysphagia,* and *dysplasia.*

SUFFIXES

In English, certain suffixes generally indicate both that a word is a noun, and that the noun represents a state of being or quality. For example, *-ness* is commonly used to change an adjective into its noun form, as with *happy* and *happiness, nice* and *niceness,* and so on. The suffix *–tion* is commonly used to transform a verb into its noun form, as with *converse* and *conversation or move* and *motion*. Thus, if readers are unfamiliar with the second form of a word, knowing the meaning of the transforming suffix can help them determine meaning.

PREFIXES FOR NUMBERS

Prefix	Definition	Examples
bi-	two	bisect, biennial
mono-	one, single	monogamy, monologue
poly-	many	polymorphous, polygamous
semi-	half, partly	semicircle, semicolon
uni-	one	uniform, unity

PREFIXES FOR TIME, DIRECTION, AND SPACE

Prefix	Definition	Examples
a-	in, on, of, up, to	abed, afoot
ab-	from, away, off	abdicate, abjure
ad-	to, toward	advance, adventure
ante-	before, previous	antecedent, antedate
anti-	against, opposing	antipathy, antidote
cata-	down, away, thoroughly	catastrophe, cataclysm
circum-	around	circumspect, circumference
com-	with, together, very	commotion, complicate
contra-	against, opposing	contradict, contravene
de-	from	depart
dia-	through, across, apart	diameter, diagnose
dis-	away, off, down, not	dissent, disappear
epi-	upon	epilogue
ex-	out	extract, excerpt
hypo-	under, beneath	hypodermic, hypothesis
inter-	among, between	intercede, interrupt
intra-	within	intramural, intrastate
ob-	against, opposing	objection
per-	through	perceive, permit
peri-	around	periscope, perimeter
post-	after, following	postpone, postscript
pre-	before, previous	prevent, preclude
pro-	forward, in place of	propel, pronoun
retro-	back, backward	retrospect, retrograde
sub-	under, beneath	subjugate, substitute
super-	above, extra	supersede, supernumerary
trans-	across, beyond, over	transact, transport
ultra-	beyond, excessively	ultramodern, ultrasonic

NEGATIVE PREFIXES

Prefix	Definition	Examples
a-	without, lacking	atheist, agnostic
in-	not, opposing	incapable, ineligible
non-	not	nonentity, nonsense
un-	not, reverse of	unhappy, unlock

EXTRA PREFIXES

Prefix	Definition	Examples
belli-	war, warlike	bellicose
bene-	well, good	benefit, benefactor
equi-	equal	equivalent, equilibrium
for-	away, off, from	forget, forswear
fore-	previous	foretell, forefathers
homo-	same, equal	homogenized, homonym
hyper-	excessive, over	hypercritical, hypertension
in-	in, into	intrude, invade
magn-	large	magnitude, magnify
mal-	bad, poorly, not	malfunction, malpractice
mis-	bad, poorly, not	misspell, misfire
mor-	death	mortality, mortuary
neo-	new	Neolithic, neoconservative
omni-	all, everywhere	omniscient, omnivore
ortho-	right, straight	orthogonal, orthodox
over-	above	overbearing, oversight
pan-	all, entire	panorama, pandemonium
para-	beside, beyond	parallel, paradox
phil-	love, like	philosophy, philanthropic
prim-	first, early	primitive, primary
re-	backward, again	revoke, recur
sym-	with, together	sympathy, symphony
vis-	to see	visage, visible

Below is a list of common suffixes and their meanings:

ADJECTIVE SUFFIXES

Suffix	Definition	Examples
-able (-ible)	capable of being	toler*able*, ed*ible*
-esque	in the style of, like	picturesque, grotesque
-ful	filled with, marked by	thankful, zestful
-ific	make, cause	terrific, beatific
-ish	suggesting, like	churlish, childish
-less	lacking, without	hopeless, countless
-ous	marked by, given to	religious, riotous

Noun Suffixes

Suffix	Definition	Examples
-acy	state, condition	accuracy, privacy
-ance	act, condition, fact	acceptance, vigilance
-ard	one that does excessively	drunkard, sluggard
-ation	action, state, result	occupation, starvation
-dom	state, rank, condition	serfdom, wisdom
-er (-or)	office, action	teacher, elevator, honor
-ess	feminine	waitress, duchess
-hood	state, condition	manhood, statehood
-ion	action, result, state	union, fusion
-ism	act, manner, doctrine	barbarism, socialism
-ist	worker, follower	monopolist, socialist
-ity (-ty)	state, quality, condition	acidity, civility, twenty
-ment	result, action	Refreshment
-ness	quality, state	greatness, tallness
-ship	position	internship, statesmanship
-sion (-tion)	state, result	revision, expedition
-th	act, state, quality	warmth, width
-tude	quality, state, result	magnitude, fortitude

Verb Suffixes

Suffix	Definition	Examples
-ate	having, showing	separate, desolate
-en	cause to be, become	deepen, strengthen
-fy	make, cause to have	glorify, fortify
-ize	cause to be, treat with	sterilize, mechanize

Review Video: English Root Words
Visit mometrix.com/academy and enter code: 896380

Denotative vs. Connotative Meaning

The **denotative** meaning of a word is the literal meaning. The **connotative** meaning goes beyond the denotative meaning to include the emotional reaction that a word may invoke. The connotative meaning often takes the denotative meaning a step further due to associations the reader makes with the denotative meaning. Readers can differentiate between the denotative and connotative meanings by first recognizing how authors use each meaning. Most non-fiction, for example, is fact-based and authors do not use flowery, figurative language. The reader can assume that the writer is using the denotative meaning of words. In fiction, the author may use the connotative meaning. Readers can determine whether the author is using the denotative or connotative meaning of a word by implementing context clues.

Review Video: Denotation and Connotation
Visit mometrix.com/academy and enter code: 310092

Nuances of Word Meaning Relative to Connotation, Denotation, Diction, and Usage

A word's denotation is simply its objective dictionary definition. However, its connotation refers to the subjective associations, often emotional, that specific words evoke in listeners and readers. Two or more words can have the same dictionary meaning, but very different connotations. Writers use diction (word choice) to convey various nuances of thought and emotion by selecting synonyms for other words that best communicate the associations they want to trigger for readers. For example, a car engine is naturally greasy; in this sense, "greasy" is a neutral term. But when a person's smile, appearance, or clothing is described as "greasy," it has a negative connotation. Some words have even gained additional or different meanings over time. For example, *awful* used to be used to describe things that evoked a sense of awe. When *awful* is separated into its root word, awe, and suffix, -ful, it can be understood to mean "full of awe." However, the word is now commonly used to describe things that evoke repulsion, terror, or another intense, negative reaction.

> **Review Video: Word Usage**
> Visit mometrix.com/academy and enter code: 197863

CONTEXT CLUES

Readers of all levels will encounter words that they have either never seen or have encountered only on a limited basis. The best way to define a word in **context** is to look for nearby words that can assist in revealing the meaning of the word. For instance, unfamiliar nouns are often accompanied by examples that provide a definition. Consider the following sentence: *Dave arrived at the party in hilarious garb: a leopard-print shirt, buckskin trousers, and bright green sneakers.* If a reader was unfamiliar with the meaning of garb, he or she could read the examples (i.e., a leopard-print shirt, buckskin trousers, and high heels) and quickly determine that the word means *clothing*. Examples will not always be this obvious. Consider this sentence: *Parsley, lemon, and flowers were just a few of the items he used as garnishes.* Here, the word *garnishes* is exemplified by parsley, lemon, and flowers. Readers who have eaten in a variety of restaurants will probably be able to identify a garnish as something used to decorate a plate.

> **Review Video: Context**
> Visit mometrix.com/academy and enter code: 613660

USING CONTRAST IN CONTEXT CLUES

In addition to looking at the context of a passage, readers can use contrast to define an unfamiliar word in context. In many sentences, the author will not describe the unfamiliar word directly; instead, he or she will describe the opposite of the unfamiliar word. Thus, you are provided with some information that will bring you closer to defining the word. Consider the following example: *Despite his intelligence, Hector's low brow and bad posture made him look obtuse.* The author writes that Hector's appearance does not convey intelligence. Therefore, *obtuse* must mean unintelligent. Here is another example: *Despite the horrible weather, we were beatific about our trip to Alaska.* The word *despite* indicates that the speaker's feelings were at odds with the weather. Since the weather is described as *horrible*, then *beatific* must mean something positive.

SUBSTITUTION TO FIND MEANING

In some cases, there will be very few contextual clues to help a reader define the meaning of an unfamiliar word. When this happens, one strategy that readers may employ is **substitution**. A good reader will brainstorm some possible synonyms for the given word, and he or she will substitute these words into the sentence. If the sentence and the surrounding passage continue to make sense, then the substitution has revealed at least some information about the unfamiliar word. Consider the sentence: *Frank's admonition rang in her ears as she climbed the mountain.* A reader unfamiliar with *admonition* might come up with some substitutions like *vow*, *promise*, *advice*, *complaint*, or *compliment*. All of these words make general sense of the sentence, though their meanings are diverse. However, this process has suggested that an admonition is some sort of message. The substitution strategy is rarely able to pinpoint a precise definition, but this process can be effective as a last resort.

Occasionally, you will be able to define an unfamiliar word by looking at the descriptive words in the context. Consider the following sentence: *Fred dragged the recalcitrant boy kicking and screaming up the stairs.* The words *dragged*, *kicking*, and *screaming* all suggest that the boy does not want to go up the stairs. The reader may assume that *recalcitrant* means something like unwilling or protesting. In this example, an unfamiliar adjective was identified.

Additionally, using description to define an unfamiliar noun is a common practice compared to unfamiliar adjectives, as in this sentence: *Don's wrinkled frown and constantly shaking fist identified him as a curmudgeon of the first order.* Don is described as having a *wrinkled frown and constantly shaking fist*, suggesting that a *curmudgeon* must be a grumpy person. Contrasts do not always provide detailed information about the unfamiliar word, but they at least give the reader some clues.

Words with Multiple Meanings

When a word has more than one meaning, readers can have difficulty determining how the word is being used in a given sentence. For instance, the verb *cleave*, can mean either *join* or *separate*. When readers come upon this word, they will have to select the definition that makes the most sense. Consider the following sentence: *Hermione's knife cleaved the bread cleanly*. Since a knife cannot join bread together, the word must indicate separation. A slightly more difficult example would be the sentence: *The birds cleaved to one another as they flew from the oak tree.* Immediately, the presence of the words *to one another* should suggest that in this sentence *cleave* is being used to mean *join*. Discovering the intent of a word with multiple meanings requires the same tricks as defining an unknown word: look for contextual clues and evaluate the substituted words.

Context Clues to Help Determine Meanings of Words

If readers simply bypass unknown words, they can reach unclear conclusions about what they read. However, looking for the definition of every unfamiliar word in the dictionary can slow their reading progress. Moreover, the dictionary may list multiple definitions for a word, so readers must search the word's context for meaning. Hence context is important to new vocabulary regardless of reader methods. Four types of context clues are examples, definitions, descriptive words, and opposites. Authors may use a certain word, and then follow it with several different examples of what it describes. Sometimes authors actually supply a definition of a word they use, which is especially true in informational and technical texts. Authors may use descriptive words that elaborate upon a vocabulary word they just used. Authors may also use opposites with negation that help define meaning.

Examples and Definitions

An author may use a word and then give examples that illustrate its meaning. Consider this text: "Teachers who do not know how to use sign language can help students who are deaf or hard of hearing understand certain instructions by using gestures instead, like pointing their fingers to indicate which direction to look or go; holding up a hand, palm outward, to indicate stopping; holding the hands flat, palms up, curling a finger toward oneself in a beckoning motion to indicate 'come here'; or curling all fingers toward oneself repeatedly to indicate 'come on', 'more', or 'continue.'" The author of this text has used the word "gestures" and then followed it with examples, so a reader unfamiliar with the word could deduce from the examples that "gestures" means "hand motions." Readers can find examples by looking for signal words "for example," "for instance," "like," "such as," and "e.g."

While readers sometimes have to look for definitions of unfamiliar words in a dictionary or do some work to determine a word's meaning from its surrounding context, at other times an author may make it easier for readers by defining certain words. For example, an author may write, "The company did not have sufficient capital, that is, available money, to continue operations." The author defined "capital" as "available money," and heralded the definition with the phrase "that is." Another way that authors supply word definitions is with appositives. Rather than being introduced by a signal phrase like "that is," "namely," or "meaning," an appositive comes after the vocabulary word it defines and is enclosed within two commas. For example, an author may write, "The Indians introduced the Pilgrims to pemmican, cakes they made of lean meat dried and mixed with fat, which proved greatly beneficial to keep settlers from starving while trapping." In this example, the appositive phrase following "pemmican" and preceding "which" defines the word "pemmican."

DESCRIPTIONS

When readers encounter a word they do not recognize in a text, the author may expand on that word to illustrate it better. While the author may do this to make the prose more picturesque and vivid, the reader can also take advantage of this description to provide context clues to the meaning of the unfamiliar word. For example, an author may write, "The man sitting next to me on the airplane was obese. His shirt stretched across his vast expanse of flesh, strained almost to bursting." The descriptive second sentence elaborates on and helps to define the previous sentence's word "obese" to mean extremely fat. A reader unfamiliar with the word "repugnant" can decipher its meaning through an author's accompanying description: "The way the child grimaced and shuddered as he swallowed the medicine showed that its taste was particularly repugnant."

OPPOSITES

Text authors sometimes introduce a contrasting or opposing idea before or after a concept they present. They may do this to emphasize or heighten the idea they present by contrasting it with something that is the reverse. However, readers can also use these context clues to understand familiar words. For example, an author may write, "Our conversation was not cheery. We sat and talked very solemnly about his experience and a number of similar events." The reader who is not familiar with the word "solemnly" can deduce by the author's preceding use of "not cheery" that "solemn" means the opposite of cheery or happy, so it must mean serious or sad. Or if someone writes, "Don't condemn his entire project because you couldn't find anything good to say about it," readers unfamiliar with "condemn" can understand from the sentence structure that it means the opposite of saying anything good, so it must mean reject, dismiss, or disapprove. "Entire" adds another context clue, meaning total or complete rejection.

SYNTAX TO DETERMINE PART OF SPEECH AND MEANINGS OF WORDS

Syntax refers to sentence structure and word order. Suppose that a reader encounters an unfamiliar word when reading a text. To illustrate, consider an invented word like "splunch." If this word is used in a sentence like "Please splunch that ball to me," the reader can assume from syntactic context that "splunch" is a verb. We would not use a noun, adjective, adverb, or preposition with the object "that ball," and the prepositional phrase "to me" further indicates "splunch" represents an action. However, in the sentence, "Please hand that splunch to me," the reader can assume that "splunch" is a noun. Demonstrative adjectives like "that" modify nouns. Also, we hand someone some*thing*—a thing being a noun; we do not hand someone a verb, adjective, or adverb. Some sentences contain further clues. For example, from the sentence, "The princess wore the glittering splunch on her head," the reader can deduce that it is a crown, tiara, or something similar from the syntactic context, without knowing the word.

Syntax to Indicate Different Meanings of Similar Sentences

The syntax, or structure, of a sentence affords grammatical cues that aid readers in comprehending the meanings of words, phrases, and sentences in the texts that they read. Seemingly minor differences in how the words or phrases in a sentence are ordered can make major differences in meaning. For example, two sentences can use exactly the same words but have different meanings based on the word order:

- "The man with a broken arm sat in a chair.
- "The man sat in a chair with a broken arm."

While both sentences indicate that a man sat in a chair, differing syntax indicates whether the man's or chair's arm was broken.

Determining Meaning of Phrases and Paragraphs

Like unknown words, the meanings of phrases, paragraphs, and entire works can also be difficult to discern. Each of these can be better understood with added context. However, for larger groups of words, more context is needed. Unclear phrases are similar to unclear words, and the same methods can be used to understand their meaning. However, it is also important to consider how the individual words in the phrase work together. Paragraphs are a bit more complicated. Just as words must be compared to other words in a sentence, paragraphs must be compared to other paragraphs in a composition or a section.

Determining Meaning in Various Types of Compositions

To understand the meaning of an entire composition, the type of composition must be considered. **Expository writing** is generally organized so that each paragraph focuses on explaining one idea, or part of an idea, and its relevance. **Persuasive writing** uses paragraphs for different purposes to organize the parts of the argument. **Unclear paragraphs** must be read in the context of the paragraphs around them for their meaning to be fully understood. The meaning of full texts can also be unclear at times. The purpose of composition is also important for understanding the meaning of a text. To quickly understand the broad meaning of a text, look to the introductory and concluding paragraphs. Fictional texts are different. Some fictional works have implicit meanings, but some do not. The target audience must be considered for understanding texts that do have an implicit meaning, as most children's fiction will clearly state any lessons or morals. For other fiction, the application of literary theories and criticism may be helpful for understanding the text.

Additional Resources for Determining Word Meaning and Usage

While these strategies are useful for determining the meaning of unknown words and phrases, sometimes additional resources are needed to properly use the terms in different contexts. Some words have multiple definitions, and some words are inappropriate in particular contexts or modes of writing. The following tools are helpful for understanding all meanings and proper uses for words and phrases.

- **Dictionaries** provide the meaning of a multitude of words in a language. Many dictionaries include additional information about each word, such as its etymology, its synonyms, or variations of the word.
- **Glossaries** are similar to dictionaries, as they provide the meanings of a variety of terms. However, while dictionaries typically feature an extensive list of words and comprise an entire publication, glossaries are often included at the end of a text and only include terms and definitions that are relevant to the text they follow.

- **Spell Checkers** are used to detect spelling errors in typed text. Some spell checkers may also detect the misuse of plural or singular nouns, verb tenses, or capitalization. While spell checkers are a helpful tool, they are not always reliable or attuned to the author's intent, so it is important to review the spell checker's suggestions before accepting them.
- **Style Manuals** are guidelines on the preferred punctuation, format, and grammar usage according to different fields or organizations. For example, the Associated Press Stylebook is a style guide often used for media writing. The guidelines within a style guide are not always applicable across different contexts and usages, as the guidelines often cover grammatical or formatting situations that are not objectively correct or incorrect.

Figurative Language

LITERAL AND FIGURATIVE MEANING

When language is used **literally**, the words mean exactly what they say and nothing more. When language is used **figuratively**, the words mean something beyond their literal meaning. For example, "The weeping willow tree has long, trailing branches and leaves" is a literal description. But "The weeping willow tree looks as if it is bending over and crying" is a figurative description—specifically, a **simile** or stated comparison. Another figurative language form is **metaphor**, or an implied comparison. A good example is the metaphor of a city, state, or city-state as a ship, and its governance as sailing that ship. Ancient Greek lyrical poet Alcaeus is credited with first using this metaphor, and ancient Greek tragedian Aeschylus then used it in *Seven Against Thebes*, and then Plato used it in the *Republic*.

FIGURES OF SPEECH

A **figure of speech** is a verbal expression whose meaning is figurative rather than literal. For example, the phrase "butterflies in the stomach" does not refer to actual butterflies in a person's stomach. It is a metaphor representing the fluttery feelings experienced when a person is nervous or excited—or when one "falls in love," which does not mean physically falling. "Hitting a sales target" does not mean physically hitting a target with arrows as in archery; it is a metaphor for meeting a sales quota. "Climbing the ladder of success" metaphorically likens advancing in one's career to ascending ladder rungs. Similes, such as "light as a feather" (meaning very light, not a feather's actual weight), and hyperbole, like "I'm starving/freezing/roasting," are also figures of speech. Figures of speech are often used and crafted for emphasis, freshness of expression, or clarity.

> **Review Video: Figure of Speech**
> Visit mometrix.com/academy and enter code: 111295

FIGURATIVE LANGUAGE

Figurative language extends past the literal meanings of words. It offers readers new insight into the people, things, events, and subjects covered in a work of literature. Figurative language also enables readers to feel they are sharing the authors' experiences. It can stimulate the reader's senses, make comparisons that readers find intriguing or even startling, and enable readers to view the world in different ways. When looking for figurative language, it is important to consider the context of the sentence or situation. Phrases that appear out of place or make little sense when read literally are likely instances of figurative language. Once figurative language has been recognized, context is also important to determining the type of figurative language being used and its function. For example, when a comparison is being made, a metaphor or simile is likely being used. This means the comparison may emphasize or create irony through the things being compared. Seven specific types of figurative language include: alliteration, onomatopoeia, personification, imagery, similes, metaphors, and hyperbole.

> **Review Video: Figurative Language**
> Visit mometrix.com/academy and enter code: 584902

ALLITERATION AND ONOMATOPOEIA

Alliteration describes a series of words beginning with the same sounds. **Onomatopoeia** uses words imitating the sounds of things they name or describe. For example, in his poem "Come Down, O Maid," Alfred Tennyson writes of "The moan of doves in immemorial elms, / And murmuring of innumerable bees." The word "moan" sounds like some sounds doves make, "murmuring" represents the sounds of bees buzzing. Onomatopoeia also includes words that are simply meant to represent sounds, such as "meow," "kaboom," and "whoosh."

> **Review Video: Alliteration**
> Visit mometrix.com/academy and enter code: 462837

PERSONIFICATION

Another type of figurative language is **personification**. This is describing a non-human thing, like an animal or an object, as if it were human. The general intent of personification is to describe things in a manner that will be comprehensible to readers. When an author states that a tree *groans* in the wind, he or she does not mean that the tree is emitting a low, pained sound from a mouth. Instead, the author means that the tree is making a noise similar to a human groan. Of course, this personification establishes a tone of sadness or suffering. A different tone would be established if the author said that the tree was *swaying* or *dancing*. Alfred Tennyson's poem "The Eagle" uses all of these types of figurative language: "He clasps the crag with crooked hands." Tennyson used alliteration, repeating /k/ and /kr/ sounds. These hard-sounding consonants reinforce the imagery, giving visual and tactile impressions of the eagle.

> **Review Video: Personification**
> Visit mometrix.com/academy and enter code: 260066

SIMILES AND METAPHORS

Similes are stated comparisons using "like" or "as." Similes can be used to stimulate readers' imaginations and appeal to their senses. Because a simile includes *like* or *as*, the device creates more space between the description and the thing being described than a metaphor does. If an author says that *a house was like a shoebox*, then the tone is different than the author saying that the house *was* a shoebox. Authors will choose between a metaphor and a simile depending on their intended tone.

Similes also help compare fictional characters to well-known objects or experiences, so the reader can better relate to them. William Wordsworth's poem about "Daffodils" begins, "I wandered lonely as a cloud." This simile compares his loneliness to that of a cloud. It is also personification, giving a cloud the human quality loneliness. In his novel *Lord Jim* (1900), Joseph Conrad writes in Chapter 33, "I would have given anything for the power to soothe her frail soul, tormenting itself in its invincible ignorance like a small bird beating about the cruel wires of a cage." Conrad uses the word "like" to compare the girl's soul to a small bird. His description of the bird beating at the cage shows the similar helplessness of the girl's soul to gain freedom.

> **Review Video: Simile**
> Visit mometrix.com/academy and enter code: 642949

A **metaphor** is a type of figurative language in which the writer equates something with another thing that is not particularly similar, instead of using *like* or *as*. For instance, *the bird was an arrow arcing through the sky*. In this sentence, the arrow is serving as a metaphor for the bird. The point of a metaphor is to encourage the reader to consider the item being described in a *different way*. Let's continue with this metaphor for a flying bird. You are asked to envision the bird's flight as being similar to the arc of an arrow. So, you imagine the flight to be swift and bending. Metaphors are a way for the author to describe an item *without being direct and obvious*. This literary device is a lyrical and suggestive way of providing information. Note that the reference for a metaphor will not always be mentioned explicitly by the author. Consider the following description of a forest in winter: *Swaying skeletons reached for the sky and groaned as the wind blew through them.* In this example, the author is using *skeletons* as a metaphor for leafless trees. This metaphor creates a spooky tone while inspiring the reader's imagination.

LITERARY EXAMPLES OF METAPHOR

A **metaphor** is an implied comparison, i.e., it compares something to something else without using "like", "as", or other comparative words. For example, in "The Tyger" (1794), William Blake writes, "Tyger Tyger, burning bright, / In the forests of the night." Blake compares the tiger to a flame not by saying it is like a fire, but by simply describing it as "burning." Henry Wadsworth Longfellow's poem "O Ship of State" (1850) uses an extended metaphor by referring consistently throughout the entire poem to the state, union, or republic as a seagoing vessel, referring to its keel, mast, sail, rope, anchors, and to its braving waves, rocks, gale, tempest, and "false lights on the shore." Within the extended metaphor, Wordsworth uses a specific metaphor: "the anchors of thy hope!"

TED HUGHES' ANIMAL METAPHORS

Ted Hughes frequently used animal metaphors in his poetry. In "The Thought Fox," a model of concise, structured beauty, Hughes characterizes the poet's creative process with succinct, striking imagery of an idea entering his head like a wild fox. Repeating "loneliness" in the first two stanzas emphasizes the poet's lonely work: "Something else is alive / Beside the clock's loneliness." He treats an idea's arrival as separate from himself. Three stanzas detail in vivid images a fox's approach from the outside winter forest at starless midnight—its nose, "Cold, delicately" touching twigs and leaves; "neat" paw prints in snow; "bold" body; brilliant green eyes; and self-contained, focused progress—"Till, with a sudden sharp hot stink of fox," he metaphorically depicts poetic inspiration as the fox's physical entry into "the dark hole of the head." Hughes ends by summarizing his vision of a poet as an interior, passive idea recipient, with the outside world unchanged: "The window is starless still; the clock ticks, / The page is printed."

> **Review Video: Metaphor**
> Visit mometrix.com/academy and enter code: 133295

HYPERBOLE

Hyperbole is excessive exaggeration used for humor or emphasis rather than for literal meaning. For example, in *To Kill a Mockingbird*, Harper Lee wrote, "People moved slowly then. There was no hurry, for there was nowhere to go, nothing to buy and no money to buy it with, nothing to see outside the boundaries of Maycomb County." This was not literally true; Lee exaggerates the scarcity of these things for emphasis. In "Old Times on the Mississippi," Mark Twain wrote, "I... could have hung my hat on my eyes, they stuck out so far." This is not literal, but makes his description vivid and funny. In his poem "As I Walked Out One Evening", W. H. Auden wrote, "I'll love you, dear, I'll love you / Till China and Africa meet, / And the river jumps over the mountain / And the salmon sing in the street." He used things not literally possible to emphasize the duration of his love.

> **Review Video: Hyperbole and Understatement**
> Visit mometrix.com/academy and enter code: 308470

LITERARY IRONY

In literature, irony demonstrates the opposite of what is said or done. The three types of irony are **verbal irony, situational irony,** and **dramatic irony**. Verbal irony uses words opposite to the meaning. Sarcasm may use verbal irony. One common example is describing something that is confusing as "clear as mud." For example, in his 1986 movie *Hannah and Her Sisters,* author, director, and actor Woody Allen says to his character's date, "I had a great evening; it was like the Nuremburg Trials." Notice these employ similes. In situational irony, what happens contrasts with what was expected. O. Henry's short story *The Gift of the Magi* uses situational irony: a husband and wife each sacrifice their most prized possession to buy each other a Christmas present. The irony is that she sells her long hair to buy him a watch fob, while he sells his heirloom pocket-watch to buy her the jeweled combs for her hair she had long wanted; in the end, neither of them can use their gifts. In dramatic irony, narrative informs audiences of more than its characters know. For example, in *Romeo and Juliet,* the audience is made aware that Juliet is only asleep, while Romeo believes her to be dead, which then leads to Romeo's death.

> **Review Video: Irony**
> Visit mometrix.com/academy and enter code: 374204

IDIOMS

Idioms create comparisons, and often take the form of similes or metaphors. Idioms are always phrases and are understood to have a meaning that is different from its individual words' literal meaning. For example, "break a leg" is a common idiom that is used to wish someone luck or tell them to perform well. Literally, the phrase "break a leg" means to injure a person's leg, but the phrase takes on a different meaning when used as an idiom. Another example is "call it a day," which means to temporarily stop working on a task, or find a stopping point, rather than literally referring to something as "a day." Many idioms are associated with a region or group. For example, an idiom commonly used in the American South is "'til the cows come home." This phrase is often used to indicate that something will take or may last for a very long time, but not that it will literally last until the cows return to where they reside.

Media

MEDIA AND FORMAT CHOICES

Effective communication depends on choosing the correct method. Media and format choices are influenced by the target audience, the budget, and the needs of the audience.

INSTRUCTIONAL VIDEOS

Instructional videos have potential for excellent two-way communication because questions and feedback can be built in. Videos can be targeted to particular audiences, and they can be paused for discussion or replayed to reinforce concepts. Viewers can see processes, including "before," "during," and "after" phases. Videos are accessible because most communities have at least one DVD player or computer. Moreover, video players and computers are continually becoming less expensive to buy and use. Disadvantages include the necessity of editing software and equipment in some cases, as well as the need for support from other print materials. There is also danger of overuse, if other media or methods are more appropriate, and higher up-front costs. Producers of instructional videos must account for the costs of script development and hiring local performers as needed.

DVDs AND CDs

Interactive DVDs and CDs, such as games, give viewers the opportunity to actively participate as they learn information. Additionally, videos are considered to be a professional method of sharing information. Compared to many other media formats, discs are comparatively inexpensive to make and are easy to transport due to their small size and weight. They are more resistant to damage and aging than older videotape technology, making them more durable. Some disadvantages include needing access to technology to play what is stored on the disc and access to certain software programs to add new content to a disc, especially if the producer wants to include video animation or audio commentary. Producers must also consider expenses concerning paid staff and production and labeling expenses. Content that would appear on DVDs and CDs can alternatively be shared through streaming services or digital files stored on a computer or other compatible device.

TELEVISION AND RADIO

Both television and radio are forms of mass media that reach many people. TV has the broadest reach and can market to the general public or be customized for target audiences, while radio only tends to reach specific target audiences. TV has the advantage of video plus audio, while radio broadcasts only feature audio. However, access to television programs is more expensive than access to radio broadcasts. A shared disadvantage is that TV and radio audiences can only interact directly during call-in programs. Additionally, programming times may be inconvenient, but tape, digital sound, and digital video recording (DVR) can remedy this. Many streaming services also provide access to these programs. Both television and radio are useful for communicating simple slogans and messages, and both can generate awareness, interest, and excitement.

NEWSPAPERS

Except for the occasional community columns, news releases, and letters to the editor, newspaper pages and features afford little opportunity for audience input or participation. However, they do reach and appeal to the general public. Cost is an advantage: hiring a PR writer and paying for a news advertisement costs much less than a radio or TV spot. Additionally, newspaper features are high-status, and audiences can reread and review them as often as they like. However, newspaper ads may have difficulty affecting the reader as deeply without audio or video, and they require a literate audience. Their publication is also subject to editors' whims and biases. Newspaper pieces combining advertising and editorial content—"advertorials"—provide inclusion of paid material, but are viewed as medium-status and cost more.

WEBSITES, BLOGS, MOBILE PHONES, AND TEXT MESSAGING

Computer literacy is required for online material, but participation potential is high via websites, e-networking, and blogging. Mobile phones and text messaging are used for enormous direct, public, two-way and one-on-one communication, with timely information and reminders. Web media need a literate public and can be tailored for specific audiences. They afford global information, are accessible by increasingly technology-literate populations, and are high-status. Web media disadvantages include the necessity of computers and people to design, manage, and supply content, as well as to provide technical support. Mobile and text media are globally popular, but appeal especially to certain demographics like teens and young adults. They are increasingly available, especially in rural regions, and are decreasing in cost. Mobile and text media disadvantages include required brevity in texts and provider messaging charges. Links to related websites and pages within existing sites are also advantages of digital media.

Public Presentations and Slideshows

Public presentations have great potential for audience participation and can directly target various audiences. They can encourage the establishment of partnerships and groups, stimulate local ownership of issues and projects, and make information public. A drawback to public presentations is that they are limited to nights, weekends, or whenever audiences are available and do not always attract the intended audience.

Another method of presentation is to use **slideshows**. These presentations are best for sophisticated audiences like professionals, civil servants, and service organizations. Well-designed slideshows are good for stimulating audience interest, selling ideas, and marketing products. Also, they are accessible online as well as in-person so they can reach a broader audience. Slideshow disadvantages include the necessity of projectors and other equipment. They are also limited to communicating more general points, outlines, and summaries rather than conveying a multitude of information in more detail.

Posters and Brochures

Both **posters** and **brochures** can target audiences of the general public and more specific public sectors. Posters are better for communicating simple slogans and messages, while brochures can include more detail and are better for printing instructional information. Both can be inexpensive to produce, especially if printed only as needed and in-house. Posters can often be printed in-house without using outside printing companies. However, it is difficult to get feedback on both posters and brochures—unless they have been broadly tested, or if their publication is accompanied by workshops and other participatory events. A disadvantage of using posters is that they are designed to draw attention and communicate quickly, as they are mostly viewed in passing. This means that their messages must be simple and communicate efficiently. A disadvantage of using brochures is that they can only be distributed to a specific, limited group or area. Posters and brochures are also only understood when audiences are literate in both written language and visual elements.

Flyers and Fact Sheets

Flyers and fact sheets have one-way communication potential because readers cannot give feedback. Their target audiences are general. Some advantages of using this form of media include flexibility: people can distribute them at meetings or events, put them on car windshields in parking lots, leave them in stores or on bulletin boards at community agencies and schools, hand them out from booths and other displays, or mail them. When printed in black and white, they can be very inexpensive. They afford recipients the convenience of being able to review them at their leisure. Organizations and individuals can produce flyers and fact sheets in-house, or even at home with desktop publishing software. Disadvantages include their limitation to single facts or tips and specific information on specified topics.

Evaluating Media Information Sources

With the wealth of media in different formats available today, users are more likely to take media at face value. However, to understand the content of media, consumers must **critically evaluate each source**.

Users should ask themselves the following questions about media sources:

- Who is delivering this message and why?
- What methods do a media source's publishers employ to gain and maintain users' attention?
- Which points of view is the media source representing?
- What are the various ways this message could be interpreted?
- What information is missing from the message?
- Is the source scholarly, i.e., peer-reviewed?
- Does it include author names and their credentials as they relate to the topic?
- Who publishes it and why?
- Who is the target audience?
- Is the language technically specific or non-technical?
- Are sources cited, research claims documented, conclusions based on furnished evidence, and references provided?
- Is the publication current?

OTHER CONSIDERATIONS FOR THE VALIDITY OF SOURCES

For books, consider whether information is **up-to-date** and whether **historical perspectives** apply. Content is more likely to be **scholarly** if publishers are universities, government, or professional organizations. Book reviews can also provide useful information. For articles, identify the author, publisher, frequency of the periodical's publication, and what kind of advertising, if any, is included. Looking for book reviews also informs users. For articles, look for biographical author information, publisher name, frequency of the periodical's publication, and whether advertising is included and, if so, whether it is for certain occupations or disciplines. For web pages, check their domain names, identify publishers or sponsors, look for the author or publisher's contact information, check dates of most recent page updates, be alert to biases, and verify the validity of the information on the webpage. The quality and accuracy of web pages located through search engines rather than library databases varies widely and requires careful user inspection. Web page recommendations from reliable sources like university faculties can help indicate quality and accuracy. Citations of websites by credible or scholarly sources also show reliability. Authors' names, relevant credentials, affiliations, and contact information support their authority. Site functionality, such as ease of navigation, ability to search, site maps, and indexes, is also a criterion to consider.

PERSUASIVE MEDIA

Advertising, public relations, and advocacy media all use **persuasion**. Advertisers use persuasion to sell goods and services. The public relations field uses persuasion to give good impressions of companies, governments, or organizations. Advocacy groups use persuasion to garner support or votes. Persuasion can come through commercials, public service announcements, speeches, websites, and newsletters, among other channels. Activists, lobbyists, government officials, and politicians use political rhetoric involving persuasive techniques. Basic techniques include using celebrity spokespersons, whom consumers admire or aspire to resemble, or conversely, "everyday people" (albeit often portrayed by actors) with whom consumers identify. Using expert testimonials lends credibility. Explicit claims of content, effectiveness, quality, and reliability—which often cannot be proven or disproven—are used to persuade. While news and advocacy messages mostly eschew humor for credibility's sake (except in political satire), advertising often persuades via humor, which gets consumer attention and associates its pleasure with advertised products and services. Qualifiers and other misleading terms, sometimes called "Weasel words," are often combined with exaggerated claims. Intensifiers, such as hyperboles, superlatives, repetitions, and sentimental appeals are also persuasive.

INTERMEDIATE TECHNIQUES

Dangerous propagandist Adolf Hitler said people suspect little lies more than big ones; hence the "Big Lie" is a persuasion method that cannot be identified without consumers' keen critical thinking. A related method is **charisma**, which can induce people to believe messages they would otherwise reject. **Euphemisms** substitute abstract, vague, or bland terms in place of more graphic, clear, and unpleasant ones. For example, the terms "layoffs" and "firing" are replaced by "downsizing," and "torture" is replaced with "intensive interrogation techniques." **Extrapolation** bases sweeping conclusions on small amounts of minor information to appeal to what consumers wish or hope. Flattery appeals to consumer self-esteem needs, such as L'Oréal's "You're worth it." Flattery is sometimes accomplished through contrast, like ads showing others' mistakes to make consumers feel superior and smarter. "Glittering generalities" refer to claims based on concepts such as beauty, love, health, democracy, freedom, and science. Persuaders use this tactic to gain consumer acceptance without consumers questioning what they mean. The opposite is name-calling to persuade consumers to reject someone or something.

American citizens love new ideas and technology. Persuaders exploit this by emphasizing the **newness** of products, services, and candidates. Conversely, they also use **nostalgia** to evoke consumers' happy memories, which they often remember more than unhappy ones. Citing "scientific evidence" is an intermediate version of the basic technique of expert testimonials. Consumers may accept this as proof, but some advertisers, politicians, and other persuaders may present inaccurate or misleading "evidence." Another intermediate technique is the "simple solution." Although the natures of people and life are complex, when consumers feel overwhelmed by complexity, persuaders exploit this by offering policies, products, or services they claim will solve complicated problems by simple means. Persuaders also use symbols, images, words, and names we associate with more general, emotional concepts like lifestyle, country, family, religion, and gender. While symbols have power, their significance also varies across individuals. For example, some consumers regard the Hummer SUV as a prestigious status symbol, while others regard it as environmentally harmful and irresponsible.

ADVANCED TECHNIQUES

Ad hominem, Latin for "against the man" attacks the person behind an idea rather than criticizing the idea itself. It operates by association: if a person is considered immoral or uneducated, then his or her ideas must be bad as well. **"Stacking the deck"** misleads by presenting only selected information that supports one position. **Apophasis**, or a false denial, allows the speaker or writer to indirectly bring attention to a flaw in an opponent's credibility. For example, a politician saying, "I won't mention my opponent's tax evasion issues" manages to mention them while seeming less accusatory. Persuaders may also use **majority belief**, making statements such as "Four out of five dentists recommend this brand" or "[insert number] people can't be wrong." In an intensified version, persuaders exploit group dynamics at rallies, speeches, and other live-audience events where people are vulnerable to surrounding crowd influences. **Scapegoating**, blaming one person or group for complex problems, is a form of the intermediate "simple solution" technique, a practice common in politics. **Timing** also persuades, like advertising flowers and candy in the weeks preceding Valentine's Day, ad campaigns preceding new technology rollouts, and politician speeches following big news events.

VISUAL MEDIA

Some images have the power to communicate more information than an entire paragraph. Images can contain several elements and be interpreted different ways, making them an effective vessel for abstract and emotionally appealing ideas. Humans are also able to understand images before they fully acquire language, meaning that images can reach more people than language can at any time. Images are also more quickly comprehended than text, making them a highly efficient method of communication. People can remember or memorize images more easily than text, also. Historically, images have been used for propaganda and subliminal messaging. Images are also used by different companies as an effective technique to entice customers to buy their products. Though images do not always contain text, they can still convey explicit and implicit meanings. An image's explicit meaning would be the most recognizable shape or concept in the image. The implicit meaning may be obscured within the image through the use of negative space, background images, or out-of-focus shapes.

INTERPRETING AND EVALUATING PERSUASIVE MEDIA

Most messages can be interpreted in different ways. They can be interpreted explicitly, where the literal meaning of the words in the message creates the meaning of the message, and no context is considered. Alternatively, other contexts can be considered alongside the explicit meaning of the message. These create alternative, not clearly stated meanings called **implicit meanings**. Politics, current events, regional norms, and even emotions are examples of contexts that can add implicit meanings to a message. These implicit meanings can change the effect a message has on its recipient. Many products have slogans with both implicit and explicit meanings. These implicit meanings must be considered to fully interpret a message.

Messages come in different forms, and each form has a unique way of communicating both explicit and implicit meanings. Images can come with captions that communicate a message, but some images carry subliminal messages. This means that their implicit meaning is received by the viewer, but the viewer is not aware of it. The term **propaganda** describes messages that advocate for a specific opinion or way of thinking. Most propaganda is politically driven and has been used during historical periods, most notably World War II. Unlike messages with hidden or veiled implicit meanings, most propaganda aggressively communicates its entire meaning and is difficult to misinterpret. Documentaries are another prominent form of communication. Documentaries are informational videos that focus on a specific figure, subject, phenomenon, or time period. While documentaries are primarily fact based and contain excerpts from interviews and testimonials, documentaries feature a limited view of their subject and sometimes attempt to persuade viewers to take action or embrace their central message. While some documentaries communicate this clearly, some hide an implicit meaning through the way they present each piece of information.

Reading Comprehension

UNDERSTANDING A PASSAGE

One of the most important skills in reading comprehension is the identification of **topics** and **main ideas**. There is a subtle difference between these two features. The topic is the subject of a text (i.e., what the text is all about). The main idea, on the other hand, is the most important point being made by the author. The topic is usually expressed in a few words at the most while the main idea often needs a full sentence to be completely defined. As an example, a short passage might be written on the topic of penguins, and the main idea could be written as *Penguins are different from other birds in many ways*. In most nonfiction writing, the topic and the main idea will be **stated**

directly and often appear in a sentence at the very beginning or end of the text. When being tested on an understanding of the author's topic, you may be able to skim the passage for the general idea by reading only the first sentence of each paragraph. A body paragraph's first sentence is often—but not always—the main **topic sentence** which gives you a summary of the content in the paragraph.

However, there are cases in which the reader must figure out an **unstated** topic or main idea. In these instances, you must read every sentence of the text and try to come up with an overarching idea that is supported by each of those sentences.

Note: The main idea should not be confused with the thesis statement. While the main idea gives a brief, general summary of a text, the thesis statement provides a **specific perspective** on an issue that the author supports with evidence.

> **Review Video: Topics and Main Ideas**
> Visit mometrix.com/academy and enter code: 407801

Supporting details are smaller pieces of evidence that provide backing for the main point. In order to show that a main idea is correct or valid, an author must add details that prove their point. All texts contain details, but they are only classified as supporting details when they serve to reinforce some larger point. Supporting details are most commonly found in informative and persuasive texts. In some cases, they will be clearly indicated with terms like *for example* or *for instance*, or they will be enumerated with terms like *first*, *second*, and *last*. However, you need to be prepared for texts that do not contain those indicators. As a reader, you should consider whether the author's supporting details really back up his or her main point. Details can be factual and correct, yet they may not be **relevant** to the author's point. Conversely, details can be relevant, but be ineffective because they are based on opinion or assertions that cannot be proven.

> **Review Video: Supporting Details**
> Visit mometrix.com/academy and enter code: 396297

An example of a main idea is: *Giraffes live in the Serengeti of Africa*. A supporting detail about giraffes could be: *A giraffe in this region benefits from a long neck by reaching twigs and leaves on tall trees*. The main idea gives the general idea that the text is about giraffes. The supporting detail gives a specific fact about how the giraffes eat.

ORGANIZATION OF THE TEXT

The way a text is organized can help readers understand the author's intent and his or her conclusions. There are various ways to organize a text, and each one has a purpose and use. Usually, authors will organize information logically in a passage so the reader can follow and locate the information within the text. However, since not all passages are written with the same logical structure, you need to be familiar with several different types of passage structure.

> **Review Video: Organizational Methods to Structure Text**
> Visit mometrix.com/academy and enter code: 606263

CHRONOLOGICAL

When using **chronological** order, the author presents information in the order that it happened. For example, biographies are typically written in chronological order. The subject's birth and childhood are presented first, followed by their adult life, and lastly the events leading up to the person's death.

Cause and Effect

One of the most common text structures is **cause and effect**. A **cause** is an act or event that makes something happen, and an **effect** is the thing that happens as a result of the cause. A cause-and-effect relationship is not always explicit, but there are some terms in English that signal causes, such as *since*, *because*, and *due to*. Furthermore, terms that signal effects include *consequently, therefore, this leads to*. As an example, consider the sentence *Because the sky was clear, Ron did not bring an umbrella*. The cause is the clear sky, and the effect is that Ron did not bring an umbrella. However, readers may find that sometimes the cause-and-effect relationship will not be clearly noted. For instance, the sentence *He was late and missed the meeting* does not contain any signaling words, but the sentence still contains a cause (he was late) and an effect (he missed the meeting).

> **Review Video: Cause and Effect**
> Visit mometrix.com/academy and enter code: 868099

Multiple Effects

Be aware of the possibility for a single cause to have **multiple effects.** (e.g., *Single cause*: Because you left your homework on the table, your dog engulfed the assignment. *Multiple effects*: As a result, you receive a failing grade, your parents do not allow you to go out with your friends, you miss out on the new movie, and one of your classmates spoils it for you before you have another chance to watch it).

Multiple Causes

Also, there is the possibility for a single effect to have **multiple causes.** (e.g., *Single effect*: Alan has a fever. *Multiple causes*: An unexpected cold front came through the area, and Alan forgot to take his multi-vitamin to avoid getting sick.) Additionally, an effect can in turn be the cause of another effect, in what is known as a cause-and-effect chain. (e.g., As a result of her disdain for procrastination, Lynn prepared for her exam. This led to her passing her test with high marks. Hence, her resume was accepted and her application was approved.)

Cause and Effect in Persuasive Essays

Persuasive essays, in which an author tries to make a convincing argument and change the minds of readers, usually include cause-and-effect relationships. However, these relationships should not always be taken at face value. Frequently, an author will assume a cause or take an effect for granted. To read a persuasive essay effectively, readers need to judge the cause-and-effect relationships that the author is presenting. For instance, imagine an author wrote the following: *The parking deck has been unprofitable because people would prefer to ride their bikes.* The relationship is clear: the cause is that people prefer to ride their bikes, and the effect is that the parking deck has been unprofitable. However, readers should consider whether this argument is conclusive. Perhaps there are other reasons for the failure of the parking deck: a down economy, excessive fees, etc. Too often, authors present causal relationships as if they are fact rather than opinion. Readers should be on the alert for these dubious claims.

Problem-Solution

Some nonfiction texts are organized to **present a problem** followed by a solution. For this type of text, the problem is often explained before the solution is offered. In some cases, as when the problem is well known, the solution may be introduced briefly at the beginning. Other passages may focus on the solution, and the problem will be referenced only occasionally. Some texts will outline multiple solutions to a problem, leaving readers to choose among them. If the author has an interest or an allegiance to one solution, he or she may fail to mention or describe accurately some of the other solutions. Readers should be careful of the author's agenda when reading a problem-solution text. Only by understanding the author's perspective and interests can one develop a proper judgment of the proposed solution.

COMPARE AND CONTRAST

Many texts follow the **compare-and-contrast** model in which the similarities and differences between two ideas or things are explored. Analysis of the similarities between ideas is called **comparison**. In an ideal comparison, the author places ideas or things in an equivalent structure, i.e., the author presents the ideas in the same way. If an author wants to show the similarities between cricket and baseball, then he or she may do so by summarizing the equipment and rules for each game. Be mindful of the similarities as they appear in the passage and take note of any differences that are mentioned. Often, these small differences will only reinforce the more general similarity.

> **Review Video: Compare and Contrast Essays**
> Visit mometrix.com/academy and enter code: 798319

Thinking critically about ideas and conclusions can seem like a daunting task. One way to ease this task is to understand the basic elements of ideas and writing techniques. Looking at the ways different ideas relate to each other can be a good way for readers to begin their analysis. For instance, sometimes authors will write about two ideas that are in opposition to each other. Or, one author will provide his or her ideas on a topic, and another author may respond in opposition. The analysis of these opposing ideas is known as **contrast**. Contrast is often marred by the author's obvious partiality to one of the ideas. A discerning reader will be put off by an author who does not engage in a fair fight. In an analysis of opposing ideas, both ideas should be presented in clear and reasonable terms. If the author does prefer a side, you need to read carefully to determine the areas where the author shows or avoids this preference. In an analysis of opposing ideas, you should proceed through the passage by marking the major differences point by point with an eye that is looking for an explanation of each side's view. For instance, in an analysis of capitalism and communism, there is an importance in outlining each side's view on labor, markets, prices, personal responsibility, etc. Additionally, as you read through the passages, you should note whether the opposing views present each side in a similar manner.

SEQUENCE

Readers must be able to identify a text's **sequence**, or the order in which things happen. Often, when the sequence is very important to the author, the text is indicated with signal words like *first*, *then*, *next*, and *last*. However, a sequence can be merely implied and must be noted by the reader. Consider the sentence *He walked through the garden and gave water and fertilizer to the plants*. Clearly, the man did not walk through the garden before he collected water and fertilizer for the plants. So, the implied sequence is that he first collected water, then he collected fertilizer, next he walked through the garden, and last he gave water or fertilizer as necessary to the plants. Texts do not always proceed in an orderly sequence from first to last. Sometimes they begin at the end and start over at the beginning. As a reader, you can enhance your understanding of the passage by taking brief notes to clarify the sequence.

MAKING PREDICTIONS

When we read literature, **making predictions** about what will happen in the writing reinforces our purpose for reading and prepares us mentally. A **prediction** is a guess about what will happen next. Readers constantly make predictions based on what they have read and what they already know. We can make predictions before we begin reading and during our reading. Consider the following sentence: *Staring at the computer screen in shock, Kim blindly reached over for the brimming glass of* *water on the shelf to her side.* The sentence suggests that Kim is distracted, and that she is not looking at the glass that she is going to pick up. So, a reader might predict that Kim is going to knock over the glass. Of course, not every prediction will be accurate: perhaps Kim will pick the glass up cleanly. Nevertheless, the author has certainly created the expectation that the water might be spilled.

As we read on, we can test the accuracy of our predictions, revise them in light of additional reading, and confirm or refute our predictions. Predictions are always subject to revision as the reader acquires more information. A reader can make predictions by observing the title and illustrations; noting the structure, characters, and subject; drawing on existing knowledge relative to the subject; and asking "why" and "who" questions. Connecting reading to what we already know enables us to learn new information and construct meaning. For example, before third-graders read a book about Johnny Appleseed, they may start a KWL chart—a list of what they *Know*, what they *Want* to know or learn, and what they have *Learned* after reading. Activating existing background knowledge and thinking about the text before reading improves comprehension.

> **Review Video: Predictions**
> Visit mometrix.com/academy and enter code: 437248

Test-taking tip: To respond to questions requiring future predictions, your answers should be based on evidence of past or present behavior and events.

EVALUATING PREDICTIONS

When making predictions, readers should be able to explain how they developed their prediction. One way readers can defend their thought process is by citing textual evidence. Textual evidence to evaluate reader predictions about literature includes specific synopses of the work, paraphrases of the work or parts of it, and direct quotations from the work. These references to the text must support the prediction by indicating, clearly or unclearly, what will happen later in the story. A text may provide these indications through literary devices such as foreshadowing. Foreshadowing is anything in a text that gives the reader a hint about what is to come by emphasizing the likelihood of an event or development. Foreshadowing can occur through descriptions, exposition, and dialogue. Foreshadowing in dialogue usually occurs when a character gives a warning or expresses a strong feeling that a certain event will occur. Foreshadowing can also occur through irony. However, unlike other forms of foreshadowing, the events that seem the most likely are the opposite of what actually happens. Instances of foreshadowing and irony can be summarized, paraphrased, or quoted to defend a reader's prediction.

> **Review Video: Textual Evidence for Predictions**
> Visit mometrix.com/academy and enter code: 261070

DRAWING CONCLUSIONS FROM INFERENCES

Inferences about literary text are logical conclusions that readers make based on their observations and previous knowledge. An inference is based on both what is found in a passage or a story and what is known from personal experience. For instance, a story may say that a character is frightened and can hear howling in the distance. Based on both what is in the text and personal knowledge, it is a logical conclusion that the character is frightened because he hears the sound of wolves. A good inference is supported by the information in a passage.

IMPLICIT AND EXPLICIT INFORMATION

By inferring, readers construct meanings from text that are personally relevant. By combining their own schemas or concepts and their background information pertinent to the text with what they read, readers interpret it according to both what the author has conveyed and their own unique perspectives. Inferences are different from **explicit information**, which is clearly stated in a passage. Authors do not always explicitly spell out every meaning in what they write; many meanings are implicit. Through inference, readers can comprehend implied meanings in the text, and also derive personal significance from it, making the text meaningful and memorable to them. Inference is a natural process in everyday life. When readers infer, they can draw conclusions about what the author is saying, predict what may reasonably follow, amend these predictions as they continue to read, interpret the import of themes, and analyze the characters' feelings and motivations through their actions.

EXAMPLE OF DRAWING CONCLUSIONS FROM INFERENCES

Read the excerpt and decide why Jana finally relaxed.

> Jana loved her job, but the work was very demanding. She had trouble relaxing. She called a friend, but she still thought about work. She ordered a pizza, but eating it did not help. Then, her kitten jumped on her lap and began to purr. Jana leaned back and began to hum a little tune. She felt better.

You can draw the conclusion that Jana relaxed because her kitten jumped on her lap. The kitten purred, and Jana leaned back and hummed a tune. Then she felt better. The excerpt does not explicitly say that this is the reason why she was able to relax. The text leaves the matter unclear, but the reader can infer or make a "best guess" that this is the reason she is relaxing. This is a logical conclusion based on the information in the passage. It is the best conclusion a reader can make based on the information he or she has read. Inferences are based on the information in a passage, but they are not directly stated in the passage.

Test-taking tip: While being tested on your ability to make correct inferences, you must look for **contextual clues**. An answer can be true, but not the best or most correct answer. The contextual clues will help you find the answer that is the **best answer** out of the given choices. Be careful in your reading to understand the context in which a phrase is stated. When asked for the implied meaning of a statement made in the passage, you should immediately locate the statement and read the **context** in which the statement was made. Also, look for an answer choice that has a similar phrase to the statement in question.

> **Review Video: Inference**
> Visit mometrix.com/academy and enter code: 379203
>
> **Review Video: Identifying Logical Conclusions**
> Visit mometrix.com/academy and enter code: 281653

MAKING CONNECTIONS TO ENHANCE COMPREHENSION

Reading involves thinking. For good comprehension, readers make **text-to-self**, **text-to-text**, and **text-to-world connections**. Making connections helps readers understand text better and predict what might occur next based on what they already know, such as how characters in the story feel or what happened in another text. Text-to-self connections with the reader's life and experiences make literature more personally relevant and meaningful to readers. Readers can make connections before, during, and after reading—including whenever the text reminds them of something similar they have encountered in life or other texts. The genre, setting, characters, plot elements, literary structure and devices, and themes an author uses allow a reader to make connections to other works of literature or to people and events in their own lives. Venn diagrams and other graphic organizers help visualize connections. Readers can also make double-entry notes: key content, ideas, events, words, and quotations on one side, and the connections with these on the other.

SUMMARIZING LITERATURE TO SUPPORT COMPREHENSION

When reading literature, especially demanding works, **summarizing** helps readers identify important information and organize it in their minds. They can also identify themes, problems, and solutions, and can sequence the story. Readers can summarize before, during, and after they read. They should use their own words, as they do when describing a personal event or giving directions. Previewing a text's organization before reading by examining the book cover, table of contents, and illustrations also aids summarizing. Making notes of key words and ideas in a graphic organizer while reading can benefit readers in the same way. Graphic organizers are another useful method; readers skim the text to determine main ideas and then narrow the list with the aid of the organizer. Unimportant details should be omitted in summaries. Summaries can be organized using description, problem-solution, comparison-contrast, sequence, main ideas, or cause-and-effect.

> **Review Video: Summarizing Text**
> Visit mometrix.com/academy and enter code: 172903

PARAPHRASING

Paraphrasing is another method that the reader can use to aid in comprehension. When paraphrasing, one puts what they have read into their own words by rephrasing what the author has written, or one "translates" all of what the author shared into their own words by including as many details as they can.

Interactions with Texts

PURPOSES FOR WRITING

In order to be an effective reader, one must pay attention to the author's **position** and **purpose**. Even those texts that seem objective and impartial, like textbooks, have a position and bias. Readers need to take these positions into account when considering the author's message. When an author uses emotional language or clearly favors one side of an argument, his or her position is clear. However, the author's position may be evident not only in what he or she writes, but also in what he or she doesn't write. In a normal setting, a reader would want to review some other texts on the same topic in order to develop a view of the author's position. If this was not possible, then you would want to at least acquire some background about the author. However, since you are in the middle of an exam and the only source of information is the text, you should look for language and argumentation that seems to indicate a particular stance on the subject.

> **Review Video: Author's Position**
> Visit mometrix.com/academy and enter code: 827954

Usually, identifying the author's **purpose** is easier than identifying his or her position. In most cases, the author has no interest in hiding his or her purpose. A text that is meant to entertain, for instance, should be written to please the reader. Most narratives, or stories, are written to entertain, though they may also inform or persuade. Informative texts are easy to identify, while the most difficult purpose of a text to identify is persuasion because the author has an interest in making this purpose hard to detect. When a reader discovers that the author is trying to persuade, he or she should be skeptical of the argument. For this reason, persuasive texts often try to establish an entertaining tone and hope to amuse the reader into agreement. On the other hand, an informative tone may be implemented to create an appearance of authority and objectivity.

An author's purpose is evident often in the organization of the text (e.g., section headings in bold font points to an informative text). However, you may not have such organization available to you in your exam. Instead, if the author makes his or her main idea clear from the beginning, then the likely purpose of the text is to inform. If the author begins by making a claim and provides various arguments to support that claim, then the purpose is probably to persuade. If the author tells a story or wants to gain the reader's attention more than to push a particular point or deliver information, then his or her purpose is most likely to entertain. As a reader, you must judge authors on how well they accomplish their purpose. In other words, you need to consider the type of passage (e.g., technical, persuasive, etc.) that the author has written and if the author has followed the requirements of the passage type.

> **Review Video: Purpose**
> Visit mometrix.com/academy and enter code: 511819

MAKING LOGICAL CONCLUSIONS ABOUT A PASSAGE

A reader should always be drawing conclusions from the text. Sometimes conclusions are **implied** from written information, and other times the information is **stated directly** within the passage. One should always aim to draw conclusions from information stated within a passage, rather than to draw them from mere implications. At times an author may provide some information and then describe a counterargument. Readers should be alert for direct statements that are subsequently rejected or weakened by the author. Furthermore, you should always read through the entire passage before drawing conclusions. Many readers are trained to expect the author's conclusions at either the beginning or the end of the passage, but many texts do not adhere to this format.

Drawing conclusions from information implied within a passage requires confidence on the part of the reader. **Implications** are things that the author does not state directly, but readers can assume based on what the author does say. Consider the following passage: *I stepped outside and opened my umbrella. By the time I got to work, the cuffs of my pants were soaked.* The author never states that it is raining, but this fact is clearly implied. Conclusions based on implication must be well supported by the text. In order to draw a solid conclusion, readers should have **multiple pieces of evidence**. If readers have only one piece, they must be assured that there is no other possible explanation than their conclusion. A good reader will be able to draw many conclusions from information implied by the text, which will be a great help on the exam.

DRAWING CONCLUSIONS

A common type of inference that a reader has to make is **drawing a conclusion**. The reader makes this conclusion based on the information provided within a text. Certain facts are included to help a reader come to a specific conclusion. For example, a story may open with a man trudging through the snow on a cold winter day, dragging a sled behind him. The reader can logically **infer** from the setting of the story that the man is wearing heavy winter clothes in order to stay warm. Information is implied based on the setting of a story, which is why **setting** is an important element of the text. If the same man in the example was trudging down a beach on a hot summer day, dragging a surf board behind him, the reader would assume that the man is not wearing heavy clothes. The reader makes inferences based on their own experiences and the information presented to them in the story.

Test-taking tip: When asked to identify a conclusion that may be drawn, look for critical "hedge" phrases, such as *likely*, *may*, *can*, and *will often*, among many others. When you are being tested on this knowledge, remember the question that writers insert into these hedge phrases to cover every possibility. Often an answer will be wrong simply because there is no room for exception. Extreme positive or negative answers (such as always or never) are usually not correct. When answering these questions, the reader **should not** use any outside knowledge that is not gathered directly or reasonably inferred from the passage. Correct answers can be derived straight from the passage.

EXAMPLE

Read the following sentence from *Little Women* by Louisa May Alcott and draw a conclusion based upon the information presented:

> *You know the reason Mother proposed not having any presents this Christmas was because it is going to be a hard winter for everyone; and she thinks we ought not to spend money for pleasure, when our men are suffering so in the army.*

Based on the information in the sentence, the reader can conclude, or **infer**, that the men are away at war while the women are still at home. The pronoun *our* gives a clue to the reader that the character is speaking about men she knows. In addition, the reader can assume that the character is speaking to a brother or sister, since the term "Mother" is used by the character while speaking to another person. The reader can also come to the conclusion that the characters celebrate Christmas, since it is mentioned in the **context** of the sentence. In the sentence, the mother is presented as an unselfish character who is opinionated and thinks about the wellbeing of other people.

> **Review Video: Drafting Conclusions**
> Visit mometrix.com/academy and enter code: 209408

COMPARING TWO STORIES

When presented with two different stories, there will be **similarities** and **differences** between the two. A reader needs to make a list, or other graphic organizer, of the points presented in each story. Once the reader has written down the main point and supporting points for each story, the two sets of ideas can be compared. The reader can then present each idea and show how it is the same or different in the other story. This is called **comparing and contrasting ideas**.

The reader can compare ideas by stating, for example: "In Story 1, the author believes that humankind will one day land on Mars, whereas in Story 2, the author believes that Mars is too far away for humans to ever step foot on." Note that the two viewpoints are different in each story that the reader is comparing. A reader may state that: "Both stories discussed the likelihood of humankind landing on Mars." This statement shows how the viewpoint presented in both stories is based on the same topic, rather than how each viewpoint is different. The reader will complete a comparison of two stories with a conclusion.

> **Review Video: Comparing Two Stories**
> Visit mometrix.com/academy and enter code: 833765

Outlining a Passage

As an aid to drawing conclusions, **outlining** the information contained in the passage should be a familiar skill to readers. An effective outline will reveal the structure of the passage and will lead to solid conclusions. An effective outline will have a title that refers to the basic subject of the text, though the title does not need to restate the main idea. In most outlines, the main idea will be the first major section. Each major idea in the passage will be established as the head of a category. For instance, the most common outline format calls for the main ideas of the passage to be indicated with Roman numerals. In an effective outline of this kind, each of the main ideas will be represented by a Roman numeral and none of the Roman numerals will designate minor details or secondary ideas. Moreover, all supporting ideas and details should be placed in the appropriate place on the outline. An outline does not need to include every detail listed in the text, but it should feature all of those that are central to the argument or message. Each of these details should be listed under the corresponding main idea.

> **Review Video: Outlining**
> Visit mometrix.com/academy and enter code: 584445

Using Graphic Organizers

Ideas from a text can also be organized using **graphic organizers**. A graphic organizer is a way to simplify information and take key points from the text. A graphic organizer such as a timeline may have an event listed for a corresponding date on the timeline, while an outline may have an event listed under a key point that occurs in the text. Each reader needs to create the type of graphic organizer that works the best for him or her in terms of being able to recall information from a story. Examples include a spider-map, which takes a main idea from the story and places it in a bubble with supporting points branching off the main idea. An outline is useful for diagramming the main and supporting points of the entire story, and a Venn diagram compares and contrasts characteristics of two or more ideas.

> **Review Video: Graphic Organizers**
> Visit mometrix.com/academy and enter code: 665513

Summarizing

A helpful tool is the ability to **summarize** the information that you have read in a paragraph or passage format. This process is similar to creating an effective outline. First, a summary should accurately define the main idea of the passage, though the summary does not need to explain this main idea in exhaustive detail. The summary should continue by laying out the most important supporting details or arguments from the passage. All of the significant supporting details should be included, and none of the details included should be irrelevant or insignificant. Also, the summary should accurately report all of these details. Too often, the desire for brevity in a summary leads to the sacrifice of clarity or accuracy. Summaries are often difficult to read because they omit all of the graceful language, digressions, and asides that distinguish great writing. However, an effective summary should communicate the same overall message as the original text.

Evaluating a Passage

It is important to understand the logical conclusion of the ideas presented in an informational text. **Identifying a logical conclusion** can help you determine whether you agree with the writer or not. Coming to this conclusion is much like making an inference: the approach requires you to combine the information given by the text with what you already know and make a logical conclusion. If the author intended for the reader to draw a certain conclusion, then you can expect the author's argumentation and detail to be leading in that direction.

One way to approach the task of drawing conclusions is to make brief **notes** of all the points made by the author. When the notes are arranged on paper, they may clarify the logical conclusion. Another way to approach conclusions is to consider whether the reasoning of the author raises any pertinent questions. Sometimes you will be able to draw several conclusions from a passage. On occasion these will be conclusions that were never imagined by the author. Therefore, be aware that these conclusions must be **supported directly by the text**.

EVALUATION OF SUMMARIES

A summary of a literary passage is a condensation in the reader's own words of the passage's main points. Several guidelines can be used in evaluating a summary. The summary should be complete yet concise. It should be accurate, balanced, fair, neutral, and objective, excluding the reader's own opinions or reactions. It should reflect in similar proportion how much each point summarized was covered in the original passage. Summary writers should include tags of attribution, like "Macaulay argues that" to reference the original author whose ideas are represented in the summary. Summary writers should not overuse quotations; they should only quote central concepts or phrases they cannot precisely convey in words other than those of the original author. Another aspect of evaluating a summary is considering whether it can stand alone as a coherent, unified composition. In addition, evaluation of a summary should include whether its writer has cited the original source of the passage they have summarized so that readers can find it.

Writing

Foundations of Grammar

THE EIGHT PARTS OF SPEECH
NOUNS

When you talk about a person, place, thing, or idea, you are talking about a **noun**. The two main types of nouns are **common** and **proper** nouns. Also, nouns can be abstract (i.e., general) or concrete (i.e., specific).

COMMON NOUNS

Common nouns are generic names for people, places, and things. Common nouns are not usually capitalized.

Examples of common nouns:

People: boy, girl, worker, manager

Places: school, bank, library, home

Things: dog, cat, truck, car

PROPER NOUNS

Proper nouns name specific people, places, or things. All proper nouns are capitalized.

Examples of proper nouns:

People: Abraham Lincoln, George Washington, Martin Luther King, Jr.

Places: Los Angeles, California; New York; Asia

Things: Statue of Liberty, Earth, Lincoln Memorial

Note: When referring to the planet that we live on, capitalize *Earth*. When referring to the dirt, rocks, or land, lowercase *earth*.

GENERAL AND SPECIFIC NOUNS

General nouns are the names of conditions or ideas. **Specific nouns** name people, places, and things that are understood by using your senses.

General nouns:

Condition: beauty, strength

Idea: truth, peace

Specific nouns:

People: baby, friend, father

Places: town, park, city hall

Things: rainbow, cough, apple, silk, gasoline

COLLECTIVE NOUNS

Collective nouns are the names for a group of people, places, or things that may act as a whole. The following are examples of collective nouns: *class, company, dozen, group, herd, team,* and *public*. Collective nouns usually require an article, which denotes the noun as being a single unit. For instance, a choir is a group of singers. Even though there are many singers in a choir, the word choir is grammatically treated as a single unit. If we refer to the members of the group, and not the group itself, it is no longer a collective noun.

Incorrect: The *choir are* going to compete nationally this year.

Correct: The *choir is* going to compete nationally this year.

Incorrect: The *members* of the choir *is* competing nationally this year.

Correct: The *members* of the choir *are* competing nationally this year.

PRONOUNS

Pronouns are words that are used to stand in for nouns. A pronoun may be classified as personal, intensive, relative, interrogative, demonstrative, indefinite, and reciprocal.

Personal: *Nominative* is the case for nouns and pronouns that are the subject of a sentence. *Objective* is the case for nouns and pronouns that are an object in a sentence. *Possessive* is the case for nouns and pronouns that show possession or ownership.

Singular

	Nominative	Objective	Possessive
First Person	I	me	my, mine
Second Person	you	you	your, yours
Third Person	he, she, it	him, her, it	his, her, hers, its

Plural

	Nominative	Objective	Possessive
First Person	we	us	our, ours
Second Person	you	you	your, yours
Third Person	they	them	their, theirs

Intensive: I myself, you yourself, he himself, she herself, the (thing) itself, we ourselves, you yourselves, they themselves

Relative: which, who, whom, whose

Interrogative: what, which, who, whom, whose

Demonstrative: this, that, these, those

Indefinite: all, any, each, everyone, either/neither, one, some, several

Reciprocal: each other, one another

> **Review Video: Nouns and Pronouns**
> Visit mometrix.com/academy and enter code: 312073

VERBS

If you want to write a sentence, then you need a verb. Without a verb, you have no sentence. The verb of a sentence indicates action or being. In other words, the verb shows something's action or state of being or the action that has been done to something.

TRANSITIVE AND INTRANSITIVE VERBS

A **transitive verb** is a verb whose action (e.g., drive, run, jump) indicates a receiver (e.g., car, dog, kangaroo). **Intransitive verbs** do not indicate a receiver of an action. In other words, the action of the verb does not point to a subject or object.

Transitive: He plays the piano. | The piano was played by him.

Intransitive: He plays. | John plays well.

A dictionary will tell you whether a verb is transitive or intransitive. Some verbs can be transitive and intransitive.

ACTION VERBS AND LINKING VERBS

Action verbs show what the subject is doing. In other words, an action verb shows action. Unlike most types of words, a single action verb, in the right context, can be an entire sentence. **Linking verbs** link the subject of a sentence to a noun or pronoun, or they link a subject with an adjective. You always need a verb if you want a complete sentence. However, linking verbs on their own cannot be a complete sentence.

Common linking verbs include *appear, be, become, feel, grow, look, seem, smell, sound,* and *taste*. However, any verb that shows a condition and connects to a noun, pronoun, or adjective that describes the subject of a sentence is a linking verb.

Action: He sings. | Run! | Go! | I talk with him every day. | She reads.

Linking:

Incorrect: I am.

Correct: I am John. | I smell roses. | I feel tired.

Note: Some verbs are followed by words that look like prepositions, but they are a part of the verb and a part of the verb's meaning. These are known as phrasal verbs, and examples include *call off, look up,* and *drop off*.

> **Review Video: Action Verbs and Linking Verbs**
> Visit mometrix.com/academy and enter code: 743142

Voice

Transitive verbs come in active or passive **voice**. If something does an action or is acted upon, then you will know whether a verb is active or passive. When the subject of the sentence is doing the action, the verb is in **active voice**. When the subject is acted upon, the verb is in **passive voice**.

Active: Jon drew the picture. (The subject *Jon* is doing the action of *drawing a picture*.)

Passive: The picture is drawn by Jon. (The subject *picture* is receiving the action from Jon.)

Verb Tenses

A verb **tense** shows the different form of a verb to point to the time of an action. The present and past tense are indicated by the verb's form. An action in the present, *I talk,* can change form for the past: *I talked*. However, for the other tenses, an auxiliary (i.e., helping) verb is needed to show the change in form. These helping verbs include *am, are, is | have, has, had | was, were, will* (or *shall*).

Present: I talk	Present perfect: I have talked
Past: I talked	Past perfect: I had talked
Future: I will talk	Future perfect: I will have talked

Present: The action happens at the current time.

Example: He *walks* to the store every morning.

To show that something is happening right now, use the progressive present tense: I *am walking*.

Past: The action happened in the past.

Example: He *walked* to the store an hour ago.

Future: The action is going to happen later.

Example: I *will walk* to the store tomorrow.

Present perfect: The action started in the past and continues into the present or took place previously at an unspecified time

Example: I *have walked* to the store three times today.

Past perfect: The second action happened in the past. The first action came before the second.

Example: Before I walked to the store (Action 2), I *had walked* to the library (Action 1).

Future perfect: An action that uses the past and the future. In other words, the action is complete before a future moment.

Example: When she comes for the supplies (future moment), I *will have walked* to the store (action completed before the future moment).

Conjugating Verbs

When you need to change the form of a verb, you are **conjugating** a verb. The key forms of a verb are singular, present tense (dream); singular, past tense (dreamed); and the past participle (have dreamed). Note: the past participle needs a helping verb to make a verb tense. For example, I *have dreamed* of this day. The following tables demonstrate some of the different ways to conjugate a verb:

Singular

Tense	First Person	Second Person	Third Person
Present	I dream	You dream	He, she, it dreams
Past	I dreamed	You dreamed	He, she, it dreamed
Past Participle	I have dreamed	You have dreamed	He, she, it has dreamed

Plural

Tense	First Person	Second Person	Third Person
Present	We dream	You dream	They dream
Past	We dreamed	You dreamed	They dreamed
Past Participle	We have dreamed	You have dreamed	They have dreamed

MOOD

There are three **moods** in English: the indicative, the imperative, and the subjunctive.

The **indicative mood** is used for facts, opinions, and questions.

> Fact: You can do this.
>
> Opinion: I think that you can do this.
>
> Question: Do you know that you can do this?

The **imperative** is used for orders or requests.

> Order: You are going to do this!
>
> Request: Will you do this for me?

The **subjunctive mood** is for wishes and statements that go against fact.

> Wish: I wish that I were famous.
>
> Statement against fact: If I were you, I would do this. (This goes against fact because I am not you. You have the chance to do this, and I do not have the chance.)

Review Video: Verb Tenses
Visit mometrix.com/academy and enter code: 269472

ADJECTIVES

An **adjective** is a word that is used to modify a noun or pronoun. An adjective answers a question: *Which one? What kind?* or *How many?* Usually, adjectives come before the words that they modify, but they may also come after a linking verb.

> Which one? The *third* suit is my favorite.
>
> What kind? This suit is *navy blue*.
>
> How many? I am going to buy *four* pairs of socks to match the suit.

ARTICLES

Articles are adjectives that are used to distinguish nouns as definite or indefinite. **Definite** nouns are preceded by the article *the* and indicate a specific person, place, thing, or idea. **Indefinite** nouns are preceded by *a* or *an* and do not indicate a specific person, place, thing, or idea. *A*, *an*, and *the* are the only articles. Note: *An* comes before words that start with a vowel sound. For example, "Are you going to get an **u**mbrella?"

    Definite: I lost *the* bottle that belongs to me.

    Indefinite: Does anyone have *a* bottle to share?

COMPARISON WITH ADJECTIVES

Some adjectives are relative and other adjectives are absolute. Adjectives that are **relative** can show the comparison between things. **Absolute** adjectives can also show comparison, but they do so in a different way. Let's say that you are reading two books. You think that one book is perfect, and the other book is not exactly perfect. It is not possible for one book to be more perfect than the other. Either you think that the book is perfect, or you think that the book is imperfect. In this case, perfect and imperfect are absolute adjectives.

Relative adjectives will show the different **degrees** of something or someone to something else or someone else. The three degrees of adjectives include positive, comparative, and superlative.

The **positive** degree is the normal form of an adjective.

    Example: This work is *difficult*. | She is *smart*.

The **comparative** degree compares one person or thing to another person or thing.

    Example: This work is *more difficult* than your work. | She is *smarter* than me.

The **superlative** degree compares more than two people or things.

    Example: This is the *most difficult* work of my life. | She is the *smartest* lady in school.

> **Review Video: Adjectives**
> Visit mometrix.com/academy and enter code: 470154

ADVERBS

An **adverb** is a word that is used to **modify** a verb, adjective, or another adverb. Usually, adverbs answer one of these questions: *When? Where? How?* and *Why?* The negatives *not* and *never* are considered adverbs. Adverbs that modify adjectives or other adverbs **strengthen** or **weaken** the words that they modify.

Examples:

    He walks *quickly* through the crowd.

    The water flows *smoothly* on the rocks.

Note: Adverbs are usually indicated by the morpheme *-ly*, which has been added to the root word. For instance, *quick* can be made into an adverb by adding *-ly* to construct *quickly*. Some words that end in *-ly* do not follow this rule and can behave as other parts of speech. Examples of adjectives ending in *-ly* include: *early, friendly, holy, lonely, silly,* and *ugly*. To know if a word that ends in *-ly* is an adjective or adverb, check your dictionary. Also, while many adverbs end in -*ly*, you need to remember that not all adverbs end in -*ly*.

Examples:

He is *never* angry.

You walked *across* the bridge.

<u>COMPARISON WITH ADVERBS</u>

The rules for comparing adverbs are the same as the rules for adjectives.

The **positive** degree is the standard form of an adverb.

Example: He arrives *soon*. | She speaks *softly* to her friends.

The **comparative** degree compares one person or thing to another person or thing.

Example: He arrives *sooner* than Sarah. | She speaks *more softly* than him.

The **superlative** degree compares more than two people or things.

Example: He arrives *soonest* of the group. | She speaks the *most softly* of any of her friends.

> **Review Video: Adverbs**
> Visit mometrix.com/academy and enter code: 713951

PREPOSITIONS

A **preposition** is a word placed before a noun or pronoun that shows the relationship between an object and another word in the sentence.

Common prepositions:

about	before	during	on	under
after	beneath	for	over	until
against	between	from	past	up
among	beyond	in	through	with
around	by	of	to	within
at	down	off	toward	without

Examples:

The napkin is *in* the drawer.

The Earth rotates *around* the Sun.

The needle is *beneath* the haystack.

Can you find "me" *among* the words?

> **Review Video: What is a Preposition?**
> Visit mometrix.com/academy and enter code: 946763

CONJUNCTIONS

Conjunctions join words, phrases, or clauses and they show the connection between the joined pieces. **Coordinating conjunctions** connect equal parts of sentences. **Correlative conjunctions** show the connection between pairs. **Subordinating conjunctions** join subordinate (i.e., dependent) clauses with independent clauses.

COORDINATING CONJUNCTIONS

The **coordinating conjunctions** include: *and, but, yet, or, nor, for,* and *so*

Examples:

>The rock was small, *but* it was heavy.

>She drove in the night, *and* he drove in the day.

CORRELATIVE CONJUNCTIONS

The **correlative conjunctions** are: *either...or* | *neither...nor* | *not only...but also*

Examples:

>*Either* you are coming *or* you are staying.

>He *not only* ran three miles *but also* swam 200 yards.

> **Review Video: Coordinating and Correlative Conjunctions**
> Visit mometrix.com/academy and enter code: 390329

SUBORDINATING CONJUNCTIONS

Common **subordinating conjunctions** include:

after	since	whenever
although	so that	where
because	unless	wherever
before	until	whether
in order that	when	while

Examples:

>I am hungry *because* I did not eat breakfast.

>He went home *when* everyone left.

> **Review Video: Subordinating Conjunctions**
> Visit mometrix.com/academy and enter code: 958913

INTERJECTIONS

Interjections are words of exclamation (i.e., audible expression of great feeling) that are used alone or as a part of a sentence. Often, they are used at the beginning of a sentence for an introduction. Sometimes, they can be used in the middle of a sentence to show a change in thought or attitude.

>Common Interjections: Hey! | Oh, | Ouch! | Please! | Wow!

Agreement and Sentence Structure

SUBJECTS AND PREDICATES

SUBJECTS

The **subject** of a sentence names who or what the sentence is about. The subject may be directly stated in a sentence, or the subject may be the implied *you*. The **complete subject** includes the simple subject and all of its modifiers. To find the complete subject, ask *Who* or *What* and insert the verb to complete the question. The answer, including any modifiers (adjectives, prepositional phrases, etc.), is the complete subject. To find the **simple subject**, remove all of the modifiers in the complete subject. Being able to locate the subject of a sentence helps with many problems, such as those involving sentence fragments and subject-verb agreement.

Examples:

The small, red <u>car</u> is the one that he wants for Christmas.
(simple subject: car; complete subject: The small, red car)

The young <u>artist</u> is coming over for dinner.
(simple subject: artist; complete subject: The young artist)

> **Review Video: Subjects**
> Visit mometrix.com/academy and enter code: 444771

In **imperative** sentences, the verb's subject is understood (e.g., [You] Run to the store), but is not actually present in the sentence. Normally, the subject comes before the verb. However, the subject comes after the verb in sentences that begin with *There are* or *There was*.

Direct:

John knows the way to the park.	Who knows the way to the park?	John
The cookies need ten more minutes.	What needs ten minutes?	The cookies
By five o'clock, Bill will need to leave.	Who needs to leave?	Bill
There are five letters on the table for him.	What is on the table?	Five letters
There were coffee and doughnuts in the house.	What was in the house?	Coffee and doughnuts

Implied:

| Go to the post office for me. | Who is going to the post office? | You |
| Come and sit with me, please? | Who needs to come and sit? | You |

PREDICATES

In a sentence, you always have a predicate and a subject. The subject tells what the sentence is about, and the **predicate** explains or describes the subject.

60

Think about the sentence *He sings*. In this sentence, we have a subject (He) and a predicate (sings). This is all that is needed for a sentence to be complete. Most sentences contain more information, but if this is all the information that you are given, then you have a complete sentence.

Now, let's look at another sentence: *John and Jane sing on Tuesday nights at the dance hall.*

<u>John and Jane</u> (subject) <u>sing on Tuesday nights at the dance hall.</u> (predicate)

SUBJECT-VERB AGREEMENT

Verbs **agree** with their subjects in number. In other words, singular subjects need singular verbs. Plural subjects need plural verbs. **Singular** is for **one** person, place, or thing. **Plural** is for **more than one** person, place, or thing. Subjects and verbs must also share the same point of view, as in first, second, or third person. The present tense ending *-s* is used on a verb if its subject is third person singular; otherwise, the verb's ending is not modified.

> **Review Video: Subject-Verb Agreement**
> Visit mometrix.com/academy and enter code: 479190

NUMBER AGREEMENT EXAMPLES:

Single Subject and Verb: *Dan* (singular subject) *calls* (singular verb) home.

Dan is one person. So, the singular verb *calls* is needed.

Plural Subject and Verb: *Dan and Bob* (plural subject) *call* (plural verb) home.

More than one person needs the plural verb *call*.

PERSON AGREEMENT EXAMPLES:

First Person: I *am* walking.

Second Person: You *are* walking.

Third Person: He *is* walking.

COMPLICATIONS WITH SUBJECT-VERB AGREEMENT
WORDS BETWEEN SUBJECT AND VERB

Words that come between the simple subject and the verb have no bearing on subject-verb agreement.

Examples:

The *joy* (singular subject) of my life *returns* (singular verb) home tonight.

The phrase *of my life* does not influence the verb *returns*.

The *question* that still remains unanswered *is* "Who are you?"
(singular subject: question; singular verb: is)

Don't let the phrase "*that still remains...*" trouble you. The subject *question* goes with *is*.

COMPOUND SUBJECTS

A compound subject is formed when two or more nouns joined by *and*, *or*, or *nor* jointly act as the subject of the sentence.

JOINED BY AND

When a compound subject is joined by *and*, it is treated as a plural subject and requires a plural verb.

Examples:

You and Jon *are* invited to come to my house.
(plural subject: You and Jon; plural verb: are)

The *pencil and paper* *belong* to me.
(plural subject: pencil and paper; plural verb: belong)

JOINED BY OR/NOR

For a compound subject joined by *or* or *nor*, the verb must agree in number with the part of the subject that is closest to the verb (italicized in the examples below).

Examples:

Today or tomorrow *is* the day.

Stan or Phil *wants* to read the book.

Neither the pen nor *the book* *is* on the desk.

Either the blanket or *pillows* *arrive* this afternoon.

INDEFINITE PRONOUNS AS SUBJECT

An indefinite pronoun is a pronoun that does not refer to a specific noun. Different indefinite pronouns may only function as a singular noun, only function as a plural noun, or change depending on how they are used.

ALWAYS SINGULAR

Pronouns such as *each*, *either*, *everybody*, *anybody*, *somebody*, and *nobody* are always singular.

Examples:

    Each (singular subject) of the runners *has* (singular verb) a different bib number.

    Is (singular verb) *either* (singular subject) of you ready for the game?

Note: The words *each* and *either* can also be used as adjectives (e.g., *each* person is unique). When one of these adjectives modifies the subject of a sentence, it is always a singular subject.

    Everybody (singular subject) *grows* (singular verb) a day older every day.

    Anybody (singular subject) *is* (singular verb) welcome to bring a tent.

ALWAYS PLURAL

Pronouns such as *both*, *several*, and *many* are always plural.

Examples:

    Both (plural subject) of the siblings *were* (plural verb) too tired to argue.

    Many (plural subject) *have tried* (plural verb), but none have succeeded.

DEPEND ON CONTEXT

Pronouns such as *some*, *any*, *all*, *none*, *more*, and *most* can be either singular or plural depending on what they are representing in the context of the sentence.

Examples:

    All (singular subject) of my dog's food *was* (singular verb) still there in his bowl.

    By the end of the night, *all* (plural subject) of my guests *were* (plural verb) already excited about coming to my next party.

OTHER CASES INVOLVING PLURAL OR IRREGULAR FORM

Some nouns are **singular in meaning but plural in form**: news, mathematics, physics, and economics.

    The *news is* coming on now.

    Mathematics is my favorite class.

Some nouns are plural in form and meaning, and have **no singular equivalent**: scissors and pants.

> Do these *pants come* with a shirt?
>
> The *scissors are* for my project.

Mathematical operations are **irregular** in their construction, but are normally considered to be **singular in meaning**.

> One plus one *is* two.
>
> Three times three *is* nine.

Note: Look to your **dictionary** for help when you aren't sure whether a noun with a plural form has a singular or plural meaning.

COMPLEMENTS

A complement is a noun, pronoun, or adjective that is used to give more information about the subject or verb in the sentence.

DIRECT OBJECTS

A direct object is a noun or pronoun that takes or receives the **action** of a verb. (Remember: a complete sentence does not need a direct object, so not all sentences will have them. A sentence needs only a subject and a verb.) When you are looking for a direct object, find the verb and ask *who* or *what*.

Examples:

> I took *the blanket*.
>
> Jane read *books*.

INDIRECT OBJECTS

An indirect object is a word or group of words that show how an action had an **influence** on someone or something. If there is an indirect object in a sentence, then you always have a direct object in the sentence. When you are looking for the indirect object, find the verb and ask *to/for whom or what*.

Examples:

> We taught the old dog (indirect object) a new trick (direct object).
>
> I gave them (indirect object) a math lesson (direct object).

Review Video: Direct and Indirect Objects
Visit mometrix.com/academy and enter code: 817385

Predicate Nominatives and Predicate Adjectives

As we looked at previously, verbs may be classified as either action verbs or linking verbs. A linking verb is so named because it links the subject to words in the predicate that describe or define the subject. These words are called predicate nominatives (if nouns or pronouns) or predicate adjectives (if adjectives).

Examples:

My <u>father</u> is a <u>lawyer</u>.
    subject   predicate nominative

Your <u>mother</u> is <u>patient</u>.
    subject   predicate adjective

Pronoun Usage

The **antecedent** is the noun that has been replaced by a pronoun. A pronoun and its antecedent **agree** when they have the same number (singular or plural) and gender (male, female, or neutral).

Examples:

Singular agreement: <u>John</u> came into town, and <u>he</u> played for us.
      antecedent   pronoun

Plural agreement: <u>John and Rick</u> came into town, and <u>they</u> played for us.
      antecedent   pronoun

To determine which is the correct pronoun to use in a compound subject or object, try each pronoun **alone** in place of the compound in the sentence. Your knowledge of pronouns will tell you which one is correct.

Example:

Bob and (I, me) will be going.

Test: (1) *I will be going* or (2) *Me will be going*. The second choice cannot be correct because *me* cannot be used as the subject of a sentence. Instead, *me* is used as an object.

Answer: Bob and I will be going.

When a pronoun is used with a noun immediately following (as in "we boys"), try the sentence **without the added noun**.

Example:

(We/Us) boys played football last year.

Test: (1) *We played football last year* or (2) *Us played football last year*. Again, the second choice cannot be correct because *us* cannot be used as a subject of a sentence. Instead, *us* is used as an object.

Answer: We boys played football last year.

> **Review Video: Pronoun Usage**
> Visit mometrix.com/academy and enter code: 666500

A pronoun should point clearly to the **antecedent**. Here is how a pronoun reference can be unhelpful if it is puzzling or not directly stated.

Unhelpful: Ron and Jim [antecedent] went to the store, and he [pronoun] bought soda.

Who bought soda? Ron or Jim?

Helpful: Jim [antecedent] went to the store, and he [pronoun] bought soda.

The sentence is clear. Jim bought the soda.

Some pronouns change their form by their placement in a sentence. A pronoun that is a **subject** in a sentence comes in the **subjective case**. Pronouns that serve as **objects** appear in the **objective case**. Finally, the pronouns that are used as **possessives** appear in the **possessive case**.

Examples:

Subjective case: *He* is coming to the show.

The pronoun *He* is the subject of the sentence.

Objective case: Josh drove *him* to the airport.

The pronoun *him* is the object of the sentence.

Possessive case: The flowers are *mine*.

The pronoun *mine* shows ownership of the flowers.

The word *who* is a subjective-case pronoun that can be used as a **subject**. The word *whom* is an objective-case pronoun that can be used as an **object**. The words *who* and *whom* are common in subordinate clauses or in questions.

Examples:

He knows who [subject] wants [verb] to come.

He knows the man whom [object] we want [verb] at the party.

CLAUSES

A clause is a group of words that contains both a subject and a predicate (verb). There are two types of clauses: independent and dependent. An **independent clause** contains a complete thought, while a **dependent (or subordinate) clause** does not. A dependent clause includes a subject and a verb, and may also contain objects or complements, but it cannot stand as a complete thought without being joined to an independent clause. Dependent clauses function within sentences as adjectives, adverbs, or nouns.

Example:

I am running (independent clause) because I want to stay in shape (dependent clause).

The clause *I am running* is an independent clause: it has a subject and a verb, and it gives a complete thought. The clause *because I want to stay in shape* is a dependent clause: it has a subject and a verb, but it does not express a complete thought. It adds detail to the independent clause to which it is attached.

> **Review Video: Independent and Dependent Clauses**
> Visit mometrix.com/academy and enter code: 556903

TYPES OF DEPENDENT CLAUSES
ADJECTIVE CLAUSES

An **adjective clause** is a dependent clause that modifies a noun or a pronoun. Adjective clauses begin with a relative pronoun (*who, whose, whom, which,* and *that*) or a relative adverb (*where, when,* and *why*).

Also, adjective clauses come after the noun that the clause needs to explain or rename. This is done to have a clear connection to the independent clause.

Examples:

I learned the reason (independent clause) why I won the award (adjective clause).

This is the place (independent clause) where I started my first job (adjective clause).

An adjective clause can be an essential or nonessential clause. An essential clause is very important to the sentence. **Essential clauses** explain or define a person or thing. **Nonessential clauses** give more information about a person or thing but are not necessary to define them. Nonessential clauses are set off with commas while essential clauses are not.

Examples:

A person who works hard at first (essential clause) can often rest later in life.

Neil Armstrong, who walked on the moon (nonessential clause), is my hero.

> **Review Video: Adjective Clauses and Phrases**
> Visit mometrix.com/academy and enter code: 520888

Adverb Clauses

An **adverb clause** is a dependent clause that modifies a verb, adjective, or adverb. In sentences with multiple dependent clauses, adverb clauses are usually placed immediately before or after the independent clause. An adverb clause is introduced with words such as *after, although, as, before, because, if, since, so, unless, when, where,* and *while*.

Examples:

When you walked outside, I called the manager. *(adverb clause: When you walked outside)*

I will go with you unless you want to stay. *(adverb clause: unless you want to stay)*

Noun Clauses

A **noun clause** is a dependent clause that can be used as a subject, object, or complement. Noun clauses begin with words such as *how, that, what, whether, which, who,* and *why*. These words can also come with an adjective clause. Unless the noun clause is being used as the subject of the sentence, it should come after the verb of the independent clause.

Examples:

The real mystery is how you avoided serious injury. *(noun clause: how you avoided serious injury)*

What you learn from each other depends on your honesty with others. *(noun clause: What you learn from each other)*

Subordination

When two related ideas are not of equal importance, the ideal way to combine them is to make the more important idea an independent clause and the less important idea a dependent or subordinate clause. This is called **subordination**.

Example:

Separate ideas: The team had a perfect regular season. The team lost the championship.

Subordinated: Despite having a perfect regular season, *the team lost the championship*.

Phrases

A phrase is a group of words that functions as a single part of speech, usually a noun, adjective, or adverb. A **phrase** is not a complete thought, but it adds detail or explanation to a sentence, or renames something within the sentence.

Prepositional Phrases

One of the most common types of phrases is the prepositional phrase. A **prepositional phrase** begins with a preposition and ends with a noun or pronoun that is the object of the preposition. Normally, the prepositional phrase functions as an **adjective** or an **adverb** within the sentence.

Examples:

Th picnic is [prepositional phrase: on the blanket].

I am sick [prepositional phrase: with a fever] today.

[prepositional phrase: Among the many flowers], John found a four-leaf clover.

Verbal Phrases

A **verbal** is a word or phrase that is formed from a verb but does not function as a verb. Depending on its particular form, it may be used as a noun, adjective, or adverb. A verbal does **not** replace a verb in a sentence.

Examples:

Correct: [verb: Walk] a mile daily.

This is a complete sentence with the implied subject *you*.

Incorrect: [verbal: To walk] a mile.

This is not a sentence since there is no functional verb.

There are three types of verbal: **participles**, **gerunds**, and **infinitives**. Each type of verbal has a corresponding **phrase** that consists of the verbal itself along with any complements or modifiers.

Participles

A **participle** is a type of verbal that always functions as an adjective. The present participle always ends with *-ing*. Past participles end with *-d*, *-ed*, *-n*, or *-t*.

Examples: [verb: dance] | [present participle: dancing] | [past participle: danced]

Participial phrases most often come right before or right after the noun or pronoun that they modify.

Examples:

> Shipwrecked on an island, [participial phrase] the boys started to fish for food.
>
> Having been seated for five hours, [participial phrase] we got out of the car to stretch our legs.
>
> Praised for their work, [participial phrase] the group accepted the first-place trophy.

GERUNDS

A **gerund** is a type of verbal that always functions as a **noun**. Like present participles, gerunds always end with *-ing*, but they can be easily distinguished from one another by the part of speech they represent (participles always function as adjectives). Since a gerund or gerund phrase always functions as a noun, it can be used as the subject of a sentence, the predicate nominative, or the object of a verb or preposition.

Examples:

> We want to be known for **teaching the poor**. [gerund — object of preposition]
>
> **Coaching this team** is the best job of my life. [gerund — subject]
>
> We like **practicing our songs** in the basement. [gerund — object of verb]

INFINITIVES

An **infinitive** is a type of verbal that can function as a noun, an adjective, or an adverb. An infinitive is made of the word *to* and the basic form of the verb. As with all other types of verbal phrases, an infinitive phrase includes the verbal itself and all of its complements or modifiers.

Examples:

    To join (infinitive) the team is my goal in life. *(noun)*

    The animals have enough food *to eat* (infinitive) for the night. *(adjective)*

    People lift weights *to exercise* (infinitive) their muscles. *(adverb)*

> **Review Video: Gerunds, Infinitives, and Participles**
> Visit mometrix.com/academy and enter code: 634263

APPOSITIVE PHRASES

An **appositive** is a word or phrase that is used to explain or rename nouns or pronouns. Noun phrases, gerund phrases, and infinitive phrases can all be used as appositives.

Examples:

    Terriers, *hunters at heart* (appositive), have been dressed up to look like lap dogs.

    The noun phrase *hunters at heart* renames the noun *terriers*.

    His plan, *to save and invest his money* (appositive), was proven as a safe approach.

    The infinitive phrase explains what the plan is.

Appositive phrases can be **essential** or **nonessential**. An appositive phrase is essential if the person, place, or thing being described or renamed is too general for its meaning to be understood without the appositive.

Examples:

    Two of America's Founding Fathers, *George Washington and Thomas Jefferson* (essential), served as presidents.

    George Washington and Thomas Jefferson, *two Founding Fathers* (nonessential), served as presidents.

ABSOLUTE PHRASES

An absolute phrase is a phrase that consists of **a noun followed by a participle**. An absolute phrase provides **context** to what is being described in the sentence, but it does not modify or explain any particular word; it is essentially independent.

Examples:

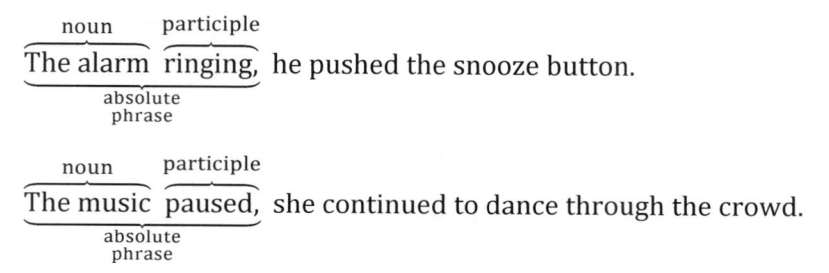

    The alarm ringing, he pushed the snooze button.
    (noun) (participle) — absolute phrase

    The music paused, she continued to dance through the crowd.
    (noun) (participle) — absolute phrase

PARALLELISM

When multiple items or ideas are presented in a sentence in series, such as in a list, the items or ideas must be stated in grammatically equivalent ways. In other words, if one idea is stated in gerund form, the second cannot be stated in infinitive form. For example, to write, *I enjoy reading and to study* would be incorrect. An infinitive and a gerund are not equivalent. Instead, you should write *I enjoy reading and studying*. In lists of more than two, all items must be parallel.

Example:

    Incorrect: He stopped at the office, grocery store, and the pharmacy before heading home.

    The first and third items in the list of places include the article *the*, so the second item needs it as well.

    Correct: He stopped at the office, *the* grocery store, and the pharmacy before heading home.

Example:

    Incorrect: While vacationing in Europe, she went biking, skiing, and climbed mountains.

    The first and second items in the list are gerunds, so the third item must be as well.

    Correct: While vacationing in Europe, she went biking, skiing, and *mountain climbing*.

> **Review Video: Parallel Construction**
> Visit mometrix.com/academy and enter code: 831988

SENTENCE PURPOSE

There are four types of sentences: declarative, imperative, interrogative, and exclamatory.

A **declarative** sentence states a fact and ends with a period.

    The football game starts at seven o'clock.

An **imperative** sentence tells someone to do something and generally ends with a period. An urgent command might end with an exclamation point instead.

    Don't forget to buy your ticket.

An **interrogative** sentence asks a question and ends with a question mark.

    Are you going to the game on Friday?

An **exclamatory** sentence shows strong emotion and ends with an exclamation point.

I can't believe we won the game!

> **Review Video: Functions of a Sentence**
> Visit mometrix.com/academy and enter code: 475974

SENTENCE STRUCTURE

Sentences are classified by structure based on the type and number of clauses present. The four classifications of sentence structure are the following:

Simple: A simple sentence has one independent clause with no dependent clauses. A simple sentence may have **compound elements** (i.e., compound subject or verb).

Examples:

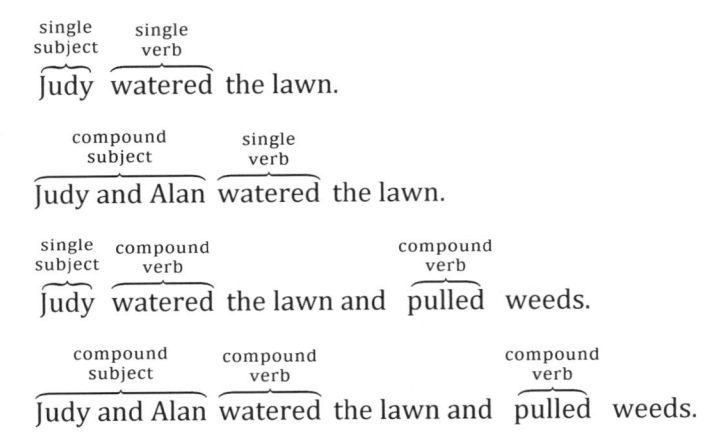

Judy (single subject) watered (single verb) the lawn.

Judy and Alan (compound subject) watered (single verb) the lawn.

Judy (single subject) watered (compound verb) the lawn and pulled (compound verb) weeds.

Judy and Alan (compound subject) watered (compound verb) the lawn and pulled (compound verb) weeds.

Compound: A compound sentence has two or more independent clauses with no dependent clauses. Usually, the independent clauses are joined with a comma and a coordinating conjunction or with a semicolon.

Examples:

The time has come (independent clause), and we are ready (independent clause).

I woke up at dawn (independent clause); the sun was just coming up (independent clause).

Complex: A complex sentence has one independent clause and at least one dependent clause.

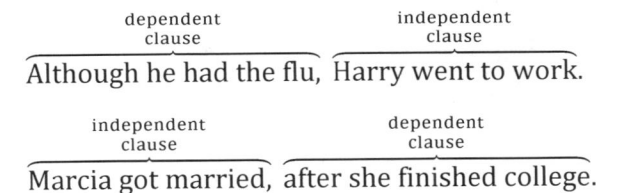

Examples:

Although he had the flu (dependent clause), Harry went to work (independent clause).

Marcia got married (independent clause), after she finished college (dependent clause).

73

Compound-Complex: A compound-complex sentence has at least two independent clauses and at least one dependent clause.

Examples:

John is my friend [independent clause] who went to India, [dependent clause] and he brought back souvenirs. [independent clause]

You may not realize this, [independent clause] but we heard the music [independent clause] that you played last night. [dependent clause]

> **Review Video: Sentence Structure**
> Visit mometrix.com/academy and enter code: 700478

Sentence variety is important to consider when writing an essay or speech. A variety of sentence lengths and types creates rhythm, makes a passage more engaging, and gives writers an opportunity to demonstrate their writing style. Writing that uses the same length or type of sentence without variation can be boring or difficult to read. To evaluate a passage for effective sentence variety, it is helpful to note whether the passage contains diverse sentence structures and lengths. It is also important to pay attention to the way each sentence starts and avoid beginning with the same words or phrases.

SENTENCE FRAGMENTS

Recall that a group of words must contain at least one **independent clause** in order to be considered a sentence. If it doesn't contain even one independent clause, it is called a **sentence fragment**.

The appropriate process for **repairing** a sentence fragment depends on what type of fragment it is. If the fragment is a dependent clause, it can sometimes be as simple as removing a subordinating word (e.g., when, because, if) from the beginning of the fragment. Alternatively, a dependent clause can be incorporated into a closely related neighboring sentence. If the fragment is missing some required part, like a subject or a verb, the fix might be as simple as adding the missing part.

Examples:

    Fragment: Because he wanted to sail the Mediterranean.

    Removed subordinating word: He wanted to sail the Mediterranean.

    Combined with another sentence: Because he wanted to sail the Mediterranean, he booked a Greek island cruise.

RUN-ON SENTENCES

Run-on sentences consist of multiple independent clauses that have not been joined together properly. Run-on sentences can be corrected in several different ways:

Join clauses properly: This can be done with a comma and coordinating conjunction, with a semicolon, or with a colon or dash if the second clause is explaining something in the first.

Example:

> **Incorrect**: I went on the trip, we visited lots of castles.
>
> **Corrected**: I went on the trip, and we visited lots of castles.

Split into separate sentences: This correction is most effective when the independent clauses are very long or when they are not closely related.

Example:

> **Incorrect**: The drive to New York takes ten hours, my uncle lives in Boston.
>
> **Corrected**: The drive to New York takes ten hours. My uncle lives in Boston.

Make one clause dependent: This is the easiest way to make the sentence correct and more interesting at the same time. It's often as simple as adding a subordinating word between the two clauses or before the first clause.

Example:

> **Incorrect**: I finally made it to the store and I bought some eggs.
>
> **Corrected**: When I finally made it to the store, I bought some eggs.

Reduce to one clause with a compound verb: If both clauses have the same subject, remove the subject from the second clause, and you now have just one clause with a compound verb.

Example:

> **Incorrect**: The drive to New York takes ten hours, it makes me very tired.
>
> **Corrected**: The drive to New York takes ten hours and makes me very tired.

Note: While these are the simplest ways to correct a run-on sentence, often the best way is to completely reorganize the thoughts in the sentence and rewrite it.

> **Review Video: Fragments and Run-on Sentences**
> Visit mometrix.com/academy and enter code: 541989

DANGLING AND MISPLACED MODIFIERS
DANGLING MODIFIERS

A dangling modifier is a dependent clause or verbal phrase that does not have a clear logical connection to a word in the sentence.

Example:

Incorrect: Reading each magazine article [dangling modifier], the stories caught my attention.

The word *stories* cannot be modified by *Reading each magazine article.* People can read, but stories cannot read. Therefore, the subject of the sentence must be a person.

Corrected: Reading each magazine article [dependent clause], I was entertained by the stories.

Example:

Incorrect: Ever since childhood [dangling modifier], my grandparents have visited me for Christmas.

The speaker in this sentence can't have been visited by her grandparents when *they* were children, since she wouldn't have been born yet. Either the modifier should be clarified or the sentence should be rearranged to specify whose childhood is being referenced.

Clarified: Ever since I was a child [dependent clause], my grandparents have visited for Christmas.

Rearranged: I have enjoyed my grandparents visiting for Christmas, ever since childhood [dependent clause].

Misplaced Modifiers

Because modifiers are grammatically versatile, they can be put in many different places within the structure of a sentence. The danger of this versatility is that a modifier can accidentally be placed where it is modifying the wrong word or where it is not clear which word it is modifying.

Example:

Incorrect: She read the book to a crowd that was filled with beautiful pictures [modifier].

The book was filled with beautiful pictures, not the crowd.

Corrected: She read the book that was filled with beautiful pictures [modifier] to a crowd.

Example:

Ambiguous: Derek saw a bus nearly hit a man <u>on his way to work</u>. *(modifier)*

Was Derek on his way to work or was the other man?

Derek: <u>On his way to work</u>, *(modifier)* Derek saw a bus nearly hit a man.

The other man: Derek saw a bus nearly hit a man <u>who was on his way to work</u>. *(modifier)*

SPLIT INFINITIVES

A split infinitive occurs when a modifying word comes between the word *to* and the verb that pairs with *to*.

Example: To *clearly* explain vs. To explain *clearly* | To *softly* sing vs. To sing *softly*

Though considered improper by some, split infinitives may provide better clarity and simplicity in some cases than the alternatives. As such, avoiding them should not be considered a universal rule.

DOUBLE NEGATIVES

Standard English allows **two negatives** only when a **positive** meaning is intended. For example, *The team was not displeased with their performance.* Double negatives to emphasize negation are not used in standard English.

Negative modifiers (e.g., never, no, and not) should not be paired with other negative modifiers or negative words (e.g., none, nobody, nothing, or neither). The modifiers *hardly, barely*, and *scarcely* are also considered negatives in standard English, so they should not be used with other negatives.

Punctuation

END PUNCTUATION

PERIODS

Use a period to end all sentences except direct questions and exclamations. Periods are also used for abbreviations.

Examples: 3 p.m. | 2 a.m. | Mr. Jones | Mrs. Stevens | Dr. Smith | Bill, Jr. | Pennsylvania Ave.

Note: An abbreviation is a shortened form of a word or phrase.

Question Marks

Question marks should be used following a **direct question**. A polite request can be followed by a period instead of a question mark.

Direct Question: What is for lunch today? | How are you? | Why is that the answer?

Polite Requests: Can you please send me the item tomorrow. | Will you please walk with me on the track.

> **Review Video: Question Marks**
> Visit mometrix.com/academy and enter code: 118471

Exclamation Marks

Exclamation marks are used after a word group or sentence that shows much feeling or has special importance. Exclamation marks should not be overused. They are saved for proper **exclamatory interjections**.

Example: We're going to the finals! | You have a beautiful car! | "That's crazy!" she yelled.

> **Review Video: Exclamation Points**
> Visit mometrix.com/academy and enter code: 199367

Commas

The comma is a punctuation mark that can help you understand connections in a sentence. Not every sentence needs a comma. However, if a sentence needs a comma, you need to put it in the right place. A comma in the wrong place (or an absent comma) will make a sentence's meaning unclear. These are some of the rules for commas:

Use Case	Example
Before a **coordinating conjunction** joining independent clauses	Bob caught three fish, and I caught two fish.
After an **introductory phrase**	After the final out, we went to a restaurant to celebrate.
After an **adverbial clause**	Studying the stars, I was awed by the beauty of the sky.
Between **items in a series**	I will bring the turkey, the pie, and the coffee.
For **interjections**	Wow, you know how to play this game.
After *yes* and *no* responses	No, I cannot come tomorrow.
Separate **nonessential modifiers**	John Frank, who coaches the team, was promoted today.
Separate **nonessential appositives**	Thomas Edison, an American inventor, was born in Ohio.
Separate **nouns of direct address**	You, John, are my only hope in this moment.
Separate **interrogative tags**	This is the last time, correct?
Separate **contrasts**	You are my friend, not my enemy.
Writing **dates**	July 4, 1776, is an important date to remember.
Writing **addresses**	He is meeting me at 456 Delaware Avenue, Washington, D.C., tomorrow morning.
Writing **geographical names**	Paris, France, is my favorite city.
Writing **titles**	John Smith, PhD, will be visiting your class today.
Separate **expressions like** *he said*	"You can start," she said, "with an apology."

Also, you can use a comma **between coordinate adjectives** not joined with *and*. However, not all adjectives are coordinate (i.e., equal or parallel).

Incorrect: The kind, brown dog followed me home.

Correct: The kind, loyal dog followed me home.

There are two simple ways to know if your adjectives are coordinate. One, you can join the adjectives with *and*: *The kind and loyal dog*. Two, you can change the order of the adjectives: *The loyal, kind dog*.

> Review Video: **Commas**
> Visit mometrix.com/academy and enter code: 786797

SEMICOLONS

The semicolon is used to connect major sentence pieces of equal value. Some rules for semicolons include:

Use Case	Example
Between closely connected independent clauses **not connected with a coordinating conjunction**	You are right; we should go with your plan.
Between independent clauses **linked with a transitional word**	I think that we can agree on this; however, I am not sure about my friends.
Between items in a **series that has internal punctuation**	I have visited New York, New York; Augusta, Maine; and Baltimore, Maryland.

> Review Video: **Semicolon Usage**
> Visit mometrix.com/academy and enter code: 370605

COLONS

The colon is used to call attention to the words that follow it. A colon must come after a **complete independent clause**. The rules for colons are as follows:

Use Case	Example
After an independent clause to **make a list**	I want to learn many languages: Spanish, German, and Italian.
For **explanations**	There is one thing that stands out on your resume: responsibility.
To give a **quote**	He started with an idea: "We are able to do more than we imagine."
After the **greeting in a formal letter**	To Whom It May Concern:
Show **hours and minutes**	It is 3:14 p.m.
Separate a **title and subtitle**	The essay is titled "America: A Short Introduction to a Modern Country."

> Review Video: **Colons**
> Visit mometrix.com/academy and enter code: 868673

PARENTHESES

Parentheses are used for additional information. Also, they can be used to put labels for letters or numbers in a series. Parentheses should be not be used very often. If they are overused, parentheses can be a distraction instead of a help.

Examples:

Extra Information: The rattlesnake (see Image 2) is a dangerous snake of North and South America.

Series: Include in the email (1) your name, (2) your address, and (3) your question for the author.

> **Review Video: Parentheses**
> Visit mometrix.com/academy and enter code: 947743

QUOTATION MARKS

Use quotation marks to close off **direct quotations** of a person's spoken or written words. Do not use quotation marks around indirect quotations. An indirect quotation gives someone's message without using the person's exact words. Use **single quotation marks** to close off a quotation inside a quotation.

Direct Quote: Nancy said, "I am waiting for Henry to arrive."

Indirect Quote: Henry said that he is going to be late to the meeting.

Quote inside a Quote: The teacher asked, "Has everyone read 'The Gift of the Magi'?"

Quotation marks should be used around the titles of **short works**: newspaper and magazine articles, poems, short stories, songs, television episodes, radio programs, and subdivisions of books or websites.

Examples:

"Rip Van Winkle" (short story by Washington Irving)

"O Captain! My Captain!" (poem by Walt Whitman)

Although it is not standard usage, quotation marks are sometimes used to highlight **irony** or the use of words to mean something other than their dictionary definition. This type of usage should be employed sparingly, if at all.

Examples:

The boss warned Frank that he was walking on "thin ice."	Frank is not walking on real ice. Instead, he is being warned to avoid mistakes.
The teacher thanked the young man for his "honesty."	The quotation marks around *honesty* show that the teacher does not believe the young man's explanation.

> **Review Video: Quotation Marks**
> Visit mometrix.com/academy and enter code: 884918

Periods and commas are put **inside** quotation marks. Colons and semicolons are put **outside** the quotation marks. Question marks and exclamation points are placed inside quotation marks when they are part of a quote. When the question or exclamation mark goes with the whole sentence, the mark is left outside of the quotation marks.

Examples:

Period and comma	We read "The Gift of the Magi," "The Skylight Room," and "The Cactus."
Semicolon	They watched "The Nutcracker"; then, they went home.
Exclamation mark that is a part of a quote	The crowd cheered, "Victory!"
Question mark that goes with the whole sentence	Is your favorite short story "The Tell-Tale Heart"?

APOSTROPHES

An apostrophe is used to show **possession** or the **deletion of letters in contractions**. An apostrophe is not needed with the possessive pronouns *his, hers, its, ours, theirs, whose*, and *yours*.

Singular Nouns: David's car | a book's theme | my brother's board game

Plural Nouns that end with -s: the scissors' handle | boys' basketball

Plural Nouns that end without -s: Men's department | the people's adventure

> **Review Video: Apostrophes**
> Visit mometrix.com/academy and enter code: 213068
>
> **Review Video: Punctuation Errors in Possessive Pronouns**
> Visit mometrix.com/academy and enter code: 221438

HYPHENS

Hyphens are used to **separate compound words**. Use hyphens in the following cases:

Use Case	Example
Compound numbers from 21 to 99 when written out in words	This team needs twenty-five points to win the game.
Written-out fractions that are used as adjectives	The recipe says that we need a three-fourths cup of butter.
Compound adjectives that come before a noun	The well-fed dog took a nap.
Unusual compound words that would be hard to read or easily confused with other words	This is the best anti-itch cream on the market.

Note: This is not a complete set of the rules for hyphens. A dictionary is the best tool for knowing if a compound word needs a hyphen.

> **Review Video: Hyphens**
> Visit mometrix.com/academy and enter code: 981632

Dashes

Dashes are used to show a **break** or a **change in thought** in a sentence or to act as parentheses in a sentence. When typing, use two hyphens to make a dash. Do not put a space before or after the dash. The following are the functions of dashes:

Use Case	Example
Set off parenthetical statements or an **appositive with internal punctuation**	The three trees—oak, pine, and magnolia—are coming on a truck tomorrow.
Show a **break or change in tone or thought**	The first question—how silly of me—does not have a correct answer.

Ellipsis Marks

The ellipsis mark has **three** periods (...) to show when **words have been removed** from a quotation. If a **full sentence or more** is removed from a quoted passage, you need to use **four** periods to show the removed text and the end punctuation mark. The ellipsis mark should not be used at the beginning of a quotation. The ellipsis mark should also not be used at the end of a quotation unless some words have been deleted from the end of the final sentence.

Example:

"Then he picked up the groceries...paid for them...later he went home."

Brackets

There are two main reasons to use brackets:

Use Case	Example
Placing **parentheses inside of parentheses**	The hero of this story, Paul Revere (a silversmith and industrialist [see Ch. 4]), rode through towns of Massachusetts to warn of advancing British troops.
Adding **clarification or detail to a quotation** that is not part of the quotation	The father explained, "My children are planning to attend my alma mater [State University]."

Review Video: Brackets
Visit mometrix.com/academy and enter code: 727546

Common Usage Mistakes

Word Confusion

Which, That, and Who

The words *which*, *that*, and *who* can act as **relative pronouns** to help clarify or describe a noun.

Which is used for things only.

> Example: Andrew's car, *which is old and rusty,* broke down last week.

That is used for people or things. *That* is usually informal when used to describe people.

> Example: Is this the only book *that Louis L'Amour wrote?*

> Example: Is Louis L'Amour the author *that wrote Western novels?*

Who is used for people or for animals that have an identity or personality.

> Example: Mozart was the composer *who wrote those operas.*

> Example: John's dog, *who is called Max,* is large and fierce.

Homophones

Homophones are words that sound alike (or similar) but have different **spellings** and **definitions**. A homophone is a type of **homonym**, which is a pair or group of words that are pronounced or spelled the same, but do not mean the same thing.

To, Too, and Two

To can be an adverb or a preposition for showing direction, purpose, and relationship. See your dictionary for the many other ways to use *to* in a sentence.

> Examples: I went to the store. | I want to go with you.

Too is an adverb that means *also, as well, very,* or *in excess.*

> Examples: I can walk a mile too. | You have eaten too much.

Two is a number.

> Example: You have two minutes left.

There, Their, and They're

There can be an adjective, adverb, or pronoun. Often, *there* is used to show a place or to start a sentence.

> Examples: I went there yesterday. | There is something in his pocket.

Their is a pronoun that is used to show ownership.

> Examples: He is their father. | This is their fourth apology this week.

They're is a contraction of *they are.*

> Example: Did you know that they're in town?

Knew and New

Knew is the past tense of *know*.

>Example: I knew the answer.

New is an adjective that means something is current, has not been used, or is modern.

>Example: This is my new phone.

Then and Than

Then is an adverb that indicates sequence or order:

>Example: I'm going to run to the library and then come home.

Than is special-purpose word used only for comparisons:

>Example: Susie likes chips more than candy.

Its and It's

Its is a pronoun that shows ownership.

>Example: The guitar is in its case.

It's is a contraction of *it is*.

>Example: It's an honor and a privilege to meet you.

Note: The *h* in honor is silent, so *honor* starts with the vowel sound *o*, which must have the article *an*.

Your and You're

Your is a pronoun that shows ownership.

>Example: This is your moment to shine.

You're is a contraction of *you are*.

>Example: Yes, you're correct.

Saw and Seen

Saw is the past-tense form of *see*.

>Example: I saw a turtle on my walk this morning.

Seen is the past participle of *see*.

>Example: I have seen this movie before.

Affect and Effect

There are two main reasons that *affect* and *effect* are so often confused: 1) both words can be used as either a noun or a verb, and 2) unlike most homophones, their usage and meanings are closely related to each other. Here is a quick rundown of the four usage options:

Affect (n): feeling, emotion, or mood that is displayed

    Example: The patient had a flat *affect*. (i.e., his face showed little or no emotion)

Affect (v): to alter, to change, to influence

    Example: The sunshine *affects* the plant's growth.

Effect (n): a result, a consequence

    Example: What *effect* will this weather have on our schedule?

Effect (v): to bring about, to cause to be

    Example: These new rules will *effect* order in the office.

The noun form of *affect* is rarely used outside of technical medical descriptions, so if a noun form is needed on the test, you can safely select *effect*. The verb form of *effect* is not as rare as the noun form of *affect*, but it's still not all that likely to show up on your test. If you need a verb and you can't decide which to use based on the definitions, choosing *affect* is your best bet.

HOMOGRAPHS

Homographs are words that share the same spelling, but have different meanings and sometimes different pronunciations. To figure out which meaning is being used, you should be looking for context clues. The context clues give hints to the meaning of the word. For example, the word *spot* has many meanings. It can mean "a place" or "a stain or blot." In the sentence "After my lunch, I saw a spot on my shirt," the word *spot* means "a stain or blot." The context clues of "After my lunch" and "on my shirt" guide you to this decision. A homograph is another type of homonym.

BANK

    (noun): an establishment where money is held for savings or lending

    (verb): to collect or pile up

CONTENT

    (noun): the topics that will be addressed within a book

    (adjective): pleased or satisfied

    (verb): to make someone pleased or satisfied

FINE

    (noun): an amount of money that acts a penalty for an offense

    (adjective): very small or thin

    (adverb): in an acceptable way

    (verb): to make someone pay money as a punishment

INCENSE

    (noun): a material that is burned in religious settings and makes a pleasant aroma

    (verb): to frustrate or anger

Lead
(noun): the first or highest position

(noun): a heavy metallic element

(verb): to direct a person or group of followers

(adjective): containing lead

Object
(noun): a lifeless item that can be held and observed

(verb): to disagree

Produce
(noun): fruits and vegetables

(verb): to make or create something

Refuse
(noun): garbage or debris that has been thrown away

(verb): to not allow

Subject
(noun): an area of study

(verb): to force or subdue

Tear
(noun): a fluid secreted by the eyes

(verb): to separate or pull apart

The Writing Process

Brainstorming
Brainstorming is a technique that is used to find a creative approach to a subject. This can be accomplished by simple **free-association** with a topic. For example, with paper and pen, write every thought that you have about the topic in a word or phrase. This is done without critical thinking. You should put everything that comes to your mind about the topic on your scratch paper. Then, you need to read the list over a few times. Next, look for patterns, repetitions, and clusters of ideas. This allows a variety of fresh ideas to come as you think about the topic.

Free Writing
Free writing is a more structured form of brainstorming. The method involves taking a limited amount of time (e.g., 2 to 3 minutes) to write everything that comes to mind about the topic in complete sentences. When time expires, review everything that has been written down. Many of your sentences may make little or no sense, but the insights and observations that can come from free writing make this method a valuable approach. Usually, free writing results in a fuller expression of ideas than brainstorming because thoughts and associations are written in complete sentences. However, both techniques can be used to complement each other.

Planning

Planning is the process of organizing a piece of writing before composing a draft. Planning can include creating an outline or a graphic organizer, such as a Venn diagram, a spider-map, or a flowchart. These methods should help the writer identify their topic, main ideas, and the general organization of the composition. Preliminary research can also take place during this stage. Planning helps writers organize all of their ideas and decide if they have enough material to begin their first draft. However, writers should remember that the decisions they make during this step will likely change later in the process, so their plan does not have to be perfect.

Drafting

Writers may then use their plan, outline, or graphic organizer to compose their first draft. They may write subsequent drafts to improve their writing. Writing multiple drafts can help writers consider different ways to communicate their ideas and address errors that may be difficult to correct without rewriting a section or the whole composition. Most writers will vary in how many drafts they choose to write, as there is no "right" number of drafts. Writing drafts also takes away the pressure to write perfectly on the first try, as writers can improve with each draft they write.

Revising, Editing, and Proofreading

Once a writer completes a draft, they can move on to the revising, editing, and proofreading steps to improve their draft. These steps begin with making broad changes that may apply to large sections of a composition and then making small, specific corrections. **Revising** is the first and broadest of these steps. Revising involves ensuring that the composition addresses an appropriate audience, includes all necessary material, maintains focus throughout, and is organized logically. Revising may occur after the first draft to ensure that the following drafts improve upon errors from the first draft. Some revision should occur between each draft to avoid repeating these errors. The **editing** phase of writing is narrower than the revising phase. Editing a composition should include steps such as improving transitions between paragraphs, ensuring each paragraph is on topic, and improving the flow of the text. The editing phase may also include correcting grammatical errors that cannot be fixed without significantly altering the text. **Proofreading** involves fixing misspelled words, typos, other grammatical errors, and any remaining surface-level flaws in the composition.

Recursive Writing Process

However you approach writing, you may find comfort in knowing that the revision process can occur in any order. The **recursive writing process** is not as difficult as the phrase may make it seem. Simply put, the recursive writing process means that you may need to revisit steps after completing other steps. It also implies that the steps are not required to take place in any certain order. Indeed, you may find that planning, drafting, and revising can all take place at about the same time. The writing process involves moving back and forth between planning, drafting, and revising, followed by more planning, more drafting, and more revising until the writing is satisfactory.

> **Review Video: Recursive Writing Process**
> Visit mometrix.com/academy and enter code: 951611

Technology in the Writing Process

Modern technology has yielded several tools that can be used to make the writing process more convenient and organized. Word processors and online tools, such as databases and plagiarism detectors, allow much of the writing process to be completed in one place, using one device.

Technology for Planning and Drafting

For the planning and drafting stages of the writing process, word processors are a helpful tool. These programs also feature formatting tools, allowing users to create their own planning tools or create digital outlines that can be easily converted into sentences, paragraphs, or an entire essay draft. Online databases and references also complement the planning process by providing convenient access to information and sources for research. Word processors also allow users to keep up with their work and update it more easily than if they wrote their work by hand. Online word processors often allow users to collaborate, making group assignments more convenient. These programs also allow users to include illustrations or other supplemental media in their compositions.

Technology for Revising, Editing, and Proofreading

Word processors also benefit the revising, editing, and proofreading stages of the writing process. Most of these programs indicate errors in spelling and grammar, allowing users to catch minor errors and correct them quickly. There are also websites designed to help writers by analyzing text for deeper errors, such as poor sentence structure, inappropriate complexity, lack of sentence variety, and style issues. These websites can help users fix errors they may not know to look for or may have simply missed. As writers finish these steps, they may benefit from checking their work for any plagiarism. There are several websites and programs that compare text to other documents and publications across the internet and detect any similarities within the text. These websites show the source of the similar information, so users know whether or not they referenced the source and unintentionally plagiarized its contents.

Technology for Publishing

Technology also makes managing written work more convenient. Digitally storing documents keeps everything in one place and is easy to reference. Digital storage also makes sharing work easier, as documents can be attached to an email or stored online. This also allows writers to publish their work easily, as they can electronically submit it to other publications or freely post it to a personal blog, profile, or website.

Outlining and Organizing Ideas

Main Ideas, Supporting Details, and Outlining a Topic

A writer often begins the first paragraph of a paper by stating the **main idea** or point, also known as the **topic sentence**. The rest of the paragraph supplies particular details that develop and support the main point. One way to visualize the relationship between the main point and supporting information is by considering a table: the tabletop is the main point, and each of the table's legs is a supporting detail or group of details. Both professional authors and students can benefit from planning their writing by first making an outline of the topic. Outlines facilitate quick identification of the main point and supporting details without having to wade through the additional language that will exist in the fully developed essay, article, or paper. Outlining can also help readers to analyze a piece of existing writing for the same reason. The outline first summarizes the main idea in one sentence. Then, below that, it summarizes the supporting details in a numbered list. Writing the paper then consists of filling in the outline with detail, writing a paragraph for each supporting point, and adding an introduction and conclusion.

Introduction

The purpose of the introduction is to capture the reader's attention and announce the essay's main idea. Normally, the introduction contains 50-80 words, or 3-5 sentences. An introduction can begin with an interesting quote, a question, or a strong opinion—something that will **engage** the reader's interest and prompt them to keep reading. If you are writing your essay to a specific prompt, your introduction should include a **restatement or summarization** of the prompt so that the reader will have some context for your essay. Finally, your introduction should briefly state your **thesis or main idea**: the primary thing you hope to communicate to the reader through your essay. Don't try to include all of the details and nuances of your thesis, or all of your reasons for it, in the introduction. That's what the rest of the essay is for!

> **Review Video: Introduction**
> Visit mometrix.com/academy and enter code: 961328

THESIS STATEMENT

The thesis is the main idea of the essay. A temporary thesis, or working thesis, should be established early in the writing process because it will serve to keep the writer focused as ideas develop. This temporary thesis is subject to change as you continue to write.

The temporary thesis has two parts: a **topic** (i.e., the focus of your essay based on the prompt) and a **comment**. The comment makes an important point about the topic. A temporary thesis should be interesting and specific. Also, you need to limit the topic to a manageable scope. These three questions are useful tools to measure the effectiveness of any temporary thesis:

- Does the focus of my essay have enough interest to hold an audience?
- Is the focus of my essay specific enough to generate interest?
- Is the focus of my essay manageable for the time limit? Too broad? Too narrow?

The thesis should be a generalization rather than a fact because the thesis prepares readers for facts and details that support the thesis. The process of bringing the thesis into sharp focus may help in outlining major sections of the work. Once the thesis and introduction are complete, you can address the body of the work.

> **Review Video: Thesis Statements**
> Visit mometrix.com/academy and enter code: 691033

SUPPORTING THE THESIS

Throughout your essay, the thesis should be **explained clearly and supported** adequately by additional arguments. The thesis sentence needs to contain a clear statement of the purpose of your essay and a comment about the thesis. With the thesis statement, you have an opportunity to state what is noteworthy of this particular treatment of the prompt. Each sentence and paragraph should build on and support the thesis.

When you respond to the prompt, use parts of the passage to support your argument or defend your position. Using supporting evidence from the passage strengths your argument because readers can see your attention to the entire passage and your response to the details and facts within the passage. You can use facts, details, statistics, and direct quotations from the passage to uphold your position. Be sure to point out which information comes from the original passage and base your argument around that evidence.

BODY

In an essay's introduction, the writer establishes the thesis and may indicate how the rest of the piece will be structured. In the body of the piece, the writer **elaborates** upon, **illustrates**, and **explains** the **thesis statement**. How writers arrange supporting details and their choices of paragraph types are development techniques. Writers may give examples of the concept introduced in the thesis statement. If the subject includes a cause-and-effect relationship, the author may explain its causality. A writer will explain or analyze the main idea of the piece throughout the body, often by presenting arguments for the veracity or credibility of the thesis statement. Writers may use development to define or clarify ambiguous terms. Paragraphs within the body may be organized using natural sequences, like space and time. Writers may employ **inductive reasoning**, using multiple details to establish a generalization or causal relationship, or **deductive reasoning**, proving a generalized hypothesis or proposition through a specific example or case.

> **Review Video: Drafting Body Paragraphs**
> Visit mometrix.com/academy and enter code: 724590

PARAGRAPHS

After the introduction of a passage, a series of body paragraphs will carry a message through to the conclusion. Each paragraph should be **unified around a main point**. Normally, a good topic sentence summarizes the paragraph's main point. A topic sentence is a general sentence that gives an introduction to the paragraph.

The sentences that follow support the topic sentence. However, though it is usually the first sentence, the topic sentence can come as the final sentence to the paragraph if the earlier sentences give a clear explanation of the paragraph's topic. This allows the topic sentence to function as a concluding sentence. Overall, the paragraphs need to stay true to the main point. This means that any unnecessary sentences that do not advance the main point should be removed.

The main point of a paragraph requires adequate development (i.e., a substantial paragraph that covers the main point). A paragraph of two or three sentences does not cover a main point. This is especially true when the main point of the paragraph gives strong support to the argument of the thesis. An occasional short paragraph is fine as a transitional device. However, a well-developed argument will have paragraphs with more than a few sentences.

METHODS OF DEVELOPING PARAGRAPHS

Common methods of adding substance to paragraphs include examples, illustrations, analogies, and cause and effect.

- **Examples** are supporting details to the main idea of a paragraph or a passage. When authors write about something that their audience may not understand, they can provide an example to show their point. When authors write about something that is not easily accepted, they can give examples to prove their point.
- **Illustrations** are extended examples that require several sentences. Well-selected illustrations can be a great way for authors to develop a point that may not be familiar to their audience.
- **Analogies** make comparisons between items that appear to have nothing in common. Analogies are employed by writers to provoke fresh thoughts about a subject. These comparisons may be used to explain the unfamiliar, to clarify an abstract point, or to argue a point. Although analogies are effective literary devices, they should be used carefully in arguments. Two things may be alike in some respects but completely different in others.

- **Cause and effect** is an excellent device to explain the connection between an action or situation and a particular result. One way that authors can use cause and effect is to state the effect in the topic sentence of a paragraph and add the causes in the body of the paragraph. This method can give an author's paragraphs structure, which always strengthens writing.

TYPES OF PARAGRAPHS

A **paragraph of narration** tells a story or a part of a story. Normally, the sentences are arranged in chronological order (i.e., the order that the events happened). However, flashbacks (i.e., an anecdote from an earlier time) can be included.

A **descriptive paragraph** makes a verbal portrait of a person, place, or thing. When specific details are used that appeal to one or more of the senses (i.e., sight, sound, smell, taste, and touch), authors give readers a sense of being present in the moment.

A **process paragraph** is related to time order (i.e., First, you open the bottle. Second, you pour the liquid, etc.). Usually, this describes a process or teaches readers how to perform a process.

Comparing two things draws attention to their similarities and indicates a number of differences. When authors contrast, they focus only on differences. Both comparing and contrasting may be done point-by-point, noting both the similarities and differences of each point, or in sequential paragraphs, where you discuss all the similarities and then all the differences, or vice versa.

BREAKING TEXT INTO PARAGRAPHS

For most forms of writing, you will need to use multiple paragraphs. As such, determining when to start a new paragraph is very important. Reasons for starting a new paragraph include:

- To mark off the introduction and concluding paragraphs
- To signal a shift to a new idea or topic
- To indicate an important shift in time or place
- To explain a point in additional detail
- To highlight a comparison, contrast, or cause and effect relationship

PARAGRAPH LENGTH

Most readers find that their comfort level for a paragraph is between 100 and 200 words. Shorter paragraphs cause too much starting and stopping and give a choppy effect. Paragraphs that are too long often test the attention span of readers. Two notable exceptions to this rule exist. In scientific or scholarly papers, longer paragraphs suggest seriousness and depth. In journalistic writing, constraints are placed on paragraph size by the narrow columns in a newspaper format.

The first and last paragraphs of a text will usually be the introduction and conclusion. These special-purpose paragraphs are likely to be shorter than paragraphs in the body of the work. Paragraphs in the body of the essay follow the subject's outline (e.g., one paragraph per point in short essays and a group of paragraphs per point in longer works). Some ideas require more development than others, so it is good for a writer to remain flexible. A paragraph of excessive length may be divided, and shorter ones may be combined.

COHERENT PARAGRAPHS

A smooth flow of sentences and paragraphs without gaps, shifts, or bumps will lead to paragraph **coherence**. Ties between old and new information can be smoothed using several methods:

- **Linking ideas clearly**, from the topic sentence to the body of the paragraph, is essential for a smooth transition. The topic sentence states the main point, and this should be followed by specific details, examples, and illustrations that support the topic sentence. The support may be direct or indirect. In **indirect support**, the illustrations and examples may support a sentence that in turn supports the topic directly.
- The **repetition of key words** adds coherence to a paragraph. To avoid dull language, variations of the key words may be used.
- **Parallel structures** are often used within sentences to emphasize the similarity of ideas and connect sentences giving similar information.
- Maintaining a **consistent verb tense** throughout the paragraph helps. Shifting tenses affects the smooth flow of words and can disrupt the coherence of the paragraph.

> **Review Video: How to Write a Good Paragraph**
> Visit mometrix.com/academy and enter code: 682127

SEQUENCE WORDS AND PHRASES

When a paragraph opens with the topic sentence, the second sentence may begin with a phrase like *first of all*, introducing the first supporting detail or example. The writer may introduce the second supporting item with words or phrases like *also*, *in addition*, and *besides*. The writer might introduce succeeding pieces of support with wording like, *another thing*, *moreover*, *furthermore*, or *not only that, but*. The writer may introduce the last piece of support with *lastly*, *finally*, or *last but not least*. Writers get off the point by presenting off-target items not supporting the main point. For example, a main point *my dog is not smart* is supported by the statement, *he's six years old and still doesn't answer to his name*. But *he cries when I leave for school* is not supportive, as it does not indicate lack of intelligence. Writers stay on point by presenting only supportive statements that are directly relevant to and illustrative of their main point.

TRANSITIONS

Transitions between sentences and paragraphs guide readers from idea to idea and indicate relationships between sentences and paragraphs. Writers should be judicious in their use of transitions, inserting them sparingly. They should also be selected to fit the author's purpose—transitions can indicate time, comparison, and conclusion, among other purposes. Tone is also important to consider when using transitional phrases, varying the tone for different audiences. For example, in a scholarly essay, *in summary* would be preferable to the more informal *in short*.

When working with transitional words and phrases, writers usually find a natural flow that indicates when a transition is needed. In reading a draft of the text, it should become apparent where the flow is disrupted. At this point, the writer can add transitional elements during the revision process. Revising can also afford an opportunity to delete transitional devices that seem heavy handed or unnecessary.

> **Review Video: Transitions in Writing**
> Visit mometrix.com/academy and enter code: 233246

Types of Transitional Words

Time	Afterward, immediately, earlier, meanwhile, recently, lately, now, since, soon, when, then, until, before, etc.
Sequence	too, first, second, further, moreover, also, again, and, next, still, besides, finally
Comparison	similarly, in the same way, likewise, also, again, once more
Contrasting	but, although, despite, however, instead, nevertheless, on the one hand... on the other hand, regardless, yet, in contrast.
Cause and Effect	because, consequently, thus, therefore, then, to this end, since, so, as a result, if... then, accordingly
Examples	for example, for instance, such as, to illustrate, indeed, in fact, specifically
Place	near, far, here, there, to the left/right, next to, above, below, beyond, opposite, beside
Concession	granted that, naturally, of course, it may appear, although it is true that
Repetition, Summary, or Conclusion	as mentioned earlier, as noted, in other words, in short, on the whole, to summarize, therefore, as a result, to conclude, in conclusion
Addition	and, also, furthermore, moreover
Generalization	in broad terms, broadly speaking, in general

Review Video: Transitional Words and Phrases
Visit mometrix.com/academy and enter code: 197796

Review Video: Transitions
Visit mometrix.com/academy and enter code: 707563

Conclusion

Two important principles to consider when writing a conclusion are strength and closure. A strong conclusion gives the reader a sense that the author's main points are meaningful and important, and that the supporting facts and arguments are convincing, solid, and well developed. When a conclusion achieves closure, it gives the impression that the writer has stated all necessary information and points and completed the work, rather than simply stopping after a specified length. Some things to avoid when writing concluding paragraphs include:

- Introducing a completely new idea
- Beginning with obvious or unoriginal phrases like "In conclusion" or "To summarize"
- Apologizing for one's opinions or writing
- Repeating the thesis word for word rather than rephrasing it
- Believing that the conclusion must always summarize the piece

Review Video: Drafting Conclusions
Visit mometrix.com/academy and enter code: 209408

Style and Form

Writing Style and Linguistic Form

Linguistic form encodes the literal meanings of words and sentences. It comes from the phonological, morphological, syntactic, and semantic parts of a language. **Writing style** consists of different ways of encoding the meaning and indicating figurative and stylistic meanings. An author's writing style can also be referred to as his or her **voice**.

Writers' stylistic choices accomplish three basic effects on their audiences:

- They **communicate meanings** beyond linguistically dictated meanings,
- They communicate the **author's attitude**, such as persuasive or argumentative effects accomplished through style, and
- They communicate or **express feelings**.

Within style, component areas include:

- Narrative structure
- Viewpoint
- Focus
- Sound patterns
- Meter and rhythm
- Lexical and syntactic repetition and parallelism
- Writing genre
- Representational, realistic, and mimetic effects
- Representation of thought and speech
- Meta-representation (representing representation)
- Irony
- Metaphor and other indirect meanings
- Representation and use of historical and dialectal variations
- Gender-specific and other group-specific speech styles, both real and fictitious
- Analysis of the processes for inferring meaning from writing

Level of Formality

The relationship between writer and reader is important in choosing a **level of formality** as most writing requires some degree of formality. **Formal writing** is for addressing a superior in a school or work environment. Business letters, textbooks, and newspapers use a moderate to high level of formality. **Informal writing** is appropriate for private letters, personal emails, and business correspondence between close associates.

For your exam, you will want to be aware of informal and formal writing. One way that this can be accomplished is to watch for shifts in point of view in the essay. For example, unless writers are using a personal example, they will rarely refer to themselves (e.g., "*I* think that *my* point is very clear.") to avoid being informal when they need to be formal.

Also, be mindful of an author who addresses his or her audience **directly** in their writing (e.g., "Readers, *like you*, will understand this argument.") as this can be a sign of informal writing. Good writers understand the need to be consistent with their level of formality. Shifts in levels of formality or point of view can confuse readers and cause them to discount the message.

Clichés

Clichés are phrases that have been **overused** to the point that the phrase has no importance or has lost the original meaning. These phrases have no originality and add very little to a passage. Therefore, most writers will avoid the use of clichés. Another option is to make changes to a cliché so that it is not predictable and empty of meaning.

Examples:

> When life gives you lemons, make lemonade.
>
> Every cloud has a silver lining.

JARGON

Jargon is **specialized vocabulary** that is used among members of a certain trade or profession. Since jargon is understood by only a small audience, writers will use jargon in passages that will only be read by a specialized audience. For example, medical jargon should be used in a medical journal but not in a New York Times article. Jargon includes exaggerated language that tries to impress rather than inform. Sentences filled with jargon are not precise and are difficult to understand.

Examples:

> "He is going to *toenail* these frames for us." (Toenail is construction jargon for nailing at an angle.)
>
> "They brought in a *kip* of material today." (Kip refers to 1000 pounds in architecture and engineering.)

SLANG

Slang is an **informal** and sometimes private language that is understood by some individuals. Slang terms have some usefulness, but they can have a small audience. So, most formal writing will not include this kind of language.

Examples:

> "Yes, the event was a blast!" (In this sentence, *blast* means that the event was a great experience.)
>
> "That attempt was an epic fail." (By *epic fail*, the speaker means that his or her attempt was not a success.)

COLLOQUIALISM

A colloquialism is a word or phrase that is found in informal writing. Unlike slang, **colloquial language** will be familiar to a greater range of people. However, colloquialisms are still considered inappropriate for formal writing. Colloquial language can include some slang, but these are limited to contractions for the most part.

Examples:

> "Can *y'all* come back another time?" (Y'all is a contraction of "you all.")
>
> "Will you stop him from building this *castle in the air*?" (A "castle in the air" is an improbable or unlikely event.)

ACADEMIC LANGUAGE

In educational settings, students are often expected to use academic language in their schoolwork. Academic language is also commonly found in dissertations and theses, texts published by academic journals, and other forms of academic research. Academic language conventions may vary between fields, but general academic language is free of slang, regional terminology, and noticeable grammatical errors. Specific terms may also be used in academic language, and it is important to understand their proper usage. A writer's command of academic language impacts their ability to communicate in an academic or professional context. While it is acceptable to use colloquialisms, slang, improper grammar, or other forms of informal speech in social settings or at home, it is inappropriate to practice non-academic language in academic contexts.

TONE

Tone may be defined as the writer's **attitude** toward the topic, and to the audience. This attitude is reflected in the language used in the writing. The tone of a work should be **appropriate to the topic** and to the intended audience. While it may be fine to use slang or jargon in some pieces, other texts should not contain such terms. Tone can range from humorous to serious and any level in between. It may be more or less formal, depending on the purpose of the writing and its intended audience. All these nuances in tone can flavor the entire writing and should be kept in mind as the work evolves.

WORD SELECTION

A writer's choice of words is a signature of their style. Careful thought about the use of words can improve a piece of writing. A passage can be an exciting piece to read when attention is given to the use of vivid or specific nouns rather than general ones.

Example:

> General: His kindness will never be forgotten.
>
> Specific: His thoughtful gifts and bear hugs will never be forgotten.

Attention should also be given to the kind of verbs that are used in sentences. Active verbs (e.g., run, swim) are about an action. Whenever possible, an **active verb should replace a linking verb** to provide clear examples for arguments and to strengthen a passage overall. When using an active verb, one should be sure that the verb is used in the active voice instead of the passive voice. Verbs are in the active voice when the subject is the one doing the action. A verb is in the passive voice when the subject is the recipient of an action.

Example:

> Passive: The winners were called to the stage by the judges.
>
> Active: The judges called the winners to the stage.

> **Review Video: Word Usage**
> Visit mometrix.com/academy and enter code: 197863

CONCISENESS

Conciseness is writing that communicates a message in the fewest words possible. Writing concisely is valuable because short, uncluttered messages allow the reader to understand the author's message more easily and efficiently. Planning is important in writing concise messages. If you have in mind what you need to write beforehand, it will be easier to make a message short and to the point. Do not state the obvious.

Revising is also important. After the message is written, make sure you have effective, pithy sentences that efficiently get your point across. When reviewing the information, imagine a conversation taking place, and concise writing will likely result.

APPROPRIATE KINDS OF WRITING FOR DIFFERENT TASKS, PURPOSES, AND AUDIENCES

When preparing to write a composition, consider the audience and purpose to choose the best type of writing. Three common types of writing are persuasive, expository, and narrative. **Persuasive**, or argumentative writing, is used to convince the audience to take action or agree with the author's claims. **Expository** writing is meant to inform the audience of the author's observations or research on a topic. **Narrative** writing is used to tell the audience a story and often allows more room for creativity. While task, purpose, and audience inform a writer's mode of writing, these factors also impact elements such as tone, vocabulary, and formality.

For example, students who are writing to persuade their parents to grant them some additional privilege, such as permission for a more independent activity, should use more sophisticated vocabulary and diction that sounds more mature and serious to appeal to the parental audience. However, students who are writing for younger children should use simpler vocabulary and sentence structure, as well as choose words that are more vivid and entertaining. They should treat their topics more lightly, and include humor when appropriate. Students who are writing for their classmates may use language that is more informal, as well as age-appropriate.

> **Review Video: Writing Purpose and Audience**
> Visit mometrix.com/academy and enter code: 146627

Modes of Writing

ESSAYS

Essays usually focus on one topic, subject, or goal. There are several types of essays, including informative, persuasive, and narrative. An essay's structure and level of formality depend on the type of essay and its goal. While narrative essays typically do not include outside sources, other types of essays often require some research and the integration of primary and secondary sources.

The basic format of an essay typically has three major parts: the introduction, the body, and the conclusion. The body is further divided into the writer's main points. Short and simple essays may have three main points, while essays covering broader ranges and going into more depth can have almost any number of main points, depending on length.

An essay's introduction should answer three questions:

1. What is the **subject** of the essay?

    If a student writes an essay about a book, the answer would include the title and author of the book and any additional information needed—such as the subject or argument of the book.

2. How does the essay **address** the subject?

    To answer this, the writer identifies the essay's organization by briefly summarizing main points and the evidence supporting them.

3. What will the essay **prove**?

This is the thesis statement, usually the opening paragraph's last sentence, clearly stating the writer's message.

The body elaborates on all the main points related to the thesis, introducing one main point at a time, and includes supporting evidence with each main point. Each body paragraph should state the point in a topic sentence, which is usually the first sentence in the paragraph. The paragraph should then explain the point's meaning, support it with quotations or other evidence, and then explain how this point and the evidence are related to the thesis. The writer should then repeat this procedure in a new paragraph for each additional main point.

The conclusion reiterates the content of the introduction, including the thesis, to remind the reader of the essay's main argument or subject. The essay writer may also summarize the highlights of the argument or description contained in the body of the essay, following the same sequence originally used in the body. For example, a conclusion might look like: Point 1 + Point 2 + Point 3 = Thesis, or Point 1 → Point 2 → Point 3 → Thesis Proof. Good organization makes essays easier for writers to compose and provides a guide for readers to follow. Well-organized essays hold attention better and are more likely to get readers to accept their theses as valid.

INFORMATIVE VS. PERSUASIVE WRITING

Informative writing, also called explanatory or expository writing, begins with the basis that something is true or factual, while **persuasive** writing strives to prove something that may or may not be true or factual. Whereas argumentative text is written to **persuade** readers to agree with the author's position, informative text merely **provides information and insight** to readers. Informative writing concentrates on **informing** readers about why or how something is as it is. This can include offering new information, explaining how a process works, and developing a concept for readers. To accomplish these objectives, the essay may name and distinguish various things within a category, provide definitions, provide details about the parts of something, explain a particular function or behavior, and give readers explanations for why a fact, object, event, or process exists or occurs.

> **Review Video: Informative Text**
> Visit mometrix.com/academy and enter code: 924964
>
> **Review Video: Argumentative Writing**
> Visit mometrix.com/academy and enter code: 561544

NARRATIVE WRITING

Put simply, **narrative** writing tells a story. The most common examples of literary narratives are novels. Non-fictional biographies, autobiographies, memoirs, and histories are also narratives. Narratives should tell stories in such a way that the readers learn something or gain insight or understanding. Students can write more interesting narratives by describing events or experiences that were meaningful to them. Narratives should start with the story's actions or events, rather than long descriptions or introductions. Students should ensure that there is a point to each story by describing what they learned from the experience they narrate. To write an effective description, students should include sensory details, asking themselves what they saw, heard, felt or touched, smelled, and tasted during the experiences they describe. In narrative writing, the details should be

concrete rather than **abstract**. Using concrete details enables readers to imagine everything that the writer describes.

> **Review Video: Narratives**
> Visit mometrix.com/academy and enter code: 280100

SENSORY DETAILS

Students need to use vivid descriptions when writing descriptive essays. Narratives should also include descriptions of characters, things, and events. Students should remember to describe not only the visual detail of what someone or something looks like, but details from other senses, as well. For example, they can contrast the feeling of a sea breeze to that of a mountain breeze, describe how they think something inedible would taste, and compare sounds they hear in the same location at different times of day and night. Readers have trouble visualizing images or imagining sensory impressions and feelings from abstract descriptions, so concrete descriptions make these more real.

CONCRETE VS. ABSTRACT DESCRIPTIONS IN NARRATIVE

Concrete language provides information that readers can grasp and may empathize with, while **abstract language**, which is more general, can leave readers feeling disconnected, empty, or even confused. "It was a lovely day" is abstract, but "The sun shone brightly, the sky was blue, the air felt warm, and a gentle breeze wafted across my skin" is concrete. "Ms. Couch was a good teacher" uses abstract language, giving only a general idea of the writer's opinion. But "Ms. Couch is excellent at helping us take our ideas and turn them into good essays and stories" uses concrete language, giving more specific examples of what makes Ms. Couch a good teacher. "I like writing poems but not essays" gives readers a general idea that the student prefers one genre over another, but not why. But when reading, "I like writing short poems with rhythm and rhyme, but I hate writing five-page essays that go on and on about the same ideas," readers understand that the student prefers the brevity, rhyme, and meter of short poetry over the length and redundancy of longer prose.

AUTOBIOGRAPHICAL NARRATIVES

Autobiographical narratives are narratives written by an author about an event or period in their life. Autobiographical narratives are written from one person's perspective, in first person, and often include the author's thoughts and feelings alongside their description of the event or period. Structure, style, or theme varies between different autobiographical narratives, since each narrative is personal and specific to its author and his or her experience.

REFLECTIVE ESSAY

A less common type of essay is the reflective essay. **Reflective essays** allow the author to reflect, or think back, on an experience and analyze what they recall. They should consider what they learned from the experience, what they could have done differently, what would have helped them during the experience, or anything else that they have realized from looking back on the experience. Reflection essays incorporate both objective reflection on one's own actions and subjective explanation of thoughts and feelings. These essays can be written for a number of experiences in a formal or informal context.

JOURNALS AND DIARIES

A **journal** is a personal account of events, experiences, feelings, and thoughts. Many people write journals to express their feelings and thoughts or to help them process experiences they have had. Since journals are **private documents** not meant to be shared with others, writers may not be concerned with grammar, spelling, or other mechanics. However, authors may write journals that they expect or hope to publish someday; in this case, they not only express their thoughts and feelings and process their experiences, but they also attend to their craft in writing them. Some authors compose journals to record a particular time period or a series of related events, such as a cancer diagnosis, treatment, surviving the disease, and how these experiences have changed or affected them. Other experiences someone might include in a journal are recovering from addiction, journeys of spiritual exploration and discovery, time spent in another country, or anything else someone wants to personally document. Journaling can also be therapeutic, as some people use journals to work through feelings of grief over loss or to wrestle with big decisions.

EXAMPLES OF DIARIES IN LITERATURE

The Diary of a Young Girl by Dutch Jew Anne Frank (1947) contains her life-affirming, nonfictional diary entries from 1942-1944 while her family hid in an attic from World War II's genocidal Nazis. *Go Ask Alice* (1971) by Beatrice Sparks is a cautionary, fictional novel in the form of diary entries by Alice, an unhappy, rebellious teen who takes LSD, runs away from home and lives with hippies, and eventually returns home. Frank's writing reveals an intelligent, sensitive, insightful girl, raised by intellectual European parents—a girl who believes in the goodness of human nature despite surrounding atrocities. Alice, influenced by early 1970s counterculture, becomes less optimistic. However, similarities can be found between them: Frank dies in a Nazi concentration camp while the fictitious Alice dies from a drug overdose. Both young women are also unable to escape their surroundings. Additionally, adolescent searches for personal identity are evident in both books.

> **Review Video: Journals, Diaries, Letters, and Blogs**
> Visit mometrix.com/academy and enter code: 432845

LETTERS

Letters are messages written to other people. In addition to letters written between individuals, some writers compose letters to the editors of newspapers, magazines, and other publications, while some write "Open Letters" to be published and read by the general public. Open letters, while intended for everyone to read, may also identify a group of people or a single person whom the letter directly addresses. In everyday use, the most-used forms are business letters and personal or friendly letters. Both kinds share common elements: business or personal letterhead stationery; the writer's return address at the top; the addressee's address next; a salutation, such as "Dear [name]" or some similar opening greeting, followed by a colon in business letters or a comma in personal letters; the body of the letter, with paragraphs as indicated; and a closing, like "Sincerely/Cordially/Best regards/etc." or "Love," in intimate personal letters.

EARLY LETTERS

The Greek word for "letter" is *epistolē*, which became the English word "epistle." The earliest letters were called epistles, including the New Testament's epistles from the apostles to the Christians. In ancient Egypt, the writing curriculum in scribal schools included the epistolary genre. Epistolary novels frame a story in the form of letters. Examples of noteworthy epistolary novels include:

- *Pamela* (1740), by 18th-century English novelist Samuel Richardson
- *Shamela* (1741), Henry Fielding's satire of *Pamela* that mocked epistolary writing.
- *Lettres persanes* (1721) by French author Montesquieu
- *The Sorrows of Young Werther* (1774) by German author Johann Wolfgang von Goethe
- *The History of Emily Montague* (1769), the first Canadian novel, by Frances Brooke
- *Dracula* (1897) by Bram Stoker
- *Frankenstein* (1818) by Mary Shelley
- *The Color Purple* (1982) by Alice Walker

BLOGS

The word "blog" is derived from "weblog" and refers to writing done exclusively on the internet. Readers of reputable newspapers expect quality content and layouts that enable easy reading. These expectations also apply to blogs. For example, readers can easily move visually from line to line when columns are narrow, while overly wide columns cause readers to lose their places. Blogs must also be posted with layouts enabling online readers to follow them easily. However, because the way people read on computer, tablet, and smartphone screens differs from how they read print on paper, formatting and writing blog content is more complex than writing newspaper articles. Two major principles are the bases for blog-writing rules: The first is while readers of print articles skim to estimate their length, online they must scroll down to scan; therefore, blog layouts need more subheadings, graphics, and other indications of what information follows. The second is onscreen reading can be harder on the eyes than reading printed paper, so legibility is crucial in blogs.

RULES AND RATIONALES FOR WRITING BLOGS

1. Format all posts for smooth page layout and easy scanning.
2. Column width should not be too wide, as larger lines of text can be difficult to read
3. Headings and subheadings separate text visually, enable scanning or skimming, and encourage continued reading.
4. Bullet-pointed or numbered lists enable quick information location and scanning.
5. Punctuation is critical, so beginners should use shorter sentences until confident in their knowledge of punctuation rules.
6. Blog paragraphs should be far shorter—two to six sentences each—than paragraphs written on paper to enable "chunking" because reading onscreen is more difficult.
7. Sans-serif fonts are usually clearer than serif fonts, and larger font sizes are better.
8. Highlight important material and draw attention with **boldface**, but avoid overuse. Avoid hard-to-read *italics* and ALL CAPITALS.
9. Include enough blank spaces: overly busy blogs tire eyes and brains. Images not only break up text but also emphasize and enhance text and can attract initial reader attention.
10. Use background colors judiciously to avoid distracting the eye or making it difficult to read.
11. Be consistent throughout posts, since people read them in different orders.
12. Tell a story with a beginning, middle, and end.

SPECIALIZED MODES OF WRITING

EDITORIALS

Editorials are articles in newspapers, magazines, and other serial publications. Editorials express an opinion or belief belonging to the majority of the publication's leadership. This opinion or belief generally refers to a specific issue, topic, or event. These articles are authored by a member, or a small number of members, of the publication's leadership and are often written to affect their readers, such as persuading them to adopt a stance or take a particular action.

RESUMES

Resumes are brief, but formal, documents that outline an individual's experience in a certain area. Resumes are most often used for job applications. Such resumes will list the applicant's work experience, certification, and achievements or qualifications related to the position. Resumes should only include the most pertinent information. They should also use strategic formatting to highlight the applicant's most impressive experiences and achievements, to ensure the document can be read quickly and easily, and to eliminate both visual clutter and excessive negative space.

REPORTS

Reports summarize the results of research, new methodology, or other developments in an academic or professional context. Reports often include details about methodology and outside influences and factors. However, a report should focus primarily on the results of the research or development. Reports are objective and deliver information efficiently, sacrificing style for clear and effective communication.

MEMORANDA

A memorandum, also called a memo, is a formal method of communication used in professional settings. Memoranda are printed documents that include a heading listing the sender and their job title, the recipient and their job title, the date, and a specific subject line. Memoranda often include an introductory section explaining the reason and context for the memorandum. Next, a memorandum includes a section with details relevant to the topic. Finally, the memorandum will conclude with a paragraph that politely and clearly defines the sender's expectations of the recipient.

Research Writing

RESEARCH WRITING

Writing for research is essentially writing to answer a question or a problem about a particular **research topic**. A **problem statement** is written to clearly define the problem with a topic before asking about how to solve the problem. A **research question** serves to ask what can be done to address the problem. Before a researcher should try to solve a problem, the researcher should spend significant time performing a **literature review** to find out what has already been learned about the topic and if there are already solutions in place. The literature review can help to re-evaluate the research question as well. If the question has not been thoroughly answered, then it is proper to do broader research to learn about the topic and build up the body of literature. If the literature review provides plenty of background, but no practical solutions to the problem, then the research question should be targeted at solving a problem more directly. After the research has been performed, a **thesis** can act as a proposal for a solution or as a recommendation to future researchers to continue to learn more about the topic. The thesis should then be supported by significant contributing evidence to help support the proposed solution.

EXAMPLE OF RESEARCH WRITING ELEMENTS

Topic	The general idea the research is about. This is usually broader than the problem itself. Example: Clean Water
Problem Statement	A problem statement is a brief, clear description of a problem with the topic. Example: Not all villages in third-world countries have ready access to clean water.
Research Question	A research question asks a specific question about what needs to be learned or done about the problem statement. Example: What can local governments do to improve access to clean water?
Literature Review	A review of the body of literature by the researcher to show what is already known about the topic and the problem. If the literature review shows that the research question has already been thoroughly answered, the researcher should consider changing problem statements to something that has not been solved.

Thesis	A brief proposal of a solution to a problem. Theses do not include their own support, but are supported by later evidence. Example: Local governments can improve access to clean water by installing sealed rain-water collection units.
Body Paragraphs	Paragraphs focused on the primary supporting evidence for the main idea of the thesis. There are usually three body paragraphs, but there can be more if needed.
Conclusion	A final wrap-up of the research project. The conclusion should reiterate the problem, question, thesis, and briefly mention how the main evidences support the thesis.

THE RESEARCH PROCESS

Researchers should prepare some information before gathering sources. Researchers who have chosen a **research question** should choose key words or names that pertain to their question. They should also identify what type of information and sources they are looking for. Researchers should consider whether secondary or primary sources will be most appropriate for their research project. As researchers find credible and appropriate sources, they should be prepared to adjust the scope of their research question or topic in response to the information and insights they gather.

USING SOURCES AND SYNTHESIZING INFORMATION

As researchers find potential sources for their research project, it is important to keep a **record** of the material they find and note how each source may impact their work. When taking these notes, researchers should keep their research question or outline in mind and consider how their chosen references would complement their discussion. **Literature reviews** and **annotated bibliographies** are helpful tools for evaluating sources, as they require the researcher to consider the qualities and offerings of the sources they choose to use. These tools also help researchers synthesize the information they find.

SYNTHESIZING INFORMATION

Synthesizing information requires the researcher to integrate sources and their own thoughts by quoting, paraphrasing, or summarizing outside information in their research project. Synthesizing information indicates that the research complements the writer's claims, ensures that the ideas in the composition flow logically, and makes including small details and quotes easier. Paraphrasing is one of the simplest ways to integrate a source. **Paraphrasing** allows the writer to support their ideas with research while presenting the information in their own words, rather than using the source's original wording. Paraphrasing also allows the writer to reference the source's main ideas instead of specific details. While paraphrasing does not require the writer to quote the source, it still entails a direct reference to the source, meaning that any paraphrased material still requires a citation.

CITING SOURCES

While researchers should combine research with their own ideas, the information and ideas that come from outside sources should be attributed to the author of the source. When conducting research, it is helpful to record the publication information for each source so that **citations** can be easily added within the composition. Keeping a close record of the source of each idea in a composition or project is helpful for avoiding plagiarism, as both direct and indirect references require documentation.

PLAGIARISM

Understanding what is considered to be plagiarism is important to preventing unintentional plagiarism. Using another person's work in any way without proper attribution is **plagiarism**.

However, it is easy to mistakenly commit plagiarism by improperly citing a source or creating a citation that is not intended for the way the source was used. Even when an honest attempt to attribute information is made, small errors can still result in plagiarized content. For this reason, it is important to create citations carefully and review citations before submitting or publishing research. It is also possible to plagiarize one's own work. This occurs when a writer has published work with one title and purpose and then attempts to publish it again as new material under a new title or purpose.

LITERATURE REVIEW

One of the two main parts of a literature review is searching through existing literature. The other is actually writing the review. Researchers must take care not to get lost in the information and inhibit progress toward their research goal. A good precaution is to write out the research question and keep it nearby. It is also wise to make a search plan and establish a time limit in advance. Finding a seemingly endless number of references indicates a need to revisit the research question because the topic is too broad. Finding too little material means that the research topic is too narrow. With new or cutting-edge research, one may find that nobody has investigated this particular question. This requires systematic searching, using abstracts in periodicals for an overview of available literature, research papers or other specific sources to explore its reference, and references in books and other sources.

When searching published literature on a research topic, one must take thorough notes. It is common to find a reference that could be useful later in the research project, but is not needed yet. In situations like this, it is helpful to make a note of the reference so it will be easy to find later. These notes can be grouped in a word processing document, which also allows for easy compiling of links and quotes from internet research. Researchers should explore the internet regularly, view resources for their research often, learn how to use resources correctly and efficiently, experiment with resources available within the disciplines, open and examine databases, become familiar with reference desk materials, find publications with abstracts of articles and books on one's topic, use papers' references to locate the most useful journals and important authors, identify keywords for refining and narrowing database searches, and peruse library catalogues online for available sources—all while taking notes.

As one searches for references, one will gradually develop an overview of the body of literature available for his or her subject. This signals the time to prepare for writing the literature review. The researcher should assemble his or her notes along with copies of all the journal articles and all the books he or she has acquired. Then one should write the research question again at the top of a page and list below it all of the author names and keywords discovered while searching. It is also helpful to observe whether any groups or pairs of these stand out. These activities are parts of structuring one's literature review—the first step for writing a thesis, dissertation, or research paper. Writers should rewrite their work as necessary rather than expecting to write only one draft. However, stopping to edit along the way can distract from the momentum of writing the first draft. If the writer is dissatisfied with a certain part of the draft, it may be better to skip to a later portion of the paper and revisit the problem section at another time.

BODY AND CONCLUSION IN LITERATURE REVIEW

The first step of a literature review paper is to create a rough draft. The next step is to edit: rewrite for clarity, eliminate unnecessary verbiage, and change terminology that could confuse readers. After editing, a writer should ask others to read and give feedback. Additionally, the writer should read the paper aloud to hear how it sounds, editing as needed. Throughout a literature review, the writer should not only summarize and comment on each source reviewed, but should also relate these findings to the original research question. The writer should explicitly state in the conclusion how the research question and pertinent literature interaction is developed throughout the body, reflecting on insights gained through the process.

> **Review Video: Drafting Conclusions**
> Visit mometrix.com/academy and enter code: 209408

SUMMARIES AND ABSTRACTS

When preparing to submit or otherwise publish research, it may be necessary to compose a summary or abstract to accompany the research composition.

A summary is a brief description of the contents of a longer work that provides an overview of the work and may include its most important details. One common type of summary is an abstract. Abstracts are specialized summaries that are most commonly used in the context of research. Abstracts may include details such as the purpose for the research, the researcher's methodology, and the most significant results of the research. Abstracts sometimes include sections and headings, where most summaries are limited to one or a few paragraphs with no special groupings.

EDITING AND REVISING

After composing a rough draft of a research paper, the writer should **edit** it. The purpose of the paper is to communicate the answer to one's research question in an efficient and effective manner. The writing should be as **concise** and **clear** as possible, and the style should also be consistent. Editing is often easier to do after writing the first draft rather than during it, as taking time between writing and editing allows writers to be more objective. If the paper includes an abstract and an introduction, the writer should compose these after writing the rest, when he or she will have a better grasp of the theme and arguments. Not all readers understand technical terminology or long words, so writers should use these sparingly. Finally, writers should consult a writing and style guide to address any industry- or institution-specific issues that may arise as they edit.

> **Review Video: Revising and Editing**
> Visit mometrix.com/academy and enter code: 674181

Information Sources

PRIMARY SOURCES

In literature review, one may examine both primary and secondary sources. Primary sources contain original information that was witnessed, gathered, or otherwise produced by the source's author. **Primary sources** can include firsthand accounts, found in sources such as books, autobiographies, transcripts, speeches, videos, photos, and personal journals or diaries. Primary sources may also include records of information, such as government documents, or personally-conducted research in sources like reports and essays. They may be found in academic books, journals and other periodicals, and authoritative databases. Using primary sources allows researchers to develop their own conclusions about the subject. Primary sources are also reliable for finding information about a person or their personal accounts and experiences. Primary sources such as photos, videos, audio recordings, transcripts, and government documents are often reliable, as they are usually objective and can be used to confirm information from other sources.

SECONDARY SOURCES

Secondary sources are sources that reference information originally provided by another source. The original source may be cited, quoted, paraphrased, or described in a secondary source. **Secondary sources** may be articles, essays, videos, or books found in periodicals, magazines, newspapers, films, databases, or websites. A secondary source can be used to reference another researcher's analysis or conclusion from a primary source. This information can inform the researcher of the existing discussions regarding their subject. These types of sources may also support the researcher's claims by providing a credible argument that contributes to the researcher's argument. Secondary sources may also highlight connections between primary sources or criticize both primary and other secondary sources. These types of secondary sources are valuable because they provide information and conclusions the researcher may not have considered or found, otherwise.

> **Review Video: Primary and Secondary Sources**
> Visit mometrix.com/academy and enter code: 383328

TYPES OF SOURCES

- **Textbooks** are specialized materials that are designed to thoroughly instruct readers on a particular topic. Textbooks often include features such as a table of contents, visuals, an index, a glossary, headings, and practice questions and exercises.
- **Newspapers** are collections of several written pieces and are primarily used to distribute news stories to their audience. In addition to news articles, newspapers may also include advertisements or pieces meant to entertain their audience, such as comic strips, columns, and letters from readers. Newspapers are written for a variety of audiences, as they are published on both the local and national levels.
- **Manuals** are instructional documents that accompany a product or explain an important procedure. Manuals include a table of contents, guidelines, and instructional content. Instructional manuals often include information about safe practices, risks, and product warranty. The instructions in manuals are often presented as step-by-step instructions, as they are meant to help users properly use a product or complete a task.
- **Electronic texts** are written documents that are read digitally and are primarily accessed online or through a network. Many electronic texts have characteristics similar to printed texts, such as a table of contents, publication information, a main text, and supplemental materials. However, electronic texts are more interactive and can be navigated more quickly. Electronic texts can also provide more accessibility, as they can be easily resized or narrated by text-to-speech software.

FINDING SOURCES

Finding sources for a research project may be intimidating or difficult. There are numerous sources available, and several research tools to help researchers find them. Starting with one of these tools can help narrow down the number of sources a researcher is working with at one time.

- **Libraries** house independent, printed publications that are organized by subject. This makes finding sources easy, since researchers can visit sections with sources relevant to their topic and immediately see what sources are available. Many libraries also offer printed journals and collections that include sources related to a common subject or written by the same author.

- **Databases** offer digital access to sources from a wide variety of libraries and online containers. To use a database, users search for keywords related to their topic or the type of source they want to use. The database then lists results related to or featuring those key words. Users can narrow their results using filters that will limit their results based on factors such as publication year, source type, or whether the sources are peer-reviewed. Database search results also list individual articles and methods of accessing the article directly. While databases help users find sources, they do not guarantee users access to each source.
- **Academic Journals** are collections of articles that cover a particular topic or fit within a certain category. These journals are often offered both online and in print. Academic journals typically contain peer-reviewed works or works that have undergone another type of reviewing process.

CREDIBILITY

There are innumerable primary and secondary sources available in print and online. However, not every published or posted source is appropriate for a research project. When finding sources, the researcher must know how to evaluate each source for credibility and relevance. Not only must the sources be reliable and relevant to the research subject, but they must also be appropriate and help form an answer to the research question. As researchers progress in their research and composition, the relevance of each source will become clear. Appropriate sources will contribute valuable information and arguments to the researcher's own thoughts and conclusions, providing useful evidence to bolster the researcher's claims. The researcher has the freedom to choose which sources they reference or even change their research topic and question in response to the sources they find. However, the researcher should not use unreliable sources, and determining a source's credibility is not always easy.

CONSIDERATIONS FOR EVALUATING THE CREDIBILITY OF A SOURCE

- The author and their purpose for writing the source
- The author's qualifications to write on the topic
- Whether the source is peer-reviewed or included in a scholarly publication
- The publisher
- The target audience
- The jargon or dialect the source is written in (e.g., academic, technical)
- The presence of bias or manipulation of information
- The date of publication
- The author's use of other sources to support their claims
- Whether any outside sources are cited appropriately in the source
- The accuracy of information presented

AUTHOR'S PURPOSE AND CREDIBILITY

Knowing who wrote a source and why they wrote it is important to determine whether a source is appropriate for a research project. The author should be qualified to write on the subject of the material. Their purpose may be to inform their audience of information, to present and defend an analysis, or even to criticize a work or other argument. The researcher must decide whether the author's purpose makes the source appropriate to use. The source's container and publisher are important to note because they indicate the source's reputability and whether other qualified individuals have reviewed the information in the source. Credible secondary sources should also reference other sources, primary or secondary, that support or inform the source's content. Evaluating the accuracy of the information or the presence of bias in a source will require careful reading and critical thinking on the part of the researcher. However, a source with excellent credentials may still contain pieces of inaccurate information or bias, so it is the researcher's responsibility to be careful in their use of each source.

Integrating References and Quotations

In research papers, one can include studies whose conclusions agree with one's position (Reed 284; Becker and Fagen 93), as well as studies that disagree (Limbaugh 442, Beck 69) by including parenthetical citations as demonstrated in this sentence. Quotations should be selective: writers should compose an original sentence and incorporate only a few words from a research source. If students cannot use more original words than quotation, they are likely padding their compositions. However, including quotations appropriately increases the credibility of the writer and their argument.

Properly Integrating Quotations

When using sources in a research paper, it is important to integrate information so that the flow of the composition is not interrupted as the two compositions are combined. When quoting outside sources, it is necessary to lead into the quote and ensure that the whole sentence is logical, is grammatically correct, and flows well. Below is an example of an incorrectly integrated quote.

> During the Industrial Revolution, many unions organized labor strikes "child labor, unregulated working conditions, and excessive working hours" in America.

Below is the same sentence with a properly integrated quote.

> During the Industrial Revolution, many unions organized labor strikes to protest the presence of "child labor, unregulated working conditions, and excessive working hours" in America.

In the first example, the connection between "strikes" and the quoted list is unclear. In the second example, the phrase "to protest the presence of" link the ideas together and successfully creates a suitable place for the quotation.

When quoting sources, writers should work quotations and references seamlessly into their sentences instead of interrupting the flow of their own argument to summarize a source. Summarizing others' content is often a ploy to bolster word counts. Writing that analyzes the content, evaluates it, and synthesizes material from various sources demonstrates critical thinking skills and is thus more valuable.

Properly Incorporating Outside Sources

Writers do better to include short quotations rather than long. For example, quoting six to eight long passages in a 10-page paper is excessive. It is also better to avoid wording like "This quotation shows," "As you can see from this quotation," or "It talks about." These are amateur, feeble efforts to interact with other authors' ideas. Also, writing about sources and quotations wastes words that should be used to develop one's own ideas. Quotations should be used to stimulate discussion rather than taking its place. Ending a paragraph, section, or paper with a quotation is not incorrect per se, but using it to prove a point, without including anything more in one's own words regarding the point or subject, suggests a lack of critical thinking about the topic and consideration of multiple alternatives. It can also be a tactic to dissuade readers from challenging one's propositions. Writers should include references and quotations that challenge as well as support their thesis statements. Presenting evidence on both sides of an issue makes it easier for reasonably skeptical readers to agree with a writer's viewpoint.

Citing Sources

Formal research writers must **cite all sources used**—books, articles, interviews, conversations, and anything else that contributed to the research. One reason is to **avoid plagiarism** and give others credit for their ideas. Another reason is to help readers find the sources consulted in the research and access more information about the subject for further reading and research. Additionally, citing sources helps to make a paper academically authoritative. To prepare, research writers should keep a running list of sources consulted, in an electronic file or on file cards. For every source used, the writer needs specific information. For books, a writer needs to record the author's and editor's names, book title, publication date, city, and publisher name. For articles, one needs the author's name, article title, journal (or magazine or newspaper) name, volume and issue number, publication date, and page numbers. For electronic resources, a writer will need the author's name, article information plus the URL, database name, name of the database's publisher, and the date of access.

Common Reference Styles

Three common reference styles are **MLA** (Modern Language Association), **APA** (American Psychological Association), and **Turabian** (created by author Kate Turabian, also known as the Chicago Manual of Style). Each style formats citation information differently. Professors and instructors often specify that students use one of these. Generally, APA style is used in psychology and sociology papers, and MLA style is used in English literature papers and similar scholarly projects. To understand how these styles differ, consider an imaginary article cited in each of these styles. This article is titled "Ten Things You Won't Believe Dragons Do," written by author Andra Gaines, included in the journal *Studies in Fantasy Fiction*, and published by Quest for Knowledge Publishing.

MLA:

Gaines, Andra. "Ten Things You Won't Believe Dragons Do". *Studies in Fantasy Fiction*, vol. 3, no. 8, Quest for Knowledge Publishing, 21 Aug. 2019.

APA:

Gaines, A. (2019). Ten Things You Won't Believe Dragons Do. *Studies in Fantasy Fiction*, *3(8)*, 42-65.

Chicago:

Gaines, Andra. "Ten Things You Won't Believe Dragons Do," *Studies in Fantasy Fiction* 3, no. 8 (2019): 42-65.

Within each of these styles, citations, though they vary according to the type of source and how its used, generally follow a structure and format similar to those above. For example, citations for whole books will probably not include a container title or a volume number, but will otherwise look very similar.

> **Review Video: Citing Sources**
> Visit mometrix.com/academy and enter code: 993637

Mathematics

Numbers

CLASSIFICATIONS OF NUMBERS

Numbers are the basic building blocks of mathematics. Specific features of numbers are identified by the following terms:

Integer – any positive or negative whole number, including zero. Integers do not include fractions $\left(\frac{1}{3}\right)$, decimals (0.56), or mixed numbers $\left(7\frac{3}{4}\right)$.

Prime number – any whole number greater than 1 that has only two factors, itself and 1; that is, a number that can be divided evenly only by 1 and itself.

Composite number – any whole number greater than 1 that has more than two different factors; in other words, any whole number that is not a prime number. For example: The composite number 8 has the factors of 1, 2, 4, and 8.

Even number – any integer that can be divided by 2 without leaving a remainder. For example: 2, 4, 6, 8, and so on.

Odd number – any integer that cannot be divided evenly by 2. For example: 3, 5, 7, 9, and so on.

Decimal number – any number that uses a decimal point to show the part of the number that is less than one. Example: 1.234.

Decimal point – a symbol used to separate the ones place from the tenths place in decimals or dollars from cents in currency.

Decimal place – the position of a number to the right of the decimal point. In the decimal 0.123, the 1 is in the first place to the right of the decimal point, indicating tenths; the 2 is in the second place, indicating hundredths; and the 3 is in the third place, indicating thousandths.

The **decimal**, or base 10, system is a number system that uses ten different digits (0, 1, 2, 3, 4, 5, 6, 7, 8, 9). An example of a number system that uses something other than ten digits is the **binary**, or base 2, number system, used by computers, which uses only the numbers 0 and 1. It is thought that the decimal system originated because people had only their 10 fingers for counting.

Rational numbers include all integers, decimals, and fractions. Any terminating or repeating decimal number is a rational number.

Irrational numbers cannot be written as fractions or decimals because the number of decimal places is infinite and there is no recurring pattern of digits within the number. For example, pi (π) begins with 3.141592 and continues without terminating or repeating, so pi is an irrational number.

Real numbers are the set of all rational and irrational numbers.

> **Review Video: Numbers and Their Classifications**
> Visit mometrix.com/academy and enter code: 461071
>
> **Review Video: Rational and Irrational Numbers**
> Visit mometrix.com/academy and enter code: 280645

THE NUMBER LINE

A number line is a graph to see the distance between numbers. Basically, this graph shows the relationship between numbers. So a number line may have a point for zero and may show negative numbers on the left side of the line. Also, any positive numbers are placed on the right side of the line. For example, consider the points labeled on the following number line:

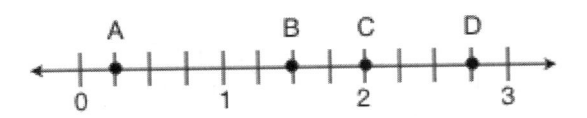

We can use the dashed lines on the number line to identify each point. Each dashed line between two whole numbers is $\frac{1}{4}$. The line halfway between two numbers is $\frac{1}{2}$.

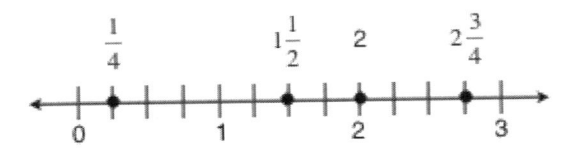

> **Review Video: Negative and Positive Number Line**
> Visit mometrix.com/academy and enter code: 816439

NUMBERS IN WORD FORM AND PLACE VALUE

When writing numbers out in word form or translating word form to numbers, it is essential to understand how a place value system works. In the decimal or base-10 system, each digit of a number represents how many of the corresponding place value—a specific factor of 10—are contained in the number being represented. To make reading numbers easier, every three digits to the left of the decimal place is preceded by a comma. The following table demonstrates some of the place values:

Power of 10	10^3	10^2	10^1	10^0	10^{-1}	10^{-2}	10^{-3}
Value	1,000	100	10	1	0.1	0.01	0.001
Place	thousands	hundreds	tens	ones	tenths	hundredths	thousandths

For example, consider the number 4,546.09, which can be separated into each place value like this:

- 4: thousands
- 5: hundreds
- 4: tens
- 6: ones
- 0: tenths
- 9: hundredths

This number in word form would be *four thousand five hundred forty-six and nine hundredths*.

> **Review Video: Number Place Value**
> Visit mometrix.com/academy and enter code: 205433

ABSOLUTE VALUE

A precursor to working with negative numbers is understanding what **absolute values** are. A number's absolute value is simply the distance away from zero a number is on the number line. The absolute value of a number is always positive and is written $|x|$. For example, the absolute value of 3, written as $|3|$, is 3 because the distance between 0 and 3 on a number line is three units. Likewise, the absolute value of -3, written as $|-3|$, is 3 because the distance between 0 and -3 on a number line is three units. So $|3| = |-3|$.

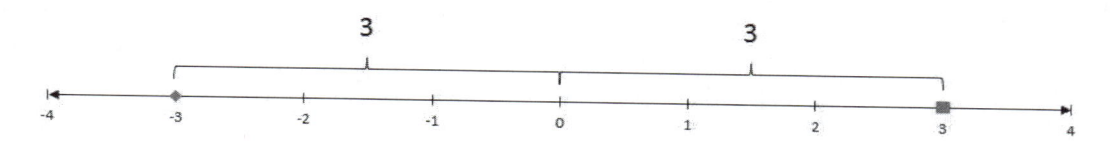

> **Review Video: Absolute Value**
> Visit mometrix.com/academy and enter code: 314669

PRACTICE

P1. Write the place value of each digit in 14,059.826

P2. Write out each of the following in words:

   (a) 29
   (b) 478
   (c) 98,542
   (d) 0.06
   (e) 13.113

P3. Write each of the following in numbers:

   (a) nine thousand four hundred thirty-five
   (b) three hundred two thousand eight hundred seventy-six
   (c) nine hundred one thousandths
   (d) nineteen thousandths
   (e) seven thousand one hundred forty-two and eighty-five hundredths

Practice Solutions

P1. The place value for each digit would be as follows:

Digit	Place Value
1	ten-thousands
4	thousands
0	hundreds
5	tens
9	ones
8	tenths
2	hundredths
6	thousandths

P2. Each written out in words would be:

(a) twenty-nine
(b) four hundred seventy-eight
(c) ninety-eight thousand five hundred forty-two
(d) six hundredths
(e) thirteen and one hundred thirteen thousandths

P3. Each in numeric form would be:

(a) 9,435
(b) 302,876
(c) 0.901
(d) 0.019
(e) 7,142.85

Operations

OPERATIONS

An **operation** is simply a mathematical process that takes some value(s) as input(s) and produces an output. Elementary operations are often written in the following form: *value operation value*. For instance, in the expression $1 + 2$ the values are 1 and 2 and the operation is addition. Performing the operation gives the output of 3. In this way we can say that $1 + 2$ and 3 are equal, or $1 + 2 = 3$.

ADDITION

Addition increases the value of one quantity by the value of another quantity (both called **addends**). For example, $2 + 4 = 6$ or $8 + 9 = 17$. The result is called the **sum**. With addition, the order does not matter, $4 + 2 = 2 + 4$.

When adding signed numbers, if the signs are the same simply add the absolute values of the addends and apply the original sign to the sum. For example, $(+4) + (+8) = +12$ and $(-4) + (-8) = -12$. When the original signs are different, take the absolute values of the addends and subtract the smaller value from the larger value, then apply the original sign of the larger value to the difference. For instance, $(+4) + (-8) = -4$ and $(-4) + (+8) = +4$.

SUBTRACTION

Subtraction is the opposite operation to addition; it decreases the value of one quantity (the **minuend**) by the value of another quantity (the **subtrahend**). For example, $6 - 4 = 2$ or $17 - 8 = 9$. The result is called the **difference**. Note that with subtraction, the order does matter, $6 - 4 \neq 4 - 6$.

For subtracting signed numbers, change the sign of the subtrahend and then follow the same rules used for addition. For example, $(+4) - (+8) = (+4) + (-8) = -4$.

MULTIPLICATION

Multiplication can be thought of as repeated addition. One number (the **multiplier**) indicates how many times to add the other number (the **multiplicand**) to itself. For example, $3 \times 2 = 2 + 2 + 2 = 6$. With multiplication, the order does not matter: $2 \times 3 = 3 \times 2$ or $3 + 3 = 2 + 2 + 2$, either way the result (the **product**) is the same.

If the signs are the same, the product is positive when multiplying signed numbers. For example, $(+4) \times (+8) = +32$ and $(-4) \times (-8) = +32$. If the signs are opposite, the product is negative. For example, $(+4) \times (-8) = -32$ and $(-4) \times (+8) = -32$. When more than two factors are multiplied together, the sign of the product is determined by how many negative factors are present. If there are an odd number of negative factors then the product is negative, whereas an even number of negative factors indicates a positive product. For instance, $(+4) \times (-8) \times (-2) = +64$ and $(-4) \times (-8) \times (-2) = -64$.

DIVISION

Division is the opposite operation to multiplication; one number (the **divisor**) tells us how many parts to divide the other number (the **dividend**) into. The result of division is called the **quotient**. For example, $20 \div 4 = 5$; if 20 is split into 4 equal parts, each part is 5. With division, the order of the numbers does matter, $20 \div 4 \neq 4 \div 20$.

The rules for dividing signed numbers are similar to multiplying signed numbers. If the dividend and divisor have the same sign, the quotient is positive. If the dividend and divisor have opposite signs, the quotient is negative. For example, $(-4) \div (+8) = -0.5$.

> **Review Video: Addition, Subtraction, Multiplication, and Division**
> Visit mometrix.com/academy and enter code: 208095

PARENTHESES

Parentheses are used to designate which operations should be done first when there are multiple operations. Example: $4 - (2 + 1) = 1$; the parentheses tell us that we must add 2 and 1, and then subtract the sum from 4, rather than subtracting 2 from 4 and then adding 1 (this would give us an answer of 3).

> **Review Video: Mathematical Parentheses**
> Visit mometrix.com/academy and enter code: 978600

EXPONENTS

An **exponent** is a superscript number placed next to another number at the top right. It indicates how many times the base number is to be multiplied by itself. Exponents provide a shorthand way to write what would be a longer mathematical expression, for example: $2^4 = 2 \times 2 \times 2 \times 2$. A number with an exponent of 2 is said to be "squared," while a number with an exponent of 3 is said to be "cubed." The value of a number raised to an exponent is called its power. So 8^4 is read as "8 to the 4th power," or "8 raised to the power of 4."

The properties of exponents are as follows:

Property	Description
$a^1 = a$	Any number to the power of 1 is equal to itself
$1^n = 1$	The number 1 raised to any power is equal to 1
$a^0 = 1$	Any number raised to the power of 0 is equal to 1
$a^n \times a^m = a^{n+m}$	Add exponents to multiply powers of the same base number
$a^n \div a^m = a^{n-m}$	Subtract exponents to divide powers of the same base number
$(a^n)^m = a^{n \times m}$	When a power is raised to a power, the exponents are multiplied
$(a \times b)^n = a^n \times b^n$ $(a \div b)^n = a^n \div b^n$	Multiplication and division operations inside parentheses can be raised to a power. This is the same as each term being raised to that power.
$a^{-n} = \dfrac{1}{a^n}$	A negative exponent is the same as the reciprocal of a positive exponent

Note that exponents do not have to be integers. Fractional or decimal exponents follow all the rules above as well. Example: $5^{\frac{1}{4}} \times 5^{\frac{3}{4}} = 5^{\frac{1}{4}+\frac{3}{4}} = 5^1 = 5$.

> **Review Video: Exponents**
> Visit mometrix.com/academy and enter code: 600998
>
> **Review Video: Laws of Exponents**
> Visit mometrix.com/academy and enter code: 532558

Roots

A **root**, such as a square root, is another way of writing a fractional exponent. Instead of using a superscript, roots use the radical symbol ($\sqrt{}$) to indicate the operation. A radical will have a number underneath the bar, and may sometimes have a number in the upper left: $\sqrt[n]{a}$, read as "the nth root of a." The relationship between radical notation and exponent notation can be described by this equation:

$$\sqrt[n]{a} = a^{\frac{1}{n}}$$

The two special cases of $n = 2$ and $n = 3$ are called square roots and cube roots. If there is no number to the upper left, the radical is understood to be a square root ($n = 2$). Nearly all of the roots you encounter will be square roots. A square root is the same as a number raised to the one-half power. When we say that a is the square root of b ($a = \sqrt{b}$), we mean that a multiplied by itself equals b: ($a \times a = b$).

A **perfect square** is a number that has an integer for its square root. There are 10 perfect squares from 1 to 100: 1, 4, 9, 16, 25, 36, 49, 64, 81, 100 (the squares of integers 1 through 10).

> **Review Video: Roots**
> Visit mometrix.com/academy and enter code: 795655

ORDER OF OPERATIONS

Order of operations is a set of rules that dictates the order in which we must perform each operation in an expression so that we will evaluate it accurately. If we have an expression that includes multiple different operations, order of operations tells us which operations to do first. The most common mnemonic for order of operations is **PEMDAS**, or "Please Excuse My Dear Aunt Sally." PEMDAS stands for parentheses, exponents, multiplication, division, addition, and subtraction. It is important to understand that multiplication and division have equal precedence, as do addition and subtraction, so those pairs of operations are simply worked from left to right in order.

For example, evaluating the expression $5 + 20 \div 4 \times (2 + 3)^2 - 6$ using the correct order of operations would be done like this:

- **P:** Perform the operations inside the parentheses: $(2 + 3) = 5$
- **E:** Simplify the exponents: $(5)^2 = 5 \times 5 = 25$
  - The equation now looks like this: $5 + 20 \div 4 \times 25 - 6$
- **MD:** Perform multiplication and division from left to right: $20 \div 4 = 5$; then $5 \times 25 = 125$
  - The equation now looks like this: $5 + 125 - 6$
- **AS:** Perform addition and subtraction from left to right: $5 + 125 = 130$; then $130 - 6 = 124$

> **Review Video: Order of Operations**
> Visit mometrix.com/academy and enter code: 259675

SUBTRACTION WITH REGROUPING

A great way to make use of some of the features built into the decimal system would be regrouping when attempting longform subtraction operations. When subtracting within a place value, sometimes the minuend is smaller than the subtrahend, **regrouping** enables you to 'borrow' a unit from a place value to the left in order to get a positive difference. For example, consider subtracting 189 from 525 with regrouping.

> **Review Video: Subtracting Large Numbers**
> Visit mometrix.com/academy and enter code: 603350

First, set up the subtraction problem in vertical form:

```
   525
-  189
```

Notice that the numbers in the ones and tens columns of 525 are smaller than the numbers in the ones and tens columns of 189. This means you will need to use regrouping to perform subtraction:

```
    5  2  5
-   1  8  9
```

To subtract 9 from 5 in the ones column you will need to borrow from the 2 in the tens columns:

```
    5  1  15
-   1  8   9
           6
```

Next, to subtract 8 from 1 in the tens column you will need to borrow from the 5 in the hundreds column:

```
    4  11  15
 -  1   8   9
    ─────────
        3   6
```

Last, subtract the 1 from the 4 in the hundreds column:

```
    4  11  15
 -  1   8   9
    ─────────
    3   3   6
```

WORD PROBLEMS AND MATHEMATICAL SYMBOLS

When working on word problems, you must be able to translate verbal expressions or "math words" into math symbols. This chart contains several "math words" and their appropriate symbols:

Phrase	Symbol
equal, is, was, will be, has, costs, gets to, is the same as, becomes	=
times, of, multiplied by, product of, twice, doubles, halves, triples	×
divided by, per, ratio of/to, out of	÷
plus, added to, sum, combined, and, more than, totals of	+
subtracted from, less than, decreased by, minus, difference between	−
what, how much, original value, how many, a number, a variable	x, n, etc.

EXAMPLES OF TRANSLATED MATHEMATICAL PHRASES

- The phrase four more than twice a number can be written algebraically as $2x + 4$.
- The phrase half a number decreased by six can be written algebraically as $\frac{1}{2}x - 6$.
- The phrase the sum of a number and the product of five and that number can be written algebraically as $x + 5x$.
- You may see a test question that says, "Olivia is constructing a bookcase from seven boards. Two of them are for vertical supports and five are for shelves. The height of the bookcase is twice the width of the bookcase. If the seven boards total 36 feet in length, what will be the height of Olivia's bookcase?" You would need to make a sketch and then create the equation to determine the width of the shelves. The height can be represented as double the width. (If x represents the width of the shelves in feet, then the height of the bookcase is $2x$. Since the seven boards total 36 feet, $2x + 2x + x + x + x + x + x = 36$ or $9x = 36$; $x = 4$. The height is twice the width, or 8 feet.)

PRACTICE

P1. Demonstrate how to subtract 477 from 620 using regrouping.

P2. Simplify the following expressions with exponents:

(a) 37^0
(b) 1^{30}
(c) $2^3 \times 2^4 \times 2^x$
(d) $(3^x)^3$
(e) $(12 \div 3)^2$

Practice Solutions

P1. First, set up the subtraction problem in vertical form:

```
   6  2  0
-  4  7  7
```

To subtract 7 from 0 in the ones column you will need to borrow from the 2 in the tens column:

```
   6  1  10
-  4  7   7
          3
```

Next, to subtract 7 from the 1 that's still in the tens column you will need to borrow from the 6 in the hundreds column:

```
   5  11  10
-  4   7   7
       4   3
```

Lastly, subtract 4 from the 5 remaining in the hundreds column:

```
   5  11  10
-  4   7   7
   1   4   3
```

P2. Using the properties of exponents and the proper order of operations:

    (a) Any number raised to the power of 0 is equal to 1: $37^0 = 1$
    (b) The number 1 raised to any power is equal to 1: $1^{30} = 1$
    (c) Add exponents to multiply powers of the same base: $2^3 \times 2^4 \times 2^x = 2^{(3+4+x)} = 2^{(7+x)}$
    (d) When a power is raised to a power, the exponents are multiplied: $(3^x)^3 = 3^{3x}$
    (e) Perform the operation inside the parentheses first: $(12 \div 3)^2 = 4^2 = 16$

Factoring

FACTORS AND GREATEST COMMON FACTOR

Factors are numbers that are multiplied together to obtain a **product**. For example, in the equation $2 \times 3 = 6$, the numbers 2 and 3 are factors. A **prime number** has only two factors (1 and itself), but other numbers can have many factors.

A **common factor** is a number that divides exactly into two or more other numbers. For example, the factors of 12 are 1, 2, 3, 4, 6, and 12, while the factors of 15 are 1, 3, 5, and 15. The common factors of 12 and 15 are 1 and 3.

A **prime factor** is also a prime number. Therefore, the prime factors of 12 are 2 and 3. For 15, the prime factors are 3 and 5.

The **greatest common factor** (**GCF**) is the largest number that is a factor of two or more numbers. For example, the factors of 15 are 1, 3, 5, and 15; the factors of 35 are 1, 5, 7, and 35. Therefore, the greatest common factor of 15 and 35 is 5.

> **Review Video: Factors**
> Visit mometrix.com/academy and enter code: 920086
>
> **Review Video: Greatest Common Factor (GCF)**
> Visit mometrix.com/academy and enter code: 838699

MULTIPLES AND LEAST COMMON MULTIPLE

Often listed out in multiplication tables, **multiples** are integer increments of a given factor. In other words, dividing a multiple by the factor will result in an integer. For example, the multiples of 7 include: $1 \times 7 = 7, 2 \times 7 = 14, 3 \times 7 = 21, 4 \times 7 = 28, 5 \times 7 = 35$. Dividing 7, 14, 21, 28, or 35 by 7 will result in the integers 1, 2, 3, 4, and 5, respectively.

The least common multiple (**LCM**) is the smallest number that is a multiple of two or more numbers. For example, the multiples of 3 include 3, 6, 9, 12, 15, etc.; the multiples of 5 include 5, 10, 15, 20, etc. Therefore, the least common multiple of 3 and 5 is 15.

> **Review Video: Multiples**
> Visit mometrix.com/academy and enter code: 626738

Rational Numbers

FRACTIONS

A **fraction** is a number that is expressed as one integer written above another integer, with a dividing line between them $\left(\frac{x}{y}\right)$. It represents the **quotient** of the two numbers "x divided by y." It can also be thought of as x out of y equal parts.

The top number of a fraction is called the **numerator**, and it represents the number of parts under consideration. The 1 in $\frac{1}{4}$ means that 1 part out of the whole is being considered in the calculation. The bottom number of a fraction is called the **denominator**, and it represents the total number of equal parts. The 4 in $\frac{1}{4}$ means that the whole consists of 4 equal parts. A fraction cannot have a denominator of zero; this is referred to as "*undefined.*"

Fractions can be manipulated, without changing the value of the fraction, by multiplying or dividing (but not adding or subtracting) both the numerator and denominator by the same number. If you divide both numbers by a common factor, you are **reducing** or simplifying the fraction. Two fractions that have the same value but are expressed differently are known as **equivalent fractions**. For example, $\frac{2}{10}, \frac{3}{15}, \frac{4}{20}$, and $\frac{5}{25}$ are all equivalent fractions. They can also all be reduced or simplified to $\frac{1}{5}$.

When two fractions are manipulated so that they have the same denominator, this is known as finding a **common denominator**. The number chosen to be that common denominator should be the least common multiple of the two original denominators. Example: $\frac{3}{4}$ and $\frac{5}{6}$; the least common multiple of 4 and 6 is 12. Manipulating to achieve the common denominator: $\frac{3}{4} = \frac{9}{12}$; $\frac{5}{6} = \frac{10}{12}$.

PROPER FRACTIONS AND MIXED NUMBERS

A fraction whose denominator is greater than its numerator is known as a **proper fraction**, while a fraction whose numerator is greater than its denominator is known as an **improper fraction**. Proper fractions have values *less than one* and improper fractions have values *greater than one*.

A **mixed number** is a number that contains both an integer and a fraction. Any improper fraction can be rewritten as a mixed number. Example: $\frac{8}{3} = \frac{6}{3} + \frac{2}{3} = 2 + \frac{2}{3} = 2\frac{2}{3}$. Similarly, any mixed number can be rewritten as an improper fraction. Example: $1\frac{3}{5} = 1 + \frac{3}{5} = \frac{5}{5} + \frac{3}{5} = \frac{8}{5}$.

> **Review Video: Proper and Improper Fractions and Mixed Numbers**
> Visit mometrix.com/academy and enter code: 211077
>
> **Review Video: Fractions**
> Visit mometrix.com/academy and enter code: 262335

ADDING AND SUBTRACTING FRACTIONS

If two fractions have a common denominator, they can be added or subtracted simply by adding or subtracting the two numerators and retaining the same denominator. If the two fractions do not already have the same denominator, one or both of them must be manipulated to achieve a common denominator before they can be added or subtracted. Example: $\frac{1}{2} + \frac{1}{4} = \frac{2}{4} + \frac{1}{4} = \frac{3}{4}$.

> **Review Video: Adding and Subtracting Fractions**
> Visit mometrix.com/academy and enter code: 378080

MULTIPLYING FRACTIONS

Two fractions can be multiplied by multiplying the two numerators to find the new numerator and the two denominators to find the new denominator. Example: $\frac{1}{3} \times \frac{2}{3} = \frac{1 \times 2}{3 \times 3} = \frac{2}{9}$.

DIVIDING FRACTIONS

Two fractions can be divided by flipping the numerator and denominator of the second fraction and then proceeding as though it were a multiplication problem. Example: $\frac{2}{3} \div \frac{3}{4} = \frac{2}{3} \times \frac{4}{3} = \frac{8}{9}$.

> **Review Video: Multiplying and Dividing Fractions**
> Visit mometrix.com/academy and enter code: 473632

MULTIPLYING A MIXED NUMBER BY A WHOLE NUMBER OR A DECIMAL

When multiplying a mixed number by something, it is usually best to convert it to an improper fraction first. Additionally, if the multiplicand is a decimal, it is most often simplest to convert it to a fraction. For instance, to multiply $4\frac{3}{8}$ by 3.5, begin by rewriting each quantity as a whole number plus a proper fraction. Remember, a mixed number is a fraction added to a whole number and a decimal is a representation of the sum of fractions, specifically tenths, hundredths, thousandths, and so on:

$$4\frac{3}{8} \times 3.5 = \left(4 + \frac{3}{8}\right) \times \left(3 + \frac{1}{2}\right)$$

Next, the quantities being added need to be expressed with the same denominator. This is achieved by multiplying and dividing the whole number by the denominator of the fraction. Recall that a whole number is equivalent to that number divided by 1:

$$= \left(\frac{4}{1} \times \frac{8}{8} + \frac{3}{8}\right) \times \left(\frac{3}{1} \times \frac{2}{2} + \frac{1}{2}\right)$$

When multiplying fractions, remember to multiply the numerators and denominators separately:

$$= \left(\frac{4 \times 8}{1 \times 8} + \frac{3}{8}\right) \times \left(\frac{3 \times 2}{1 \times 2} + \frac{1}{2}\right)$$

$$= \left(\frac{32}{8} + \frac{3}{8}\right) \times \left(\frac{6}{2} + \frac{1}{2}\right)$$

Now that the fractions have the same denominators, they can be added:

$$= \frac{35}{8} \times \frac{7}{2}$$

Finally, perform the last multiplication and then simplify:

$$= \frac{35 \times 7}{8 \times 2} = \frac{245}{16} = \frac{240}{16} + \frac{5}{16} = 15\frac{5}{16}$$

DECIMALS

Decimals are one way to represent parts of a whole. Using the place value system, each digit to the right of a decimal point denotes the number of units of a corresponding *negative* power of ten. For example, consider the decimal 0.24. We can use a model to represent the decimal. Since a dime is worth one-tenth of a dollar and a penny is worth one-hundredth of a dollar, one possible model to represent this fraction is to have 2 dimes representing the 2 in the tenths place and 4 pennies representing the 4 in the hundredths place:

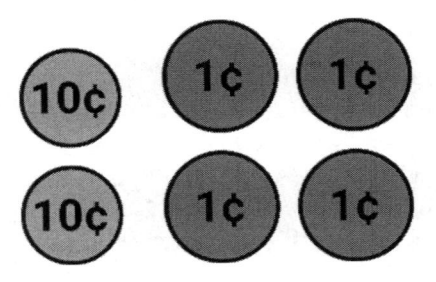

To write the decimal as a fraction, put the decimal in the numerator with 1 in the denominator. Multiply the numerator and denominator by tens until there are no more decimal places. Then simplify the fraction to lowest terms. For example, converting 0.24 to a fraction:

$$0.24 = \frac{0.24}{1} = \frac{0.24 \times 100}{1 \times 100} = \frac{24}{100} = \frac{6}{25}$$

> **Review Video: Decimals**
> Visit mometrix.com/academy and enter code: 837268

OPERATIONS WITH DECIMALS
ADDING AND SUBTRACTING DECIMALS

When adding and subtracting decimals, the decimal points must always be aligned. Adding decimals is just like adding regular whole numbers. Example: $4.5 + 2.0 = 6.5$.

If the problem-solver does not properly align the decimal points, an incorrect answer of 4.7 may result. An easy way to add decimals is to align all of the decimal points in a vertical column visually. This will allow one to see exactly where the decimal should be placed in the final answer. Begin adding from right to left. Add each column in turn, making sure to carry the number to the left if a column adds up to more than 9. The same rules apply to the subtraction of decimals.

> **Review Video: Adding and Subtracting Decimals**
> Visit mometrix.com/academy and enter code: 381101

MULTIPLYING DECIMALS

A simple multiplication problem has two components: a **multiplicand** and a **multiplier**. When multiplying decimals, work as though the numbers were whole rather than decimals. Once the final product is calculated, count the number of places to the right of the decimal in both the multiplicand and the multiplier. Then, count that number of places from the right of the product and place the decimal in that position.

For example, 12.3×2.56 has a total of three places to the right of the respective decimals. Multiply 123×256 to get 31,488. Now, beginning on the right, count three places to the left and insert the decimal. The final product will be 31,488.

> **Review Video: Multiplying Decimals**
> Visit mometrix.com/academy and enter code: 731574

DIVIDING DECIMALS

Every division problem has a **divisor** and a **dividend**. The dividend is the number that is being divided. In the problem $14 \div 7$, 14 is the dividend and 7 is the divisor. In a division problem with decimals, the divisor must be converted into a whole number. Begin by moving the decimal in the divisor to the right until a whole number is created. Next, move the decimal in the dividend the same number of spaces to the right. For example, 4.9 into 24.5 would become 49 into 245. The decimal was moved one space to the right to create a whole number in the divisor, and then the same was done for the dividend. Once the whole numbers are created, the problem is carried out normally: $245 \div 49 = 5$.

> **Review Video: Dividing Decimals**
> Visit mometrix.com/academy and enter code: 560690
>
> **Review Video: Dividing Decimals by Whole Numbers**
> Visit mometrix.com/academy and enter code: 535669

PERCENTAGES

Percentages can be thought of as fractions that are based on a whole of 100; that is, one whole is equal to 100%. The word **percent** means "per hundred." Percentage problems are often presented in three main ways:

- Find what percentage of some number another number is.
  - Example: What percentage of 40 is 8?
- Find what number is some percentage of a given number.
  - Example: What number is 20% of 40?
- Find what number another number is a given percentage of.
  - Example: What number is 8 20% of?

There are three components in each of these cases: a **whole** (W), a **part** (P), and a **percentage** (%). These are related by the equation: $P = W \times \%$. This can easily be rearranged into other forms that may suit different questions better: $\% = \frac{P}{W}$ and $W = \frac{P}{\%}$. Percentage problems are often also word problems. As such, a large part of solving them is figuring out which quantities are what. For example, consider the following word problem:

In a school cafeteria, 7 students choose pizza, 9 choose hamburgers, and 4 choose tacos. What percentage of student choose tacos?

To find the whole, you must first add all of the parts: $7 + 9 + 4 = 20$. The percentage can then be found by dividing the part by the whole $\left(\% = \frac{P}{W}\right): \frac{4}{20} = \frac{20}{100} = 20\%$.

> **Review Video: Percent Increase vs. Percent of Whole**
> Visit mometrix.com/academy and enter code: 130715

CONVERTING BETWEEN PERCENTAGES, FRACTIONS, AND DECIMALS

Converting decimals to percentages and percentages to decimals is as simple as moving the decimal point. To *convert from a decimal to a percentage*, move the decimal point **two places to the right**. To *convert from a percentage to a decimal*, move it **two places to the left**. It may be helpful to remember that the percentage number will always be larger than the equivalent decimal number. For example:

$$0.23 = 23\% \quad 5.34 = 534\% \quad 0.007 = 0.7\%$$
$$700\% = 7.00 \quad 86\% = 0.86 \quad 0.15\% = 0.0015$$

To convert a fraction to a decimal, simply divide the numerator by the denominator in the fraction. To convert a decimal to a fraction, put the decimal in the numerator with 1 in the denominator.

Multiply the numerator and denominator by tens until there are no more decimal places. Then simplify the fraction to lowest terms. For example, converting 0.24 to a fraction:

$$0.24 = \frac{0.24}{1} = \frac{0.24 \times 100}{1 \times 100} = \frac{24}{100} = \frac{6}{25}$$

Fractions can be converted to a percentage by finding equivalent fractions with a denominator of 100. For example,

$$\frac{7}{10} = \frac{70}{100} = 70\% \qquad \frac{1}{4} = \frac{25}{100} = 25\%$$

To convert a percentage to a fraction, divide the percentage number by 100 and reduce the fraction to its simplest possible terms. For example,

$$60\% = \frac{60}{100} = \frac{3}{5} \qquad 96\% = \frac{96}{100} = \frac{24}{25}$$

> **Review Video: Converting Decimals to Fractions and Percentages**
> Visit mometrix.com/academy and enter code: 986765
>
> **Review Video: Converting Fractions to Percentages and Decimals**
> Visit mometrix.com/academy and enter code: 306233
>
> **Review Video: Converting Percentages to Decimals and Fractions**
> Visit mometrix.com/academy and enter code: 287297

RATIONAL NUMBERS

The term **rational** means that the number can be expressed as a ratio or fraction. That is, a number, r, is rational if and only if it can be represented by a fraction $\frac{a}{b}$ where a and b are integers and b does not equal 0. The set of rational numbers includes integers and decimals. If there is no finite way to represent a value with a fraction of integers, then the number is **irrational**. Common examples of irrational numbers include: $\sqrt{5}$, $(1 + \sqrt{2})$, and π.

> **Review Video: Rational and Irrational Numbers**
> Visit mometrix.com/academy and enter code: 280645

PRACTICE

P1. What is 30% of 120?

P2. What is 150% of 20?

P3. What is 14.5% of 96?

P4. Simplify the following expressions:

(a) $\frac{2}{5} \div \frac{4}{7}$

(b) $\frac{7}{8} - \frac{8}{16}$

(c) $\frac{1}{2} + \left(3\left(\frac{3}{4}\right) - 2\right) + 4$

(d) $0.22 + 0.5 - (5.5 + 3.3 \div 3)$

(e) $\frac{3}{2} + (4(0.5) - 0.75) + 2$

P5. Convert the following to a fraction and to a decimal: (a) 15%; (b) 24.36%

P6. Convert the following to a decimal and to a percentage. (a) $\frac{4}{5}$; (b) $3\frac{2}{5}$

P7. A woman's age is thirteen more than half of 60. How old is the woman?

P8. A patient was given pain medicine at a dosage of 0.22 grams. The patient's dosage was then increased to 0.80 grams. By how much was the patient's dosage increased?

P9. At a hotel, $\frac{3}{4}$ of the 100 rooms are occupied today. Yesterday, $\frac{4}{5}$ of the 100 rooms were occupied. On which day were more of the rooms occupied and by how much more?

P10. At a school, 40% of the teachers teach English. If 20 teachers teach English, how many teachers work at the school?

P11. A patient was given blood pressure medicine at a dosage of 2 grams. The patient's dosage was then decreased to 0.45 grams. By how much was the patient's dosage decreased?

P12. Two weeks ago, $\frac{2}{3}$ of the 60 customers at a skate shop were male. Last week, $\frac{3}{6}$ of the 80 customers were male. During which week were there more male customers?

P13. Jane ate lunch at a local restaurant. She ordered a $4.99 appetizer, a $12.50 entrée, and a $1.25 soda. If she wants to tip her server 20%, how much money will she spend in all?

P14. According to a survey, about 82% of engineers were highly satisfied with their job. If 145 engineers were surveyed, how many reported that they were highly satisfied?

P15. A patient was given 40 mg of a certain medicine. Later, the patient's dosage was increased to 45 mg. What was the percent increase in his medication?

P16. Order the following rational numbers from least to greatest: 0.55, 17%, $\sqrt{25}$, $\frac{64}{4}$, $\frac{25}{50}$, 3.

P17. Order the following rational numbers from greatest to least: 0.3, 27%, $\sqrt{100}$, $\frac{72}{9}$, $\frac{1}{9}$, 4.5

P18. Perform the following multiplication. Write each answer as a mixed number.

(a) $\left(1\frac{11}{16}\right) \times 4$

(b) $\left(12\frac{1}{3}\right) \times 1.1$

(c) $3.71 \times \left(6\frac{1}{5}\right)$

P19. Suppose you are making doughnuts and you want to triple the recipe you have. If the following list is the original amounts for the ingredients, what would be the amounts for the tripled recipe?

$1\frac{3}{4}$	cup	Flour	$1\frac{1}{2}$	Tbsp	Butter
$1\frac{1}{4}$	tsp	Baking powder	2	large	Eggs
$\frac{3}{4}$	tsp	Salt	$\frac{3}{4}$	tsp	Vanilla extract
$\frac{3}{8}$	cup	Sugar	$\frac{3}{8}$	cup	Sour cream

Practice Solutions

P1. The word *of* indicates multiplication, so 30% of 120 is found by multiplying 120 by 30%. Change 30% to a decimal, then multiply: $120 \times 0.3 = 36$

P2. The word *of* indicates multiplication, so 150% of 20 is found by multiplying 20 by 150%. Change 150% to a decimal, then multiply: $20 \times 1.5 = 30$

P3. Change 14.5% to a decimal before multiplying. $0.145 \times 96 = 13.92$.

P4. Follow the order of operations and utilize properties of fractions to solve each:

(a) Rewrite the problem as a multiplication problem: $\frac{2}{5} \times \frac{7}{4} = \frac{2 \times 7}{5 \times 4} = \frac{14}{20}$. Make sure the fraction is reduced to lowest terms. Both 14 and 20 can be divided by 2.

$$\frac{14}{20} = \frac{14 \div 2}{20 \div 2} = \frac{7}{10}$$

(b) The denominators of $\frac{7}{8}$ and $\frac{8}{16}$ are 8 and 16, respectively. The lowest common denominator of 8 and 16 is 16 because 16 is the least common multiple of 8 and 16. Convert the first fraction to its equivalent with the newly found common denominator of 16: $\frac{7 \times 2}{8 \times 2} = \frac{14}{16}$. Now that the fractions have the same denominator, you can subtract them.

$$\frac{14}{16} - \frac{8}{16} = \frac{6}{16} = \frac{3}{8}$$

(c) When simplifying expressions, first perform operations within groups. Within the set of parentheses are multiplication and subtraction operations. Perform the multiplication first to get $\frac{1}{2} + \left(\frac{9}{4} - 2\right) + 4$. Then, subtract two to obtain $\frac{1}{2} + \frac{1}{4} + 4$. Finally, perform addition from left to right:

$$\frac{1}{2} + \frac{1}{4} + 4 = \frac{2}{4} + \frac{1}{4} + \frac{16}{4} = \frac{19}{4} = 4\frac{3}{4}$$

(d) First, evaluate the terms in the parentheses $(5.5 + 3.3 \div 3)$ using order of operations. $3.3 \div 3 = 1.1$, and $5.5 + 1.1 = 6.6$. Next, rewrite the problem: $0.22 + 0.5 - 6.6$. Finally, add and subtract from left to right: $0.22 + 0.5 = 0.72$; $0.72 - 6.6 = -5.88$. The answer is -5.88.

(e) First, simplify within the parentheses, then change the fraction to a decimal and perform addition from left to right:

$$\frac{3}{2} + (2 - 0.75) + 2 =$$

$$\frac{3}{2} + 1.25 + 2 =$$

$$1.5 + 1.25 + 2 = 4.75$$

P5. (a) 15% can be written as $\frac{15}{100}$. Both 15 and 100 can be divided by 5: $\frac{15 \div 5}{100 \div 5} = \frac{3}{20}$

When converting from a percentage to a decimal, drop the percent sign and move the decimal point two places to the left: $15\% = 0.15$

(b) 24.36% written as a fraction is $\frac{24.36}{100}$, or $\frac{2436}{10,000}$, which reduces to $\frac{609}{2500}$. 24.36% written as a decimal is 0.2436. Recall that dividing by 100 moves the decimal two places to the left.

P6. (a) Recall that in the decimal system the first decimal place is one tenth: $\frac{4 \times 2}{5 \times 2} = \frac{8}{10} = 0.8$

Percent means "per hundred." $\frac{4 \times 20}{5 \times 20} = \frac{80}{100} = 80\%$

(b) The mixed number $3\frac{2}{5}$ has a whole number and a fractional part. The fractional part $\frac{2}{5}$ can be written as a decimal by dividing 5 into 2, which gives 0.4. Adding the whole to the part gives 3.4.

To find the equivalent percentage, multiply the decimal by 100. $3.4(100) = 340\%$. Notice that this percentage is greater than 100%. This makes sense because the original mixed number $3\frac{2}{5}$ is greater than 1.

P7. "More than" indicates addition, and "of" indicates multiplication. The expression can be written as $\frac{1}{2}(60) + 13$. So, the woman's age is equal to $\frac{1}{2}(60) + 13 = 30 + 13 = 43$. The woman is 43 years old.

P8. The first step is to determine what operation (addition, subtraction, multiplication, or division) the problem requires. Notice the keywords and phrases "by how much" and "increased."

"Increased" means that you go from a smaller amount to a larger amount. This change can be found by subtracting the smaller amount from the larger amount: 0.80 grams− 0.22 grams = 0.58 grams.

Remember to line up the decimal when subtracting:

$$\begin{array}{r} 0.80 \\ -\ 0.22 \\ \hline 0.58 \end{array}$$

P9. First, find the number of rooms occupied each day. To do so, multiply the fraction of rooms occupied by the number of rooms available:

$$\text{Number occupied} = \text{Fraction occupied} \times \text{Total number}$$
$$\text{Number of rooms occupied today} = \frac{3}{4} \times 100 = 75$$
$$\text{Number of rooms occupied} = \frac{4}{5} \times 100 = 80$$

The difference in the number of rooms occupied is: $80 - 75 = 5$ rooms

P10. To answer this problem, first think about the number of teachers that work at the school. Will it be more or less than the number of teachers who work in a specific department such as English? More teachers work at the school, so the number you find to answer this question will be greater than 20.

40% of the teachers are English teachers. "Of" indicates multiplication, and words like "is" and "are" indicate equivalence. Translating the problem into a mathematical sentence gives $40\% \times t = 20$, where t represents the total number of teachers. Solving for t gives $t = \frac{20}{40\%} = \frac{20}{0.40} = 50$. Fifty teachers work at the school.

P11. The decrease is represented by the difference between the two amounts:

$$2 \text{ grams} - 0.45 \text{ grams} = 1.55 \text{ grams}.$$

Remember to line up the decimal point before subtracting.

$$\begin{array}{r} 2.00 \\ -\ 0.45 \\ \hline 1.55 \end{array}$$

P12. First, you need to find the number of male customers that were in the skate shop each week. You are given this amount in terms of fractions. To find the actual number of male customers, multiply the fraction of male customers by the number of customers in the store.

$$\text{Actual number of male customers} = \text{fraction of male customers} \times \text{total customers}$$
$$\text{Number of male customers two weeks ago} = \frac{2}{3} \times 60 = \frac{120}{3} = 40$$
$$\text{Number of male customers last week} = \frac{3}{6} \times 80 = \frac{1}{2} \times 80 = \frac{80}{2} = 40$$

The number of male customers was the same both weeks.

P13. To find total amount, first find the sum of the items she ordered from the menu and then add 20% of this sum to the total.

$$\$4.99 + \$12.50 + \$1.25 = \$18.74$$

$$\$18.74 \times 20\% = (0.20)(\$18.74) = \$3.748 \approx \$3.75$$

$$\text{Total} = \$18.74 + \$3.75 = \$22.49$$

P14. 82% of 145 is $0.82 \times 145 = 118.9$. Because you can't have 0.9 of a person, we must round up to say that 119 engineers reported that they were highly satisfied with their jobs.

P15. To find the percent increase, first compare the original and increased amounts. The original amount was 40 mg, and the increased amount is 45 mg, so the dosage of medication was increased by 5 mg (45− 40 = 5). Note, however, that the question asks not by how much the dosage increased but by what percentage it increased.

$$\text{Percent increase} = \frac{\text{new amount} - \text{original amount}}{\text{original amount}} \times 100\%$$

$$= \frac{45 \text{ mg} - 40 \text{ mg}}{40 \text{ mg}} \times 100\% = \frac{5}{40} \times 100\% = 0.125 \times 100\% = 12.5\%$$

P16. Recall that the term rational simply means that the number can be expressed as a ratio or fraction. Notice that each of the numbers in the problem can be written as a decimal or integer:

$$17\% = 0.1717$$
$$\sqrt{25} = 5$$
$$\frac{64}{4} = 16$$
$$\frac{25}{50} = \frac{1}{2} = 0.5$$

So, the answer is 17%, $\frac{25}{50}$, 0.55, 3, $\sqrt{25}$, $\frac{64}{4}$.

P17. Converting all the numbers to integers and decimals makes it easier to compare the values:

$$27\% = 0.27$$
$$\sqrt{100} = 10$$
$$\frac{72}{9} = 8$$
$$\frac{1}{9} \approx 0.11$$

So, the answer is $\sqrt{100}$, $\frac{72}{9}$, 4.5, 0.3, 27%, $\frac{1}{9}$.

> **Review Video: Ordering Rational Numbers**
> Visit mometrix.com/academy and enter code: 419578

P18. For each, convert improper fractions, adjust to a common denominator, perform the operations, and then simplify:

(a) Sometimes, you can skip converting the denominator and just distribute the multiplication.

$$\left(1\frac{11}{16}\right) \times 4 = \left(1 + \frac{11}{16}\right) \times 4$$
$$= 1 \times 4 + \frac{11}{16} \times 4$$
$$= 4 + \frac{11}{16} \times \frac{4}{1}$$
$$= 4 + \frac{44}{16} = 4 + \frac{11}{4} = 4 + 2\frac{3}{4} = 6\frac{3}{4}$$

(b)

$$\left(12\frac{1}{3}\right) \times 1.1 = \left(12 + \frac{1}{3}\right) \times \left(1 + \frac{1}{10}\right)$$
$$= \left(\frac{12}{1} \times \frac{3}{3} + \frac{1}{3}\right) \times \left(\frac{10}{10} + \frac{1}{10}\right)$$
$$= \left(\frac{36}{3} + \frac{1}{3}\right) \times \frac{11}{10}$$
$$= \frac{37}{3} \times \frac{11}{10}$$
$$= \frac{407}{30} = \frac{390}{30} + \frac{17}{30} = 13\frac{17}{30}$$

(c)

$$3.71 \times \left(6\frac{1}{5}\right) = \left(3 + \frac{71}{100}\right) \times \left(6 + \frac{1}{5}\right)$$
$$= \left(\frac{300}{100} + \frac{71}{100}\right) \times \left(\frac{6}{1} \times \frac{5}{5} + \frac{1}{5}\right)$$
$$= \frac{371}{100} \times \left(\frac{30}{5} + \frac{1}{5}\right)$$
$$= \frac{371}{100} \times \frac{31}{5}$$
$$= \frac{11501}{500} = \frac{11500}{500} + \frac{1}{500} = 23\frac{1}{500}$$

P19. Fortunately, some of the amounts are duplicated, so we do not need to convert every amount.

$$1\frac{3}{4} \times 3 = (1 \times 3) + \left(\frac{3}{4} \times 3\right)$$
$$= 3 + \frac{9}{4}$$
$$= 3 + 2\frac{1}{4}$$
$$= 5\frac{1}{4}$$

$$1\frac{1}{4} \times 3 = (1 \times 3) + \left(\frac{1}{4} \times 3\right)$$
$$= 3 + \frac{3}{4}$$
$$= 3\frac{3}{4}$$

$$\frac{3}{4} \times 3 = \frac{3}{4} \times 3$$
$$= \frac{9}{4}$$
$$= 2\frac{1}{4}$$

$$\frac{3}{8} \times 3 = \frac{3}{8} \times 3$$
$$= \frac{9}{8}$$
$$= 1\frac{1}{8}$$

$$1\frac{1}{2} \times 3 = 1 \times 3 + \frac{1}{2} \times 3$$
$$= 3 + \frac{3}{2}$$
$$= 3 + 1\frac{1}{2}$$
$$= 4\frac{1}{2}$$

$$2 \times 3 = 6$$

So, the result for the triple recipe is:

$5\frac{1}{4}$	cup	Flour	$4\frac{1}{2}$	Tbsp	Butter
$3\frac{3}{4}$	tsp	Baking powder	6	large	Eggs
$2\frac{1}{4}$	tsp	Salt	$2\frac{1}{4}$	tsp	Vanilla extract
$1\frac{1}{8}$	cup	Sugar	$1\frac{1}{8}$	cup	Sour cream

Proportions and Ratios

PROPORTIONS

A proportion is a relationship between two quantities that dictates how one changes when the other changes. A **direct proportion** describes a relationship in which a quantity increases by a set amount for every increase in the other quantity, or decreases by that same amount for every decrease in the other quantity. Example: Assuming a constant driving speed, the time required for a car trip increases as the distance of the trip increases. The distance to be traveled and the time required to travel are directly proportional.

Inverse proportion is a relationship in which an increase in one quantity is accompanied by a decrease in the other, or vice versa. Example: the time required for a car trip decreases as the speed increases and increases as the speed decreases, so the time required is inversely proportional to the speed of the car.

> **Review Video: Proportions**
> Visit mometrix.com/academy and enter code: 505355

RATIOS

A **ratio** is a comparison of two quantities in a particular order. Example: If there are 14 computers in a lab, and the class has 20 students, there is a student to computer ratio of 20 to 14, commonly written as 20: 14. Ratios are normally reduced to their smallest whole number representation, so 20: 14 would be reduced to 10: 7 by dividing both sides by 2.

> **Review Video: Ratios**
> Visit mometrix.com/academy and enter code: 996914

CONSTANT OF PROPORTIONALITY

When two quantities have a proportional relationship, there exists a **constant of proportionality** between the quantities; the product of this constant and one of the quantities is equal to the other quantity. For example, if one lemon costs $0.25, two lemons cost $0.50, and three lemons cost $0.75, there is a proportional relationship between the total cost of lemons and the number of lemons purchased. The constant of proportionality is the **unit price**, namely $0.25/lemon. Notice that the total price of lemons, t, can be found by multiplying the unit price of lemons, p, and the number of lemons, n: $t = pn$.

WORK/UNIT RATE

Unit rate expresses a quantity of one thing in terms of one unit of another. For example, if you travel 30 miles every two hours, a unit rate expresses this comparison in terms of one hour: in one hour you travel 15 miles, so your unit rate is 15 miles per hour. Other examples are how much one ounce of food costs (price per ounce) or figuring out how much one egg costs out of the dozen (price per 1 egg, instead of price per 12 eggs). The denominator of a unit rate is always 1. Unit rates are used to compare different situations to solve problems. For example, to make sure you get the best deal when deciding which kind of soda to buy, you can find the unit rate of each. If soda #1 costs $1.50 for a 1-liter bottle, and soda #2 costs $2.75 for a 2-liter bottle, it would be a better deal to buy soda #2, because its unit rate is only $1.375 per 1-liter, which is cheaper than soda #1. Unit rates can also help determine the length of time a given event will take. For example, if you can paint 2 rooms in 4.5 hours, you can determine how long it will take you to paint 5 rooms by solving for the unit rate per room and then multiplying that by 5.

> **Review Video: Rates and Unit Rates**
> Visit mometrix.com/academy and enter code: 185363

SLOPE

On a graph with two points, (x_1, y_1) and (x_2, y_2), the **slope** is found with the formula $m = \frac{y_2 - y_1}{x_2 - x_1}$, where $x_1 \neq x_2$ and m stands for slope. If the value of the slope is **positive**, the line has an *upward direction* from left to right. If the value of the slope is **negative**, the line has a *downward direction* from left to right. Consider the following example:

A new book goes on sale in bookstores and online stores. In the first month, 5,000 copies of the book are sold. Over time, the book continues to grow in popularity. The data for the number of copies sold is in the table below.

# of Months on Sale	1	2	3	4	5
# of Copies Sold (In Thousands)	5	10	15	20	25

So, the number of copies that are sold and the time that the book is on sale is a proportional relationship. In this example, an equation can be used to show the data: $y = 5x$, where x is the number of months that the book is on sale. Also, y is the number of copies sold. So, the slope of the corresponding line is $\frac{\text{rise}}{\text{run}} = \frac{5}{1} = 5$.

> **Review Video: Finding the Slope of a Line**
> Visit mometrix.com/academy and enter code: 766664

FINDING AN UNKNOWN IN EQUIVALENT EXPRESSIONS

It is often necessary to apply information given about a rate or proportion to a new scenario. For example, if you know that Jedha can run a marathon (26.2 miles) in 3 hours, how long would it take her to run 10 miles at the same pace? Start by setting up equivalent expressions:

$$\frac{26.2 \text{ mi}}{3 \text{ hr}} = \frac{10 \text{ mi}}{x \text{ hr}}$$

Now, cross multiply and solve for x:

$$26.2x = 30$$
$$x = \frac{30}{26.2} = \frac{15}{13.1}$$
$$x \approx 1.15 \text{ hrs } or \text{ 1 hr 9 min}$$

So, at this pace, Jedha could run 10 miles in about 1.15 hours or about 1 hour and 9 minutes.

> **Review Video: Cross Multiply Fractions**
> Visit mometrix.com/academy and enter code: 893904

PRACTICE

P1. Solve the following for x.

(a) $\frac{45}{12} = \frac{15}{x}$

(b) $\frac{0.50}{2} = \frac{1.50}{x}$

(c) $\frac{40}{8} = \frac{x}{24}$

P2. At a school, for every 20 female students there are 15 male students. This same student ratio happens to exist at another school. If there are 100 female students at the second school, how many male students are there?

P3. In a hospital emergency room, there are 4 nurses for every 12 patients. What is the ratio of nurses to patients? If the nurse-to-patient ratio remains constant, how many nurses must be present to care for 24 patients?

P4. In a bank, the banker-to-customer ratio is 1:2. If seven bankers are on duty, how many customers are currently in the bank?

P5. Janice made $40 during the first 5 hours she spent babysitting. She will continue to earn money at this rate until she finishes babysitting in 3 more hours. Find how much money Janice earns per hour and the total she earned babysitting.

P6. The McDonalds are taking a family road trip, driving 300 miles to their cabin. It took them 2 hours to drive the first 120 miles. They will drive at the same speed all the way to their cabin. Find the speed at which the McDonalds are driving and how much longer it will take them to get to their cabin.

P7. It takes Andy 10 minutes to read 6 pages of his book. He has already read 150 pages in his book that is 210 pages long. Find how long it takes Andy to read 1 page and also find how long it will take him to finish his book if he continues to read at the same speed.

Practice Solutions

P1. Cross multiply, then solve for x:

(a)
$$45x = 12 \times 15$$
$$45x = 180$$
$$x = \frac{180}{45} = 4$$

(b)
$$0.5x = 1.5 \times 2$$
$$0.5x = 3$$
$$x = \frac{3}{0.5} = 6$$

(c)
$$8x = 40 \times 24$$
$$8x = 960$$
$$x = \frac{960}{8} = 120$$

P2. One way to find the number of male students is to set up and solve a proportion.

$$\frac{\text{number of female students}}{\text{number of male students}} = \frac{20}{15} = \frac{100}{\text{number of male students}}$$

Represent the unknown number of male students as the variable x: $\frac{20}{15} = \frac{100}{x}$

Cross multiply and then solve for x:

$$20x = 15 \times 100$$
$$x = \frac{1500}{20}$$
$$x = 75$$

P3. The ratio of nurses to patients can be written as 4 to 12, 4:12, or $\frac{4}{12}$. Because four and twelve have a common factor of four, the ratio should be reduced to 1:3, which means that there is one nurse present for every three patients. If this ratio remains constant, there must be eight nurses present to care for 24 patients.

P4. Use proportional reasoning or set up a proportion to solve. Because there are twice as many customers as bankers, there must be fourteen customers when seven bankers are on duty. Setting up and solving a proportion gives the same result:

$$\frac{\text{number of bankers}}{\text{number of customers}} = \frac{1}{2} = \frac{7}{\text{number of customers}}$$

Represent the unknown number of patients as the variable x: $\frac{1}{2} = \frac{7}{x}$.

To solve for x, cross multiply: $1 \times x = 7 \times 2$, so $x = 14$.

P5. Janice earns $8 per hour. This can be found by taking her initial amount earned, $40, and dividing it by the number of hours worked, 5. Since $\frac{40}{5} = 8$, Janice makes $8 in one hour. This can also be found by finding the unit rate, money earned per hour: $\frac{40}{5} = \frac{x}{1}$. Since cross multiplying yields $5x = 40$, and division by 5 shows that $x = 8$, Janice earns $8 per hour.

Janice will earn $64 babysitting in her 8 total hours (adding the first 5 hours to the remaining 3 gives the 8-hour total). Since Janice earns $8 per hour and she worked 8 hours, $\frac{\$8}{\text{hr}} \times 8 \text{ hrs} = \$64$. This can also be found by setting up a proportion comparing money earned to babysitting hours. Since she earns $40 for 5 hours and since the rate is constant, she will earn a proportional amount in 8 hours: $\frac{40}{5} = \frac{x}{8}$. Cross multiplying will yield $5x = 320$, and division by 5 shows that $x = 64$.

P6. The McDonalds are driving 60 miles per hour. This can be found by setting up a proportion to find the unit rate, the number of miles they drive per one hour: $\frac{120}{2} = \frac{x}{1}$. Cross multiplying yields $2x = 120$ and division by 2 shows that $x = 60$.

Since the McDonalds will drive this same speed, it will take them another 3 hours to get to their cabin. This can be found by first finding how many miles the McDonalds have left to drive, which is $300 - 120 = 180$. The McDonalds are driving at 60 miles per hour, so a proportion can be set up to determine how many hours it will take them to drive 180 miles: $\frac{180}{x} = \frac{60}{1}$. Cross multiplying yields

$60x = 180$, and division by 60 shows that $x = 3$. This can also be found by using the formula $D = r \times t$ (or distance = rate × time), where $180 = 60 \times t$, and division by 60 shows that $t = 3$.

P7. It takes Andy 10 minutes to read 6 pages, $\frac{10}{6} = 1\frac{2}{3}$ minutes, which is 1 minute and 40 seconds.

Next, determine how many pages Andy has left to read, $210 - 150 = 60$. Since it is now known that it takes him $1\frac{2}{3}$ minutes to read each page, that rate must be multiplied by however many pages he has left to read (60) to find the time he'll need: $60 \times 1\frac{2}{3} = 100$, so it will take him 100 minutes, or 1 hour and 40 minutes, to read the rest of his book.

Measurement Principles

PRECISION, ACCURACY, AND ERROR

Precision: How reliable and repeatable a measurement is. The more consistent the data is with repeated testing, the more precise it is. For example, hitting a target consistently in the same spot, which may or may not be the center of the target, is precision.

Accuracy: How close the data is to the correct data. For example, hitting a target consistently in the center area of the target, whether or not the hits are all in the same spot, is accuracy.

Note: it is possible for data to be precise without being accurate. If a scale is off balance, the data will be precise, but will not be accurate. For data to have precision and accuracy, it must be repeatable and correct.

	Precise	Imprecise
Accurate	hits clustered in center	hits scattered around center
Inaccurate	hits clustered off-center	hits scattered off-center

Approximate error: The amount of error in a physical measurement. Approximate error is often reported as the measurement, followed by the ± symbol and the amount of the approximate error.

Maximum possible error: Half the magnitude of the smallest unit used in the measurement. For example, if the unit of measurement is 1 centimeter, the maximum possible error is $\frac{1}{2}$ cm, written as ± 0.5 cm following the measurement. It is important to apply significant figures in reporting maximum possible error. Do not make the answer appear more accurate than the least accurate of your measurements.

ROUNDING AND ESTIMATION

Rounding is reducing the digits in a number while still trying to keep the value similar. The result will be less accurate, but will be in a simpler form, and will be easier to use. Whole numbers can be rounded to the nearest ten, hundred or thousand.

When you are asked to estimate the solution to a problem, you will need to provide only an approximate figure or **estimation** for your answer. In this situation, you will need to round each number in the calculation to the level indicated (nearest hundred, nearest thousand, etc.) or to a level that makes sense for the numbers involved. When estimating a sum **all numbers must be rounded to the same level**. You cannot round one number to the nearest thousand while rounding another to the nearest hundred.

> **Review Video: Rounding and Estimation**
> Visit mometrix.com/academy and enter code: 126243

SCIENTIFIC NOTATION

Scientific notation is a way of writing large numbers in a shorter form. The form $a \times 10^n$ is used in scientific notation, where a is greater than or equal to 1 but less than 10, and n is the number of places the decimal must move to get from the original number to a. Example: The number 230,400,000 is cumbersome to write. To write the value in scientific notation, place a decimal point between the first and second numbers, and include all digits through the last non-zero digit ($a = 2.304$). To find the appropriate power of 10, count the number of places the decimal point had to move ($n = 8$). The number is positive if the decimal moved to the left, and negative if it moved to the right. We can then write 230,400,000 as 2.304×10^8. If we look instead at the number 0.00002304, we have the same value for a, but this time the decimal moved 5 places to the right ($n = -5$). Thus, 0.00002304 can be written as 2.304×10^{-5}. Using this notation makes it simple to compare very large or very small numbers. By comparing exponents, it is easy to see that 3.28×10^4 is smaller than 1.51×10^5, because 4 is less than 5.

> **Review Video: Scientific Notation**
> Visit mometrix.com/academy and enter code: 976454

PRACTICE

P1. Round each number to the indicated degree:

  (a) Round to the nearest ten: 11; 47; 118

  (b) Round to the nearest hundred: 78; 980; 248

  (c) Round each number to the nearest thousand: 302; 1,274; 3,756

P2. Estimate the solution to $345,932 + 96,369$ by rounding each number to the nearest ten thousand.

P3. A runner's heart beats 422 times over the course of six minutes. About how many times did the runner's heart beat during each minute?

Practice Solutions

P1. (a) When rounding to the nearest ten, anything ending in 5 or greater rounds up. So, 11 rounds to 10, 47 rounds to 50, and 118 rounds to 120.

(b) When rounding to the nearest hundred, anything ending in 50 or greater rounds up. So, 78 rounds to 100, 980 rounds to 1000, and 248 rounds to 200.

(c) When rounding to the nearest thousand, anything ending in 500 or greater rounds up. So, 302 rounds to 0, 1,274 rounds to 1,000, and 3,756 rounds to 4,000.

P2. Start by rounding each number to the nearest ten thousand: 345,932 becomes 350,000, and 96,369 becomes 100,000. Then, add the rounded numbers: 350,000 + 100,000 = 450,000. So, the answer is approximately 450,000. The exact answer would be 345,932 + 96,369 = 442,301. So, the estimate of 450,000 is a similar value to the exact answer.

P3. "About how many" indicates that you need to estimate the solution. In this case, look at the numbers you are given. 422 can be rounded down to 420, which is easily divisible by 6. A good estimate is 420 ÷ 6 = 70 beats per minute. More accurately, the patient's heart rate was just over 70 beats per minute since his heart actually beat a little more than 420 times in six minutes.

Units of Measurement

Metric Measurement Prefixes

Giga-: one billion (1 *giga*watt is one billion watts)
Mega-: one million (1 *mega*hertz is one million hertz)
Kilo-: one thousand (1 *kilo*gram is one thousand grams)
Deci-: one-tenth (1 *deci*meter is one-tenth of a meter)
Centi-: one-hundredth (1 *centi*meter is one-hundredth of a meter)
Milli-: one-thousandth (1 *milli*liter is one-thousandth of a liter)
Micro-: one-millionth (1 *micro*gram is one-millionth of a gram)

Measurement Conversion

When converting between units, the goal is to maintain the same meaning but change the way it is displayed. In order to go from a larger unit to a smaller unit, multiply the number of the known amount by the equivalent amount. When going from a smaller unit to a larger unit, divide the number of the known amount by the equivalent amount.

For complicated conversions, it may be helpful to set up conversion fractions. In these fractions, one fraction is the **conversion factor**. The other fraction has the unknown amount in the numerator. So, the known value is placed in the denominator. Sometimes, the second fraction has the known value from the problem in the numerator and the unknown in the denominator. Multiply the two fractions to get the converted measurement. Note that since the numerator and the denominator of the factor are equivalent, the value of the fraction is 1. That is why we can say that the result in the new units is equal to the result in the old units even though they have different numbers.

It can often be necessary to chain known conversion factors together. As an example, consider converting 512 square inches to square meters. We know that there are 2.54 centimeters in an inch and 100 centimeters in a meter and that we will need to square each of these factors to achieve the conversion we are looking for.

$$\frac{512 \text{ in}^2}{1} \times \left(\frac{2.54 \text{ cm}}{1 \text{ in}}\right)^2 \times \left(\frac{1 \text{ m}}{100 \text{ cm}}\right)^2 = \frac{512 \text{ in}^2}{1} \times \left(\frac{6.4516 \text{ cm}^2}{1 \text{ in}^2}\right) \times \left(\frac{1 \text{ m}^2}{10{,}000 \text{ cm}^2}\right) = 0.330 \text{ m}^2$$

Review Video: Measurement Conversions
Visit mometrix.com/academy and enter code: 316703

COMMON UNITS AND EQUIVALENTS

METRIC EQUIVALENTS

1000 μg (microgram)	1 mg
1000 mg (milligram)	1 g
1000 g (gram)	1 kg
1000 kg (kilogram)	1 metric ton
1000 mL (milliliter)	1 L
1000 μm (micrometer)	1 mm
1000 mm (millimeter)	1 m
100 cm (centimeter)	1 m
1000 m (meter)	1 km

Review Video: Metric System Conversions
Visit mometrix.com/academy and enter code: 163709

DISTANCE AND AREA MEASUREMENT

Unit	Abbreviation	US equivalent	Metric equivalent
Inch	in	1 inch	2.54 centimeters
Foot	ft	12 inches	0.305 meters
Yard	yd	3 feet	0.914 meters
Mile	mi	5280 feet	1.609 kilometers
Acre	ac	4840 square yards	0.405 hectares
Square Mile	sq. mi. or mi.²	640 acres	2.590 square kilometers

CAPACITY MEASUREMENTS

Unit	Abbreviation	US equivalent	Metric equivalent
Fluid Ounce	fl oz	8 fluid drams	29.573 milliliters
Cup	c	8 fluid ounces	0.237 liter
Pint	pt.	16 fluid ounces	0.473 liter
Quart	qt.	2 pints	0.946 liter
Gallon	gal.	4 quarts	3.785 liters
Teaspoon	t or tsp.	1 fluid dram	5 milliliters
Tablespoon	T or tbsp.	4 fluid drams	15 or 16 milliliters
Cubic Centimeter	cc or cm³	0.271 drams	1 milliliter

WEIGHT MEASUREMENTS

Unit	Abbreviation	US equivalent	Metric equivalent
Ounce	oz	16 drams	28.35 grams
Pound	lb	16 ounces	453.6 grams
Ton	tn.	2,000 pounds	907.2 kilograms

Volume and Weight Measurement Clarifications

Always be careful when using ounces and fluid ounces. They are not equivalent.

1 pint = 16 fluid ounces	1 fluid ounce ≠ 1 ounce
1 pound = 16 ounces	1 pint ≠ 1 pound

Having one pint of something does not mean you have one pound of it. In the same way, just because something weighs one pound does not mean that its volume is one pint.

In the United States, the word "ton" by itself refers to a short ton or a net ton. Do not confuse this with a long ton (also called a gross ton) or a metric ton (also spelled *tonne*), which have different measurement equivalents.

$$1 \text{ US ton} = 2000 \text{ pounds} \quad \neq \quad 1 \text{ metric ton} = 1000 \text{ kilograms}$$

Practice

P1. Perform the following conversions:

(a) 1.4 meters to centimeters

(b) 218 centimeters to meters

(c) 42 inches to feet

(d) 15 kilograms to pounds

(e) 80 ounces to pounds

(f) 2 miles to kilometers

(g) 5 feet to centimeters

(h) 15.14 liters to gallons

(i) 8 quarts to liters

(j) 13.2 pounds to grams

Practice Solutions

P1. (a) $\frac{100 \text{ cm}}{1 \text{ m}} = \frac{x \text{ cm}}{1.4 \text{ m}}$ Cross multiply to get $x = 140$

(b) $\frac{100 \text{ cm}}{1 \text{ m}} = \frac{218 \text{ cm}}{x \text{ m}}$ Cross multiply to get $100x = 218$, or $x = 2.18$

(c) $\frac{12 \text{ in}}{1 \text{ ft}} = \frac{42 \text{ in}}{x \text{ ft}}$ Cross multiply to get $12x = 42$, or $x = 3.5$

(d) $15 \text{ kilograms} \times \frac{2.2 \text{ pounds}}{1 \text{ kilogram}} = 33 \text{ pounds}$

(e) $80 \text{ ounces} \times \frac{1 \text{ pound}}{16 \text{ ounces}} = 5 \text{ pounds}$

(f) $2 \text{ miles} \times \frac{1.609 \text{ kilometers}}{1 \text{ mile}} = 3.218 \text{ kilometers}$

(g) 5 feet $\times \frac{12 \text{ inches}}{1 \text{ foot}} \times \frac{2.54 \text{ centimeters}}{1 \text{ inch}} = 152.4$ centimeters

(h) 15.14 liters $\times \frac{1 \text{ gallon}}{3.785 \text{ liters}} = 4$ gallons

(i) 8 quarts $\times \frac{1 \text{ gallon}}{4 \text{ quarts}} \times \frac{3.785 \text{ liters}}{1 \text{ gallon}} = 7.57$ liters

(j) 13.2 pounds $\times \frac{1 \text{ kilogram}}{2.2 \text{ pounds}} \times \frac{1{,}000 \text{ grams}}{1 \text{ kilogram}} = 6{,}000$ grams

Instructional Support

Evaluating Student Writing

The evaluation of student writing should be structured to include three basic goals:

- To provide students with a description of the effectiveness of their response
- To provide a pathway for potential improvement
- To help students learn to evaluate themselves

To fulfill these goals, it is necessary for the concept of evaluation to be broadened beyond correcting or judging students. Any teacher response to a student's response should be considered part of the evaluation. In responding to student's responses, a teacher may use written or taped comments, dialogue with students, or conferencing between teacher and students to discuss classroom performance. Students may be asked to evaluate themselves and a teacher, and students can review past progress and plan directions for potential improvement.

Components of Formulating a Teacher's Response

There are seven basic components of a teacher's response to be considered:

- **Praise** provides positive reinforcement for the student. Praise should be specific enough to bolster the student's confidence.
- **Describing** provides feedback on a teacher's responses to student responses. This is best done in a conversational, non-judgmental mode.
- **Diagnosing** is determining the student's unique set of strengths, attitudes, needs, and abilities. This evaluation should take into consideration all elements of the student.
- **Judging** is evaluating the level, depth, insightfulness, completeness, and validity of a student's responses. This evaluation will depend on the criteria implied in the instructional approach.
- **Predicting** anticipates the potential improvement of a student's responses based on specific criteria.
- **Recordkeeping** is the process of recording a student's reading interests, attitudes, and use of literary strategies to chart student progress across time. Both qualitative and quantitative assessments may be used.
- **Recognition** acknowledges a student's growth and progress.

Literary Tests and Assessments

Literary tests are measures of a student's individual performance. Literary assessments are measures of performance of a group of students without reference to individuals. Tests take into consideration what the teacher has taught the students, whereas assessments do not.

For either tests or assessments, the teacher needs a clear purpose on which to base questions or activities. Students should be told of the purpose of the tests or assessments so they will know what to expect. Tests should be used sparingly as one tool among many that can be used to evaluate students. Tests should encourage students on formulation of responses rather than rote answers. They should evaluate students on the basis of their responses rather than correct answers. Improvement over time may be noted and the students praised for specific responses.

STANDARDIZED ACHIEVEMENT TESTS

These multiple-choice tests measure students' ability to understand text passages or apply literary concepts to texts. Although these tests are widely used, they have many limitations. They tend to be based on a simplistic model that ignores the complex nature of a reader's engagement with a text. These tests also do not measure students' articulation of responses. The purpose of these tests is to rank students in group norms so that half the students are below the norm.

To accurately measure a student's abilities, teachers should employ open-ended written or oral-response activities. In developing such tests, teachers must know what specific response patterns they wish to measure. The steps involved in measuring these response patterns must be clearly outlined. Teachers may wish to design questions that encourage personal expressions of responses. This would obviate the pitfall of testing primarily facts about literature rather than how students relate and use this information to engage texts.

ASSESSING ATTITUDES TOWARD LITERATURE

An important element in teaching literature is to understand the attitudes of students about reading and studying text. This may be done by group or individual interviews encouraging students to discuss their feelings about literature. Another way to measure attitudes is with a paper-and-pencil rating scale using six- or eight-point Liker scales. This type of assessment can be refined to explore preferences in form and genre.

Another type of assessment is done by using semantic scales to indicate students' interest (or lack thereof) in reading in general and favored forms and genres.

Questionnaires can be developed to learn more about students' habits regarding literature. Typical questions could be: Do you use the library regularly? Do you read books or magazines? What types of reading do you do? Comparisons before and after instruction can indicate the effect of the instruction on habits and attitudes about literature.

CLASSROOM-BASED RESEARCH

Teachers can conduct their own informal descriptive research to assess the effects of their teaching on students' responses. This allows teachers an opportunity to review and reflect on their instructional methods and results. This research can take many forms, including the following:

- An analysis of students' perceptions of guided response activities to determine which were most effective
- An analysis of students' small- and large-group discussions
- A teacher self-analysis of taped, written, or conference feedback to students' writing
- Interviews with students about their responses and background experiences and attitudes
- Evaluating students' responses to texts commonly used in their instruction

These are only a few possibilities for effective classroom-based research. Any research that provides insight into student needs and preferences can be a valuable tool.

Conducting Classroom Research

Teachers must always keep in mind the purposes driving the research. Evaluation itself is relatively easy; the challenge is using the evaluations to help both students and teachers to grow and become better at what they are doing.

- Create a research question related to literature instruction or responses.
- Summarize the theory and research related to the topic.
- Describe the participants, setting, tasks, and methods of analysis.
- Summarize the results of the research in a graph, table, or report.
- Interpret or give reasons for the results.
- Draw conclusions from the results that suggest ways to improve instruction and evaluation of students.

Assessing Instructional Methods

Assessing instructional methods within a school, district, or state can help determine instructional goals and techniques relative to overall system goals. Results can indicate needed changes in the curriculum and can help an accreditation process measure the quality of an English or literature program.

An effective assessment usually includes interviews, questionnaires, and classroom observation. Trained observers rate the general type of instruction being provided (e.g., lectures, modeling and small groups), the focus of instruction (e.g., novels, poetry, drama et cetera), the critical approach used, the response strategies used and the response activities employed. Observers may also analyze the statements of goals and objectives in a curriculum, as well as the scope and sequence of the curriculum. Additionally, interviews of both students and teachers are helpful in getting firsthand accounts of instruction and results.

Building and Supporting of Arguments

A curriculum that is project-based begins with explicit questions meant to stimulate the curiosity of students and serve as a basis for launching various research ideas and directions. Teachers can see that curricular units provide a valuable advantage in motivating students with regard to developing hypotheses, finding research information in many sources of data in order to confirm or argue the hypotheses, and in developing arguments which are based upon understanding certain intended concepts. The internet can provide a wealth of information but can also provide challenges for teachers. Students with literacy challenges have difficulties finding information, identifying relevant information and then reading that which they find. These challenges may at times be linked to the inability of a student to draw conceptual parallels in content and then translate them into an internet search.

Culturally-Relevant Approaches

Teachers should develop learning environments that are reflective of their students' social, cultural and linguistic experiences. These serve as instructors, mediators, guides, consultants and advocates for students in helping them to find a way that is most effective to connect their cultural and community-based knowledge to their learning experiences in the classroom. A key criterion for teaching that is culturally relevant is nurturing and supporting competence in cultures both at school and at home. Teachers should use the student's home cultural experience as a base on which to build skills and increase knowledge. Content that is learned in this manner becomes more significant to the student and helps facilitate a transfer of school learning to real-life.

SUMMATIVE ASSESSMENT

Summative assessment is carried out less frequently by the teacher; it is appropriate for checking knowledge at the end of a unit of study or at the end of the course. Whereas formative assessment is an assessment *for* learning, in that it helps the teacher to make positive adjustments to the course, summative assessment is an assessment *of* learning. It is likely that the means of summative assessment will be affected by the performance of students on formative assessments. It is important that summative assessments provide a comprehensive evaluation of students' mastery of the material, such that every area of knowledge is questioned and every skill is tested. Also, summative assessment should include questions of varying difficulty, so that students can distinguish themselves.

CHARISMATIC AUTHORITY

Max Weber defined charismatic authority as legitimate power that an individual earns by his or her personal merit. There is no set of objective values for measuring charisma, and each society may have a different standard by which charismatic authority is assigned. A leader may combine charismatic authority with traditional or legal authority, as for instance in the case of John F. Kennedy. Other recent charismatic leaders include Cesar Chavez, Martin Luther King, and Mahatma Gandhi. Charismatic authority may be wielded in subcultures and cults, as in the cases of David Koresh or Charles Manson, and, unlike the other forms of authority, it may easily disappear.

LITERACY DIFFERING ACROSS CONTENT AREAS

Studies have shown that it is impossible to separate practices in the classroom such as strategies for activating prior knowledge from the larger cultural and social contexts in which the practices exist. Researchers say that a need exists for adolescent literacy that includes the adolescent's literacy practices beyond the confines of the classroom setting, their expanded conceptions of text such as the internet, and the relationship that exists between the development of identity and literacy. However, the need for additional research in the teaching and learning of context in secondary schools still exists. For instance, more study is needed on the interactions between student and teacher, and between student and student; also on how students perceive themselves as readers, what their interests are at a particular time, and how institutional configurations affect the daily events occurring both in and out of school.

READING DISORDER

Students who have a reading disorder have problems with their reading skills. Their skills are significantly below that which is normal for the student's age, intelligence, and education. The poor reading skills can cause problems with the student's academic success and in other areas of life. Signs associated with reading disorders include poor word recognition in reading, very slow reading, or making many mistakes. They may also show poor comprehension. Students who suffer from reading disorders normally have low self-esteem, social problems, and a higher drop-out rate in school. Reading disorders may be associated with conduct disorder, attention deficit disorder, depression, or other learning disorders. Reading disorders are usually brought to the attention of a child's parents in kindergarten or the first grade, when reading instruction becomes a very important facet of teaching.

SELECTING TESTS

When selecting tests, care should be taken to ensure the test is not biased or offensive with regard to race, sex, native language, geographic region, or ethnic origin, as well as other factors. Those who develop tests are expected to show sensitivity to the test-takers' demographic. Steps can be taken during test development and documentation to minimize the influence of cultural factors on the test scores. These may include evaluating the items for offensiveness and cultural dependency, and using statistics to identify differential item difficulty. Questions to ask include: "Were the tests analyzed statistically for bias?" "What method was used?" "How were the items selected for the final version?" "Should the test be used with non-native English speakers?"

SOCIAL CLASS AND FAMILY BACKGROUND VARIABLES IN EMERGENT LITERACY

The social class and family background variables are prominent in emergent literacy research. Numerous studies have addressed links between parental occupation, income, and children's achievements. One finding is that there are wide variations in children's achievements, regardless of social class in relation to a child's early literacy experiences. Specific factors in family environments such as parental interest, positive attitudes, and modeling have been identified as major predictors of academic success despite social class or educational levels. There is considerable variation among family environments in the status and value given to books, the presence of materials for writing, and the time that is spent reading and writing. Studies have shown that early readers tend to come from homes with more pencils, paper, and books, and that have mothers who read more often.

SOCIAL LEARNING AND MEDIATION

Along with genetic analysis, social learning and mediation are the three major components of a sociocultural approach to literacy. Social learning refers to the social origin of mental functioning. Vygotsky said that every function in the child's cultural development appears first on the social level and later on the individual level. The first development is between people and the second is inside the child. Vygotsky also believed the development occurred through such means as apprenticeship learning, or interaction with teachers and peers. This view looks at learning not as an isolated act of cognition but rather a process of gaining entry to a discourse of practitioners. Mediation is the notion that all human activity is mediated through signs or tools. It is not so much the tools, such as computers or writing, by themselves as it is how they transform human action in a fundamental way.

MULTILITERACIES

A great deal of interest has risen around the world in the future of literacy teaching through so-called "multiliteracies." The multiliteracies argument is that our personal, public, and working lives are currently changing in some very significant ways and that these changes have the effect of transforming cultures and the ways in which we communicate. The ramification of this is that the way literacy is now taught will become obsolete and what counts for literacy must also change. Multiliteracies has at its heart two major and closely related changes. First is the growing significance of cultural and linguistic diversity. This is reinforced every day by modern media. Each day, both globally and in our local communities, we have to negotiate differences that are interconnected with our working and community lives. As this happens, English is becoming a world language. The second major shift is the influence of new communications technologies.

LITERACY STARTING AT HOME

Children's school readiness is influenced by their parents' educational levels. The higher the parents' education, the more likely the child will succeed in school. Children who are raised in literate homes are likely to enter first grade with several thousand hours of 1-to-1 pre-reading experience. Children have a better chance of becoming fully literate adults if they are encouraged to read at home. Studies have shown that improving parents' skills positively affects their children's language development. Without parental support, the cycle of under-education will continue in families from generation to generation. With support from family literacy programs, children who may have otherwise been educationally and developmentally behind their peers came into school on par with their peers.

Phonemic Awareness

Different levels of phonemic awareness in terms of abilities include:

- Hearing rhymes and alliteration as measured by knowing nursery rhymes.
- Doing tasks such as comparing and contrasting the sounds of words for rhyme and alliteration, also known as oddity tasks.
- Blending and splitting syllables.
- Performing phonemic segmenting such as counting out the number of phonemes contained in a word.
- Performing tasks of phoneme manipulation such as adding or deleting a particular phoneme.

Instruction in phonemic awareness might include:

- Engaging preschool children in activities that direct their attention to sounds in words, such as rhyming games.
- Teaching segmentation and blending.
- Combining letter-sound relationship instruction with segmentation and blending.
- Sequencing examples systematically when teaching blending and segmentation.

Children of kindergarten age require development of phonemic awareness by hearing, identifying, and manipulating phonemes or individual sounds within spoken words. Once children acquire knowledge of letters, they can be taught to perform activities to isolate phonemes and achieve phoneme segmentation by pointing to or manipulating letters along with sounds. Blending and segmentation in phonemic awareness is important because they provide a foundation for skills such as spelling. Studies have shown that phonemic awareness can be acquired with as little as 20 hours of instruction, although some children might require more instruction in order to accurately segment words. The individual students should be assessed to verify that the instruction was successful. More instruction might be required for some children than others.

Phonemic awareness is difficult because:

- There are about 40 phonemes or sound units in the English language despite there being only 26 letters in the alphabet.
- There are 250 different spellings representing distinct sounds such as "f," which may be represented as "ph" or "gh."
- Phonemes, or sound units, are not necessarily obvious. They must be learned. The sounds that make up words are not distinctly separate from one other, a state referred to as being "coarticulated." Additionally, words such as "fat" and "hat" are said to have different phonemes "f" and "h" in English despite little difference in sound to distinguish the words. These are called a "minimal pair." If no minimal pair can be found to demonstrate two distinct sounds, these sounds may be termed "allophones," which are variant sounds not recognized by a speaker as distinct and as such are not significantly different in language. They are therefore looked upon as being the same.

Sing-Songs

Rhyme is a prominent feature of many songs. Listening to and singing songs helps make children aware of the phonemic nature of spoken language. Songs that help children to manipulate sounds in words are most effective in having children pay attention to a language's sound structure. Manipulating sounds in words can be challenging for those children in the early stages of phonemic awareness development, so children should be given many opportunities to learn the songs before they start trying to manipulate the sounds. One way this can be done is to play tapes of such songs during transitional activities such as snack time or clean-up time in order to help children become more familiar with sound play.

Social Constructivism

Social constructivism is a variant of cognitive constructivism that puts an emphasis on the collaborative nature of learning. This theory was developed by Soviet psychologist Lev Vygotsky. He was a cognitivist but he rejected postulations by other cognitivists such as Piaget and Perry which said that separating learning from its social context was possible. Vygotsky theorized that all cognitive functions originate and must be explained as products of social interactions and that learning was not simply the accommodation and assimilation of new knowledge attained by those learning. Instead, he felt it was the process by which learners were integrated into a community of knowledge. Vygotsky believed that the cultural development of children appears first on the social level and only later inside the child. This applies equally in voluntary attention to logical memories and forming concepts. Higher functions come from actual relationships between people, Vygotsky postulated.

Stages of Reading for Young Children

Children gain literacy through emergent, beginning, and fluent stages. The emergent stage is marked by children noticing environmental print, showing interest in books, pretending to read, and using picture cues and predictable patterns in books in order to retell a story. They also can identify some letters, reread books with patterns that are predictable, and recognize up to 10 familiar words. The beginning stage will show the child identifying letter names and sounds; matching written and spoken words; using the beginning, middle, and ending sounds to decode words; recognizing as many as 100 high-frequency words; reading slowly, word by word; and self-correcting while they are reading. The fluent stage features automatic identification with most words, reading with expression, reading at about 100 words per minute or more, preferring to read silently, recognizing up to 300 high-frequency words, and often reading independently making inferences.

Reading Proficiency at a Young Age

There is strong evidence that young people who are not fluent readers and writers by the end of the third grade may never catch up with their peers. One study found that first graders who were not on grade level by the end of the year stood a 1-in-10 chance of never having proficiency at grade level in reading. A governor of Indiana indicated that the determination of how many new prison beds to build was based, in part, on the number of second graders who do not read at second grade level. The number of future prison beds in California depends on numbers of children who do not go past the fourth grade reading level.

Lexical Affixes

Lexical affixes, also known as semantic affixes, are bound elements that appear as affixes, but function as incorporated nouns within verbs and as elements of compound nouns. In other words, they are similar to word roots or stems in function, but are similar to affixes in form. Although they are similar to incorporated nouns, lexical affixes differ in that they never occur in freestanding nouns. They always appear as affixes. Such affixes are relatively rare. Lexical suffixes often bear little or no resemblance to free nouns with similar meaning. When used, lexical suffixes usually have more general meanings. For instance, a language may have a lexical suffix that means water in a general sense, but not have a noun equivalent referring to water in general. Instead, it may have several nouns with more specific meanings, such as saltwater or groundwater.

FORM FUNCTION OF ORAL LANGUAGE

The form function of oral language consists of phonology, morphology, and syntax. Phonology is the system of phonemes or sounds in language. Morphology is the system of rules governing word structure and organization. Many sounds have no meaning by themselves; these are phonemes. Every morpheme, however, has meaning on its own, as a root word, or attached to a root word as a prefix, suffix, or word ending. In English, the normal sentence is structured as subject + verb + object. Syntax refers to the way in which words are combined into sentences. Students with an understanding of syntax can comprehend how the various parts of a sentence relate to one another other.

WRITING AND COOPERATIVE WRITING

Specific instruction in writing for different reasons and audiences as well as instruction in strategies to help clarify and enrich language expression is crucial. Language mechanical skills such as usage, capitalization, and grammar can be taught and integrated into the students' own writing through the process of editing. For instance, students might study the use of adjectives and adverbs, and then write descriptive compositions. Cooperative learning can be a very effective upper elementary reading and writing instruction if used properly. Students should generally work in groups of four or five members that stay together for six-to-eight weeks. Each group might be presented a lesson on main idea and the students can work in groups to practice such a skill.

WORD IDENTIFICATION

The identification or recognition of words is the ability of students to develop an automaticity when reading isolated words. Automaticity refers to the speed and accuracy with which students are able to read these isolated words. Automatic words recognition is an important part of literacy because the level of students' abilities to recognize known words and decode or determine unfamiliar words can affect how fluently the students may read, and fluency is essential for comprehension. It should be remembered that building meaning is the goal of any literacy endeavor. Developing strong word recognition skills is also critical for students who, for whatever reason, did not develop strong phonological awareness in early childhood. These students may need to rely more heavily on their vocabularies and less on decoding skills.

NEWSPAPERS

Students learn when they are motivated and the topics they study hold interest and relevance to their lives. Many classrooms are using newspapers as a source for motivational and timely resources. It is a concept that dates back to 1795 when the Portland Eastern Herald in Maine published an editorial that put forth the role that newspapers can play in helping to deliver, extend, and enrich the curriculum. Classrooms around the world are using newspapers to complement text books and other relevant resources for a variety of disciplines. Newspapers featuring articles, editorials, and advertising help students apply literacy and numeracy skills as well as appreciate the importance of studying history and current affairs. Studies have shown that students who use newspapers score higher on reading comprehension tests and develop stronger critical thinking skills.

First Grade Reading Comprehension

The process of learning to read is not a linear one. Students need not learn decoding before they learn to comprehend. Both skills should be taught at the same time, beginning at the earliest stages of instruction for reading. Comprehension strategies can be taught using both material that is read to children and material that they read for themselves. Before reading, teachers can delineate the reason for the reading: reviewing vocabulary, encouraging children to predict what stories are about, or activating background knowledge. Teachers can direct children's attention to subtle or difficult portions of the text during reading, point out difficult words and ideas and ask children to find problems and solutions. After reading, children can be taught particular metacognitive strategies such as asking themselves regularly whether what is being read makes sense.

Reciprocal Teaching

In many ways, reciprocal teaching is the aggregation of four separate comprehension strategies: summarizing, questioning, clarifying, and predicting. Summarizing presents the ability to identify and integrate the information that is most important in a text. Text can be summarized across sentences and paragraphs, and also across passages. When students start the reciprocal teaching procedures they are usually focused on sentences and paragraphs. Questioning reinforces the strategy of summarizing. When students identify questions, they identify a kind of information that is important enough to provide substance for a question, then post the information in question form. Clarifying is important for students with comprehension difficulty. They are taught to be alert to the effects of comprehension impediments and to take the necessary measures to restore meaning. Predicting is when students predict what the author will discuss next in the text.

What is most important in reading education is turning out readers who can understand the meaning in texts. Reciprocal teaching is a scaffolded discussion technique for instilling some of the methods that good readers can use to comprehend text through questioning, clarifying, summarizing, and predicting. Teaching students the four strategies gives them the tools that great readers use in meeting their text-reading goals. Thus, it is the four strategies that are taught rather than reading skills. These multiple strategies help students to read by giving them a choice of strategies to be used in reading. The scaffolding gives support to help the students connect what they know and can do with what they need to do in order to be successful at learning a particular lesson. This also gives the students a chance to support each other and foster a sense of community among classmates.

The word "reciprocal" in reciprocal teaching is somewhat misleading in that it does not entail students doing the teaching. But the students use a set of four strategies—summarizing, clarifying, predicting, and questioning—to improve reading comprehension. That improvement is the ultimate goal. Other aspects of the method include:

- The teacher scaffolds instruction of the strategy by guiding, modeling, and applying the strategies.
- It guides students to become metacognitive and reflective in the use of strategies.
- It helps students monitor their comprehension of reading.
- It uses the social nature of learning in order to improve and scaffold the comprehension of reading.
- The instruction is presented through different classroom settings including whole group, guided reading groups, and literature circles.

Student Note-Taking

Reading for certain information and then taking notes are perhaps the most challenging steps in the process of solving information problems. Students in grades 3-8 require many developmentally-appropriate chances to locate information before the techniques are mastered. Note-taking consists of identifying keywords and related words, skimming and scanning, and extracting needed information. These steps begin after students define and narrow the task, construct researchable questions, and find the right sources. After students build researchable questions from the information needed to finish a task or solve an information problem, the questions can be transferred to graphic organizers or data charts. This can allow them to focus on the key words. Skimming and scanning will help them make use of the text with less time and effort. Information may be extracted and recorded with different forms of note-taking, including citation, summary, quotation, and paraphrasing.

Test-Taking Strategies

A reason for test anxiety and poor performance on tests is often a lack of preparation. Children often know about a test in advance. Some teachers also tell parents when tests will be given. Knowing when the test is scheduled and what will be covered can help give the child a study schedule to prepare for the test. One schedule is for the student to study nightly for several nights before the test. Teachers may encourage parents to determine how long the child can be expected to concentrate at a given sitting. The parent should also be encouraged by the teacher to ask the child what material might be on the test and to go over questions at the end of chapters and sections. Maps, charts, and diagrams should receive special attention. A sample test can be developed from this information, which can even make studying fun.

Students should follow directions carefully. Have the student listen and read the directions to the test so they understand what is expected of them. Teachers need to make sure the students understand vocabulary words and concepts in the directions. Words appearing in the test directions that are common should be introduced to students as part of the process of test preparation. Ensure that the students understand what they are to do. If students have questions, they should be encouraged to ask the teacher before the test starts. Listening and reading activities that will provide practice for following directions can be incorporated into the classroom. Students must know how to budget their time for the test. They should work fast but comfortably. Students can practice this.

Before the Test Strategy

Before a test students should:

- Begin to study the material a few days before the test and take study breaks every 20-30 minutes.
- Take time to do some kind of physical activity that will help reduce tension and stress.
- Eat a good breakfast the morning of the test and get a good night's sleep the night before the test.
- Skim the material and determine which parts are best understood and which ones are still difficult.
- Read a sentence or two and reread what they don't understand.
- Pick out main ideas or key terms and think up possible test questions by themselves.
- Read aloud and study with a partner or parent. While reading, the students should listen to themselves.
- Think about what important points the teacher talked about during class.
- Remain motivated and positive.

Emphasis on Literacy in Content Areas

Attention should be paid to literacy in content areas for several reasons. The 2003 National Assessment of Educational Progress Reading Report shows that general test scores have improved over recent years, but very few young people in the United States can read at proficient or advanced levels. Most can decode and answer simple comprehension questions, but few can synthesize ideas, interpret the information they receive, or critique the ideas they read about, especially when they work with expository texts. Also, literacy in content areas has consequences that go beyond the ability to understand a subject-matter text. Advanced or specialized literacy forms are tools that signify success, both academically and socially, and can be important for economic, social, and political success beyond school.

Cubing

Cubing is a literacy strategy in which students are able to explore topics from six separate dimensions or viewpoints. The student can:

1. Provide a description of the particular topic.
2. Compare the topic to a different topic.
3. Associate the topic with something else and provide specific reasons for the choice.
4. Analyze the topic and tell how the topic came about.
5. Give an explanation of what the topic comprises after analysis.
6. Provide an argument for or against the topic.

The teacher chooses a topic related to the thematic unit and students are divided into six groups. Students brainstorm about their dimension ideas and then use a quick write or quick draw. These are shared with the class and are attached to the sides of a cube box. This strategy can be applicable to subjects such as social studies.

Multimedia Literacy

Multimedia literacy is an aspect of literacy that is being recognized as technology expands how people communicate with each other. Literacy, as a concept, emerged as a measure of how one can read or write. It means today that someone reads or writes at a level that is adequate to communicate. Multimedia calls for a more fundamental meaning of literacy when looked upon at a societal level. Multimedia is the use of several different media to send or receive information. These include text, audio, graphics, animation, virtual reality, computer programming, and robotics. The basic literacy of reading and writing is often handled by computer these days and provides a foundation for more advanced levels of multimedia literacy.

Film and Television as Teaching Tools

Television and film can help students explore cultural context and are easily integrated into the curriculum. They are entertaining media and allow for a great deal of flexibility in techniques of teaching and material. Surveys indicate that more teachers than ever are integrating television and videotapes into their curricula. Teachers are seeking quality programming with the appropriate structure and length, as well as advance information that allows them to preview the programming. Also found in the surveys was that both teachers and students are becoming more media savvy as they use camcorders and other video production equipment with increased frequency. That effect is likely to grow even further with such mobile video platforms as digital cameras and cell phones.

Electronic Textbooks

Technology is commonly used in learning situations, such as elementary science students watching a video of an experiment being performed, middle school students manipulating commercial software that helps them prepare for a rapidly-changing technological workplace, and high school students playing interactive chemistry games on the internet that score their manipulations of chemical equations and formulas such as those used to solve problems in real life. Technology can help a child who is blind to hear audible descriptions that allow him or her to understand procedures and participate in a particular portion of class. Students who have physical disabilities can complete computer activities with commercial software that has adaptive devices to permit the student to independently complete a task. Students who are hard of hearing can use CDs or internet videos with captions.

LESSON IDEAS THAT MAKE USE OF TECHNOLOGY

Various lessons can be enriched by the use of technology. This includes:

- Digital presentations. Students can show their learning in a digital presentation. They might create a website or create a stand-alone presentation. Students should cite their sources of information as with any research project. They should also be taught the importance of seeking permission for copyrighted matter.
- Have students read books online. Thousands of books are available online at websites such as Online Books Page.
- Have web quests. This is an activity that is good for language arts and exploration of literature. The quests list sets of questions and tasks on which students can perform internet research.
- Word processing. Word processing programs are good for projects that would require having multiple drafts.

CONTENT-SPECIFIC LESSON IDEAS USING TECHNOLOGY

Technology can be used in lessons for a host of content areas. Some examples include:

- Language arts. The internet can be used to look at photos described in novels and can provide information about the social fabric of the community, helping students to learn the context.
- Mathematics. Spreadsheets can be used to calculate distance, speed, and travel time between two cities. The data can be exposed in several forms to help foster the understanding of variables.
- Science. The internet can be used to view topographic and satellite maps to help determine an area's rock formations.
- Physical education. The internet can be used to watch basketball techniques in slow motion to help improve shooting form.

LITERACY ACTIVITY IN WHICH STUDENTS REPORT THE NEWS

Students are told to be reporters and report the news for their school. They are told that they will need to report on local news, world news, national news, sports, entertainment, and weather. The reporter should visit various news websites to gather information for the stories. The stories must be accurate, informative, and interesting. The audience is the students' fifth grade class so it must be in language they can understand. The teacher functions as the editor. In this exercise, the student learns the parts of the newspaper: the headline, the lead, quotes, body, and ending. There should be pre-writing planning and collection of information. The student gets a "beat" to cover, finds a story, and writes about it.

Recursive Strategies for Composing Texts

The framework for composing texts includes planning, drafting, revision, and proofreading. Many recursive strategies lie inside these components. Planning refers to the ways in which a writer might think about what he or she wants to do and how it could be done. It involves using outlines, seeking other opinions and perspectives, and research. It is recursive in that writers invent throughout the act of writing, planning, revising, and editing. Drafting refers to the different versions of a text before closure. Writers discover as a result of writing a draft, and then draft some more. Some view revision as a way to see the text from different perspectives. Revision is also rethinking ideas and how they may be conveyed. Proofreading refers to decisions that writers make to produce writing in which the words and punctuation are correct, along with flowing sentence structure and diction.

Making Learning Personal

Assignments that make learning personal are often very effective in helping students appreciate studying and completing those assignments. Such work often lets students look into their family, community, and cultural experiences and gain a better appreciation of both their own and their peers' backgrounds. Family tree projects in social studies classes are an example because of the great diversity of most American schools. These projects or others such as historical ones in which family members are sought out may often bring out values that the students might not otherwise appreciate and can also foster closer family relationships. Making assignments personal and valuable gives students a great incentive to appreciate studying about a subject and to find learning as a quest.

Working with Recent Immigrant Students

American schools have been a major agent for helping those children and youth who recently arrived in this country with adapting to the civic and social demands of their new homes. Classroom lessons and socialization on the school yard take place. But sometimes the home culture teachings and expectations are contrasted with those of American schools. This can lead to labeling children as disabled when no disability actually exists. These students do have issues with psychosocial stress as they attempt to adapt. A transition that is successful to one's new country requires a secure cross-cultural identity. How much of each culture forms this identity depends on the person's needs, skills, experience, education, and support. Recognition of these transitioning needs and support are among the strategic help that can be given to these children.

Students may display behaviors in their cultures that are different from those in the American mainstream; thus, they are at risk for being labeled by uninformed educators as having behaviors that are "wrong." Teachers should familiarize themselves with a student's home culture's values and practices. There should be an awareness of differences that promotes understanding, tolerance, acceptance, and celebration of others and their ways. Information on other cultures can be found in many textbooks and travel books, and on various websites. Another way to develop familiarity with a student's cultural background is the use of a "cultural informant." This is someone who might be familiar with the group and their ways, such as teachers or other successful members of that cultural group.

Culture Capsule

A culture capsule is a biliteracy activity that is usually prepared outside class by students, but presented during class for about five or 10 minutes. It consists of a paragraph or two and explains one minimal difference between an American custom and that of another culture's custom. It also includes several photos and other information that is relevant. These capsules can be used in addition to role playing. Students may act out a part of another culture. Essentially the capsule is a brief description of some aspect of the target culture followed by contrasting information from the students' native language culture. These are done orally with teachers giving a brief talk on the chosen cultural point and then leading a discussion on cultures.

TEACHING ABOUT CULTURE

When teaching about culture, whether local, domestic, or international, it is often helpful to keep the following in mind:

- **Validating Information Sources** - Cultural information can vary based on the source and is often laced with bias, which are often harmful or misleading. It is best to use official, and up-to-date sources to ensure accuracy.
- **Learning Objectives** – Culture is a broad topic and it is woven throughout a society. Specificity of instruction is often helpful when approaching culture. Make sure to have well-defined topics for discussion and research. Common breakdowns of cultural analysis includes geography, industry, politics, ethics, food, clothing, language, history, art, and many more topics. Make sure to direct students toward focused topics for deeper knowledge when discussing a broad topic such as culture.
- **Cultural Exposure** – Especially when discussing unfamiliar cultures, it's helpful to establish an appreciation for other cultures by having students experience that culture firsthand. These can be highly motivating ways to participate in another culture: sharing cultural food, wearing cultural clothing, watching videos and films, and viewing artwork from that culture. This can help prime students to be more receptive to discussions about that culture's history or other, more challenging topics.
- **Assessment** – Assessing a student's cultural knowledge can be challenging without clearly defined goals. Traditional tests may not enable the teacher to see a student's views on or investment in a topic such as a culture. Presentations are useful for having a student demonstrate their knowledge and their attitudes or appreciation for a culture. Keep in mind that assessments should be valid and repeatable, so a rubric is necessary for assessment with presentations.

MEASURING CHANGES IN ATTITUDES OVER FOREIGN CULTURES

Students often are hesitant to intermingle with people of other cultures. A common aspect of human behavior is to avoid the unknown, which includes encountering 'strange behaviors' of people from other cultures. A common goal of a cultural education is that students can become more globally aware and comfortable with people from different cultures. As students encounter more cultures and become more culturally-aware, there should be developments in their behavior indicating comfort with diverse peer groups.

These are two common indicators:

- **Social distance scales** - This is to measure the degree to which one separates oneself socially from members of another culture. For instance: Would a person be willing to marry, have as a close friend, have as an acquaintance, or work with someone from another culture?

- **Semantic differential scales** – This type of scale judges a person's predispositions about a company, race, product, etc. by requiring a person to choose from a range between two opposite choices. An example would be to consider a specific brand of shoes. The semantic differential scale might require a person to examine the following pairs: clean/dirty, casual/dressy, cheap/expensive, and masculine/feminine. Some options may be neutral, but this gives the examiner a good view of how the test-taker feels about the subject in general. This can be applied to analyzing a person's view of another culture to gauge their predispositions, which all people have, and to address them well in class.

DEVELOPING PERSONAL RELATIONSHIPS WITH NEWLY ARRIVED IMMIGRANTS

Students need to feel welcomed and valued by their teacher. A direct verbal communication may not be feasible, but there are other methods of showing acceptance and personal warmth toward students. This will help relieve anxiety and can promote an enthusiasm to learn academics and American patterns of behavior. Smiles are a good way to reach different cultural, ethnic, and linguistic groups. Also, teachers should take time to talk with the youngsters, even through an interpreter. Having students talk about their prior life will help the teacher become more familiar with their concerns and enable the teacher to emotionally support the new students. The teacher may also answer questions about schools and what is needed to live here in America. The teacher may also discuss how he or she can help make the transition easier.

BECOMING ACQUAINTED WITH A STUDENT'S STRENGTHS AND NEEDS

An important part of planning and organizing for instruction is acquiring an understanding of the students. It is useful, early in the school year, to learn as much as possible about the students, what their interests, learning abilities, and learning styles are. As a teacher talks directly with each student, information is provided about how that student perceives himself or herself as a learner. Also useful is:

- Give oral or written diagnostic questionnaires or surveys to assess the students' current abilities, interests, and attitudes.
- Consult other personnel, student portfolios, and the students' records from previous years.
- Consider the potential for using previously successful adaptations with each student, and plan other adaptations to address the specific needs for learning.

INVENTORY OF STUDENTS' LEARNING STYLES

A teacher wants to know what types of learning styles a student has as well as answers to other questions. These are the answers teachers must use to determine how instruction may be personalized for the students. This can also be surprising information for the students as well. An inventory of student learning styles can build self-esteem by helping the student to discover his or her strengths, learn about the areas in which more effort is required, and appreciate the differences among fellow students. A number of published inventories are available to help students determine their learning strengths. Inventories may also be found for free on the internet.

Learning Style Terminology

Within-class ability grouping in classrooms	Research tends to support within-class ability grouping, grouping those with like abilities, as helping most students learn. It is generally flexible and not as stigmatizing as other groups. If such groups are considered, teachers might want only two such groups to make management of the grouping process easier.
Cooperative learning	Cooperative learning is an instructional strategy in which students are put into heterogeneous groups. It is perhaps one of the best researched innovations in recent times and can have dramatic student achievement effects when implemented properly.
Individualized instruction	Individualized instruction or one-on-one instruction is the best way to deal with individual student difference, but it is very difficult to accomplish. Computer-assisted instruction may change that.

Continuous Progress with Respect to Class Groupings

Continuous progress generally means that children remain with their classroom peers in an age cohort, despite having met or surpassed specific grade-level achievement expectations. This term is usually associated with an emphasis on the individualized curriculum, so that teaching and learning tasks are responsive to previous experience, and on the rate of progress of the child despite age. This practice is sometimes referred to as social promotion. The main reason for this practice is that there might be a stigmatizing effect on children if removed from their age cohort. Like ungraded approaches, the programs that are focused on continuous progress are not aimed at maximizing the educational benefits of children of different abilities and ages being together. Instead, their goal is to let the children progress without being made to meet expectations of achievement.

Implications of Different Age Grouping Schemes

Grouping practices might seem to have slight distinctions but there are significant implications in practice. Ungraded or nongraded approaches indicate that age is not a good indicator of what children are ready to learn. It emphasizes regrouping children for class based on perceived readiness to acquire skills and knowledge instead of age. Its main goal is of homogenizing children for instruction based on achievement rather than age. Combined grade groupings and continuous progress practices do not intend to increase a sense of family within class or to encourage children to share knowledge and experience, but mixed-age grouping does take advantage of heterogeneity of experience and skills in a group of children.

Safe Learning Environments

Most incidents of school violence or serious disruption begin as less serious behavior that has escalated to the point of requiring attention. Many aggressive or disruptive behaviors that spiraled out of control could have been prevented by early and appropriate classroom responses. A well-documented knowledge base exists on how to prevent misbehavior escalation in the classrooms. A number of the programs that integrate those findings into classroom management packages have become available. Most rely on principles of effectively managing the classroom including:

- Multiple options that rely on various strategies and responses for maintaining an effective learning environment.
- Emphasizing the positive.
- Teaching responsibility.
- Decelerating emotional conflict.

- Consistently communicating appropriate behavior.
- Early responses that let the student know what the school and classroom rules are and that they will be enforced.

BOOK CLUBS

Activities in which school book clubs can grow together as a group include:

- Letting the group name themselves. Let them decide on a club mascot.
- Allowing each club to keep a group reading notebook or journal where they track their readings. Perhaps they might decorate the journal if they so wish.
- Allowing groups to decide upon projects that are inquiry-based. For example, a group might decide to explore something of specific interest to them and search for the information.

After these steps are taken, teachers should explain the process and allow some class time so that students may discuss the activities and establish their first groups. Those students who are not interested in this voluntary activity can read on their own.

COMMON LANGUAGE DISORDERS:

Stuttering	Stuttering is an interruption in the rhythm or flow of speech that is characterized by hesitations, repetitions, or prolongation of sounds, syllables, words, or phrases.
Articulation disorders	Articulation disorders are difficulties with the way sounds are formed and put together. They are usually characterized by substituting one sound for another (wabbit for rabbit), omitting a sound (han for hand), or distorting sounds.
Voice disorders	Voice disorders are characterized by pitches that are inappropriate, such as being too high, too low, never changing or breaking, excessive or inadequate volume, or vocal qualities such as harsh, hoarse, nasal, or breathy.
Aphasia	Aphasia is the loss of speech and language abilities as a result of a head injury or stroke.
Delayed language	Delayed language is characterized by a marked slowness in grammar and vocabulary development that is needed to express and understand ideas and thoughts.

DYSLEXIA

Dyslexia is a brain difference, not a defect, that makes it excessively hard to learn language. A child with dyslexia will have problems from the very beginning in learning to understand speech and being understood. The child might need to describe what he or she wants, might have trouble sequencing words, or may speak words in an incorrect order. A child may have problems positioning letters when he or she enters school. Dyslexia is difficult to recognize because many of its manifestations are part of the natural maturing process of young children. When children get stuck in these stages and it lasts for an abnormally long period, parents and teachers should recognize this as a possible problem. But a dyslexic mind may have exceptional ability for singing or playing a musical instrument at an early age.

VARIOUS STUDENT ASSESSMENT SYSTEMS

Assessment system types include norm-referenced, criterion-referenced, and individual or alternative assessments. Criterion-referenced systems are those in which an individual's performance is compared to a certain learning objective of performance standard rather than the performance of other students. Norm-referenced systems are those in which student performance is compared to a "norm group," which may be a national sample that represents a diverse cross-section of students. These tests usually sort students and measure achievement based on some performance criterion. An individual assessment is one focusing on the individual student, such as a portfolio assessment. This is a portfolio of the student's classroom work. Alternative assessments are those requiring students to respond to a question rather than a set of responses.

WIDE-RANGE ACHIEVEMENT TEST

The Wide-Range Achievement Test is one of a number of standardized achievement assessments to determine a child's cognitive ability. It is designed for individuals ages 5-75. It contains scoring for reading, spelling, and math. It provides up to 30 minutes for each of the three forms. The test uses a single-level format as well as alternative forms. These alternative forms may be used individually or with one another in order to provide a more qualitative assessment of academic skills. The reading subtest includes letter naming and word pronunciation out of context. The spelling subtest asks the student to write his or her own name, and then write words as they are directed. The mathematical portion includes counting, reading problems, number symbols, and written computation.

STUDENT READING INVENTORY

To administer a student reading inventory, certain materials would be needed such as a stop watch to time the student, a copy of all readings for both the student and the teacher, and comprehension questions for scoring purposes. Steps to be taken when administering the inventory include:

- Explain to students that this is not a test. Tell them that this inventory is really to tell how the teacher can teach them better.
- Set the timer.
- Begin the timer as the student reads the first excerpt aloud.
- Score errors on the teacher's copy.
- Stop the timer when the student stops and record the total time.
- Give the comprehension questions and record the answers.

FORMATIVE ASSESSMENT

A formative assessment is a diagnostic use of assessment to provide feedback to teachers and students over the course of instruction. That is in contrast to a summative assessment, which usually happens after a period of instruction and requires making judgments about the learning that has occurred, such as with a test score or paper. Assessments in general include teacher observation, classroom instruction, or an analysis of student work, including homework and tests. Assessments are formative when the information is used to adapt teaching and learning to meet the needs of the students. When teachers know how students are progressing and where they are having difficulties, they can use this information to make needed instructional adjustments, such as reteaching, alternative instruction approaches, or offering more practice opportunities.

INFORMAL ASSESSMENT

Although there are no uniformly accepted definitions for formal and informal assessments, informal can mean techniques that are easily put into classroom routines, and learning activities to measure a student's learning outcome. Informal assessment can be used without interfering with instructional time. The results can be an indicator of the skills or subjects that interest a student, but they do not provide comparison to a broader group like standardized tests. Informal tests require clear understanding of the levels of a student's abilities. Informal assessments seek identification of a student's strengths and weaknesses without a regard to norms or grades. Such assessments may be done in structured or unstructured manners. Structured ones include checklists or observations. Unstructured assessments are those such as student work samples or journals.

Authentic Assessment

Authentic assessment asks students to apply their skills and knowledge the same way that they would be used in real-world situations. It is a performance-based assessment that requires each student to exhibit his or her in-depth knowledge and understanding through a mastery demonstration. It is an assessment of authentic learning, which is the type of learning in which activities and materials are framed in real-life contexts. The underlying assumption of such an approach is that the material is meaningful to students, and thus more motivating and deeply processed. Some of the terms or concepts that are related to authentic learning include contextual learning and theme-based curriculum.

Constructed-Response Tests as Opposed to Selected-Response

Constructed-response tests are a type of non-multiple-choice exam that requires some type of written or oral response. Selected-response tests consist of questions to be answered from a predetermined list of answers, with formats that include multiple choice, true/false, matching, or fill in the blanks. Each type of test has its benefits. Selected-response formats allow more questions to be asked in shorter time periods. Scoring is faster and it is easy to create comparable test forms. Since selected-response tests can normally be answered quickly, more items that covers several content areas can be administered in a short period of time. They can also be machine-scorable tests that allow quicker and more objective scoring. Constructed-response tests have the potential for gathering deeper information about a student's knowledge and understanding of a content area. Constructed-response items are more time consuming and allow fewer items to be covered.

Portfolio Assessments

A portfolio can be thought of as a scrapbook or photo album that records the progress and activities of the program and those who participate in it. It showcases them to interested parties both inside and outside of the program. Portfolios can be used to examine and measure progress by documenting the learning as it takes place. They extend beyond test scores to include a substantive picture of what a student is doing and experiencing. Portfolios are useful in documenting progress in higher-order goals such as applying skills and synthesizing experience beyond what standardized or norm-based tests can do. The portfolio contents are sometimes known as "evidence" or "artifacts." They can include drawings, writing, photos, video, audio tapes, computer discs, and copies of program-specific or standardized tests.

Portfolio assessment is best used for the following:

- Evaluating programs with flexible or individualized outcomes or goals.
- Allowing individuals and programs in the community to be involved in their own change and decisions to change.
- Giving information that provides a meaningful insight into behavioral change.
- Providing tools to ensure communications and accountability to a wide range of audiences. These participants, such as families or community members, may not be sophisticated in interpreting statistical data and can better appreciate more visual or experiential evidence of success being achieved.
- Assessing some of the more important and complex aspects of many constructs.

Portfolio assessment has these disadvantages:
- It can be very time-intensive for teachers to evaluate, especially if the portfolios must be done in addition to traditional grading and tests.
- Having to develop an individualized criteria may be unfamiliar or difficult at first.
- The portfolio could just be a collection of miscellaneous artifacts that does not show growth or progress if the goals and criteria are unclear.
- As is the case with other forms of qualitative data, the data that is used from portfolio assessments can be difficult to analyze or to aggregate in order to see progress or change in the individual student.

Portfolios used for assessment have certain essential characteristics including:
- Having multiple data sources including both people and artifacts. People can be teachers, participants, or community members. Artifacts can be test scores, drawings, writings, videotapes, or audiotapes.
- Having authentic evidence that is related to program activities.
- Being dynamic and capturing change and growth. Portfolios should include different stages of mastery which will allow a much deeper understanding of the change process.
- Being explicit in that participants should know what is expected of them.
- Being integrated, meaning having the evidence to establish a connection between program activities and life experiences.
- Being based on ownership, or having the participant help to determine what evidence to include to show that the goals are being met.
- Being multipurposed, or allowing for assessment of the effectiveness of the program while also assessing the performance of the participant.

Portfolio assessments are not as useful for the following situations:
- Evaluating programs that have very concrete, uniform purposes or goals. For instance, it would not be necessary to compile a portfolio for a programs such as immunizing children by the age of five because the immunizations are the same and the evidence is usually straightforward and clear.
- Allowing a teacher to rank participants or a program in a quantitative or standardized way, even though evaluators or staff members of the program might be able to make subjective judgments on that which is relative.
- Comparing participants or programs to standardized norms. Portfolios can and often do include some kinds of standardized test scores along with other types of evidence. However, this is not the main purpose in using portfolio assessments.

The main factors that guide the design and development of a portfolio are:
- Purpose. The primary concern is understanding the purpose that is to be served by the portfolio. This will define guidelines for collecting materials. For instance, is the goal to report progress? To identify special needs? For program accountability? For all such reasons?
- Assessment criteria. The next step is to decide on the criteria standards, such as what will be considered a success, and what strategies are needed to meet the goals. Items are then selected to provide evidence of meeting said criteria or making progress with respect to the goals which have been set.
- Evidence. A number of considerations in collecting data are needed. What are the sources of evidence? How often should evidence be collected? How can sense be made of the evidence?

MISCUE ANALYSIS

A miscue analysis is an assessment in which a child reads a story aloud and the teacher checks for errors in the recognition and comprehension of words. Such an analysis might be performed in the following manner:

- The teacher instructs the student that they will read a passage aloud without the teacher's help.
- A videotape or audiotape should be made for analysis after the session.
- After reading the teacher marks all miscues, including insertions, mispronunciations, omissions, and corrections by the student.
- The teacher records the miscues by writing what the text said in one column and what the reader said in another.
- The miscues are analyzed using criteria, including whether the miscue went with the preceding context and whether it was corrected.
- Percentages are calculated based on the total number of miscues.

JOURNALS

Journals let students write an ongoing record of thoughts, ideas, experiences, and reflections on a given topic. They go beyond the demands of usual written assignments as they promote integration of personal thoughts and expression with materials for a class. Journals provide a systematic means of collecting evidence and documenting learning for self-evaluation and reflections. Journals can be structured or free-form. Structured journals are when students are given specific questions, a set of guidelines, or a target on which to base their writing. Free-form lets students record thoughts and feelings with little direction. Whatever the form, journals are valuable in assessing a student's ability to observe, challenge, doubt, question, explore, and solve problems.

VALIDITY AND RELIABILITY

A test is valid when it measures what it is supposed to measure. The validity of a test depends on the purpose for which it is to be used. For instance, a thermometer might measure temperature, but it cannot measure barometric pressure. A test is reliable when it yields results that are consistent. A test may be reliable and valid, valid and unreliable, reliable and invalid, or neither valid nor reliable. A test must be reliable for it to measure validity and the validity of a test is constrained by its reliability. If a test does not consistently measure a construct or domain, then it may not be expected to have a high degree of validity.

TYPES OF TEST VALIDITY INCLUDE:

- Face validity. This asks the question: Does the test measure what should be measured?
- Content validity. This asks: Is the full content of the concept being defined included in the measure? It must include a broad sample of what is tested, emphasize material that is important and, require skills that are appropriate.
- Criterion validity. This asks: Is the measure consistent with what is already known and expected? There are two subcategories, which are predictive and concurrent.
- Predictive validity predicts a known association between the construct being measured and something else.
- Concurrent validity is associated with indicators that pre-exist or with something that already measures the same concept.
- Construct validity. This shows the measure that relates to a number of other measures that are specified.
- Discriminant validity. This type does not associate with unrelated constructs.

THREATS TO THE INTERNAL VALIDITY OF A TEST

Factors affecting how valid a test is by itself include:

- History. Outside events that happen during the course of what is being studied may influence the results. It does not make the test less accurate.
- Maturation. Change due to aging or development between or within groups may affect validity.
- Instrumentation. The reliability is questioned because of a calibration change in a measuring device or changes in human ability to measure difference, such as fatigue or experience.
- Testing. Test-taking experience affects results. This refers to either physical or mental changes, such as changes in the attitude or physiological response of a participant after repeated measures.
- Statistical regression. This is the tendency to regress towards the mean, making some scores higher or lower.

If a measure is not reliable, some variation will occur between repeated measures.

ADDITIONAL THREATS TO THE INTERNAL VALIDITY OF A TEST

A test may have the following threats to its internal validity:

- Selection. Participants in a group may be alike in certain ways, but will respond differently to the independent variable.
- Mortality. Participants drop out of a test, making the group unequal. Who drops out and why can be a factor.
- Interaction. Two or more threats can interact, such as selection-maturation when there is a difference between age groups causing groups to change at different ages.
- Contamination. This is when a comparison group in some way impacts another group, causing an increase of efforts. This is also called "compensatory rivalry."

CONVENTIONAL VIEWS OF TEST RELIABILITY

Views in recent decades on test reliability include:

- Temporal stability. This refers to implementing the same form of testing on two or more separate occasions to the same group of students. This is not practical as repeated measurements are likely to result in higher scores on later tests after students become familiar with the format.
- Form equivalence. This is relative to two different test forms based on the same content, administered once to the same group of students.
- Internal consistency. This relates to the coefficient of test scores obtained from a single test. When no pattern is found in the student responses, the test is probably too difficult and the students resorted to randomly guessing at the answers.
- Reliability is a necessary but insufficient condition for a test to be valid. The test might reflect consistent measurement but it may not be especially valid.

Conventional Views of Test Validity

Some conventional views on test validity in recent years include:

- Face validity. This means that a test is valid at face value. As a check on face validity, psychometricians traditionally sent test items to teachers for modification. This was abandoned for a long time because of its vagueness and subjectivity. But face validity returned in the 1990s in another form, with validity defined as making common sense, being persuasive, and appearing right to the reader.
- Content validity. This draws inferences from test scores to a large domain of items that are similar to those on a test. The concern with content validity is a sample-population representation, meaning that the knowledge and skills covered by the test should be representative of the larger knowledge and skill domain.

Regression Analysis with Respect to Test Validity

Regression analysis can be used to establish validity of the criteria of a test. An independent variable may be used as a predictor of the dependent variable, which is the criterion variable. The correlation coefficient between them is known as the validity coefficient. For instance, test scores are the criterion variable. It is hypothesized that if the student passes the test, he or she would meet the criteria of knowing all the specific subject matter. Criterion validity values prediction over explanation. Prediction is concerned with mathematical or non-casual dependence, whereas explanation pertains to casual or logical dependence. For instance, one can predict the weather based on the mercury height in a thermometer. The mercury could satisfy the criterion validity as a predictor. Yet one cannot say why the weather changes because of the mercury's height.

Two Sources of Test Invalidity

Two particular threats to test validity are known as "construct underrepresentation" and "construct-irrelevant variance." The first term indicates that the task being measured in the assessment fails to include important discussions or facets of the construct. So the test results will indicate a student's abilities within only a portion of the construct intended to be measured by the test. The second term means that a test measures too many variables. Many of these variables are irrelevant to the interpreted construct. This can take two forms. "Construct-irrelevant easiness" occurs when outside clues in format permit some individuals to respond correctly or appropriately in ways which are irrelevant to the assessed construct. "Construct-irrelevant difficulty" occurs when outside aspects make it more difficult for individuals to respond correctly.

Evaluating a Child for Reading Problems

Parents whose children are being tested for reading problems should be assured by teachers or reading specialists that the evaluation:

- Uses the native language such as Spanish or sign language unless it is clearly impossible to do so.
- Does not discriminate against the child because he or she has some type of disability or comes from a background that is racially or culturally different.
- Is administered by evaluators who know how to give the tests they decide to use.
- Will be used to determine if the child has a disability and to select the educational program that fits the child's needs. These decisions cannot be based solely on one evaluation.

Conjoint Behavioral Consultation

Conjoint behavioral consultation (CBC) is a partnership model of service delivery in which parents, educators, other primary caregivers, and service providers all work in collaboration to meet the developmental needs of children, address their concerns, and achieve success by promoting the competencies of all parties concerned. CBC creates an opportunity for families and schools to work together for a common interest and to build upon and promote the capabilities and strengths of the family members and school personnel. Individual needs are identified and acted upon using an organized approach that is data-based and that has mutual and collaborative interactions between parents and children, along with the guidance and assistance of consultants such as school psychologists.

Conjoint behavioral consultant partnerships (CBC) can be implemented through four stages: needs identification, needs analysis, plan development, and plan evaluation. Three of these stages use interviews to structure the decisions to be made. Overall, the goal is to effectively address the needs and desires of parents and teachers for the children. Specific objectives include:

- Addressing concerns as they happen across, rather than only within individual settings.
- Enhancing home-school partnerships to benefit student learning and performance.
- Establishing joint responsibility for solving problems.
- Improving communications between children, families, and school personnel.
- Assessing needs in a comprehensive and functional way.
- Promoting continuity and consistency among agents of change and across various settings.
- Providing opportunities for parents to become empowered using strength-based orientation.

READING FIRST PROFESSIONAL DEVELOPMENT PROGRAMS

Training in the five essential components of reading instruction is one of the most important elements of a quality professional development plan under the Reading First initiative. Teachers should learn effective strategies for providing explicit and systematic instruction for each component. Those components are:

- Phonemic awareness. Teachers should understand the difference between phonemic awareness and phonics. Phonemic awareness focuses on hearing sounds and learning how those sounds are put together.
- Phonics. Teachers should be trained in explicit and systematic phonics instruction based on scientifically based reading research.
- Fluency. Teachers will learn the various techniques for reading fluency, such as teacher modeling, repeating reading aloud, and choral reading.
- Reading vocabulary. Teachers can learn several effective techniques for teaching vocabulary.
- Reading comprehension. Professional development can give teachers certain comprehension strategies to help students understand what they read.

THERE ARE CERTAIN REQUIREMENTS FOR IMPLEMENTING FEDERAL READING FIRST PROFESSIONAL DEVELOPMENT PLANS. THEY INCLUDE:

- The plans must be closely aligned with the principles of scientifically-based reading research and the five essential components of reading instruction. The programs must provide instruction in scientifically-based reading instructional materials, programs, strategies, and approaches. Also, the programs must train teachers in the appropriate use of assessment tools and in the analysis and interpretation of gathered data.

- An eligible professional development provider must deliver the professional development program. To be eligible, the provider must be able to train teachers, including special education teachers, in reading instruction that is grounded in scientifically-based reading research.
- Teachers must be instructed in teaching all components of reading instruction and must understand how the components are related, the progression in which they should be taught, and the underlying structure of the English language.

SINCE READING FIRST IS A FEDERAL INITIATIVE, MANY STATES MAY HAVE SIMILAR STATE GUIDELINES FOR CARRYING OUT THE INITIATIVE, SUCH AS SUMMER READING PROGRAMS. SOME GUIDELINE EXAMPLES MIGHT INCLUDE:

- The use of Reading First-approved core, supplemental, and intervention programs.
- Daily 90-minute uninterrupted reading instructional blocks. This would include systematic delivery of explicit instruction using approved core reading program material.
- Intervention services provided for students who are below the mastery of reading skills.
- Evidence of teacher's use of data to drive instruction. Reports on the program developed by the state will include information on the number of students served, the summer school teacher credentials, student achievement gain, and percentage of students meeting end of grade benchmarks at the beginning and end of the summer program.

CONVEYING HIGH EXPECTATIONS TO STUDENTS

Researchers have found certain ways that a school may let students know that the school's expectations of them are high:

- Establish policies that emphasize how important it is to achieve academically. This can be done by notifying parents if students are not meeting the academic expectations or setting minimally acceptable achievement levels for students to participate in sports or extracurricular activities.
- Use slogans that communicate high expectations for the students such as "Yes we can."
- Protect instructional time and discourage tardiness, absenteeism, and interruptions.
- Provide insistent coaching to students who experience difficulty with learning tasks. Researchers say that excusing children from trying hard to succeed in academics because it is not fair or because it is hopeless to expect any more does not really help students in learning. It detracts from academic skills and can also lower motivation and self-esteem.

PROBLEM-SOLVING PROCESS

A problem-solving process can be used with methods to assess or measure how well the curriculum is meeting students' needs so that changes in the curriculum can be made. The process includes:

- Identify the problem to be solved. For instance, a marked underachievement in reading.
- Identify alternative solutions to the problem, such as a new reading method.
- Implement new programs and test alternative solutions. Revise unsuccessful solutions.
- Terminate the problem. This includes revising unsuccessful instructional programs. When making changes in a student's instructional program, teachers should be aware of various alterable characteristics of instruction that are under the direct control of the teacher.

EVOLUTIONARY CHANGES AND REVOLUTIONARY CHANGES

Instructional changes can be viewed as either revolutionary or evolutionary. Revolutionary changes are those with major modifications in an instructional program. Evolutionary changes are minor ones. Evolutionary changes may be made in certain parts of the instructional plan such as time, activity, materials, or motivation. A revolutionary change could include the method of instruction from a language experience approach to direct instruction. Technically sound achievement indicators for such decisions include the number of words read correctly for reading, and the number of correct letter sequences in two minutes or the number of words spelled in two minutes for spelling. For written expression, the indicators could be the number of words written, the number of correctly spelled words, or the number of correct word sequences in two minutes.

Effective Curricula that are Culturally Responsive

Effective curricula that are culturally responsive share certain characteristics. These include:

- The curriculum is integrated and interdisciplinary. It does not rely on one-time activities or "sprinkling" the traditional curriculum with a few minority individuals.
- It is authentic, connected to the child's real life, and child-centered. It uses materials from the child's culture and history to illustrate concepts and principles.
- It develops critical thinking skills.
- It often incorporates strategies that use cooperative learning, whole language instruction, and self-esteem building, and it recognizes diverse styles of learning.
- It is supported by appropriate staff development and pre-service preparation.
- It is part of a coordinated strategy. Successful implementation requires a school climate that is receptive and recognizes that the hidden curriculum in any school can be a powerful ally or a powerful enemy.

Assessing Curriculum Materials for Cultural Relevance

A number of criteria should be evaluated when looking for curriculum materials that are culturally relevant. Teachers should look for invisibility, stereotyping, selectivity, imbalance, unreality, isolation, language bias, and fragmentation. Also to be looked for in books is the inappropriate treatment of African Americans, Native Americans, Asian Americans, and Hispanic Americans, especially when the "one size fits all view" is expressed. This is where instructional material reflects through generalization that there is a single Hispanic, African, Asian, or Native culture. The sidebar approach also should be avoided. This is where a few isolated events relevant to ethnic experiences are relegated to a box or sidebar that is set apart from the rest of the text.

Facilitator in Culturally-Relevant Approaches to Education

A teacher can become a facilitator in transferring school knowledge to that of real life by involving a student's home culture in learning. Ways to do this include:

- Have students share artifacts from home that are reflective of their culture.
- Have students write about traditions that their families share.
- Have students research different aspects of their culture.
- Have members of the community who share a culture with your students speak to the class on various subjects.
- Involve the class in making something relevant to other cultures (such as a piñata for studying the Hispanic culture.)

Critically Analyzing School Wide Reading Programs

When critically looking at goals and needs, schools should recognize that the ultimate goal is better results. Measuring progress, being accountable for results, and making changes based on reliable data are vital aspects of school wide improvement. Many school leaders look upon this process as a work in progress. Continuous data-driven accountability involves teams of teachers and reading specialists engaging in the following activities:

- Combine information from multiple measurements on all groups of students.
- Organize data to clarify strengths and needs of the school as a whole.
- Disaggregate information on students to determine whether some subgroups are experiencing common problems.
- Keep alert to the implications of the quality of education supported by the school as a whole.

CONTINUOUS PROGRESS MONITORING

Continuous monitoring that allows analysis of school wide programs such as reading gives the faculty and staff a sense of ownership by putting accountability in their hands. Few surprises exist in continuous monitoring because the school is in control of its own assessment. Teachers and school leaders score many of their own tests so they learn the results immediately. As teams of reading specialists and classroom teachers examine the data, they look for information about different aspects of the subject within the school. With data analysis, questions may be asked such as: Are there grades with an especially strong or weak showing in the subject? Are non-English or limited-English speakers improving their use of test materials?

READING SPECIALIST

Reading specialists help staff develop knowledge of literacy theory and instructions. They are consultants and collaborating teachers for classroom teachers, aides, parents, and other teachers such as special education, speech, music, and art. Some schools have chosen to replace reading specialists with teaching assistants who lack specialized literacy training. When this happens, a grave injustice is done to students, teachers, and the literacy program. Reading specialists provide expert instruction to learners who differ in language, learning style, culture, and ability. They share effective learning strategies and practices with school staff and parents, and they serve as experts for the school and district on information about reading and literacy instruction.

HOME-SCHOOL CONNECTIONS

Schools are now opening their doors more as community resources to serve students and families. So-called "full-service" schools show that they are paying attention to the students' holistic needs as well as their academic needs. These schools offer health, counseling, social service, and other programs to support learning and growth. Some community-initiated activities are also transforming schools. These communities are taking responsibility to use information about schools to offer new ways to improve schools. They are working with schools on recurring problems. The schools are beginning to change in ways that bring more voices to the table when it comes to decision-making.

There are a number of concrete steps that community members can take to help schools improve and especially to help more children to read. Community members can:

- Become a learning partner or tutor. The citizen can tutor a child in the child's own neighborhood or in a local elementary school. Volunteers might read with or to a child for 30 minutes a week for at least eight weeks, and could also take the child to the library to get him or her a library card.

- Volunteer to serve as a community coordinator for a community reading program. A number of organizations can work to recruit tutors. This person can also work with local schools to match community members and children.
- Ask organizations to help support community reading programs. Local businesses can be encouraged to donate supplies or allow employees time off to volunteer in school.

IMPACT OF FAMILY BACKGROUND ON EDUCATION

The exact nature of the impact parental education and social economic status has on student achievement is unknown, although it does have an impact. Studies have found that parental education and family socioeconomic status alone are not necessarily predictors of how students will achieve academically. Studies have found that parental education accounts for about a quarter of the variance in student test scores while socioeconomic status accounts for slightly more than a quarter. Other research indicates that dysfunctional home environments, low expectations from parents, parenting that is ineffective, differences in language and high mobility levels may account for the low achievement levels among those students that come from lower socioeconomic levels. Other impacts that family culture has on a student's performance might include cultural dispositions that end up isolating a student from his or her peer group. One of the most reliable ways of addressing family or socioeconomic background is by increasing the student's awareness of their future, whether that be in education or a particular career path. Having the student start thinking about his or her future will help to set and achieve short-term goals that will naturally lead into their long-term goals.

PROGRESS MONITORING

Progress monitoring is a classroom-based assessment for reading instruction that evaluates how well a child is learning based upon a systematic review by teachers of children who perform academic tasks equivalent to those which are a part of the student's daily classroom instruction. Unlike a one-time test for proficiency, this type of ongoing assessment helps to determine whether students are making sufficient progress or require more help in achieving grade-level reading objectives. Progress monitoring should have certain benchmarks to ensure reliability and validity. Progress monitoring can assess the efficacy of various components of a student's instruction in reading such as in phonemic awareness, phonics, fluency, vocabulary and reading comprehension.

SOCRATIC QUESTIONING

Socratic questioning is at the heart of critical thinking skills. It is more than just having a one-word answer or expressing agreement or disagreement. Socratic questions force students to make assumptions, sort through both relevant and irrelevant points and, additionally, explain those points. This instruction can take many different forms including:

- Raising basic issues.
- Probing beneath the surface of matters.
- Pursuing areas of thought fraught with problems.
- Helping students find the structure of their own thinking.
- Helping students develop clarity, accuracy and relevance.
- Helping students make judgments by reasoning on their own.
- Helping students to think about evidence, conclusions, assumptions, implications, points of view, concepts and interpretations.

METADISCURSIVE

Research shows that teaching in content areas should include teaching students to be metadiscursive, meaning that they should not only be able to be part of many different discourse communities but that they should also know why and how it is that they are taking part as well as what those engagements mean for them and others in the realm of larger power relationships and social position.

This does not mean that the historical limitations in integrating content literacy should be ignored. Teaching content literacy should still focus on the knowledge and beliefs of students and teachers, which requires considering questions such as how teachers balance the notion of subject-matter literacy as a metadiscursive practice while encountering probable resistance from students who have become comfortable with the notion that content area learning is a matter of rote memory and information reproduction.

TRADE BOOKS

Trade books are instructional materials written specifically for students but are not textbooks, per se. They may be used to help improve reading skills, develop knowledge of content areas and further understand the world. Trade books can be a valued complement to teaching and curriculum. They may also affect the appreciation which a student has for content-related literature. These books should not replace thorough instruction in reading skills, however. Trade books also are not an alternative to teaching concepts of content areas, but rather, these texts can help students understand concepts by putting them into an appropriate context. Teachers can use strategies such as this to help develop better reading skills and help students comprehend the text.

DRAMATIC ACTIVITIES AS SCAFFOLDING FOR ELEMENTARY AND ENGLISH AS A SECOND LANGUAGE INSTRUCTION

Elementary and English as a Second Language classes can receive scaffolding for effective literacy from dramatic activities. Researchers have found that scaffolded play with students of elementary age allow them to participate in language learning in an active way. Students may also be more motivated to discuss, organize, rewrite and perform in the dramatic presentation.

Students have also become more engaged when there were interwoven activities involving literature, drama, music and movement, even for at-risk students in grades K-3. Activities involving bilingual children in which their own cultural experiences are called upon and valued also helps motivate and support literacy and meaningful learning environments.

LEARNING CULTURE

Students learning about culture should be taught to react appropriately in social situations. They should be able to describe a pattern in the culture and recognize a pattern when it is illustrated. Additionally, they should be able to explain these patterns and predict how a pattern is likely to apply in a given situation. Students learning culture should describe or manifest an attitude that is important for making oneself acceptable in a foreign society. They should evaluate the form of a statement concerning a culture pattern and describe or demonstrate defensible methods of analyzing a sociocultural whole. They should identify basic human responses which signify that that which is being taught is understood.

KEEPING EXPECTATIONS HIGH FOR RECENT IMMIGRANT STUDENTS

It is common for some teachers to become frustrated upon seeing that they are unable to reach one or more of their students. Becoming more culturally informed can help enhance their teaching repertoire. This information can also help teachers realize that these students may have trouble under the teaching of any skilled instructor. But the belief that is expressed in a student helps to create persistence and motivation on their part. Linguistic as well as academic achievements in the United States are often only realized because of the patience, tolerance and encouragement which American teachers display. Effort is promoted by teachers who are supportive and who create a valuing, welcoming and accepting educational setting.

Support Services for Recent Immigrant Students

Schools can help recent immigrants feel welcome and supported while developing positive identities that are cross-cultural. Schools have many ways to assist their students in learning the curriculum and adapting to American culture and habits. For example, a recent arrival can be partnered with another student who speaks his or her language or dialect, even if they are not necessarily of the same nationality or heritage. Cross-age tutoring is also an option that might be considered. Candidates include someone from the student's culture or region, other recent immigrants, or an accepting and helpful American youngster. Hiring paraprofessionals who speak the student's language can also be helpful.

Between-Class Ability Approach to Grouping

Between-class ability grouping is not a strategy in which all students can learn. Students at the top level seem to benefit but those in the middle and lower levels may not. It is nonetheless a popular practice in American education. The problem may lie more with the method of grouping than with the concept itself. Ability groups are mostly determined by standardized testing or basic skills tests. But students may not have uniform knowledge of, and aptitude for, the various content areas. Another problem, research demonstrates, is that teachers' expectations and the quality of instruction are often lower for lower-track groups in between-class grouping. Students may also lower their own expectations when placed in a lower-level group. This may affect self-concept in academic achievement, and thus, affect the teacher's expectations.

Combined Grade Classes

Combined classes are those which include more than one grade level in a classroom. These classes are sometimes referred to as split classes, blended classes or double-year classes. These classes will usually include the required curriculum for each of the two grades that are represented, yet some class activities may take place with children who are from both of the combined grades. This type of grouping takes place more frequently in smaller schools, yet on occasion in larger schools when the number of children in different age groups tends to have fluctuated. The main purpose of such classes appears to be maximizing resource use with regard to personnel and space instead of capitalizing on the diversity of ability and experience within the groups of mixed ages.

Valuing Correct Answers

One of the most effective points that can be made to help establish a safe learning environment for students is to emphasize that errors are friends rather than faults. Students often apologize for not knowing something. They can be reassured that no one knows everything and that everyone has something to learn. Teachers can teach them to value their correct answers rather than dwelling on the errors that they made, and point out patterns of errors as well. For example, they can be taught to count the number of questions about which they were correct, thus offering positive reinforcement. Even if a student gets one item correct and the remainder incorrect, the student can be told that they have already learned something.

Peer Mediation Programs

Peer mediation uses a group of student mediators who are taught a negotiation procedure that is interest-based, along with problem-solving and communicational strategies to help settle disagreements without confrontation or violent actions. Students come to mediation on a voluntary basis and are guided by the peer mediators to move from blaming one another to coming up with solutions that are acceptable to all parties. Peer mediation often is put in place as part of a broader program for conflict resolution. Peer mediation can substantially change how students approach conflicts and settle them. Students who are involved in peer mediation oftentimes express a greater desire to help friends avoid fights and solve their problems.

ALTERNATIVES TO TECHNOLOGICAL MEANS AND REDUCING STUDENT DISRUPTION

Little data exists demonstrating that punitive "zero tolerance" policies have significantly improved school safety or student behavior. Researchers have begun to discover that which is and is not efficacious in preventing school violence. The programs that seem to be most effective are proactive rather than reactive, involving families, students, teachers and communities. They include a number of components that help address the complexity of school violence and disruption. There is far more data available supporting the effectiveness of bullying prevention programs, anger management or peer mediation programs than there is to support how well violence and disruption is stemmed by technological means such as surveillance cameras or metal detectors.

EYE COORDINATION PROBLEMS

Four general types of eye coordination problems can affect a young reader – astigmatism, eye-hand coordination, visual motor problems, esophoria, and other conditions. Children will get into postures that are distorted while trying to get one eye to function. They will often put their head down on their arms, covering an eye with their hand or rotating their head so that their nose bridge interferes with one eye's vision. Esophoria is another eye coordination problem that tends to turn eyes inward. A child will see objects smaller than they really are. The only way that a child can view the object as larger is to move it closer to him or her.

DISCREPANCY CRITERIA AND ASSUMPTIONS ABOUT UNIQUE TYPES OF POOR READING

Most state and federal guidelines for identifying those with reading disabilities have as a foundation an ability-achievement discrepancy. It is usually operationalized as an IQ-achievement discrepancy. An assumption behind such guidelines has been that poor readers with discrepancies or the reading disabled, have a unique type of poor reading, different from other poor reading types. Such criteria have been attacked by reading disability researchers, who argue that there are many similarities between those who read poorly and have discrepancies and poor readers who have no discrepancies such as children whose IQs are on level with their reading ability but are not low enough for them to be termed intellectually disabled. Both groups seem to have problems with word decoding and phonological functions and little evidence is present to support the notion that poor readers with discrepancies can eventually perform better than those with none.

ASSUMPTIONS OF INTRINSIC PROCESSING DISORDER AND PROCESSING TESTS

An educational diagnosis of reading disorders normally employs processing tests, which test memory, language ability, and visual and auditory processing. Poor readers do have certain difficulties in certain processing measures such as decoding words and phonological processing. These tests can provide early identification of reading problems and also help plan an educational program for the student. The problem is that word decoding and phonological processing measures are not always emphasized in identification of reading disabilities in schools. Many such measures lack validity and reliability and interpretations of these tests also present problems. A poor performance on these tests is most often interpreted as evidence of a processing disorder intrinsic to the reader, but researchers emphasize that processing is shaped not only by innate characteristics such as genetics but also experiences such as reading in class.

Scoring an Informal Reading Inventory

Once written comprehension questions are chosen, a teacher will want to determine the number of errors that are permissible for the students. Students are often graded and grouped into three categories: independent (the student can read on their own), instructional (the student could read if classroom help is available) and frustration (the student will most likely find this piece too difficult even in a classroom setting). Where the child falls on that scale depends upon the amount of errors per 100 words that the student commits. For example, an "independent" reader might commit one or two errors per 100 words and score 90 percent or higher on comprehension questions.

Running Records

Running records give teachers an important tool for making decisions on appropriate grouping, materials and support when taken over time in early literacy training. They are based on structured observations of children's reading and writing behaviors and exemplify authentic assessment which is critical with emergent readers as they come across new reading material.

The student reads from a text and the teacher watches closely, coding behaviors on a sheet of paper. Words that are accurately read are given a check. Errors receive a line with reader behaviors recorded above the line and teacher actions recorded below. A goal of the running records for this level would be to help students develop a "self-extending" system, which indicates that children learn to apply strategies of self-monitoring and self-correction on more difficult texts for extended amounts of text.

Certain points should be remembered when taking and scoring running records. These include:

- Running records must be analyzed to offer data for instructional use in addition to being scored.
- Consider what text the student reads, up to and including the error when analyzing a substitution.
- Do not make professional judgments base on the results of one running record. Reviewing the analysis and accuracy of scores of a number of running records is the only way to understand a student's reading process.
- Individual errors are studied for gaining insight into the reader's process.
- When analyzing a record, circle the cues that the reader used and not the ones that were neglected.

Observation

Observation is one of the most powerful techniques that a teacher has. The purpose is to build a picture of a student's personal, social and cognitive development and how they are making progress in their learning. Only when a number of cameos, vignettes, snapshots, notes or indicators exist can teachers start looking for patterns in student behavior and make judgments about their performance. Dating such records will help record the contexts along with observed achievement characteristics in order to build a historical profile that is useful. Supporting and acknowledging students working at different levels requires flexibility and tailoring to the individual student. The formats should suit the particular activities, reflect the activities' goals and support the recording of different levels and rates of students' work.

Reliability of Performance, Portfolio, and Responsive Evaluations

Some scholars and testing experts argue that performance, portfolio and responsive evaluations—where tasks vary greatly from student to student and where multiple tasks may be simultaneously evaluated—are not reliable. A difficulty cited is that there is more than one source of errors in measuring performance assessment. For instance, a writing skill test score might have its reliability affected by graders, or other such factors. There may also be confusion about diversity of reliability indices. Nonetheless, different reliability measures share a common thread. One such commonality is constituted in measurement procedures in situations such as internal consistency. Oftentimes for convenience in computing, the reliability index is based upon a single data collection. The ultimate reference, however, should go beyond just one testing occasion to other such occasions.

Performance Factors that Reading Specialists Might Look at in Consultation with Teachers

Teachers may look for specific performance factors that can be passed along to the reading specialist or others for assessment in order to decide if a child needs modified reading instruction. These factors are:

- Continuous improvement. Are the student's grades improving, stagnating or declining?
- Comparative performance. Do the results show that the student is doing well in comparison to other children in comparable settings?
- Absolute performance. Do the results show the student is reaching the school's desired level of performance?
- Small-group performance. Do the results show that children of a similar group as the student (limited English, Title I students) are making better progress that that of the student in question?

Student Peer Training

Students have long had informal, untrained peer helping networks. Students share their concerns with each other naturally while at lunch, after school and while talking on the phone at home. The seriousness of the problems discussed have changed somewhat in today's world. Students may likely know someone who was pregnant or suicidal, who had a drug problem, was being abused or who had an eating disorder but many of these students with such problems do not seek adult help, resulting in a crisis in which a student's coping mechanisms are not effective, and thus many students in the end obtain little or no help from professionals. Peer programs offer the ability to increase the student's skill in responding and helping friends, and train students to know when there is a crisis and to whom the peer may be referred.

Curriculum-Based Assessment

Instructional strategies are not fail-proof with regard to teaching students new skills. There are, however, a number of data-based strategies that have been identified that when used with an objective and systematic assessment can lead to a curriculum that will help improve student performance. Such an assessment is termed a curriculum-based assessment. These are models of assessment that emphasize a direct relationship to the student's curriculum. These assessments use measures from the curriculum to evaluate the effectiveness of instruction and to determine what changes to the instruction can lead to more effective teaching methods and improved student achievement. The assessment provides information on how the student's behavior changes on a generic task of constant difficulty. Increases in the behavior being measured on equivalent forms of the task would represent growth academically.

Data Sources to Critically Analyze School-Wide Programs

Data sources such as aligned instructional benchmarks and assessments can be used to critically analyze school wide programs such as reading so that appropriate changes can be made to meet students' goals and needs. Many schools have linked aligned instructional benchmarks to broader objectives that are periodically measured by their state's assessment programs. Schools, through aligned assessments, can examine results for several purposes to track absolute progress, compare against benchmark goals and to find patters that reveal progress or weaknesses over time. An ongoing analysis of data can determine adjustments that are timely. Aligned information can let educators examine instructional variations that might make a difference in academic achievements. This allows educators to ask what should be done at various levels within the classroom or school to prevent problems identified by the data.

Promoting Collaboration Among Colleagues

The reading specialist in a school setting provides a wide variety of services, many of which are in a collaborative effort with colleagues. The specialist works with teachers to promote and develop the literacy program as well as developing thinking strategies in the classroom. As a diagnostician, the specialist administers both group and individual evaluations of reading achievement and recommends activities to build comprehension. For intervention, the specialist works with teachers as well as students and small groups for providing instruction and for building competencies in literacy. In addition, the reading specialist works with the staff and parents in order to promote various events in order to gather support for the literacy program and which support literacy as a whole.

Parental Expectations and Children's Classroom Outcomes

Various research has found that parental expectations have a significant impact upon school performance as well as being critical to achievement in academics. High expectations from parents are usually found in association with higher levels of educational attainment. Parenting practices that are effective and associated with high levels of academic achievement include expectations that children receive high numerical grades of their schoolwork. Additionally, research indicates that child rearing beliefs, ways to academically enrich home environments and standards of behavior that are acceptable both in and out of school are likewise important to achieving academically. Insofar as behavior is concerned, the children who succeed have greater adaptability to conforming with behavioral standards at school; something many have already learned through parental expectations.

Reading Poetry

Some general guidelines for reading poetry may be summarized as follows:

- Understand the relationship of the title to the work. Does the title suggest anything about the subject?
- Ascertain who the "speaker" of the poem is. Determine what type of narrative is employed.
- Know the major theme or argument which dominates the work.
- Poems deal with private or individual matters or subjects in the public spectrum. Determine which the poem is addressing.
- What type of meter is used in the poem? Is rhyme employed as a device?
- Carefully examine the poem for figurative language and note how it is used.
- Be aware of the poems historical and cultural setting in order to place the meaning in context.
- Notice whether the poem fits a formally defined genre within poetry.

Oral Questioning

One easy way for teachers to conduct a formative assessment in class is to briefly quiz students on the material covered. Indeed, whether it is to be done for a grade or not, it is generally useful to recapitulate the previous day's lesson at the beginning of class. Oftentimes, this can be best accomplished by allowing students to articulate the material, and to critique one another's understanding. Some probing questions from the teacher can ensure that the recent material is understood in the context of the material that has already been learned. It is not always necessary to formally grade students on their participation or performance in an informal question-and-answer session; the main thing is to develop an idea of the students' progress.

NYSTCE Practice Test #1

Questions 1–13 are based on the passage and graph below:

A child's educational atmosphere has a profound effect on his or her future. One of the greatest advantages—or disadvantages—a student may face is undoubtedly the size of his or her class. Ideally, class sizes should allow for a teacher to adequately meet the learning needs of each student, with time for answering questions and making sure everyone is on the same page. But in today's education crisis, more and more students are being squeezed into classrooms, stretching teachers to educate a large number of children with a wide variety of learning abilities, aptitudes, and educational needs, not to mention a variety of backgrounds that affect their learning.

A study done on early elementary students found that those in smaller classes scored significantly better on reading than those in larger classes. When these students graduated from high school, they were also more likely to complete college entrance exams. Significantly, minorities and lower income students in the smaller classes were particularly more likely to take steps toward a college education. Clearly class size had an impact.

While adding new technology or upgrading to state-of-the-art facilities can benefit students, very few of these improvements have the same long-term effect as giving students more teacher time and attention. Lowering the student-to-teacher ratio is crucial to improving education.

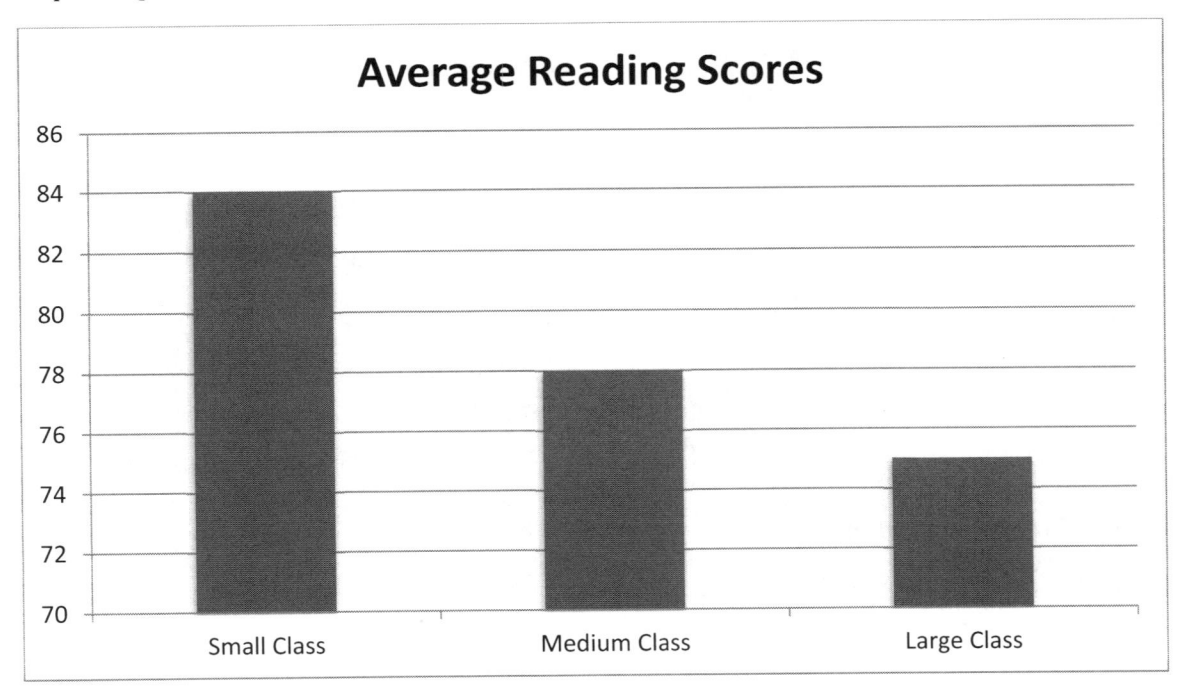

Average Reading Scores

Class Size	Average Reading Score
Small Class	84
Medium Class	78
Large Class	75

1. What is the meaning of the word "profound" in the first sentence?
  a. Wise
  b. Immense
  c. Challenging
  d. Confusing

2. **Which of the following best represents the main idea of this passage?**
   a. "A child's educational atmosphere has a profound effect on his or her future."
   b. "One of the greatest advantages…is undoubtedly the size of his or her class."
   c. "A study done on early elementary students found that those in smaller classes scored significantly better…"
   d. "While adding…long-term effect as giving students more teacher time and attention."

3. **Where in this passage is the topic sentence?**
   a. The first sentence of the passage
   b. The second sentence in the passage
   c. The third sentence of the passage
   d. The fifth sentence of the passage

4. **What is the meaning of the word "aptitudes" in the fourth sentence?**
   a. Classes
   b. Interests
   c. Abilities
   d. Needs

5. **From the passage, one can infer that _____.**
   a. Lowering class sizes is an effective way to improve student learning.
   b. Adding new technology to the classroom can significantly improve test scores.
   c. Class size has little effect on graduation rates.
   d. Students in smaller classes are more likely to obtain postgraduate degrees.

6. **What is the tone of this passage?**
   a. Informative
   b. Persuasive
   c. Entertaining
   d. Warning

7. **Of the following, which best restates the main idea of this passage?**
   a. Smaller class sizes promote better learning.
   b. Students from small classes are more likely to attend college.
   c. Children have differing needs and so they need individualized education.
   d. Teachers cannot effectively manage large classes.

8. **Which paragraph of the passage gives examples of how lowering class size affects students?**
   a. This information is not included in the passage.
   b. This information is stated in the first paragraph.
   c. This information is given in the second paragraph.
   d. This information is stated in the third paragraph.

9. **Which of the following is not an effect of smaller class sizes, according to the passage?**
   a. higher percentage of students taking college entrance exams
   b. higher percentage of students graduating from high school
   c. higher percentage of minorities seeking college education
   d. higher reading scores

10. This passage identifies which of the following as beneficial to students?
   a. Low student-to-teacher ratio
   b. New technology
   c. State-of-the-art facilities
   d. All of the above

11. According to the passage, which of the following test scores were higher in the smaller classes?
   a. All-around academics
   b. Mathematics
   c. Reading
   d. Reading and mathematics

12. According to the chart, what was the average reading score of students in the medium-sized class?
   a. 75
   b. 78
   c. 84
   d. This information cannot be determined from the chart.

13. According to the chart, students in the small class outscored students in the large class by how many points, on average?
   a. 6
   b. 9
   c. 12
   d. This information cannot be determined from the chart.

14. Which of the following is a sentence fragment rather than a complete sentence?
   a. That's nice.
   b. You must try.
   c. One of these people.
   d. Everybody has problems.

15. Which of the following choices correctly completes this sentence? "____ are many people who share ____ opinion."
   a. Their; there
   b. Their; their
   c. There; their
   d. There; there

16. Which of the following sentences uses every word correctly for the intended meaning?
   a. "She was deeply affected by the music."
   b. "The music had a profound affect upon the child."
   c. "Their goal is to affect change in smooth transitions."
   d. "Punishment did not seem to effect him one bit."

17. For the following sentence, which version accurately places all the words?
   a. "Wear will you ware the designer wheres you bought?"
   b. "Where will you wear the designer wares you bought?"
   c. "Ware will you where the designer wears you bought?"
   d. "Were will you weir the designer wheres you bought?"

18. What is a characteristic of a fact as opposed to an opinion?
   a. It can vary among sources.
   b. It has been or can be proven.
   c. It communicates emotions.
   d. It communicates a thought.

19. Which of the following sentences has an error in subject-verb agreement?
   a. Diligence and patience is required for this job.
   b. Hannah and her sisters were all at the dinner.
   c. Every one of the students has to take the test.
   d. A group of people was waiting at the building.

20. Of these, which choice demonstrates standard subject-verb agreement?
   a. They wondered where you was.
   b. My friends and I am going there.
   c. I go today and she go tomorrow.
   d. He has gone, but they have not.

21. Which of these choices includes an example of the present perfect verb tense?
   a. By the time we got there, they had already left.
   b. I have often wondered what happened to them.
   c. Even as we speak, they are still working on that.
   d. After they left, we noticed how early it still was.

22. Among the following, which sentence includes a verb in the future tense?
   a. If you do it alone, you will not have finished it by tomorrow.
   b. If you need help, we will be glad to help you with that work.
   c. If you had needed help then, you could have asked us then.
   d. If you need help with it right now, we are still glad to assist.

Questions 23–27 are based on the passage below:

A teacher has an immense set of responsibilities to juggle, but also has access to a number of resources. Multiple people or organizations are available to aid teachers in their work or to augment the educational experiences of the students. One of these resources is the Library Media Center (LMC), which serves both to provide a broader education for students and to share the teaching tasks of the teacher.

The Library Media Center serves to educate students on multiple topics: research, technology, information literacy, and many others. Students are able to obtain hands-on experience in discovering information and learning how to find what they need. The librarian and other library staff guide the students during their time in the LMC, giving the teacher time to focus on other needs such as planning.

The instruction given in the LMC not only offers an extra learning opportunity, but also carries back to the classroom. Teachers can use the resources and instruction that the LMC offers to enrich their lessons, link various subjects together, and engage students more deeply in learning. The school library is more than merely a place to read books; it sparks learning.

23. Where in this passage is the main idea stated?
   a. The first sentence
   b. The second sentence
   c. The third sentence
   d. The entire first paragraph

24. Which of these choices is the best example of a topic sentence in this passage?
   a. The first sentence in the first paragraph
   b. The second sentence in the first paragraph
   c. The first sentence in the second paragraph
   d. The second sentence in the second paragraph

25. Which of the following is a synonym for the word "juggle" in the first sentence?
   a. Succeed
   b. Balance
   c. Waver
   d. Toss

26. What is the meaning of the word "augment" in the second sentence?
   a. Increase
   b. Correct
   c. Change
   d. Color

27. Which of the following most accurately restates the main idea of the passage?
   a. Teachers cannot carry the teaching burden alone, so library staff help them.
   b. There are many resources available for teachers if they know where to look.
   c. Libraries serve to educate students in many ways as well as assisting teachers in their jobs.
   d. A library is more than just a place to find books.

Answer the following three questions based on the graphic below.

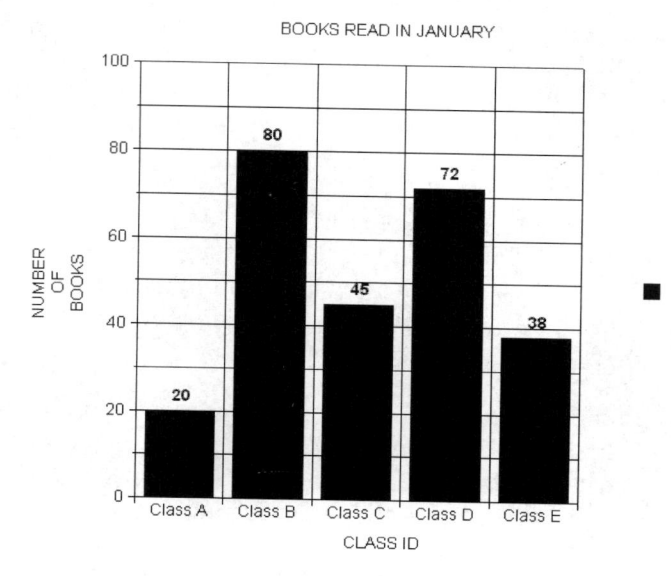

BOOKS READ IN JANUARY

Class	Number of Books
Class A	20
Class B	80
Class C	45
Class D	72
Class E	38

28. Which class read the most books in the month of January?
   a. Class A
   b. Class B
   c. Class D
   d. Class E

29. What is the relationship between Classes A and B in terms of how many books each class read?
   a. Class B read four times as many books as Class A.
   b. Class A read four times as many books as Class B.
   c. Class B read twice as many books as Class A.
   d. Class A read twice as many books as Class B.

30. What is the total number of books read by all five classes during January?
   a. 145
   b. 110
   c. 255
   d. 155

31. Of the following, which type of graphic can be used equally well to show change in values over time, and also to compare values occurring at the same time?
   a. Bar graph
   b. Line graph
   c. Pie chart
   d. Table

32. **If you wanted to depict visually how much of its budget the government spends on different departments, e.g., military, health and human services, etc., which graphic would be most useful?**
    a. Tabular form
    b. A line graph
    c. A bar graph
    d. A pie chart

33. **Of the following verbs, which is regular with respect to endings for all tenses?**
    a. To be
    b. To go
    c. To run
    d. To walk

34. **Which of these verbs is not correctly conjugated in terms of present, past, and perfect tense endings?**
    a. Write, wrote, written
    b. Swim, swam, swum
    c. Do, did, done
    d. Run, ran, ran

35. **In the sentence, "It's only me," what is true about the use of the pronoun "me"?**
    a. It may be tolerated in casual speech, but not in formal writing.
    b. It is considered acceptable in both spoken and written English.
    c. It is technically correct because the pronoun is an object pronoun.
    d. It is technically correct because the pronoun is a subject pronoun.

36. **Which of the following versions of this sentence is correct?**
    a. Its time for the snake to shed it's skin.
    b. It's time for the snake to shed it's skin.
    c. It's time for the snake to shed its skin.
    d. Its time for the snake to shed its skin.

37. **Fill in the blank in this sentence with the correct choice:**
    "Jacqueline, ____ loves picnics, has suggested that we all eat outside."
    a. whom
    b. which
    c. who
    d. that

38. **Which of the following is an example of correct demonstrative pronoun use?**
    a. This was a great meal last week.
    b. That is beautiful weather today.
    c. These over there are the nicest.
    d. Those are the ones that I want.

39. Among the following sentences, which one uses the correct modifier?
   a. When Todd and Jimmy race, Todd is the best runner.
   b. Out of all the candidates, she was the better choice.
   c. In math class, Sue is a better student than Jeffrey is.
   d. He scored highest on the first of the two tests given.

40. Which choice correctly fills in the blank in this sentence?
   The runt of the litter is the _____ of the four puppies.
   a. Small
   b. Smaller
   c. Smallish
   d. Smallest

41. Of these choices, which one is a complete sentence and not a fragment?
   a. "Coming soon to a location near you."
   b. "The best and brightest in our nation."
   c. "Leave them alone."
   d. "Everybody who registers to compete."

42. In the following, what choice is an example of a run-on sentence?
   a. I know what you mean I have had the exact same experience.
   b. Time flies when we are busy, and we are busy all of the time.
   c. They live on a mountaintop; they can see the city from there.
   d. Jim watched the football game, but Jerry was not interested.

43. Among these, which one shows correct sentence division?
   a. While the Japanese bow the Americans shake hands.
   b. The children played while the grandparents watched.
   c. His car could not be fixed he had to buy another one.
   d. We write in English words they write computer code.

44. Which of these sentences is punctuated correctly?
   a. Run and play now children.
   b. Marietta has her hands full: she has ten children.
   c. You may not like it, however, that is the way it is.
   d. We got along well; and we became good friends.

45. Of the following sentences, which has correct punctuation?
   a. We are, by the way, quite concerned.
   b. She is, for your information an expert.
   c. They did on the other hand, plan first.
   d. Why, you are the first, to mention this.

46. Among these choices, which sentence(s) are accurately punctuated?
   a. Many people believe this is true. But, the facts show it is a myth.
   b. Many people believe this is true; but, the facts show it is a myth.
   c. Many people believe this is true, but the facts show it is a myth.
   d. Many people believe this is true but the facts show it is a myth.

47. The punctuation is correct in which of the following sentence versions?
    a. "Wow! How great to see you! where have you been?"
    b. "Wow! how great to see you! where have you been?"
    c. "Wow! how great to see you! Where have you been?"
    d. "Wow! How great to see you! Where have you been?"

48. Which of these versions of the sentence capitalizes all words correctly?
    a. She hoped to practice her japanese in Tokyo, though many citizens wanted to practice their english.
    b. She hoped to practice her Japanese in Tokyo, though many citizens wanted to practice their English.
    c. She hoped to practice her Japanese in tokyo, though many citizens wanted to practice their English.
    d. She hoped to practice her japanese in tokyo, though many citizens wanted to practice their english.

49. In which of the following choices do all words have proper capitalization?
    a. The queen of England is Her Majesty Queen Elizabeth II.
    b. The Queen of England is her majesty queen Elizabeth II.
    c. The Queen of England is her Majesty Queen Elizabeth II.
    d. The queen of england is her majesty queen Elizabeth II.

50. In the context of each of these sentences, which commonly shared word is correctly spelled?
    a. The police officer was sighted for improper conduct.
    b. The police officer was sighted pursuing the suspects.
    c. The police officer sighted the motorist for a violation.
    d. The police officer sighted several instances for proof.

51. Which version spells all words correctly in the context of the sentence?
    a. I new you meant slightly used when you said knew.
    b. I knew you meant slightly used when saying knew.
    c. I new you meant slightly used when you said new.
    d. I knew you meant slightly used when you said new.

52. Of the following, which sentence version spells every word correctly for the context?
    a. If it hurt your feelings, I didn't mean to. I know how you feel to.
    b. If it hurt your feelings, I didn't mean too. I know how you feel to.
    c. If it hurt your feelings, I didn't mean to. I know how you feel too.
    d. If it hurt your feelings, I didn't mean too. I know how you feel too.

53. Which of these choices applies a capitalization rule correctly?
    a. The Golden Gate Bridge
    b. The Golden Gate bridge
    c. The Golden gate Bridge
    d. The golden gate bridge

54. What version of this sentence correctly spells every word?
    a. We didn't no there were know lifeguards on duty.
    b. We didn't know there were know lifeguards then.
    c. We didn't know there were no lifeguards on duty.
    d. We didn't no there were no lifeguards there then.

55. What is the value of the underlined digit in 8,706?
    a. 70
    b. 700
    c. 7
    d. 7000

56. In which place value is the digit 2 in 9,452.8?
    a. Ones
    b. Hundreds
    c. Tens
    d. Tenths

57. What is 788 rounded to the nearest ten?
    a. 789
    b. 800
    c. 790
    d. 780

58. What is 3,895,399 rounded to the nearest thousand?
    a. 3,896,000
    b. 5,000
    c. 3,895,000
    d. 3,895,400

59. How many meters are equivalent to 7,200 cm?
    a. 720,000
    b. 72
    c. 720
    d. 7.2

60. A homeowner is ordering fencing material to place a fence around her property. The lot is rectangular with a length of 385 feet, and the width is 295 feet. Which of the following is the best estimate of the minimum amount of fencing material she should order?
    a. 1600 feet
    b. 700 feet
    c. 1400 feet
    d. 1200 feet

61. Ms. Robinson has a busy afternoon delivering gifts to family members. First, she drives 5.1 miles to her mother's house. Then she drives 7.2 miles to her aunt's house followed to 13.9 miles to her brother's house. Finally drives 14.6 miles on the return trip home. What is the best estimate of the total miles Ms. Robinson drives on her trip?

   a. 29 miles
   b. 41 miles
   c. 39 miles
   d. 42 miles

62. The ticket sales for Monday through Friday of a school fundraiser are 120, 240, 81, 29, and 350. What was the total number of tickets sold?

   a. 720
   b. 810
   c. 820
   d. 819

63. Chen is planning a trip from San Francisco to Los Angeles that has a distance of 262 miles. If he stops off at his grandparents, it will add an additional 49 miles to his trip. How long is Chen's trip if he visits his grandparents?

   a. 213 miles
   b. 311 miles
   c. 310 miles
   d. 360 miles

64. Fifty-three pies are donated for the sports fundraiser. If 17 pies are sold the first day, how many pies remain?

   a. 47
   b. 37
   c. 46
   d. 36

65. What is the difference between 73,752 and 63,721?

   a. 10,031
   b. 10,131
   c. 10,020
   d. 10,021

66. Felicia's new job requires extensive travel. If she is required to be out of town on business for 157 of 365 days this year, how many days is Felicia in town?

   a. 208
   b. 209
   c. 218
   d. 532

67. The music club is selling raffle tickets as a fundraiser. Two students each sold 75 tickets on Monday. Three students each sold 45 tickets on Tuesday. And one student sold 95 tickets on Wednesday. How many tickets were sold in all?
   a. 305
   b. 335
   c. 215
   d. 380

68. What is 1200×1200?
   a. 1,440,000
   b. 14,400,000
   c. 144,000
   d. 14,400

69. A local theater group rents an auditorium with 25 rows of 40 seats each. How many seats does the auditorium contain?
   a. 1,000
   b. 800
   c. 900
   d. 1200

70. What is the remainder when 150 is divided by 11?
   a. 1
   b. 3
   c. 5
   d. 7

71. An employer is dividing a $5000 bonus evenly between 20 employees. What is the amount each employee receives?
   a. $200
   b. $500
   c. $250
   d. $150

72. Ethan finances a car for $32,460. He is paying for the car in 60 equal monthly payments. How much is his car payment each month?
   a. $431
   b. $441
   c. $531
   d. $541

73. If Mr. Jackson drives at 55 mph for 3 hours, how far does he drive?
   a. 175 miles
   b. 145 miles
   c. 155 miles
   d. 165 miles

74. Marshall buys $12\frac{1}{4}$ yards of material for a backdrop for the school play. If he only uses $8\frac{2}{3}$ yards, how much of the material remains?

   a. $3\frac{1}{2}$
   b. $3\frac{7}{12}$
   c. $4\frac{1}{12}$
   d. $3\frac{5}{12}$

75. What is the sum of $\frac{1}{2} + \frac{1}{3} + \frac{1}{4}$?

   a. $1\frac{1}{12}$
   b. 1
   c. $1\frac{1}{6}$
   d. $1\frac{1}{4}$

76. Mr. Nelson stocks shelves for a big box store. On Thursday night he stocks 505 jars of tomato sauce that weighed 1.09 pounds each. What is the total weight of tomato sauce that Mr. Nelson stocked?

   a. 550.45 pounds
   b. 50.50 pounds
   c. 545.95 pounds
   d. 540.45 pounds

77. Mr. Screen drove 412.5 miles in his new car on only 12.5 gallons of gasoline. How many miles per gallon did his new car get?

   a. 31 mpg
   b. 33 mpg
   c. 35 mpg
   d. 37 mpg

78. Ms. Snead's classroom contains 24 students. If 8 of the students have pets, approximately what percent of the students have pets?

   a. 0.16%
   b. 16%
   c. 0.33%
   d. 33%

79. Marcie finished 25% of her math problems on the bus. If Marcie finished 8 problems, how many homework problems did she have?

   a. 24
   b. 48
   c. 16
   d. 32

80. If 60% of Ms. Feece's students prefer apple slices to carrot sticks, what fraction of her students prefer apple slices?
   a. $\frac{2}{3}$
   b. $\frac{3}{5}$
   c. $\frac{2}{5}$
   d. $\frac{5}{8}$

81. What is 0.0037 written as a percent?
   a. 3.7%
   b. 0.037%
   c. 37%
   d. 0.37%

82. For a student with a haptic learning style, which reading-related activity is most applicable?
   a. Writing a paper about a literary work the student read
   b. Sculpting a model of a character or author in literature
   c. Listening to a recording of the literary work read aloud
   d. Choreographing and performing a dance about a work

83. Which of these instructional activities is most related to activating student background knowledge?
   a. Assigning students to write about something in their lives similar to what they read
   b. Assigning students to look for examples in real life of things they are reading about
   c. Assigning students to drill repeatedly as practice to learn reading vocabulary words
   d. Assigning students to watch a movie adapted from their required reading material

84. If a student wants to find comprehensive background information about a reading topic, which instructional resource is most useful?
   a. Glossary
   b. Thesaurus
   c. Dictionary
   d. Encyclopedia

85. When can students best summarize some text they have been assigned or have chosen to read?
   a. While they skim the text for the first time
   b. Before they skim the text for the first time
   c. During their first-time reading of that text
   d. After they have read that text thoroughly

86. In the Question-Answer Relationship (QAR) reading comprehension strategy, which type of question is it if the teacher asks students, "How would you feel if what happened in this story happened to you?"
   a. "Right There"
   b. "On Your Own"
   c. "Author and You"
   d. "Think and Search"

87. When monitoring student reading progress, which teacher activity is most related to lesson planning?
    a. Reteaching specific skills in which students are shown most deficient
    b. Allowing more time to teach skills where students are least proficient
    c. Eliminating skills all students have fully mastered from the next exam
    d. Designing quizzes to reflect instructional proportions in various areas

88. A teacher collects information on student progress in reading through formative assessment to inform her planning and instruction. Which resulting teacher action most involves instruction?
    a. The teacher writes a new lesson using different strategies.
    b. The teacher revises the calendar to address critical needs.
    c. The teacher adjusts the pace to fit students' learning rates.
    d. The teacher writes shorter quizzes to give more frequently.

89. When teachers instruct students in writing, which of the following is most appropriate?
    a. Students should draft before editing and proofreading it.
    b. Students should draft and edit their writing concurrently.
    c. Students should proofread their writing while they edit it.
    d. Students should do all three at once, as a holistic process.

90. Teachers must help students focus their writing to make it effective. Among the following related necessary features, which one is most critical of all to focus in writing?
    a. Topic
    b. Purpose
    c. Main idea
    d. Organization

91. Among the following factors, which is most related to focused writing?
    a. Perfect grammar and spelling
    b. Evocative choices of words
    c. Smooth sentence connections
    d. A significant unifying perspective

92. A middle school English teacher has assigned her class to cooperative learning groups for a writing exercise wherein each student edits his/her first draft of a short story. The teacher asks her teaching assistant to supervise one small group. Which feedback that the assistant can give the teacher would be most useful?
    a. The quality of student collaborations
    b. The students who seem to write best
    c. The things students needed help with
    d. The story she found the most creative

93. A student learning to vary his writing has demonstrated skill in varying sentence length. Now he is trying to vary sentence types, but he is unsure whether he is producing complete sentences or not. Which type of resource would help him with this most?
    a. Dictionaries, online and/or in hardcopies
    b. Online and/or hardcopy grammar books
    c. Word processor program grammar check
    d. Imitating sentences by authors of classics

94. Within technology that supports student writing, which characteristic related to word processing software programs is often lacking in public schools today?
    a. Portable hardware
    b. Bundled software
    c. Facilitated revision
    d. Typing vs. writing

95. If a teacher wants to conduct formative assessment of student progress in writing skills to inform lesson planning, upcoming testing, and ongoing instruction, which format would likely give the best information?
    a. Pop quiz
    b. Oral test
    c. Formal exam
    d. Writing sample

96. Monitoring student writing progress informs the teacher's planning, assessment, and instruction. Of these teacher decisions that student data will inform, which is most related to assessment?
    a. How much time to spend with each writing skill
    b. How frequently to gather progress information
    c. How to identify strategies for each writing skill
    d. How to group students for working on writing

97. Which of the following statements is most accurate about problem-solving as it relates to K–4 math instruction?
    a. It is a discrete topic and a component of the math program.
    b. It is a goal far less important than others in math instruction.
    c. It is a process that should pervade the whole math program.
    d. It is a set of math concepts and skills that students can learn.

98. In an elementary school class, the majority of students understand the concept of multiplication after several days of instruction. However, three students are having difficulty. The teacher asks his teaching assistant to help them. Which action by the assistant will most assist these students in grasping the concept?
    a. Have them add several sets of three pennies to a pile one set at a time.
    b. Give them calculators and show them how to use them for multiplying.
    c. Have them reread the textbook chapter and then ask her any questions.
    d. Give them worksheets with a few simple multiplication problems to do.

99. Mickey, a high school student, just started his first after-school part-time job. His classmate Alonzo started a part-time job last summer and has continued it since school started. Mickey wants to know if he receives the hourly wages promised for all the hours he works. Alonzo wants to know the cumulative results of small raises he has received quarterly over the past nine months. Which resources or procedures can each of them use?
   a. Both students should use graphic organizers to get answers
   b. Mickey can add and subtract; Alonzo can multiply and divide
   c. Each student should use real money he can count, add, etc.
   d. Multiplication and division for Mickey; Alonzo can make a graph

100. Mr. Kirk, a new teacher at a public high school, has been teaching a trigonometry course when he discovers a number of students know how to look up numbers in a table, plot these values as points, and connect them to make a graph, but they have no idea what a sine or function is. He decides to consult his mentor about how to explain these concepts, and then add some lessons to help students understand them. Student information has informed Mr. Kirk most in which areas?
   a. Planning and instruction
   b. Planning, teaching, testing
   c. Instruction and assessment
   d. Planning and assessment

Answer Key and Explanations for Test #1

1. B: *Profound* means "great or intense." While the word can be used to describe wisdom or challenges, it does not actually mean "wise" (a) or "challenging" (c). "Confusing" (d) is a synonym for "confound," not "profound."

2. B: This sentence best expresses the main idea; option (a) provides additional information supporting it; option (c) elaborates on it; and option (d) elaborates on the opening sentence of the second paragraph, which can also be considered the topic sentence of the second paragraph.

3. B: Topic sentences are often, but not always, the first sentences. In this case, the first sentence (a) introduces the subject but the second sentence is actually the topic sentence. The third sentence (c) supports the topic sentence by adding some information. The fifth sentence (d) is more appropriately the second paragraph's topic sentence rather than the topic sentence of the whole passage.

4. C: An *aptitude* is "a natural ability to do something." This is somewhat similar to interests (b) but refers more to a student's actual talent or skill rather than what he or she enjoys. It does not refer to a student's classes (a) or needs (d).

5. A: The passage implies that small class sizes may be responsible for improved test scores, and thus improved learning. New technology (b) is mentioned as a potential benefit, but the passage does not specify what kind of benefit. The passage does not mention graduation rates (c), though it refers to students who do graduate. The passage discusses impact on college education, but makes no mention of postgraduate work (d).

6. B: The last sentence of the passage gives an action statement, preceded by arguments to support it. Thus, this is a persuasive passage, trying to convince the reader of something. While it contains information, the tone is not merely informative (a). It is meant to persuade, not entertain (c) or warn (d).

7. A: This is the best restatement of the main idea. Option (b) makes an assumption that is not fully backed up by the passage, option (c) states a supporting piece of information on the topic, and option (d) makes another assumption not supported by the passage.

8. C: The second paragraph describes the study on class sizes, detailing how they can affect test scores and college entrance.

9. B: The passage mentions that students who graduate high school are more likely to pursue college, but does not discuss high school graduation rates.

10. D: The passage mentions all three as beneficial to students, although the low student-to-teacher ratio is supposed to be most beneficial.

11. C: The second paragraph mentions that students in smaller classes scored higher on reading. The passage does not mention all-around academics (a) or mathematics (b, d).

12. B: The chart shows that the average reading scores were 84 for the small class (c), 78 for the medium class (b), and 75 for the large class (a).

13. B: Students in the small class had an average reading score of 84, while students in the large class averaged 75. This is a difference of 9.

14. C: Sentence completeness is not determined by sentence length: option (a) is a complete sentence as it has a subject ("That") and verb ("is") in the contraction "That's." Sentence (b) is also complete, with a subject, auxiliary verb, and verb. Sentence (d) has a subject, verb, and object and is complete. However, option (c) is a sentence fragment because it has no verb—only a subject noun, preposition, demonstrative adjective, and object noun.

15. C: "There," in addition to being a preposition indicating place, is used as a pronoun in existential clauses like this one to indicate something's existence. "Their" is the possessive case of the third person plural pronoun "they." Hence option (a) reverses the correct choice, and options (b) and (d) incorrectly use the same word for both meanings and parts of speech.

16. A: As a noun, an effect is a result: choice (b) should be "a profound effect." As a verb, effect means to accomplish, bring about, or produce: choice (c) should be "to effect smooth transitions." As a verb, affect means to influence or change: choice (d) should be "to affect him" and choice (a) correctly uses the verb form.

17. B: "Where" is an adverb indicating place, "wear" is a verb meaning "to dress in or have on something" (e.g., clothing, a smile or frown, etc.), and "wares" is a plural noun meaning "products for sale." "Were" (d) is the third-person plural, or second-person singular and plural, past tense of the verb "to be." A "weir" (d) is a noun meaning "a small dam, fence, or net in a stream or river," and does not belong anywhere in this sentence. Choices (a), (c), and (d) place all of these words incorrectly.

18. B: To help students distinguish facts from opinions, teachers can explain that opinions can vary from one source or individual to another, and even within one source or individual (a); and that opinions communicate emotions (c) and/or thoughts (d), whereas facts have been or can be proven (b) and are invariably true.

19. A: Two or more subjects joined by "and" (i.e., "Diligence and patience" here) require a plural verb, so the verb in this sentence should be "are," not "is." For the same reason, choice (b) correctly uses the plural "were." However, the subject of choice (c) is "one," not "students," so the auxiliary verb is correctly "has," not "have." The subject of choice (d) is "group," a mass noun, not "people," a count noun, so the auxiliary verb "was" is correct, not "were."

20. D: The third person singular "He" takes "has," and the third person plural takes "have." In option (a), the second person "you" takes "were" (past tense) or "are" (present tense) whether singular or plural, so "was" is incorrect. In option (b), two subjects connected by "and" take plural "are," not singular "am." In option (c), first person singular "I" does take "go," but third person singular "she" needs the form "goes." The -s ending is only added to verbs with third person singular subjects, not first or second person.

21. B: In choice (a), "had… left" is an example of the past perfect verb tense. In choice (b), "have… wondered" is an example of the present perfect verb tense. In choice (c), "are… working" is an example of the present progressive (or continuous) verb tense. In choice (d), "left," "noticed," and "was" are all examples of verbs in the past tense.

22. B: In this sentence, "need" is in the present tense, and "will be" is in the future tense. In option (a), "do" is in the present tense, and "will [not] have finished" is in the future perfect tense. In option (c), "had needed" and "could have asked" are in the past perfect tense. In option (d), "need" and "are" are both in the present tense.

23. C: The main idea can be found in the third sentence of the first paragraph. The first two sentences bring up the subject of helping teachers and giving students an improved educational experience, but the Library Media Center is not mentioned until the third sentence.

24. C: The first sentence of the second paragraph is the best example of a topic sentence as it states the main topic of the paragraph. The first two sentences of the first paragraph (a, b) provide some background for the subject but do not mention the topic. The second sentence in the second paragraph (d) gives details that support that paragraph's topic sentence.

25. B: The word *juggle* here refers to the teacher's need to balance many different responsibilities. While the teacher undoubtedly hopes to succeed, that is not the meaning of the word here. A juggler may waver (c) as he or she tosses (d) balls, but the literal meaning of juggling does not apply here.

26. A: To *augment* something is to increase it or make it greater. While the library may correct some misinformation (a) or change a student's education (c), these are not the meaning of *augment*. "Color" (d) is *pigment*, not *augment*.

27. C: This is the best restatement of the main idea. Choices (a) and (b) restate information from the first two sentences, but the main idea is found in the third sentence. Choice (d) restates a detail from the final paragraph.

28. B: The graph shows that Class B read 80 books in January. This is more than any of the other classes, whose totals were 20, 45, 32, and 78 respectively. Hence Class A (a), Class D (c), and Class E (d) are all incorrect as none of these classes read as many books in January as Class B did.

29. A: Class A read 20 books and Class B read 80 books. Because 80 = 4 × 20, Class B read four times as many books as Class A did, not vice versa (b). For option (c) to be correct, either Class B would have read 40 books instead of 80, or Class A would have read 40 books instead of 20. For option (d) to be correct, either Class A would have read 160 books while Class B remained at 80, or Class B would have read 10 books while Class A remained at 20.

30. C: To get the total, use addition: 80 + 20 + 45 + 72 + 38 = 255. Choice (a) is the sum of books read by Classes A, B, and C, omitting the numbers of books read by Classes D and E. Choice (b) is the sum of books read by Classes D and E, omitting the numbers of books read by Classes A, B, and C. Choice (d) is the sum of books read by Classes C, D, and E, omitting the numbers of books read by Classes A and B.

31. A: A bar graph shows change over time when each bar represents a value from a different time. It also compares concurrent values when each bar represents the same variable's value for different people, places, or things—e.g., the amount of rainfall during the same year in different countries. Line graphs (b) show change over time by identifying values at different times, not multiple values at once because the line connects separate points in time. A pie chart (c) shows proportions or parts of a whole. A table (d) typically lists data without images showing differences over time or comparing values.

32. D: A pie chart, also called a circle graph, divides a round "pie" into wedge-shaped segments whose sizes represent percentages or proportions of the whole. This makes it easy to visualize and compare how a total amount is distributed among parts. Tables (a) are better for viewing numbers or words directly; line graphs (b) are better for showing differences by time, place, frequency, or another variable; and bar graphs can be used like line graphs, or to show differences among variables occurring simultaneously.

33. D: The verb "to walk" is regular, i.e., it is conjugated with regular endings: walk, walks, walking, walked. "To be" (a) is irregular: am, is, are, were. "To go" (b) is also irregular, with past tense being "went" rather than "goed" (which is not a word). "To run" is irregular, with run in present tense and ran in past, but "have run" and "had run" (not ran) in present perfect and past perfect tenses.

34. D: The verb "to run" is "run" in present tense ("I run every day"), "ran" in past tense ("She ran home") and "have/has/had run" in perfect tense ("He had run to the mailbox"). The other choices are all irregular verbs, conjugated correctly here.

35. A: Many English grammar experts tolerate the common but incorrect use of "me," "him," "her," "them," and similar object pronouns instead of subject pronouns. A subject pronoun can be the sentence subject (e.g., "I am here"), or rename the subject (e.g., "It is only I"). Object pronouns are objects (e.g., "Dogs like me"). In formal writing, "I" is correct here, not "me." Thus choice (b) is incorrect. Because "me" is an object pronoun but is technically incorrect, choice (c) is wrong. Because "me" is incorrect and is not a subject pronoun, choice (d) is wrong.

36. C: The possessive case of the pronoun "it" is correctly spelled "its" without an apostrophe, just as the possessive form of "him" is "his" with no apostrophe. "It's" is a contraction of the pronoun "it" and the verb "is," used correctly in options (b) and (c). Option (a) uses both incorrectly by omitting the apostrophe from the contraction and adding it to the possessive. Although option (d) uses the possessive correctly, it uses the contraction incorrectly by omitting the apostrophe.

37. C: The pronoun "who" refers to a person as the sentence or phrase subject (Jacqueline in this case). The pronoun "whom" (a) refers to a person as a sentence or phrase object (e.g., "Whom did you choose?"). The pronouns "which" (b) and "that" (d) refer to a thing rather than to a person.

38. D: Demonstrative pronouns can stand alone to replace nouns. (When modifying nouns, they are demonstrative adjectives, e.g., "This meal was great"). "Those" is plural and refers correctly to "the ones." However, "This" (a) should be "That" as it refers to a meal last week; conversely, "That" (b) should be "This" as it refers to weather today. "These" (c) should be "Those" as it refers to things "over there." "These" would refer to things right here.

39. C: Comparative modifiers show a difference between two things (or places or people)—Sue and Jeffrey in this case. Superlative modifiers show differences between more than two. Therefore, choice (a) should use "better," not "best," as only two people are compared; choice (b) should use "best," not "better," as she was the choice "Out of all the candidates"; and choice (d) should use "higher," not "highest," as only two test scores are compared.

40. D: Grammatically, these adjectives follow a logical progression showing increasing degrees of the attribute: the original is small (a); the comparative, indicating more small, is smaller and is used to compare two things (b); and the superlative, indicating most small, is smallest (d). Smallish (c) is also an adjective based on small, but not comparative or superlative; rather, it indicates approximation, i.e., sort of small or somewhat small.

41. C: This is a complete sentence with an implied subject (you), verb, and object. Choice (a) is a sentence fragment with a verb, adverb, preposition, article, object, and preposition, but no subject. Choice (b) is a fragment with subjects and a prepositional phrase, but no verb. Choice (d) is a fragment as it has a subject modified by a dependent clause containing a verb, but the subject has no accompanying verb to create the necessary independent clause.

42. A: This is a run-on sentence because it contains two independent clauses, but no connection or division. To be correct, these can be divided into two sentences by a period; remain one sentence divided by a semicolon; or be joined by a comma and a coordinating conjunction, e.g., "because," "since," or "as." Choice (b) correctly divides two independent clauses with a comma plus coordinating conjunction "and." Choice (c) correctly divides two independent clauses with a semicolon. Choice (d) correctly connects two independent clauses with a comma and coordinating conjunction "but."

43. B: This sentence is correct: "while," as a subordinating conjunction, introduces the subordinate (dependent) clause. However, when the subordinate clause comes first (a), a comma should separate it from the following independent clause. The run-on sentence (c) needs a semicolon to divide it; a comma plus a coordinating conjunction like "so" (or a semicolon plus "therefore," "thus," "hence," etc. plus a comma); or a period, making two sentences. Run-on (d) needs either a period, a semicolon, or a comma plus a conjunction like "and" or "but." (Shorter sentences can omit the comma or conjunction.)

44. B: Sentence (a) omits a comma before "children" to indicate the first part is addressing them. Without the comma, they become the object of the verb "play." Sentence (b) is punctuated correctly: a semicolon separates independent clauses when the second one explains or completes the first. Sentence (c) incorrectly uses a comma before "however" instead of a semicolon. Conversely, sentence (d) incorrectly uses a semicolon before "and" instead of a comma.

45. A: Phrases that interrupt the flow of a sentence ("by the way" in this case) should be set off by commas. Sentence (b) has the first comma, but omits the second to set off "for your information." Sentence (c) has the second comma, but omits the first to set off "on the other hand." A comma should follow an introductory word like "Why," but there should be no comma after "first" (d).

46. C: When joining two independent clauses within one sentence via a coordinating conjunction like "but," a comma should precede the "but." These two clauses can also be correctly divided into two separate sentences. However, there should not be a comma or any other punctuation following "But" when it begins the second sentence (b). Conversely, omitting punctuation before "but" within the same sentence (d) is incorrect.

47. D: The first letter of the first word in any sentence must always be capitalized, no matter what that word is. This includes the first word of a new sentence within a quotation, as in this example, which contains two separate sentences following the exclamation "Wow!" Choice (a) capitalizes only the first new sentence, choice (b) capitalizes neither new sentence, and choice (c) capitalizes only the second new sentence.

48. B: Proper nouns, e.g., the name of the city Tokyo, always have capitalized initial letters. Not only proper nouns, but also verbs, adjectives, and other parts of speech derived from proper nouns—e.g., "Japanese" and "English"—also always have their first letters capitalized. Option (a) fails to capitalize these language names, option (c) fails to capitalize the city name, and option (d) fails to capitalize all of these.

49. A: Formal titles of people, positions, occupations, etc. that come before or after proper names are capitalized. However, nouns naming positions and/or occupations are not capitalized as their titles are. Therefore, choice (a) is correct. Choice (b) incorrectly capitalizes the noun "queen" at the beginning and fails to capitalize the titles "Her Majesty" and "Queen [Elizabeth II]." Choice (c) incorrectly capitalizes the noun "queen" and fails to capitalize "Her" in the title. Choice (d) fails to capitalize the proper noun "England" and the title words "Her Majesty" and "Queen."

50. B: In this sentence, "sighted" means seen and is spelled correctly. In option (a), the word should be spelled "cited" and means officially summoned to appear in court or issued a citation (ticket). In option (c), it should also be "cited," with the same or similar meaning as option (a). In option (d), it should again be spelled "cited," but in this case it means made reference to as examples, support, confirmation, or proof.

51. D: The spelling "knew" indicates the past tense of the verb "to know"; the spelling "new" indicates the adjective meaning novel, recent, original, not old, etc. These two meanings cannot be spelled alike or interchangeably. Choice (a) misspells both words; choice (b) misspells only "new" as "knew"; and choice (c) misspells only "knew" as new."

52. C: This is a surprisingly common error today. The first instance is the preposition "to," meaning in order, and used as the first word of verb infinitives. The second instance is the adverb "too," meaning excessively, or (as in this case) also. Option (a) misspells the second instance, option (b) misspells both, option (c) is correct, and option (d) misspells the first instance.

53. A: As the name of a landmark structure, this phrase is a proper noun. Not only proper nouns (i.e., names), but also adjectives derived from proper nouns (e.g., "Golden") should have their initial letters capitalized. "Bridge" is part of the whole name and is included in this capitalization rule (b). The same applies to "Gate" (c). Because all three of the name's words should be capitalized, choice (d) is incorrect.

54. C: The first instance, meaning be aware or cognizant of, is spelled "know"; the second instance, meaning not any, is spelled "no." Option (a) reverses these spellings, option (b) misspells the second instance, option (c) spells both correctly, and option (d) misspells the first instance.

55. B: The place value is assigned by the position of the digit. The places to the left of the decimal are ones, tens, hundreds, then thousands, respectively. Since the digit 7 is in the third place to the left of the implied decimal, it's in the hundreds place. The value of this digit is 7×100, which is 700.

56. A: The place value of a digit depends on its location in relation to the decimal point. The places to the left of the decimal are ones, tens, then hundreds, respectively. The places to the right of the decimal are tenths, hundredths, and thousandths, respectively. Since the digit 2 is in the first position to the left of the decimal point, its place value is ones.

57. C: The place value of a digit depends on its location in relation to the decimal point. The places to the left of the decimal are ones, tens, then hundreds, respectively. To round a number to a certain place value, look at the digit to the immediate right. If the digit to the right is 5 or more, round up by adding one. If the digit is less than five, round down by keeping the same digit. For this problem, the digit in the tens place is 8. The digit to its immediate right is 8. Since 8 is greater than 5, round up: 788 rounded to the nearest ten is 790.

58. C: The place value of a digit depends on its location in relation to the decimal point. The places to the left of the decimal are ones, tens, hundreds, then thousands, respectively. To round a number to a certain place value, look at the digit to the immediate right. If the digit to the right is 5 or more, round up by adding one. If the digit is less than five, round down by keeping the same digit. For this problem, the digit in the thousands place is 5. The digit to its immediate right is 3. Since 3 is less than 5, round down: 3,895,399 rounded to the nearest thousand is 3,895,000.

59. B: Since 1 meter equals 100 centimeters, the conversion factor is 100. Since a centimeter is shorter than a meter, we divide by the conversion factor. So, 7,200 centimeters equal $7,200 \div 100$ or 72 meters.

60. C: The length of the fence is equal to the perimeter of the rectangular property. The perimeter of the property is equal to the sum of twice the length and twice the width. The length is approximately 400 feet, and the width is approximately 300 feet, so $2(400) + 2(300) = 1400$ feet.

61. B: A quick estimate of the total miles can be obtained by rounding each leg of the trip to the nearest whole mile and finding the sum: $5 + 7 + 14 + 15 = 41$ miles.

62. C: The total number of tickets sold is equal to the sum of the tickets sold each day. The total is equal to $120 + 240 + 81 + 29 + 350$ or 820 tickets.

63. B: The length of Chen's trip is equal to the sum of the original distance and the additional miles to see his grandparents. Then the total equals $262 + 49$ or 311 miles.

64. D: The amount of pies remaining is equal to the difference between the number of pies donated and the number of pies sold. Then, the amount equals $53 - 17$ or 36 pies.

65. A: This is ordinary subtracting with no borrowing: $73{,}752 - 63{,}721 = 10{,}031$.

66. A: The number of day's Felicia is in town is equal to the difference between the number of days in a year and the number of days she travels. The number of days equals $365 - 157$ or 208 days.

67. D: The number of tickets sold is the sum of the tickets sold by each of the students. This sum is $75 + 75 + 45 + 45 + 45 + 95 = 380$ tickets.

68. A: To multiply numbers ending in zero, first multiply the numbers (ignoring the zeros) and then add the zeros after the last digit of the product. Then $12 \times 12 = 144$ and adding the four zeros yields 1,440,000.

69. A: The number of seats in the auditorium is equal to the product of the number of rows and the number of seats per row. The number of seats equals 25×40 or 1,000 seats.

70. D: Since 11 is not a factor of 150, there is a remainder when 150 is divided by 11. Since $11 \times 13 = 143$, and $150 - 143 = 7$, the remainder is 7.

71. C: The amount received by each employee is equal to the total amount of the bonus divided by the number of employees. The amount each employee receives equals $\$5{,}000 \div 20 = \$250$.

72. D: The amount of Ethan's car payment is equal to the cost of the car divided by the number of payments. The car payment equals $\$32{,}460 \div 60$ or $\$541$.

73. D: The distance travelled is equal to the product of the rate of travel and the time of travel. Since $55 \times 3 = 165$, Mr. Jackson drives 165 miles.

74. B: The amount of material remaining is equal to $12\frac{1}{4} - 8\frac{2}{3}$. First, convert both mixed numbers to improper fractions: $\frac{49}{4} - \frac{26}{3}$. Next convert to a common denominator: $\frac{147}{12} - \frac{104}{12}$. Finally, subtract the numerators and convert back to a mixed number: $\frac{147}{12} - \frac{104}{12} = \frac{43}{12} = 3\frac{7}{12}$.

75. A: To add these fractions, rewrite each fraction as an equivalent fraction over the least common denominator: $\frac{6}{12} + \frac{4}{12} + \frac{3}{12} = \frac{13}{12}$ or $1\frac{1}{12}$.

76. A: The total weight of the tomato sauce Mr. Nelson stocked is equal to the product of the number of jars and the weight of each jar. The total weight equals 505×1.09 or 550.45 pounds.

77. B: The number of miles per gallon is the quotient of the number of miles driven and the number of gallons of gasoline. The number of miles per gallon equals 412.5 ÷ 12.5 or 33 mpg.

78. D: This question is basically asking, "What percent of 24 is 8?" Let n represent *what percent*, and replace the *of* with a multiplication symbol and the *is* with an equal sign. Then we have $n \times 24 = 8$. To solve this equation, divide both sides by 24. Then $n = 8 \div 24 = 0.3333$. This is in decimal form. To convert a decimal to a percent, move the decimal point two places to the right and add the percent symbol. Then the decimal 0.3333 is 33.33%. Rounded to the nearest percent, this is 33%.

79. D: This question is asking, "8 is 25% of what number?" Let n represent *what number*, and replace the *of* with a multiplication sign and the *is* with an equal sign. But first, we need to convert the 25% to a decimal. Remove the percent sign and move the decimal point two places to the left. Then we have $8 = 0.25 \times n$. To solve this equation, divide both sides by 0.25. Then $8 \div 0.25 = n$, so $n = 32$. Marcie had 32 homework problems.

80. B: To covert a percent to a fraction, remove the percent symbol and place the number over one hundred. Then 60% is represented by the fraction $\frac{60}{100}$, which reduces to $\frac{3}{5}$.

81. D: To convert a decimal to a percent, move the decimal point two places to the right and add the percent symbol. Thus 0.0037 equals 0.37%.

82. B: A haptic learning style is one in which the student learns best through tactile contact (e.g., touching, feeling, manipulating, and shaping things using the hands). Writing a paper (a) is most applicable for a student with a verbal learning style, learning best through reading and writing. Listening to a recording (c) is most applicable for a student with an auditory learning style, learning better through hearing than through seeing. Dance (d) is most applicable for a student with a kinesthetic learning style, learning best though physical movement.

83. A: Activating students' previous experiences and knowledge and connecting new learning to these makes reading material more meaningful to them. One way is having students identify similarities between and relate things in their reading and personal lives. Having them seek examples in real life (b) helps students apply reading more than relate it to prior knowledge. Drilling (c) is better for memorizing, e.g., new vocabulary, irregular spellings/verbs, etc., than for activating prior knowledge. Movies (d) make reading matter multisensory, reducing verbal demand, rather than accessing prior experience.

84. D: An encyclopedia offers the most comprehensive information about a variety of academic and other subjects. A glossary (a) is a list that a text includes of vocabulary words or specialized terminology used specifically in that text, with definitions—not a comprehensive information source. A thesaurus (b) provides synonyms and antonyms for words. A dictionary (c) provides spellings, pronunciations, definitions, and usage examples of most words in a language—not limited to text-specific words, and not including other information unrelated to words.

85. D: Students can gain some comprehension of the overall topic of text while skimming it for the first time (a), but cannot summarize while skimming. Before skimming (b), they can get a general idea what text is about by previewing the title, heading(s), table of contents, illustrations, etc., but not summarize actual main ideas. They cannot summarize during first reading (c) as they have not finished it yet. Summarizing is an effective comprehension and retention strategy only after students have thoroughly read the text (d).

86. B: In the QAR strategy, "Right There" (a) questions ask students to find a single correct answer in text. "Author and You" (c) questions ask students to relate text to their existing knowledge. "Think and Search" (d) questions ask students to recall facts directly from text, usually in multiple locations. "On Your Own" (b) questions ask students to respond from their own experience and knowledge rather than the text.

87. B: Using student reading progress information to allow more time for the instruction that students need most is more related to lesson planning than the other choices. Using this information for reteaching (a) is more related to instruction. Using it for eliminating mastered skills from an exam (c) and for designing quizzes in proportion to amounts of instruction (d) are both more related to assessment.

88. C: Writing a new lesson using different strategies (a) that might be more effective most involves planning. Revising the calendar to allow more time for instruction to meet critical student needs (b) also involves planning most. Adjusting the instructional pace to fit student learning rates better (c) involves instruction the most among these choices. Writing shorter quizzes to administer more often (d) to divide new learning into smaller and more manageable amounts most involves assessment.

89. A: The best way to teach students to write is to instruct them first to compose rough drafts, then to edit their drafts. After editing, once they have achieved a final draft, only then should they proofread their work for mechanical and typing or handwriting errors and correct these. Some students with especial writing gifts or talents may be capable of choices (b), (c), or (d), but they are the minority. Most students (and other writers) must learn and apply the process in sequential steps (a).

90. B: Although writers and writing students must focus on a specific topic (a) and/or main idea (c), either or both of these alone are insufficient. They must moreover know why they are writing about these, and what they want their writing to communicate about them—i.e., their purpose for writing (b). Focus interacts reciprocally with organization (d): focus determines structural choices, and good writers make use of suitable organizational choices to reinforce focus. (The same applies to other writing features.)

91. D: As experienced writers and teachers advise, if students determine a perspective from which to write, they can establish a clear focus before starting to make writing unified and coherent, and discover what message they want to communicate. In other words, determining perspective helps them find their purpose for writing. Perfect mechanics (a), effective word choice (b), and smoothly connected sentences (c) demonstrate good technical skills in writing, but are useless if the writing is not focused and unified by some central viewpoint or idea, i.e., the student's reason for writing.

92. C: The writing exercise focused on students editing their own drafts. Though they were assigned to cooperative learning groups, how well they collaborated (a) is not the most useful information for the teacher. Neither is identifying exemplary student writers (b), nor identifying the most creative writing (d). To help the teacher plan ongoing instruction best, her assistant can inform her of what kinds of help she observed the students needed in editing their own writing.

93. B: Dictionaries will help a student with word meanings, spellings, pronunciations, and usage, but not with sentence structure. The grammar check functions in word processing programs (c) are typically unreliable: they frequently detect some errors but not others; try to "correct" already acceptable constructions; and, lacking artificial intelligence, also lack the informed judgment of knowledgeable humans. The greatest authors (e.g., Shakespeare) frequently break grammatical rules with the expertise to do so effectively (d). Grammar books and guides (b) supply rules for writing complete sentences.

94. A: Word processing software presents a great boon to most students in public schools. However, many schools today lack accompanying computer hardware that is portable, durable, and cost-effective. Technology companies have produced and continue developing tablet computers and similar devices as solutions, but most public schools do not have these yet. Spell-check, style-check and other related software programs typically bundled (b) with word processing programs offer added advantages to students. Word processing programs facilitate revision (c), another advantage. Many students having fine motor deficits can learn to type more easily than handwrite (d), which is another asset.

95. D: A pop quiz (a) or an oral test (b) may yield some information about what students do and do not know about writing, but will not show their actual use of writing skills. Formal examinations (c) are typically not used as formative assessments during instruction, but as summative assessments after instruction. However, writing samples (d) require students to demonstrate and enable teachers to evaluate how students are writing at the time, progress made, skills mastered, and skills or areas needing more instruction.

96. B: How often to collect information on student progress is most related to assessment among these choices. How much time to spend on each writing skill (a) is more related to planning. Identifying strategies (both to use and to teach) for each writing skill (c) is more related to instruction. Grouping students (d) is more related to planning.

97. C: According to education experts, in K–4 math instruction, problem-solving is not a separate topic or part of a math program (a), but is among the foremost goals of math instruction (b). It is a process that should spread throughout the whole math program (c), and it supplies the context wherein students can learn math concepts and skills, rather than actually being those math concepts and skills (d).

98. A: Giving the students a hands-on learning activity using concrete objects that are also familiar will make the abstract math concept simpler for them to understand. Concrete, manipulative objects are important for teaching abstract concepts to younger students who typically do not yet think abstractly. Calculators (b) do not explain the concept. Rereading the textbook and asking questions (c) does not provide concrete objects or hands-on learning. These three students cannot apply the concept by working even simple problems (d) until they first understand it.

99. D: Graphic organizers (a) can make differences, similarities, and relationships more visual, but will not necessarily help these students with what they want to know. Mickey can determine whether his hours worked times pay per hour equals his total wages by multiplying and/or dividing; Alonzo can determine how much his raises have added to his earnings by graphing them across the time period. Choice (b) cites the wrong math procedures for what each student wants to determine. Counting real money (c) will not efficiently or practically give them the data they want as simple computations and graphing will.

100. A: Informed by student progress data, Mr. Kirk's decision to consult his mentor about how to explain these concepts is most related to instruction, while his decision to add lessons with this instruction is most related to planning. Neither decision is related to assessment.

NYSTCE Practice Test #2

Questions 1–9 are based on the passage below:

Classroom Management

While each teacher has a unique method of classroom management and cannot be completely categorized as one certain type, most tend toward one of four main styles. These styles depend on the amount of control and involvement a teacher takes. A teacher with both high involvement and high control is Authoritative. An Authoritarian teacher also exhibits a high level of control, but low involvement. Some teachers exhibit high involvement but low control. These teachers are termed Indulgent. Finally, a Permissive teacher has low involvement and low control. The style a teacher uses determines, to a significant degree, both the environment of the classroom and the success of the teaching.

An Authoritative teacher provides a stable environment with clear expectations. Rules are enforced and the teacher is invested in the students, who learn to be responsible and to take on leadership. Students under Authoritarian teachers, on the other hand, can feel uncared for, as behavior is strictly enforced but the teacher may not take time to explain rules and concepts or truly invest in the individuals. Indulgent teachers take time to talk to students and help them but rules are feebly enforced. Students know their teacher cares for them, but this style can lead to a chaotic environment that hampers learning. Permissive teachers allow excess freedom for students and give little direction, which can result in poor behavior and lack of learning.

While each style can have benefits, the Authoritative style is typically the most effective for student learning because it provides an orderly and caring atmosphere. Students know they must behave but they also know the teacher cares about them and will take time to explain concepts and listen to questions. The strictness is tempered by kindness, and students not only learn better but also grow better emotionally in an Authoritative environment.

1. Which of the following is the most accurate meaning of *feebly*, as used in the fourth sentence of Paragraph 2?
   a. Weakly
   b. In a senile fashion
   c. Haphazardly
   d. Rarely

2. The word *tempered* in the last sentence is closest in meaning to which related word?
   a. The noun temper, meaning the heat of anger
   b. The adjective temperate, meaning moderate
   c. The noun temper, meaning one's disposition
   d. The adjective temperamental, meaning sensitive

3. Of these choices, where is the main idea of this article best expressed?
    a. In the article's title
    b. In the first sentence of the first paragraph
    c. In the last sentence of the first paragraph
    d. In the last sentence of the last paragraph

4. What can be stated about the topic sentences in this selection?
    a. The first sentence of each paragraph is that paragraph's topic sentence.
    b. None of the three paragraphs has a true topic sentence, only a main idea.
    c. The first and third paragraphs begin with a topic sentence, while the second paragraph has no clear topic sentence.
    d. Each paragraph concludes with the topic sentence.

5. Where in the article are the results of the different classroom management styles discussed?
    a. All three paragraphs
    b. Paragraph 3
    c. Paragraphs 1 and 3
    d. Paragraphs 2 and 3

6. Which two classroom management styles exhibit a low level of involvement?
    a. Authoritative and Indulgent
    b. Authoritarian and Indulgent
    c. Authoritarian and Permissive
    d. Indulgent and Permissive

7. Which sentence in the first paragraph is the best example of a topic sentence?
    a. The first sentence
    b. The second sentence
    c. The final sentence
    d. None of these

8. What best describes the sequence of the paragraphs in this article?
    a. Main Idea, Supporting Details, Summary
    b. Problem, Solution, Summary
    c. Introduction, Cause, Effect
    d. Introduction, Supporting Details, Application

9. What kind of graph would be best to depict the number of teachers using each style of classroom management in a particular school?
    a. A line graph
    b. A bar graph
    c. A scatter plot
    d. A Venn diagram

Questions 10–18 are based on the passage below:

While the pros and cons of using technology in teaching have been argued for decades, it is undoubtedly an integral part of the classroom now. Teachers are expected to utilize technology to further the education of their students, both in the classroom and out. This can provide new ways not only to teach, but also to engage students in their own learning. Yet it can also provide new challenges.

Nearly every school has a wide range of student backgrounds; economic backgrounds, ethnic/cultural backgrounds, and learning styles can vary greatly, along with other details like level of parental involvement. This variety can make it tricky when using technology, especially out of the classroom. For instance, an idea to host an online forum for homework help may seem advantageous, but some students may not have Internet access or a computer. Even students who can access the forum may need other methods, such as video for those who need auditory teaching along with the text.

Despite these challenges, technology brings a host of opportunities to enhance learning and enable students to participate more in their education. Students can connect with teachers and other students outside the classroom, expand their research competence, and be more "hands-on" rather than simply listening to a lecture. Despite technology's drawbacks of cost and challenge to implement, the potential for educational enhancement is immense.

10. Which of the following is the best meaning for *host*, as seen in the first sentence of the third paragraph?
   a. Supporting role
   b. Dearth
   c. Multitude
   d. Exclusive selection

11. A suitable synonym for the word *competence* in the second sentence of the third paragraph would be which of these choices?
   a. Victory
   b. Knowledge
   c. Aggression
   d. Ability

12. Which sentence serves as the most direct introductory statement?
   a. The opening sentence of the first paragraph
   b. The second sentence of the first paragraph
   c. The first sentence of the second paragraph
   d. The entire second paragraph

13. What is the best restatement of the main idea of the text?
   a. There are both positive and negative aspects of technology.
   b. Different student backgrounds make it a challenge to use technology in education.
   c. The benefits of using technology in education outweigh the challenges.
   d. Students can have many new experiences with technology that would be impossible without it.

14. Regarding summary statements, which choice is most accurate about this text?
   a. The entire first paragraph is a summary statement.
   b. There is no summary statement in this selection.
   c. The entire last paragraph is a summary statement.
   d. The final sentence is a summary statement.

15. Which paragraph(s) of this text name the drawbacks of using technology in schools?
   a. The first and second paragraphs
   b. The second and third paragraphs
   c. The second paragraph only
   d. All three paragraphs

16. What is the tone of this selection?
   a. Persuasive
   b. Confrontational
   c. Informative
   d. Concerned

17. Is the final sentence of the selection a fact or an opinion, and does it show bias?
   a. Fact, bias
   b. Opinion, bias
   c. Fact, no bias
   d. Opinion, no bias

18. How can the three paragraphs of the text be described?
   a. Introduction, Argument and Counterargument, Summary
   b. Introduction, Counterargument, Argument and Summary
   c. Argument, Counterargument, Summary
   d. Introduction, Argument, Counterargument

19. Which version of the sentence below uses all three homophones (words that sound alike) correctly?
   a. Their going back to there house over they're.
   b. There going back to they're house over their.
   c. They're going back to their house over there.
   d. Their going back to there house over they're.

20. Of the following choices, which sentence demonstrates correct use of the preposition?
   a. It was an agreement among all of the neighbors.
   b. We heard disagreements between many friends.
   c. The couple kept this a secret among themselves.
   d. The group had no consensus between members.

21. Which sentence does not err in choosing commonly confused words?
   a. "Rather than directly name the scandal, she made an illusion."
   b. "His description of grace made an allusion to his late mother."
   c. "The author's illusion to the past required history knowledge."
   d. "Her belief in a perfect marriage turned out to be an allusion."

Answer the following three questions based on the graphic below.

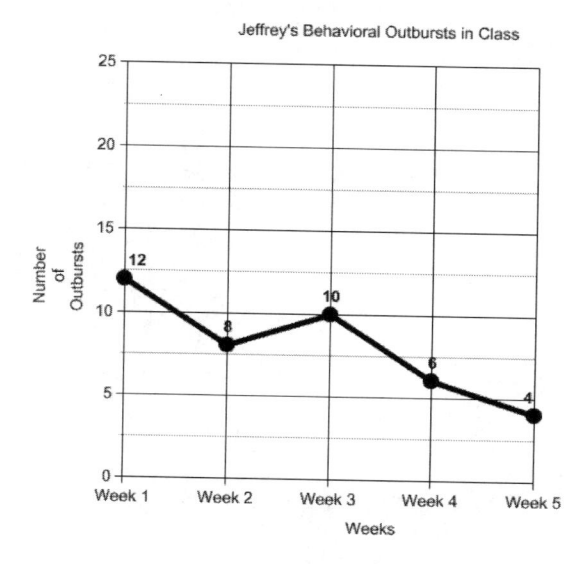

Jeffrey's Behavioral Outbursts in Class

Week 1: 12, Week 2: 8, Week 3: 10, Week 4: 6, Week 5: 4

22. This student received an intervention to reduce behavioral outbursts in class. What effect has this had by the fifth week, according to the graph's data?
    a. His outbursts have decreased by one-third of what they were.
    b. His outbursts have decreased to one-third of what they were.
    c. His outbursts have decreased by one-half of what they were.
    d. His outbursts have decreased to one-half of what they were.

23. What is the overall pattern of the target behavior over the five weeks shown?
    a. Decreasing overall, with one increase from Week 2 to Week 3
    b. Increasing overall, with one decrease from Week 3 to Week 4
    c. Decreasing overall, with instability shown by interim changes
    d. Increasing overall, with two decreases between Weeks 1 to 5

24. Using the graphed values, what is the average number of outbursts Jeffrey had over the weeks shown?
    a. 40
    b. 12
    c. 8
    d. 4

25. An audiogram is a line graph used to show the loudness levels at which someone can hear different frequencies (i.e., higher, middle, and lower pitches) of sound. How does this differ from more common uses of line graphs?
    a. The points connected by lines are all recorded at the same time.
    b. There are two lines, one for each ear; other graphs use one line.
    c. Other line graphs show a continuous line with no discrete points.
    d. There is no difference; all line graphs are made in this same way.

Answer the following question by interpreting the graphic shown below:

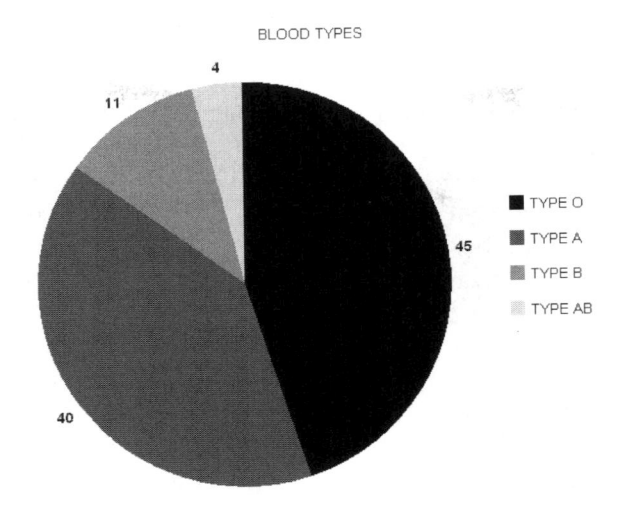

BLOOD TYPES

- TYPE O — 45
- TYPE A — 40
- TYPE B — 11
- TYPE AB — 4

26. Based on this pie chart, which of the following statements is true?
   a. More people have Type O blood than all other types combined.
   b. More people have Type O blood than Types A and B combined.
   c. More people have Types O and AB blood than A and B combined.
   d. More people have Type O blood than Types B and AB combined.

27. Among the following statements for grades 3–4 students, which is an example of opinion?
   a. Jean's shoes are red; Jane's are white.
   b. Red shoes are better than black shoes.
   c. A cheetah can run faster than a horse.
   d. Dogs have a better sense of smell than people.

28. "Everybody has ___ own copy of the book." Which word(s) correctly fill(s) in the blank?
   a. His or her
   b. Their
   c. Your
   d. Our

29. Which sentence has correct subject-verb agreement?
   a. Bart and Lisa takes the first turn.
   b. Both of them takes the first turn.
   c. Lisa or Marge takes the first turn.
   d. Either of them take the first turn.

30. Of the following sentences, which is in the present tense?
   a. Today we will take the test.
   b. Yesterday we took the test.
   c. We take this test each year.
   d. We have taken many tests.

31. Which of these is an example of the future tense?
   a. We will complete that by tomorrow.
   b. We will have done it by next month.
   c. We had finished before the deadline.
   d. We were going to finish it next week.

32. Which of these sentences uses the past tense of the verb?
   a. Teddy prepares a delicious gourmet meal.
   b. Teddy prepared a delicious meal for us all.
   c. Teddy is preparing a delicious meal for us.
   d. Teddy has prepared for us this delicious meal.

33. Of the following, which contains a verb in the present perfect tense?
   a. Danny said that he had already finished his homework.
   b. Danny says that he has already finished his homework.
   c. Danny says he will have finished his homework by then.
   d. Danny says that he is finishing his homework right now.

34. Which of the following has a present progressive verb tense?
   a. Joyce and Eric are heading up our new committee.
   b. Joyce and Eric will be heading our new committee.
   c. Joyce and Eric have headed up our new committee.
   d. Joyce and Eric had been heading a new committee.

35. Which version of this sentence uses the past perfect progressive verb tense?
   a. Manuel is improving his grades steadily so far this year.
   b. Manuel was improving his grades steadily all last year.
   c. Manuel has been improving his grades steadily all year.
   d. Manuel had been improving his grades steadily all year.

36. In English, which subject person, number, and verb tense always has a verb with an -s ending?
   a. First person, singular, present tense
   b. Third person, plural, past tense
   c. Second person, plural, present tense
   d. Third person, singular, present tense

37. In which choice does the reflexive pronoun agree with the noun it renames?
   a. Now it's every boy for themself.
   b. It's now every girl for himself.
   c. Now it's every group for itself.
   d. It's now each team for themselves.

38. Among these choices, which demonstrates pronoun-antecedent and subject-verb agreement?
   a. The one who should apologize is he, not she.
   b. The person responsible for this task are you.
   c. The people who have to do the job are them.
   d. When asked who did it, Sylvia said it was her.

39. **In which sentence does the pronoun agree with its antecedent?**
   a. The payment was divided between Ralph and I.
   b. They gave identical payments to Ralph and me.
   c. They divided a payment between he and Ralph.
   d. The money was divided among they and Ralph.

40. **"They described their best attorney, which was my uncle." What is true about the relative pronoun?**
   a. It should be "who."
   b. It should be "that."
   c. It should be "whom."
   d. It is correctly "which."

41. **Which of the following sentences is correct?**
   a. The house is sinking on it's foundation.
   b. Simone says that the building is her's.
   c. The family agrees the house is theirs.
   d. If you want to fix it, its your job.

42. **Of the following, which version of the sentence uses demonstrative pronouns appropriately?**
   a. This book here is better than that book here.
   b. This book there is better than that book here.
   c. This book there is better than that book there.
   d. This book here is better than that book there.

43. **The student's reading skills were poor, but his writing skills were _____. What word correctly completes this sentence?**
   a. worst
   b. worse
   c. worser
   d. poorest

44. **"The hostess with the mostest" is a familiar American English expression. Though it was intended to create humor and a rhyme, what else is true about the word "mostest"?**
   a. It is an acceptable superlative form outside of this expression.
   b. It is incorrect because it is the superlative rather than the comparative form.
   c. It is incorrect to use as the superlative because it is redundant.
   d. It is superfluous, but it is acceptable outside of this expression.

45. **Which of the following is an example of a complete sentence?**
   a. Let's go.
   b. Let's go when the rain.
   c. Let's go even though they say.
   d. Let's go because all the other guests.

46. Which of these choices is a sentence fragment?
   a. The city was beautiful.
   b. With bright lights, the city was beautiful.
   c. We visited the beautiful city with its bright lights.
   d. The beautiful city we visited with all the bright lights.

47. Of the following versions, which is an example of a run-on sentence?
   a. Jack loves to write he would write in every class if he could.
   b. Jack loves to write; he would write in every class if he could.
   c. Jack loves to write. He would write in every class if he could.
   d. As Jack loves to write, he would write in each class if he could.

48. Which of the following sentences is grammatically correct?
   a. We are going Tuesday won't you come with us?
   b. We are sorry you can't attend we will miss you.
   c. We will go on Tuesday; won't you come along?
   d. We are sorry you cannot go, will bring pictures.

49. The punctuation is correct in which of the following?
   a. They asked for permission, however, he refused.
   b. They asked for permission; however, he refused.
   c. They asked for permission, however; he refused.
   d. They asked for permission, however he refused.

50. Which of the following sentences contains correct standard capitalization?
   a. The Mayor and Councilmembers discussed a new ordinance regarding pedestrian traffic.
   b. After the accident, Mayor Wells discussed a new ordinance with his councilmembers.
   c. Concerned for the safety of citizens, mayor Wells and his councilmembers discussed a new ordinance.
   d. Mayor Wells met with the Councilmembers to discuss a new ordinance for pedestrian safety.

51. Which word is spelled incorrectly?
   a. Subtle
   b. Ubiquitous
   c. Pinnicle
   d. Malicious

52. Which of the following sentences contains correct standard capitalization?
   a. Johnny famously stated, "If it does not fit, you must acquit."
   b. Johnny famously stated, "if it does not fit, you must acquit."
   c. Johnny famously said that if it did not fit, "You must acquit."
   d. Johnny famously stated need for acquittal "If it does not fit."

53. With respect to capital letters, which phrase below is incorrect?
   a. draconian laws
   b. herculean feat
   c. quixotic behavior
   d. german lullaby

54. Among the following sentences, which spells the common word correctly for its context?
    a. "The name identifies county verses state government."
    b. "The implications of acting verses waiting are unclear."
    c. "The lengthy epic poem contains a great many verses."
    d. "The Army verses Navy game was anticipated by fans."

55. What is the value of the underlined digit in 23,0<u>8</u>5?
    a. 8000
    b. 800
    c. 80
    d. 8

56. In the number 376.1, what is the hundreds digit?
    a. 7
    b. 3
    c. 1
    d. 6

57. What is 125,420 rounded to the nearest hundred?
    a. 400
    b. 500
    c. 125,000
    d. 125,400

58. How many inches are in 4 feet?
    a. 48
    b. 36
    c. 24
    d. 12

59. How many meters are equivalent to 336 millimeters?
    a. 336,000
    b. 33,600
    c. 3.36
    d. 0.336

60. The length of a rectangular room is 14.2 feet and the width is 9.6 feet. Using estimating, what is the minimum amount of carpeting that will completely cover the floor in this room?
    a. 135 ft²
    b. 140 ft²
    c. 143 ft²
    d. 148 ft²

61. A square has side lengths of 5.8 cm. Estimate the perimeter of the square to the nearest whole centimeter.
    a. 34 cm
    b. 33 cm
    c. 24 cm
    d. 23 cm

62. What is the sum of 12 + 18 + 14 + 16?
   a. 40
   b. 60
   c. 59
   d. 50

63. Add 4,670,897 + 56,905 + 709,846.
   a. 5,437,648
   b. 5,437,638
   c. 5,436,648
   d. 4,437,648

64. Ms. Robinson buys a coat that is originally marked $225. If she receives a $45 discount, what is the sale price of the coat?
   a. $190
   b. $185
   c. $170
   d. $180

65. Ms. Wise receives $5,695 in prize money after taxes. She deposits $1,200 in savings and purchases a vacation cruise package for $3,975. She donates the remaining amount to charity. How much does Ms. Wise donate to charity?
   a. $520
   b. $515
   c. $510
   d. $505

66. Chloe buys 3 CDs at $7 each and 4 t-shirts at $8 each. If she pays for these items with an $100 bill, how much money does she have left?
   a. $43
   b. $57
   c. $53
   d. $47

67. The enrollment of Lincoln High school is as follows: Freshmen 334, Sophomores 410, Juniors 312, and Seniors 345. What is the total enrollment?
   a. 1,491
   b. 1,401
   c. 1,301
   d. 1.472

68. Find 325 × 1,000.
   a. 3,250
   b. 3,250,000
   c. 32,500
   d. 325,000

69. A storage unit contains 3 pallets of 8 boxes. If each box contains 10 laptop computers, how many computers does the storage unit contain?

    a. 210
    b. 240
    c. 225
    d. 230

70. What is the remainder when 3500 is divided by 120?

    a. 20
    b. 30
    c. 40
    d. 50

71. Divide 864 by 24.

    a. 28
    b. 26
    c. 36
    d. 46

72. The Jewel Corporation has a profit of $156,168. If the profit is divided evenly among 324 employees, how much does each employee receive?

    a. $482
    b. $582
    c. $472
    d. $478

73. Mr. Miller bought a refrigerator for $2,160. He agreed to make 12 equal monthly payments. How much more than $100 will each payment be?

    a. $180
    b. $160
    c. $80
    d. $60

74. If it takes $1\frac{1}{2}$ teaspoons of sugar to make 1 cup of hot lemonade, how much is needed to make 16 cups of hot lemonade?

    a. 12 teaspoons
    b. 24 teaspoons
    c. 18 teaspoons
    d. 28 teaspoons

75. What is the product of $\frac{6}{11} \times \frac{11}{9}$?

    a. $\frac{1}{3}$
    b. $\frac{2}{3}$
    c. $\frac{2}{9}$
    d. $\frac{4}{9}$

76. Mr. Elliott bought 1.25 pounds of nails. If the cost is $4.08 per pound, what was the cost of the nails?
    a. $5.01
    b. $5.10
    c. $6.00
    d. $6.10

77. If the cost of hamburger is $1.39 per pound, what is the cost of 5 pounds of hamburger?
    a. $6.95
    b. $5.95
    c. $6.85
    d. $6.55

78. A survey of 200 high school students reveals that only 5% prefer strawberry ice cream over chocolate ice cream. How many students prefer strawberry ice cream?
    a. 20
    b. 15
    c. 10
    d. 5

79. Ms. Marejo paid $52 for a dress from the clearance rack. If the dress was 20% off, what was the list price?
    a. $65
    b. $260
    c. $62.40
    d. $41.60

80. Convert 125% to a decimal.
    a. 1.25
    b. 12.5
    c. 0.125
    d. 0.00125

81. Convert 3.25 to a mixed number.
    a. $2\frac{4}{5}$
    b. $3\frac{1}{5}$
    c. $3\frac{1}{4}$
    d. $3\frac{1}{2}$

82. An elementary school teacher assigns a teaching assistant to work with small groups of beginning reading students to help them learn irregular sight word spellings (e.g., is, are, were, the, who, what, know, etc.). Which instructional procedure would best meet this need?
    a. Reading words in context
    b. Drilling for memorization
    c. Relating texts to real lives
    d. Picture-to-word matching

83. To analyze the sequence of a story plot, which learning activity would most benefit a student with a predominantly visual learning style?
    a. Oral summary
    b. Written outline
    c. Manipulative(s)
    d. Drawn timeline

84. A class includes students with disabilities, gifted students, average students, and a variety of reading levels. To support reading, which type of instructional resources would afford the most benefits to the most students?
    a. Printed materials
    b. Pictorial materials
    c. Multimedia materials
    d. Manipulative materials

85. An ELL student from another country speaks excellent conversational English and has mastered the basics of reading written English, but has comprehension difficulties owing to insufficient knowledge of general English vocabulary. Which resource would be most helpful to this student?
    a. Desk dictionary
    b. Word thesaurus
    c. Textbook glossaries
    d. Encyclopedia

86. In a lesson for grades 3–8 on skimming nonfictional text for comprehension, which choice represents the best sequence of instruction?
    a. Explain how students can use skimming, define the goal for skimming the specific lesson text, conduct a think-aloud while modeling how to skim, collect student questions and feedback, have students practice, model using keywords in questions, get student questions and feedback, repeat modeling and student practice.
    b. Conduct a think-aloud while modeling how to skim, repeat modeling and student practice, define the goal for skimming the specific lesson text, explain how students can use skimming, have students practice, collect student questions and feedback, repeat modeling and student practice, model using keywords in questions.
    c. Model using keywords in questions, conduct a think-aloud while modeling how to skim, explain how students can use skimming, have students practice, repeat modeling and student practice, collect student questions and feedback, define the goal for skimming the specific lesson text, get student questions and feedback.
    d. Define the goal for skimming the specific lesson text, model using keywords in questions, explain how students can use skimming, have students practice, collect student questions and feedback, conduct a think-aloud while modeling how to skim, repeat modeling and student practice, get student questions and feedback.

87. A teacher has assigned reading of informational social studies and science texts to middle school students. To encourage them to think critically about their reading, as well as to model questioning skills, the teacher prompts students by asking open-ended questions. Which choice is a good example of such a question(s)?
   a. "What subject was covered in this text?"
   b. "What are some facts? Some opinions?"
   c. "Did you understand all of the reading?"
   d. "Does the author give supporting data?"

88. A teacher of a class with a wide range of backgrounds, reading levels, and reading skills wants to differentiate her lesson plans, instructional strategies, and assessment methods to meet every student's needs best. Which way of collecting information on their reading progress will best help her do this?
   a. A whole-class test
   b. Current Lexile levels
   c. Small-group projects
   d. Individual observations

89. During classroom instruction, a teacher conducted formative assessments aligned to state standards, finding all students demonstrate high comprehension rates with grade-level reading. But on the state reading test two months later, nearly half of the students scored below grade level in comprehension. This test used different texts, but all texts were grade-level. What is the most likely reason for this change?
   a. Assessment instruments used were different.
   b. Each assessment used different sets of texts.
   c. There was no ongoing formative assessment.
   d. The summative assessment is always harder.

90. During which component of the writing process should a student remove extraneous content, add missing necessary information, and rearrange the order of some paragraphs?
   a. Planning
   b. Proofing
   c. Drafting
   d. Editing

91. A student working on a composition is going through the entire document and correcting grammar, spelling, punctuation, and capitalization as needed. In which stage of the writing process should this student be?
   a. Proofreading a final draft
   b. Editing an intermediate draft
   c. Revising a first or rough draft
   d. Proofreading the rough draft

92. Students should find a focus before writing, and they can also improve their focus during revision. To guide revisions for reinforcing focus, teachers and students can pose questions. Which of these is not a good guiding question for this purpose?
   a. What is the most important point in your composition?
   b. Does your composition keep focus on your main point?
   c. Regardless of why, do you know what you write about?
   d. Did you use ideas that do not reinforce the main point?

93. Writing research identifies characteristics of "mature" writers to which writing students can aspire. Which of the following behaviors demonstrates one of these characteristics?
   a. Planning during writing from one sentence to another
   b. Setting a goal during planning for direction and focus
   c. Revising in spots as needed to give better information
   d. Planning and revising as separate parts of the process

94. Among the following technological resources, which would best support writing for students who cannot manually operate writing implements or computer keyboards but can read, hear, and speak?
   a. Speech-to-text computer software programs
   b. Text-to-speech computer software programs
   c. Communication boards or voice synthesizers
   c. Large-print text and/or magnification devices

95. Which of these would present the most difficulty for students to look up words in a standard dictionary?
   a. Not knowing the meanings of words
   b. Not knowing words' pronunciations
   c. Not knowing the spellings for words
   d. Not knowing words' parts of speech

96. The principal, faculty, and staff of a public school are interested in how their students' writing skills compare to those of other public-school students in the same grades nationwide. Which type of assessment would give them this information?
   a. A criterion-referenced test
   b. A classroom writing test
   c. A formative assessment
   d. A norm-referenced test

97. A 4th-grade teacher introduces the math topic of decimals to the class. Together they preview their textbook chapter on decimals. The teacher assigns small groups of students to generate questions to which they want answers. Which of the following examples is the least helpful question to guide them at this stage of their learning?
   a. "How are decimals important to us in our everyday lives?"
   b. "How can decimals be whole numbers and also fractions?"
   c. "In the number 467.912, which digit is in the hundredths?"
   d. "Can we make fractions decimals, and decimals fractions?"

98. Which statement is true about the arithmetic examples below?

   I. 375 ÷ 5 = 75
   II. 5 × 75 = 375
   III. 75 + 5 = 375
   IV. 375 − 5 = 370

   a. Sample III is incorrect and Sample II corrects it.
   b. Sample I is incorrect and Sample IV corrects it.
   c. Sample II is incorrect and Sample III corrects it.
   d. Sample IV is incorrect and Sample III corrects it.

99. A teaching assistant identifies a "teachable moment" when two kindergarten students are arguing about whose toy is bigger. Which resource can she provide in showing them how to settle the dispute objectively?

   a. Computer
   b. Graph
   c. Chart
   d. Ruler

100. To assess early math learning in young children, which is/are the most appropriate material(s)?

   a. Cookies or candies
   b. Marbles or pennies
   c. Simple worksheets
   d. An arithmetic exam

Answer Key and Explanations for Test #2

1. A: *Feeble* means weak, infirm, or unable to walk. It can refer to physical or mental frailty. However, when meaning senile (b), it is more commonly compounded to "feeble-minded." The sentence is not referring to memory loss but to weakness in enforcing classroom management. Both haphazard (c) and rare (d) could fit the context of the sentence, but do not match the meaning of feeble.

2. B: The verb *to temper* means to moderate, tone down, or change, e.g., literally to temper glass or metal, or "to temper emotion with reason." Its meaning is closest to that of the adjective temperate, meaning moderate, e.g., a temperate climate or disposition, rather than the noun temper meaning the heat of anger (a); the noun temper meaning one's disposition (c), e.g., "she has an even temper"; or the adjective temperamental, meaning sensitive, moody, or irritable (d). The sentence is explaining that strictness is made more moderate, or balanced, by kindness.

3. C: The main idea that a teacher's classroom management style affects the classroom environment and success of teaching is stated in the last sentence of the first paragraph. The title (a) identifies the topic of classroom management but not the main idea of the four styles. The first sentence of the first paragraph (c) introduces the topic. The last sentence of the last paragraph (d) gives supporting details on one classroom management style.

4. C: The first and third paragraphs begin with a statement that introduces the topic of that paragraph. The second paragraph discusses the four classroom management styles and begins with the first one rather than introducing the topic, so the first sentence of each is not a topic sentence (a). Two paragraphs do have a topic sentence, not just a main idea, so answer choice (b) is incorrect. The topic sentences are not at the conclusion of each paragraph (d).

5. D: The first paragraph defines the classroom management styles but does not describe the results. The second paragraph gives examples of results ("[Students] learn to be responsible and take on leadership."). The third paragraph also gives examples ("students not only learn better but also grow better emotionally").

6. C: The first paragraph states that an Authoritarian teacher exhibits high control and low involvement, while a Permissive teacher has low control and low involvement. Authoritative and Indulgent teachers both have high levels of involvement.

7. A: The opening sentence is a good example of a topic sentence. It also introduces the piece. The second sentence (b) adds details to the first sentence. The final sentence (c) gives the thesis statement of the paragraph, but is not the topic sentence.

8. D: The first paragraph introduces the topic, briefly describing each of the four classroom management styles. The second paragraph goes into more detail on each style, describing the effect each has on the students and class environment. The final paragraph suggests which style is most effective for positive outcomes. This paragraph is more of an application of previous material than a summary of it (a). No true problem and solution are mentioned (b), and neither are a cause and effect (c).

9. B: A bar graph gives a clear visual depiction of how many teachers fall under each category, allowing the viewer to easily compare the four styles and see which ones are used most or least. A line graph (a) is best for showing how values change, which is not applicable for a one-time value. A scatter plot (c) shows each individual value, which is useful for tracking trends but makes it difficult to see how many teachers fall under each category since each teacher is listed separately. A Venn diagram (d) is useful for showing overlap between categories, but unless the teachers could be measured to exhibit a certain percentage of various styles, this graph could not be used here.

10. C: *Host* means a large number, though it can also mean one who entertains guests or an organism that supports another. This sentence is referring to the many opportunities afforded by technology, not to hospitality or biology (a). "Dearth" (b) is the opposite of the correct meaning, and "exclusive selection" cannot be inferred from the word or context.

11. D: This sentence refers to students' "research competence." While competence can include knowledge (b), here it is referring to skill or ability in researching. While *competence* and *compete* have similar etymology, this term is not referring to being victorious (a) or aggressive (c).

12. A: The opening sentence introduces the topic of technology in education and the fact that it has both pros and cons. The rest of the passage builds on this. The second sentence (b) expounds on the first. The second paragraph (c, d) deals with challenges of implementing technology, which is only part of the passage's subject.

13. C: This choice best restates the main idea. Choice (a) is not specific enough, making the general statement that technology has both pros and cons, but not mentioning that the passage is referring to technology use in schools or that the pros outweigh the cons. Choice (b) restates the main point of the second paragraph and choice (d) restates ideas from the third paragraph.

14. D: The first paragraph (a) introduces the topic, but does not summarize it. Most of the last paragraph (c) is on the topic of the benefits of technology, rather than summarizing the entire passage. Only the last sentence summarizes the two contrasting ideas (the pros and cons). Since there is a summary statement, choice (b) is incorrect.

15. B: The first paragraph introduces the subject. It mentions that there are "challenges" to implementing technology, but does not name them. The second paragraph is devoted to these challenges, and the final sentence of the third paragraph summarizes the subject, specifically mentioning two of the drawbacks. So, the second and third paragraphs both discuss the drawbacks.

16. A: The passage makes the argument that although technology has challenges, its benefits outweigh the challenges. This is a persuasive text, stating both sides of an issue and then indicating which is best. It is not confrontational (b) because it does not condemn anyone for holding the opposite opinion. It is not just informative (c), because it does not merely offer facts and allow the reader to draw his own opinion. And it is not concerned (d) because it does not have an emotional tone.

17. D: The final sentence sums up the selection, briefly restating the arguments for and against technology, and agrees with the pro side. Because an argument can be made for each side of the case, this is an opinion, although it is backed up by facts. Because it gives equal time to each side and uses factual information to fairly support each side, it is not biased.

18. B: The first paragraph introduces the subject, stating that there are two sides but not giving any details for either side. Based on the final sentence, which states that the pros of technology outweigh the cons, we can say that pro-technology is the main Argument and anti-technology (or the argument that the drawbacks outweigh the benefits) is the Counterargument. So, the second paragraph is the Counterargument since it focuses on the challenges of implementing technology.

The third paragraph gives the Argument, stating reasons technology should be implemented in education, and ends with a Summary sentence that restates the arguments and gives a conclusion.

19. C: "They're" is a contraction of "they are," i.e., the third person plural pronoun as a subject with the present tense plural of the verb "to be." "Their" is the possessive case of the third person plural pronoun "they," modifying the noun "house." And "there" is an adverb indicating place. The other choices use either three (a), (b) or two (d) of these homophones incorrectly.

20. A: The preposition "among" is used only with three or more persons, places, or things; the preposition "between" is used only with two persons, places, or things. "All of the neighbors" indicates more than two people, so "among" is correct (a). "Many friends" indicates more than two, so "between" is incorrect (b). "The couple" means two people, so "among" is incorrect (c). "The group" indicates more than two, so "between" is incorrect (d).

21. B: An allusion is a reference, often indirect, implicit, casual, or passing; an illusion is a false perception or impression. Therefore, option (a) should be "allusion," option (b) is correct, option (c) should be "allusion," and option (d) should be "illusion." (Illusion can also mean a very thin, transparent fabric, or jewelry with almost invisible string.)

22. B: In Week 1, the number of outbursts was 12; in Week 5, it was four. Because four is one-third of 12, the outbursts have decreased to one-third of what they were. They have not decreased by one-third of what they were (a), which would be a decrease of four, i.e., 12 – 4 = 8. If they had decreased by half of what they were, half of 12 is six, so 12 – 6 = 6. If they had decreased to half of what they were, they would also be six in Week 5.

23. A: The line graph shows an overall descending pattern, meaning the number of outbursts is decreasing weekly overall. However, the number increased from eight in Week 3 to 10 in Week 4 before resuming the pattern of decreasing. The line overall goes down, so the pattern is not increasing (b), (d). Multiple changes between Weeks 1 and 5 indicating instability (c) do not exist on this graph; there is only one change in Week 3, while all other weeks after Week 1 show decreases.

24. C: To find the average, first add all of the numbers of outbursts each week: 12 + 8 + 10 + 6 + 4 = 40. Then divide this sum by five weeks: 40 ÷ 5 = 8. So, 40 (a) is the sum of all outbursts over all five weeks, 12 (b) is the number of outbursts in Week 1, and 12 is also the largest number in any week shown. Four (d) is the number of outbursts in Week 5, and the smallest number in any week shown.

25. A: The more common uses of line graphs record points at different times, so the line connecting those points shows variation over time. Audiograms differ by recording each point during the same hearing test. The line connecting those points shows variation in hearing levels across different frequencies instead of variation over time. Many line graphs use two or more lines (b), color-coded (and/or dashed, broken, etc.) for differentiation. All line graphs plot and connect distinct data points (c). Because choice (a) is correct, choice (d) is incorrect.

26. D: The chart shows 45 percent of people have Type O blood, so the other three types total 55 percent, making option (a) incorrect. Forty percent have Type A and 11 percent have Type B blood, which adds to 51 percent, so option (b) is incorrect. Forty-five percent Type O plus four percent Type AB blood equals 49 percent, whereas 40 percent Type A and 11 percent Type B equals 51 percent, so option (c) is incorrect. However, 40 percent with Type B plus four percent with Type AB equals 44 percent, whereas 45 percent have Type O blood, which makes option (d) correct.

27. B: Choices (a), (c), and (d) are all statements of fact, i.e., they have been and/or can be proven, and they are consistently true. Choice (b) is a statement of opinion, i.e., it varies depending on the person making the statement, it can vary for the same individual if s/he changes her/his opinion, and it expresses a thought or emotion.

28. A: "Everybody" is singular and requires these singular pronouns to agree; "their" (b) and "our" (d) are plural. Although "your" (c) can be singular or plural, it would go with a plural subject like "All of you" or a singular subject like "One of you," but does not fit with "Everybody," which refers to the third person rather than the second (c) or first person (d). (Note: If "his or her" becomes stilted, make the subject plural, e.g., "All students have their own copies.")

29. C: Using "or" between two nouns, proper nouns, or pronouns indicates a singular subject and verb (takes). "And" indicates plural subjects and a plural verb (take), so option (a) should be "take," option (b) should be "take," option (c) is correct, and option (d) should be "takes."

30. C: "We take" is the present tense of "to take" with a first-person plural subject. The predicate in choice (a) is in the future tense "will take." Future tense always uses auxiliary verb(s) "will," "will be ___ing," etc. The past tense is "took" (b). "(We) have taken" (d) is the present perfect tense.

31. A: Future tense is generally indicated by an auxiliary verb like "will" plus the plain or uninflected form of the verb. Auxiliary verbs "will" and "have" plus the perfect form of the verb "done" (b) indicate the future perfect tense. Auxiliary verb plus past verb form "Had finished" (c) indicates the past perfect tense. Auxiliary plus participle "were going" (d) indicates the past progressive (aka past continuous) tense.

32. B: Sentence (a) uses the present tense of the verb "to prepare." Sentence (b) uses the past tense of this verb, so this is the correct choice for the question. Sentence (c) uses the present progressive tense (also called the present continuous tense). Sentence (d) uses the present perfect tense.

33. B: Choice (a) contains the past tense "said" and the past perfect "had... finished." The other choices all use "to say" in the present tense, "says." Choice (b) uses the present perfect tense of "to finish," "has finished." Choice (c) uses the future perfect tense, "will have finished." Choice (d) uses the present progressive (aka continuous) tense "is finishing."

34. A: This is an example of the present progressive (or present continuous) tense, indicating something that is currently ongoing. Option (b) is an example of the future progressive tense, indicating something that will be ongoing in the future. Option (c) is an example of the present perfect tense, indicating something that has occurred in the past before the present. Option (d) is an example of the past perfect progressive tense, indicating something ongoing in the past before something subsequent, also in the past.

35. D: Version (a) uses the present progressive tense ("is improving"). Version (b) uses the past progressive tense ("was improving"). Version (c) uses the present perfect progressive tense ("has been improving"). Version (d) uses the past perfect progressive tense ("had been improving").

36. D: A verb modifying a noun in the third person singular (a pronoun like he, she, it, or any other singular noun or other word) in the present tense is the only combination that always has an -s ending on the verb, e.g., is, has, does, goes, walks, likes, sees, thinks, feels, wakes, sleeps, etc. Examples with a regular verb are, of choice (a), "I walk"; of choice (b), "They walked"; and of (c), "You walk." Only choice (d) would be "She walks," "He walks," or "It walks."

37. C: The reflexive pronoun "itself" correctly renames the noun "group" by agreeing with its neutral gender. "Themself" is not a word (a), "himself" disagrees with the feminine gender "girl" (b), and "themselves" disagrees with the singular "team" (d).

38. A: Each of these pronouns agrees with the antecedent "one," as each can replace that subject grammatically. In option (b), singular subject "person" and pronoun "you" agree, but the verb "are" disagrees with subject "person," instead incorrectly agreeing with pronoun "you." The third person plural pronoun to agree with "people… are" (c) is "they," not "them." Similarly, the third person feminine singular pronoun referring to Sylvia and agreeing with "it was" is "she," not "her" (d).

39. B: To test pronoun-antecedent agreement when the pronoun is the object, make it the *only* object: since we would write, "They gave the payment to me," not "to I," we would not change the form just because the pronoun is compounded with another object, like Ralph (a). The same applies to "Ralph and him" or "him and Ralph," not "he and Ralph" (c); and to "Ralph and them" or "them and Ralph," not "they and Ralph" (d).

40. A: The correct relative pronoun to refer to "their best attorney" and "was my uncle" is "who." "That" (b) is used with nonrestrictive more than restrictive clauses, but both "that" and "which" are used with things whereas "who" is more appropriate with people. "Whom" (c) is only used as an object—direct (e.g., "Whom do you choose?") or indirect (e.g., "To whom did you give it?")—not a relative pronoun. Because choice (a) is correct, choice (d) is incorrect.

41. C: Possessive pronouns differ from possessive proper nouns in that, whereas both nouns and proper nouns take "–'s" endings when possessive (e.g., "the woman's hat," "the man's house," "Mary's hat," "Walter's house," etc.), pronouns do not. Hence option (a) should be written "its foundation," option (b) should be "hers," option (c) is correctly "theirs," and option (d) should be "it's."

42. D: Use the demonstrative pronoun "here" to refer to things closer at hand, and "there" to refer to things farther away. Do not use "here" for both (a), "there" for both (c), or use each for the opposite meanings (b) of those identified.

43. B: The correct comparative modifier meaning more than bad is "worse." "Worst" (a) is the superlative, not the comparative, and is not used when comparing only two things. "Worser" (c) is not a real word: it is redundant because *-er* denotes more, but "worse" already means more bad. "Poorest" (d), like "worst," is the superlative form and inappropriate here.

44. C: In describing quantity, relative to words like "few," "little," "some," "much," "many," etc., the comparative meaning a greater amount or number is "more," and the superlative meaning the ultimate quantity is "most." Hence "mostest" is redundant. It is not acceptable outside of this expression (a), nor acceptable despite being superfluous (d). It is the superlative form rather than comparative (b), but this does not make it incorrect.

45. A: Complete sentences can be brief as long as they contain a subject, a verb, and express a complete thought. Choice (b) is a sentence fragment with an incomplete dependent clause lacking a verb (e.g., "when the rain STOPS"). Choice (c) needs either a phrase or clause to complete "they say" (e.g., "we should not," "not to go"), or another verb replacing "say" (e.g., "refuse," "protest," "complain," "criticize," "laugh," "joke") needing no object. Choice (d) needs either a verb completing "guests" (e.g., "went," "are going," "will go," "are there"), or "of" inserted ("because OF all the other guests").

46. D: Choices (a), (b), and (c) are all complete sentences as each has a subject and verb and expresses a complete thought. However, choice (d) has a subject ("city") but no verb. Unlike in choice (c), "we visited" are not the subject and verb in choice (d), but modify "city" as does the rest ("with…"). To complete this fragment, the subject needs its own predicate (e.g., "The beautiful city we visited with all the bright lights was a popular destination" or "…had a large population," etc.).

47. A: This is an example of a run-on sentence, which combines two independent clauses without the necessary division of punctuation and/or a conjunction. This can be corrected by dividing the clauses with a semicolon (b), separating them with a period into two sentences (c), or making one clause dependent/subordinate by adding a subordinating conjunction and separating it from the independent clause with a comma (d). Or a comma plus conjunction (e.g., ", and" or ", so") can join these clauses.

48. C: This sentence correctly connects two independent clauses with a semicolon. The other choices are all run-on sentences. Option (a) can be corrected with a semicolon or period between "Tuesday" and "won't." Option (b) can use the same between "attend" and "we," or a comma plus conjunction "and." Option (d) needs either a period or semicolon plus "we" before "will."

49. B: When connecting two independent clauses using "however" as a conjunctive adverb, punctuate with a semicolon before "however" and a comma after it. Using a comma before "however" (a) incorrectly creates a comma splice. Choice (c) reverses the correct punctuation sequence. By omitting the comma after "however," choice (d) alters the meaning: it reads as if they asked for permission no matter how he refused.

50. B: Neither "mayor" nor "councilmembers" are capitalized when used as a common noun, so (a) and (d) are incorrect. When used as a proper noun, "mayor" should be capitalized, so (c) is incorrect.

51. C: The correct spelling is "pinnacle." All of the other words are spelled correctly.

52. A: The first letter of the first word in a sentence should always be capitalized. This rule also applies to the first letter of the first word in any full quotation, regardless of whether it appears in the middle of another sentence. Hence option (b) is incorrect. However, a partial quotation and/or one that continues the sentence containing it should not begin with a capital letter, so options (c) and (d) are both incorrect.

53. D: Although adjectives derived from proper nouns are normally capitalized, choices (a), (b), and (c) here are exceptions: over time, these have become so commonly used that they no longer need to be capitalized, although it is still common to use capitalization. However, adjectives derived from proper nouns like country names, e.g., German (d), French, English, etc. are still capitalized at all times.

54. C: The spelling "verses" indicates the plural noun, singular "verse," meaning a line of poetry, song lyrics, or Biblical scripture. In sentences (a), (b), and (d), the correct spelling should be "versus," meaning against, contrasting with, or opposing. Though both words originate from the same Latin source, their English meanings have evolved to be very different.

55. C: The place value is assigned by the position of the digit. The places to the left of the decimal are ones, tens, hundreds, then thousands, respectively. Since the digit 8 is in the second place to the left of the implied decimal, it's in the tens place. The value of this digit is 8×10, which is 80.

56. B: The place value of a digit depends on its location in relation to the decimal point. The places to the left of the decimal are ones, tens, then hundreds, respectively. The places to the right of the decimal are tenths, hundredths, and thousandths, respectively. Since the digit 3 is in the third position to the left of the decimal point, its place value is hundreds.

57. D: The place value of a digit depends on its location in relation to the decimal point. The places to the left of the decimal are ones, tens, then hundreds, respectively. To round a number to a certain place value, look at the digit to the immediate right. If the digit to the right is 5 or more, round up by adding one followed by a zero. If the digit is less than five, round down by keeping the same digit followed by a zero. For this problem, the digit in the hundreds place is 4. The digit to its immediate right is 2. Since 2 is less than 5, round down. So, 125,420 rounded to the nearest hundred is 125,400.

58. A: Since 1 foot equals 12 inches, the conversion factor is 12. Since a foot is longer than an inch, we multiply by the conversion factor, so 4 feet equal 4×12 or 48 inches.

59. D: Since 1 meter equals 1,000 millimeters, the conversion factor is 1,000. Since a millimeter is shorter than a meter, we divide by the conversion factor, so 336 millimeters equal $336 \div 1,000$ or 0.336 feet.

60. B: The area of the rectangular room equals the amount of carpeting needed. The area of a rectangle equals the product of the length and the width. The length of the room is approximately 14 feet, and the width of the room is approximately 10 feet. The area of this room is approximately 140 ft².

61. C: The perimeter of a square is found by the equation $p = 4s$ where p represents the perimeter and s represents the length of the sides. The side length is approximately equal to 6 cm. The perimeter of this square is found by $p = 4(6) = 24$ cm.

62. B: The sum can be found by adding the digits in the ones column ($2 + 8 + 4 + 6 = 20$), and then carrying the 2 to the tens column and adding the digits ($2 + 1 + 1 + 1 + 1 = 6$). Then the sum is 60. Alternately, $12 + 18 = 30$ and $14 + 16 = 30$, so $30 + 30 = 60$.

63. A: The sum is found by adding the ones column ($7 + 5 + 6 = 18$) and carrying the 1 to the tens column. Then add the tens column ($1 + 9 + 0 + 4 = 14$) and carry the 1 to the hundreds column. Then add the hundreds column ($1 + 8 + 9 + 8 = 26$) and carry the 2 to the thousands column. Then add the thousands column ($2 + 0 + 6 + 9 = 17$) and carry the 1 to the ten thousands column. Then add the ten thousands column ($1 + 7 + 5 + 0 = 13$) and carry the 1 to the hundred thousands column. Then add the hundred thousands column ($1 + 6 + 7 = 14$) and carry the 1 to the millions columns. Then, add the millions column ($1 + 4 = 5$). Pulling the digits all together in their proper places yields 5,437,648.

64. D: The sale price is equal to the difference between the original amount and the discount. The sale price equals $225 − $45 or $180.

65. A: The amount Ms. Wise donates to charity is equal difference between the original amount of prize money and the sum of the savings deposit and cost of the cruise package. Then, the amount she donates equals $5,695 − ($1,200 + $3,975) or $520.

66. D: The amount of money Chloe has left is equal to the difference between the amount of money she started with and the amount of money she spends. The amount she spends equals 3($7) + 4($8) or $53. The amount she has left equals $100 − $53 or $47.

67. B: The total enrollment is the sum of the enrollments of the individual classes. The enrollment is equal to 334 + 410 + 312 + 345 = 1,401.

68. D: To multiply numbers ending in zero, first multiply the numbers ignoring the zeros and then add the zeros after the last digit of the product. Then 325 × 1 = 325 and adding the three zeros yields 325,000.

69. B: The number of computers in the storage unit is the product of the number of pallets, the number of boxes, and the number of computers in each box. The number of computers equals 3 × 8 × 10 or 240 computers.

70. A: Since 120 × 29 = 3480 and 120 × 30 = 3600 (which is more than 3500), the remainder is 3500 − 3480 = 20.

71. C: To divide 864 by 24, the first step is to divide 86 by 24. Since 24 × 3 = 72, the divisor 24 goes into 86 three times. Then place the 72 under the 86 and subtract. Then 86 − 72 = 14. Now bring down the 4, and determine how many times 24 goes into 144. Since 24 × 6 = 144, the divisor 24 goes into 144 six times. Then place the 144 under the 144 and subtract to get zero. This means that 864 ÷ 24 = 36.

72. A: The amount of money each employee receives is equal to the quotient between $156,168 and 324. Then $156,168 ÷ 324, which is $482.

73. C: The amount of the monthly payment is the quotient of the cost divided by the number of payments. The payment equals $2160 ÷ 12 or $180. The payment of $180 is $80 over $100.

74. B: The amount of sugar needed is equal to the product of the number of cups of lemonade needed and the amount of sugar per cup. The amount of sugar needed is equal to $16 \times 1\frac{1}{2} = 16 \times \frac{3}{2} = 24$ teaspoons.

75. B: When multiplying fractions, first try to cancel factors in the numerators with factors in the denominators. Then multiply the numerators and denominators and reduce: $\frac{6}{11} \times \frac{11}{9} = \frac{2}{1} \times \frac{1}{3} = \frac{2}{3}$.

76. B: The cost of the nails is equal to the product of the pounds of nails and the cost per pound. The cost equals 1.25 × $4.08 or $5.10.

77. A: The cost of the hamburger is the product of the number of pounds and the cost per pound. The cost equals $1.39 × 5 or $6.95.

78. C: This question is basically asking, "What is 5% of 200?" Let n represent *what*, and replace the *of* with a multiplication symbol and the *is* with an equal sign. But first, we need to convert the 5% to a decimal. Remove the percent sign and move the decimal point two places to the left. Then we have $n = 0.05 \times 200 = 10$. This means that only 10 of the 200 students prefer strawberry ice cream over chocolate.

79. A: Since the dress was 20% off, $52 is 80% of the list price. Then, this question is asking, "$52 is 80% of what number?" Let n represent *what number*, and replace the *of* with a multiplication sign and the *is* with an equal sign. But first, we need to convert the 80% to a decimal. Remove the percent sign and move the decimal point two places to the left. Then we have $52 = 0.80 \times n$. To solve this equation, divide both sides by 0.80: $52 ÷ 0.80 = n$, so $n = 65$. Thus, the list price of the dress was $65.

80. A: To covert a percent to a decimal, remove the percent symbol and move the decimal point two places to the left. So 125% equals 1.25.

81. C: To convert a decimal to a fraction, move the decimal point two places to the right, place the number over 100, and simplify the fraction. Then 3.25 equals $3\frac{25}{100}$, which simplifies to $3\frac{1}{4}$.

82. B: Students cannot decode irregular words that do not follow phonics (letter-sound) rules. To recognize these on sight, children must simply memorize them; drilling is best. Reading words in context (a) is inappropriate for beginning readers who have not memorized these words. Relating text to real life (c) is important to reading instruction, but unrelated to learning irregular words. Pictures (d) help beginning readers, but most irregular words (see examples in the question) are function words and/or express abstract concepts, and cannot be pictured like concrete meanings (e.g., dog, cat, house, etc.).

83. D: Students with visual learning styles learn best from things they can see, e.g., videos, pictures, diagrams, drawings, etc. A timeline drawing shows plot sequence visually. An oral plot summary (a) would benefit students with auditory learning styles, who learn best from things they can hear. A written outline (b) would benefit students with verbal learning styles, who learn best from things they can read and write. Manipulatives (c) would benefit students with haptic (tactile) learning styles, who learn best from things they can touch, feel, move, and rearrange.

84. C: The more modalities and media the learning materials include, the more they can address a larger number of varied student needs. There are two reasons for this: (1) if one modality or medium is not effective for certain students, then another one will be; (2) presenting the same information redundantly and through different modalities makes learning more effective for all students than presenting it through only one (a), (b), (d).

85. A: A dictionary will help the student look up unfamiliar words encountered when reading. A thesaurus (b) provides synonyms and antonyms for given words, which would help students vary their word choice when writing, but would not help this student learn general English vocabulary for reading. Textbook glossaries (c) would help the student learn vocabulary and terminology specific to each text, but not general English vocabulary found in other reading. An encyclopedia (d) would provide extensive information about subject content, not vocabulary.

86. A: The best sequence is: explain skimming enables students to find text parts important to them and disregard others. Identify the goal for skimming the lesson's specific text. Model skimming, narrating with a think-aloud (e.g., "Let's look for this in the table of contents first," etc.). Collect students' questions and feedback. Invite students to practice locating information in a caption, diagram, graph, or under a heading. Model (with think-aloud) finding keywords in questions about text to guide skimming. Get student questions and feedback. Continue modeling and student practice until students demonstrate successful skimming for information.

87. B: This is a good example because it requires critical thinking for students to differentiate facts vs. opinions; it is also open-ended, allowing a variety of valid responses. Choice (a) requires only factual knowledge and a limited response range. Choice (c) can be answered yes or no, so not open-ended; to improve it, follow "no" responses with, "What did you not understand?" or" What questions do you have?" Choice (d) is also a yes or no question; it can be improved by following "yes" responses with, "How do the data support the author's viewpoint?"

88. D: Of the choices given, the best way to get information for differentiating instruction for individual students is through observations of individual students (d) with detailed observational notes of their specific reading needs and strengths. A whole-class test (a) will yield different individual student scores and even need and strength areas, but less information about specific students. Lexile levels (b), when available, help identify texts at suitable reading levels for each student rather than inform instructional differentiation. Small-group projects (c) yield group, not individual, student results.

89. C: Differences between assessment instruments (a), different (yet both grade-level) texts (b), and even the greater difficulty of standardized summative assessments than of classroom formative assessments (d) cannot explain such a significant discrepancy. The most likely cause is the two months between the teacher's classroom formative assessments and the state reading test: formative assessment must be ongoing to show current student status, which can change over time, so monitoring must be continuous.

90. D: The activities described are part of the editing component of the writing process. The planning (a) part occurs before the student starts writing and includes activities like brainstorming ideas, establishing focus, doing research, making outlines, etc. The drafting (c) component involves producing a rough draft before progressing to any editing actions. The proofing (b) or proofreading component involves checking and correcting all writing and typing mechanics in the final draft, after drafting and editing.

91. A: Proofreading to correct mechanics is the last step for a student before turning in a composition. Editing (b) does not involve proofreading, but rather entails removing, adding, changing, and rearranging content as needed to produce a logical, coherent, cohesive, unified piece. Revising a rough draft (c) is like editing. Proofreading is only done with the last draft, not the first or rough draft (d).

92. C: Good questions that teachers and students can use during writing revisions include identifying the most important point (a); whether the piece remains focused throughout on that most important point (b); and whether the student included ideas that detract from, weaken, or do not strengthen their central focus (d). Before and during writing, students should ask themselves not only what they write about, but moreover why they write about it (c).

93. B: Writing researchers find that "mature" writers do not plan during writing by letting one sentence dictate the next (a). They see their work as a whole, and plan and revise recursively, instead of only revising in certain places and/or concentrating on giving information (c) in a linear fashion. They plan and revise globally throughout the entire writing process (d). They focus their writing in part by setting a goal, so their planning and revising are then goal-directed (b).

94. A: Speech-to-text software programs enable students who cannot manually write or type but can speak to dictate compositions to computers and have these programs convert their spoken words to printed text. Text-to-speech software programs (b) would support students who can write and type but cannot speak. Communication boards and voice synthesizers (c) would support writing for students who cannot write, type, or speak. Large-print text and/or magnification devices (d) would support writing for students with impaired vision.

95. C: Students need not know every letter of the correct spelling of a word in order to look it up in a standard dictionary, but they must know the initial letter. For example, many Greek-derived words are spelled beginning with *ps-* but pronounced beginning with /s/; the "p" is silent. A few phonetic dictionaries, enabling lookup by pronunciation respelling, have been published to address this. Not knowing word meanings (a) is a perfect reason for looking them up in a regular dictionary, which will also provide their pronunciations (b) and parts of speech (d).

96. D: Norm-referenced tests are standardized, so the performance of all students in the nation or state is measured the same way. They refer to a norm, i.e., student scores are compared to the average scores of a normative sample of students as representative of most students in the country/state. Criterion-referenced tests (a) do not compare student scores to any such norm, but only against a preset performance criterion. Classroom writing tests (b) enable comparing among classmates, not with students nationwide. Formative assessments (c) typically only measure learning during instruction within a classroom.

97. C: Question (a) is good for meeting the standard of applying mathematics to real life. Question (b) is good for students to learn the conceptual relationship of decimals and fractions as different yet equivalent ways of expressing parts of a whole. Question (d) is good for students to learn how to convert fractions to decimals and vice versa. Question (c) is better asked by the teacher than by students—and not at this stage of their learning, but only after they understand place value.

98. A: Sample III uses the plus sign, but gives the product of multiplication instead of the sum of addition. Sample II corrects this error. Samples I, II, and IV are correct as they are (b), (c), (d). Samples I and II reverse each other by dividing (I) and multiplying (II) the same values. If Sample III were corrected, then Samples III and IV would reverse each other by adding (III) and subtracting (IV) the same values.

99. D: Young children tend to focus on only one attribute of objects to the exclusion of others—e.g., height but not width, number of pieces rather than overall size or amount, etc. A computer (a) is overkill; a graph (b) or chart (c) is irrelevant. By providing a ruler (d) and then showing them how to measure both toys, the assistant can teach the children how to use an objective measurement.

100. B: An arithmetic exam (d) is inappropriate to assess early math learning in young children, who may not even be able to write numbers or letters yet. Similarly, even very simple worksheets (c) are not developmentally appropriate. Familiar concrete objects are best for instructing and assessing abstract concepts with very young students. However, cookies or candies (a) are problematic as young children are likely to eat them. Marbles or pennies (b) are better for demonstrating and practicing adding, subtracting, comparing, etc.

NYSTCE Practice Test #3

1. Which of the following related words is most synonymous with *wordy*?
   a. Verbal
   b. Verbose
   c. Verbiage
   d. Verbatim

2. Of the following sentences, which one uses all words correctly?
   a. "I am going too see my sister's new house."
   b. "My sister bought a house, and we did to."
   c. "I will go to see my sister's new house too."
   d. "My sister is coming too our new house to."

3. Which of the following uses accurate word forms?
   a. "You must site your sources in research papers."
   b. "Her child's smile was a beautiful sight for her."
   c. "He used a telescoping cite to aim his weapon."
   d. "They plan to inspect the job sight next month."

4. Which of the following sentences demonstrates choice of the correct word form?
   a. "Paint was Liz's art media of choice."
   b. "The medium cost of all drinks at the coffee shop was $3.89."
   c. "He expressed himself through the media of clay and marble."
   d. "She used both online and print medium to spread her message."

Questions 5–21 are based on the passage below:

Teaching Gifted Students

One challenge that comes with classes of any size is different abilities of learners. Some students grasp certain subjects quickly, while others struggle. While it is vital to recognize those who are in danger of falling behind, the gifted students can slip through the cracks because it sometimes seems that they don't need as much help. Approximately one in twenty of the nation's students is enrolled in a gifted and talented program, but many gifted students remain in regular classes or attend schools without such programs. Teachers have the challenge of first identifying and then assisting gifted students so they are able to succeed.

A common misconception is that gifted students excel in their classes. While learning often comes more easily, they can also be distracted or bored. A troublemaker who saunters into class late and then distracts others may simply be a gifted child who is not being mentally stimulated and seeks a way to occupy his mind. Another student may be failing the class because she doesn't complete her homework—not because she doesn't understand it but because she isn't interested in the material that doesn't challenge her. Teachers face the monumental task of keeping students from every range of ability and work ethic on track so that they learn.

One way to tailor education to gifted students in a class filled with mixed aptitudes is to have tiered learning: offering various levels of learning difficulty. Obviously, this creates additional effort for instructors, but it is simpler than personally tutoring the advanced students. Another way to teach to different levels is to offer the most difficult instruction first in a class period, and then provide differentiated instruction on other levels. This may appear tantamount to teaching multiple classes but can become feasible with practice. Yet another option is to allow student grouping, both with other gifted students and with those who may be struggling. Gifted students can encourage each other, wrestle through challenges, and bounce ideas off each other. Additionally, they can solidify the concepts in their minds by working with classmates who need assistance. Finally, a teacher can simply keep a supply of challenging activities and worksheets handy to occupy gifted students when they grow bored.

It can take trial and error to find the method that works best for each class with its unique group of students. It is important to remember that gifted students are still children. They are not necessarily more motivated to learn or more likely to have a good work ethic. It is crucial to assess them as individuals to find out how best to help them excel. As a teacher learns more about his or her students, he or she will be more able to teach all students as well as possible.

5. From the context in the third sentence of the second paragraph, which is the best definition of the word *saunters*?
    a. Slinks
    b. Races
    c. Strolls
    d. Gallops

6. From the context in the first sentence of the third paragraph, which is the best synonym for the word *tailor*?
   a. Sew
   b. Teach
   c. Customize
   d. Change

7. Which of the following phrases is the best synonym for the word *tantamount*, as seen in the fourth sentence of the third paragraph?
   a. Most important
   b. Almost as much
   c. Much more than
   d. Being equal with

8. Where in this text is a statement of the main idea?
   a. In the title
   b. In the first sentence of the first paragraph
   c. In the last sentence of the first paragraph
   d. In the last sentence of the last paragraph

9. Which of the following can be said about the third paragraph?
   a. There is no topic sentence.
   b. This is a counterargument against the main idea.
   c. This is a comparison and contrast paragraph.
   d. This is a narrative paragraph.

10. What type of organizational pattern can be seen in this passage?
    a. Comparison and contrast
    b. Cause and effect
    c. Classification
    d. Explanation

11. Which of the following is/are most like an introductory statement in this text?
    a. The title
    b. The first sentence of the first paragraph
    c. The final sentence of the first paragraph
    d. The final sentence of the final paragraph

12. According to the information provided, a gifted child may cause trouble because _____.
    a. he/she is late to class.
    b. the work is too easy.
    c. he/she has not finished his/her homework.
    d. he/she is not being mentally stimulated.

13. Which option allows gifted students to bounce ideas off each other?
   a. Tiered learning
   b. Differentiated instruction
   c. Student grouping
   d. Challenging activities and worksheets

14. Based on the information in the text, what proportion of the students in the US attend gifted programs?
   a. 3 percent
   b. 5 percent
   c. 10 percent
   d. cannot be determined

15. The author of the passage states, "It is important to remember that gifted students are still children." Is this fact or opinion?
   a. Fact, because students are legally minors
   b. Fact, because teachers are required to study childhood development
   c. Opinion, because some students in the programs are over 18
   d. Opinion, because this is the author's personal view of what is important

16. Which of the following is a misconception mentioned in the passage?
   a. Gifted students can be troublemakers.
   b. Gifted students excel in class.
   c. Gifted students always complete their homework.
   d. All gifted students learn the same way.

17. One teaching technique is to offer what level of instruction first?
   a. The easiest
   b. The middle-of-the-road
   c. The most difficult
   d. The most engaging

18. Which of the following teaching strategies is NOT mentioned in the text?
   a. Varying levels of instruction
   b. Grouping gifted students with classmates who need assistance
   c. Using a different textbook for gifted students
   d. Offering extra activities and worksheets

19. Which of the following is NOT mentioned as a challenge that teachers face?
   a. Identifying gifted students
   b. Assisting gifted students so they can succeed
   c. Teaching students of varying abilities in the same class
   d. Getting gifted students to complete homework

20. What kind of passage would be best for choosing which of the teaching methods is most effective for a given group of students?
   a. Comparison and contrast
   b. Cause and effect
   c. Classification
   d. Explanation

21. To show the number of students who learn best from the various types of instruction, which kind of graphic would be most suitable?
   a. Line graph
   b. Pie chart
   c. Venn diagram
   d. Cartesian graph

Answer the following five questions based on the graphic below.

Some high school students who want to attend college in a certain region of the country are researching how many public and private schools they might apply to in a four-state area. Answer the following questions based on the graphic below.

Number of Postsecondary Institutions

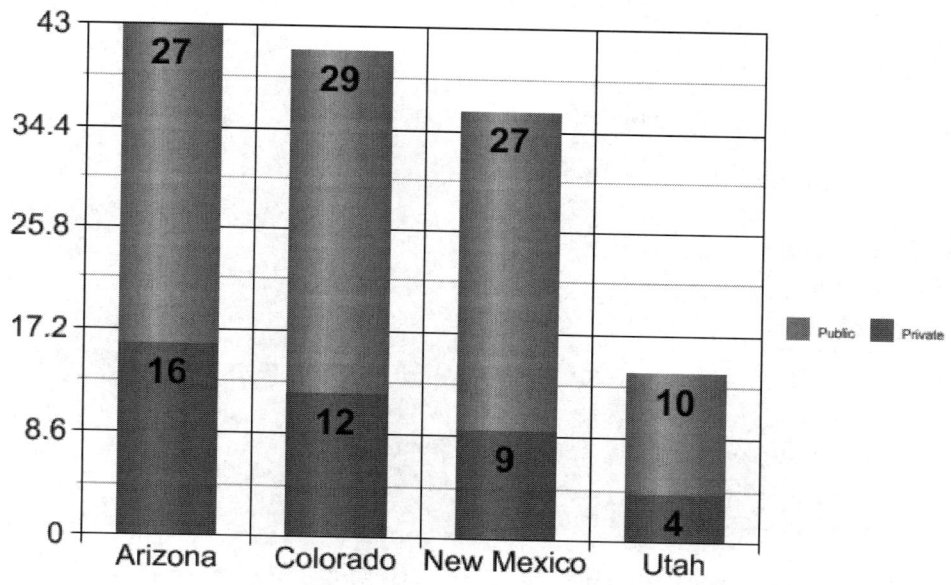

State	Public	Private
Arizona	16	27
Colorado	12	29
New Mexico	9	27
Utah	4	10

SOURCE: National Center for Education Statistics, Integrated Postsecondary Education Data System (IPEDS): Fall 2002

22. According to the graph data, what is true about the number of public universities and colleges in the states shown?
   a. Arizona and New Mexico have an equal number.
   b. Colorado has fewer than Arizona or New Mexico.
   c. Arizona has more than Colorado or New Mexico.
   d. Utah has one-third as many of these as Colorado does.

23. Which is correct about the number of private higher education institutions in the states displayed?
    a. New Mexico has exactly half as many as Arizona.
    b. Colorado has three times as many as Utah has.
    c. Arizona has 50 percent more of them than Colorado.
    d. Utah has more than one-half of New Mexico's.

24. What is correct about the availability of public vs. private postsecondary schools in these four states?
    a. Only one of these states has more private institutions.
    b. Two states have more public schools, and two have more private schools.
    c. There are more private institutions in all of these states.
    d. There are more public institutions in all of these states.

25. Which of the states shown has the smallest total number of higher education institutions?
    a. New Mexico
    b. Colorado
    c. Arizona
    d. Utah

26. Which state has one-third as many private schools as it has public schools?
    a. Colorado
    b. New Mexico
    c. Utah
    d. Arizona

27. Of the following sentences, which represents a fact rather than an opinion?
    a. "Michelle is a whole lot taller at age 13 than Howie."
    b. "Michelle, like any girl aged 13, is taller than Howie."
    c. "Michelle is four inches taller at age 13 than Howie."
    d. "Michelle is uncomfortable being taller than Howie."

28. Which of the following sentences demonstrates subject-verb agreement?
    a. "The beautiful shores of Hawaii is where I call home."
    b. "Neither Harriet nor her sister are going to visit him."
    c. "The people of the Iroquois Nation are in agreement."
    d. "Only one of these islands have a civilized population."

29. The subjects and verbs agree throughout which of these sentences?
    a. "When Stephen and his little sister walk to school, they hold hands."
    b. "Every time that she become embarrassed, her face gets bright red."
    c. "The entire family leave for a summer vacation when school is over."
    d. "The applicant's background and experience fits the job description."

30. In the choices below, which correctly demonstrates the past perfect tense?
   a. She found her lost dog four days after the dog had disappeared.
   b. She is absolutely overjoyed now that she had found her lost dog.
   c. After this incident, she is going to install a lock on the gate.
   d. They appreciated the support of friends while they will be missing their dog.

31. Which of the following sentences has the verb in the present tense?
   a. The toddler has behaved well for several hours now.
   b. The toddler had thrown a major tantrum yesterday.
   c. The toddler wants to participate in adults' activities.
   d. The toddler cooperated with directions more today.

32. Of the following, which choice uses the future verb tense?
   a. Lana specializes in mechanical engineering.
   b. Lana will soon acquire an advanced degree.
   c. Lana has worked in this field for many years.
   d. Lana had always been interested in the field.

33. Which sentence correctly uses the present perfect verb tense?
   a. We have delayed the meeting for you latecomers.
   b. We had planned to start the meeting an hour ago.
   c. We have ask what we should do next.
   d. We are ending the meeting later owing to this delay.

34. In which tense and for which verbs does the *-d* or *-ed* ending apply?
   a. Present perfect tense of all verbs
   b. Past perfect with irregular verbs
   c. The simple past tense of all verbs
   d. The simple past for regular verbs

35. Which of the following sentences shows disagreement between pronoun and antecedent?
   a. "The person who is at fault here is you."
   b. "They are the people who voted for us."
   c. "Students must finish their tests today."
   d. "We have met the enemy and he is us."

36. Of the following examples, which has pronoun-antecedent agreement?
   a. The members of the committee gave their votes.
   b. She liked the way her self-portrait portrayed him.
   c. Mr. Davis wanted to supervise everything herself.
   d. Susie asked her brother to give him a ride home.

37. "The one in charge of this group is ___." Which pronoun completes this sentence to agree grammatically with its antecedent?
   a. her
   b. you
   c. him
   d. me

38. Which of the following uses of possession is correct?
    a. The hat is Mary's, but Sue says it is her's.
    b. This hat is Mary's, but Sue says it is hers.
    c. This hat is Marys, but Sue says it is her's.
    d. This hat is Marys, but Sue says it is hers.

39. Among the following, which version uses the correct relative pronoun?
    a. Thank you for your advice, who really helped.
    b. Thank you for your advice, that really helped.
    c. Thank you for your advice, what really helped.
    d. Thank you for your advice, which really helped.

40. If you had a dog on a leash right next to you, and a man had another dog on a leash across the park from you, how would you correctly describe both pets using demonstratives?
    a. This is my dog, and that is his dog.
    b. This is my dog, and this is his dog.
    c. That is my dog, and that is his dog.
    d. That is my dog, and this is his dog.

41. "Ted is the _____ employee in the company." Which word correctly completes this sentence?
    a. efficientest
    b. more efficient
    c. most efficient
    d. efficienter

42. "Curiouser and curiouser," remarks Alice in Lewis Carroll's *Alice's Adventures in Wonderland* (1865). Which statement is most accurate about this use of the comparative form?
    a. It is grammatically correct; comparatives use -er endings.
    b. It is grammatically incorrect, but it invokes poetic license.
    c. It is grammatically incorrect, and it indicates poor writing.
    d. It is grammatically correct, but it is excessively repetitive.

43. Which of the following is a complete sentence?
    a. Through the yard, up over the fence, and out into the street.
    b. Climbed up over the fence and ran out into the street.
    c. Climbed over the fence and ran out into the street.
    d. Climbing the fence, he ran into the street.

44. Among these, which choice is an example of a sentence fragment?
    a. Chaos occurred.
    b. After the law passed, chaos occurred.
    c. After the law had finally been passed.
    d. Chaos occurred after the law passed.

45. Of the following examples, which is or has a run-on sentence?
   a. Your assignment is written on the board and printed in the handout you will find materials in the back.
   b. You will find materials in the back, and your assignment is written on the board and printed in the handout.
   c. Your assignment is written on the board and printed in the handout; you will find materials in the back.
   d. The materials are in the back, and your assignment is written on the board and printed in the handout.

46. Which of these sentences is correctly divided?
   a. I know you want to play your new game but you must finish your homework first.
   b. I know you want to play your new game but, you must finish your homework first.
   c. I know you want to play your new game; but, you must finish your homework first.
   d. I know you want to play your new game, but you must finish your homework first.

47. Of the following, which choice demonstrates correct punctuation?
   a. Our visitors hailed from Alamo, Tennessee, Moscow, Idaho, Springfield, Michigan, and other locations.
   b. Our visitors hailed from Alamo; Tennessee, Moscow; Idaho, Springfield; Michigan, and other locations.
   c. Our visitors hailed from Alamo, Tennessee; Moscow, Idaho; Springfield, Michigan; and other locations.
   d. Our visitors hailed from Alamo Tennessee, Moscow Idaho, Springfield Michigan, and other locations.

48. Which of the following versions of this sentence is punctuated correctly?
   a. If I like it, and I think I will, I will give it a good review, you can count on that.
   b. If I like it, and I think I will, I will give it a good review; you can count on that.
   c. If I like it, and I think I will; I will give it a good review, you can count on that.
   d. If I like it; and I think I will; I will give it a good review; you can count on that.

49. Where is an example of both correct punctuation and correct capitalization in this sentence?
   a. We are in America; they are in Europe.
   b. We are in America; They are in Europe.
   c. We are in America, They are in Europe.
   d. We are in America, they are in Europe.

50. Correct capitalization is represented in which of the following choices?
   a. The supreme court ruled that this action was Constitutional.
   b. The Supreme Court ruled the action defied the constitution.
   c. The Supreme Court ruled that this action was constitutional.
   d. The Supreme court ruled the action defied the Constitution.

51. Which of the following sentences incorporates standard capitalization?
    a. That practice is prohibited by four Federal Regulations.
    b. Teachers are Federally Mandated Reporters of neglect.
    c. The Federal Trade Commission prohibited that practice.
    d. This practice is banned by the federal trade commission.

52. Which of the following sentences has correct capitalization and spelling?
    a. Sherif Jones stopped when he saw a car with a flat tire.
    b. Spotting a woman with a flat tire, sheriff Jones pulled over quickly.
    c. The sheriff stopped to help the woman with a flat tire.
    d. As soon as he saw the car with a flat tire, the sherif stopped.

53. Among these, which version of the sentence spells all words correctly?
    a. A lot of the funds allotted for that project were misappropriated.
    b. Allot of the funds allotted for that project were misappropriated.
    c. Alot of the funds allotted for that project were misappropriated.
    d. Alot of the funds alotted for that project were misappropriated.

54. Which of these sentences correctly spells the word with the common sound?
    a. Charlie was the friend who came to my aide.
    b. Charlie just got hired as a White House aide.
    c. Charlie was on the scene giving needed aide.
    d. Charlie is now working as a White House aid.

55. How many times greater is the underlined digit than the digit in the one's place in 4,444?
    a. 100
    b. 400
    c. 44
    d. 10

56. In the number 4,708.9, what is the tenths digit?
    a. 7
    b. 0
    c. 9
    d. 8

57. What is 49,249 rounded to the nearest hundred?
    a. 49,200
    b. 200
    c. 49,250
    d. 49,300

58. How many centimeters are in 6 meters?
    a. 0.06
    b. 600
    c. 60
    d. 6000

59. How many kilograms are equivalent to 58.6 grams?
   a. 58,600
   b. 5,860
   c. 0.586
   d. 0.0586

60. A contractor is trying to estimate the height of a six-story building. If each story is 11.7 feet high, estimate the height of the building.
   a. 72 feet
   b. 74 feet
   c. 76 feet
   d. 78 feet

61. A square has side lengths of 12.8 cm. Estimate the area of the square to the nearest whole square centimeter.
   a. 155 cm²
   b. 179 cm²
   c. 144 cm²
   d. 169 cm²

62. What is the sum of $200 + 300 + 400 + 500$?
   a. 1,300
   b. 1,600
   c. 1,400
   d. 1,500

63. Add $686 + 455 + 295 + 613$.
   a. 2,049
   b. 2,039
   c. 2,139
   d. 2,149

64. What is $1,250 - 449$?
   a. 829
   b. 819
   c. 811
   d. 801

65. TJ's savings account balance is $3,281. If he withdrawals $425 for a new gaming system, what is his remaining balance?
   a. $2,866
   b. $3,856
   c. $2,856
   d. $2,286

66. Mr. Miller buys two gallons of tea at $3 per gallon, three loaves of bread at $2 per loaf, and six cans of tuna at two cans for $2. What was the total cost of the food?

   a. $20
   b. $18
   c. $21
   d. $24

67. Madison Public Library bought 1,243 new books in the last two years. The number of new fiction books was 703. The number of reference books was 123. The rest of the books were nonfiction books. How many nonfiction books did the library purchase?

   a. 663
   b. 417
   c. 476
   d. 561

68. Find 724×201.

   a. 15,204
   b. 145,524
   c. 2,172
   d. 1,448,724

69. What is $4 \times 1 \times 2 \times 5 \times 3$?

   a. 150
   b. 135
   c. 120
   d. 105

70. What is $36,000 \div 900$?

   a. 4
   b. 40
   c. 6
   d. 60

71. Divide 29400 by 245.

   a. 120
   b. 122
   c. 130
   d. 132

72. Marcus does yard work after school. If earns $8 per hour and works 20 hours a week over a period of 12 weeks, how much does he earn?

   a. $1,920
   b. $1,940
   c. $1,960
   d. $1,980

73. A city in California charges a fine of $49 for each mile a speeder is driving above the speed limit. Tina received a $882 fine for speeding. How many miles per hour above the speed limit was she traveling?
   a. 16 mph
   b. 24 mph
   c. 20 mph
   d. 18 mph

74. Which of the following fractions is equivalent to 0.2?
   a. $\frac{2}{9}$
   b. $\frac{1}{6}$
   c. $\frac{1}{5}$
   d. $\frac{2}{7}$

75. What is $\frac{3}{4} \div \frac{3}{8}$?
   a. 2
   b. $\frac{1}{2}$
   c. $\frac{9}{32}$
   d. 3

76. Ms. Fishburn fills her gas tank for her road trip to her sister's house. If she buys 20.7 gallons of gasoline at $2.30 per gallon, what was the cost of the gasoline?
   a. $48.81
   b. $48.71
   c. $47.61
   d. $47.71

77. Ms. Ferguson's checking account balance is $1,507.23. If she makes purchase of $36.07, $120.00, and $490.09, what is her new account balance?
   a. $861.07
   b. $860.07
   c. $859.07
   d. $859.03

78. A recent poll of a city of 25,000 showed that 70% of the adult residents are in favor of building a new community center. How many of the residents are not in favor of building a new community center?
   a. 1,750
   b. 7,500
   c. 17,500
   d. 23,250

79. Mr. Franklin sold a $16,000 used car to a customer. If his commission is 4%, what is his commission?
   a. $640
   b. $6,400
   c. $6,600
   d. $600

80. How is the decimal 2.07 written as a percent?
   a. 20.7%
   b. 2.07%
   c. 0.0207%
   d. 207%

81. What is 0.1 written as fraction?
   a. $\frac{1}{100}$
   b. $\frac{1}{10}$
   c. $\frac{1}{11}$
   d. $\frac{1}{20}$

82. A teacher asks the teaching assistant to show a video as instructional material to a whole class. Time prohibits pausing, rewinding, or replaying. Which of the following is NOT an advantage of this?
   a. Engages more sensory modalities
   b. More interesting to many students
   c. More chance for analysis and review
   d. Circumvents difficulties with reading

83. A teacher's assistant helps the teacher with young students by using pictures to teach them simple words. Which is the best way of presenting this information?
   a. First present the word alone, and then show the picture alone.
   b. Present each picture and word on the same sheet, card, or screen.
   c. First show the picture by itself, then present the word by itself.
   d. Present each picture and word together on two separate cards.

84. A student whose parents emigrated from Puerto Rico has learned cultural background from them, but they had little formal education. After reading a brief passage in a social studies text about Puerto Rico, the student is eager to learn more about its history. Which instructional resource would offer this information and also support reading?
   a. Educational film
   b. Dictionary entry
   c. Location photos
   d. An encyclopedia

85. To help several ELL students whose native languages are Spanish, Italian, and French to increase their English language vocabulary, their teacher encourages them to learn more about the many cognates among English and these languages. Which resource would be most handy for them to research English word origins?
   a. Dictionary
   b. Text glossary
   c. Encyclopedia
   d. Grammar guide

86. Among reading comprehension strategies, which can teachers best use before, during, and after students read text?
   a. Skimming an assigned text
   b. Monitoring understanding
   c. Activating prior knowledge
   d. Reviewing or summarizing

87. Among metacognitive strategies that students can use to monitor their reading comprehension, which student example reflects the strategy of identifying the content of a comprehension difficulty?
   a. "I don't understand how this is done. By its title, the next chapter may tell; I'll read it."
   b. "Rereading about this character in Chapter 1 may help me explain his actions later on."
   c. "The author must mean an important event when s/he writes that it was a 'milestone.'"
   d. "I don't understand what the author means when s/he describes that as a 'milestone.'"

88. To inform ongoing planning, instruction, and assessment, a 1st-grade teacher collects information about the students' reading progress. Which student behavior is most likely to indicate difficulty with phonological skills?
   a. A student reading aloud skips words without self-correcting.
   b. A student cannot identify sounds to go with all print letters.
   c. A student can sound out words but cannot remember them.
   d. A student can read around 100 common words by mid-year.

89. When using the words correct per minute (WCPM) procedure to assess reading fluency, at which level should teachers select text for monitoring student progress?
   a. The student's goal level
   b. The student's grade level
   c. The student's instructional level
   d. The student's independent level

90. Which of the following most accurately describes the writing process as students must understand it?
   a. Finite
   b. Linear
   c. Recursive
   d. Spontaneous

91. When students use word processing programs for writing, in which stage of the process should they make the most use of the program's spell-check and grammar-check features?
    a. Planning stage
    b. Proofreading stage
    c. Revision stage
    d. Drafting stage

92. To help students establish focus for writing, the RAFT strategy is an acronym for which of these?
    a. Role, audience, format, task
    b. Reading, action, form, text
    c. Reflect, answer, fit, topic
    d. Review, ask, find, test

93. A formula that helps students create a focus statement, which may also be their topic sentence (or thesis statement in formal papers) to help them focus their writing, is: topic + focus = focus statement. Here is an example: "Our school must try to be more environmentally responsible." Which choice accurately identifies the topic and/or focus in this statement?
    a. This entire sentence is the topic, but it does not indicate any focus.
    b. This entire sentence is the focus, but it does not identify any topic.
    c. "Our school" is the focus, and the rest of the sentence is the topic.
    d. "Our school" is the topic, and the rest of the sentence is the focus.

94. A teacher reviews a student's rough draft and provides feedback that the student is writing only simple sentences. The student is perplexed about how to write compound, complex, and compound-complex sentences. To which of these resources does the teacher direct the student?
    a. A desk dictionary
    b. An encyclopedia
    c. A grammar guide
    d. Library database

95. Which statement is true about a K–12 comprehensive system for the assessment of student writing?
    a. Measures used need not be valid or reliable.
    b. Measures used are not necessarily related to writing goals.
    c. Measures used are all one type of data source.
    d. Measures used inform instructional decisions.

96. Among the following, which form of assessment data can a teacher best use to review individual students' writing progress throughout an entire school year?
    a. Reading assessments
    b. Formative assessments
    c. Summative assessments
    d. Student writing portfolios

97. Of the following, which use of math skills for everyday situations is most related to a student's application of math for an English class?
 a. To determine the value of an unknown number
 b. To determine scores needed to get from B to A
 c. To determine the area of the school auditorium
 d. To determine supplies needed for PTA meeting

98. A student is struggling to grasp the concept of multiplication. Which of the following techniques could the teacher use to help the student understand?
 a. Going over basic multiplication problems side by side
 b. Grouping beads into four clusters of three to demonstrate multiplying four by three
 c. Using coins to show that nickels are five times the worth of pennies
 d. Using flashcards with multiplication facts

99. A class is being introduced to the concept of percentages. Which of the following examples is a good question at the beginning of the lesson?
 a. "How do we use percentages when we're shopping?"
 b. "How can we convert percentages to decimals?"
 c. "Which is greater: 80% or ¾?"
 d. "Why do some percentages include decimals?"

100. Which of these math assessment tasks would be the most appropriate for kindergarten students?
 a. Completing a series like 72, 87, ___, 117, ___
 b. Circling six like items out of a total 10 in a picture
 c. A word problem requiring students to add three 2-digit numbers
 d. Writing 421 in words

Answer Key and Explanations for Test #3

1. B: All these words derive from "verb," but their meanings and parts of speech vary. Verbose (b) means wordy, i.e., using many or excessive words in writing or speech. Verbal (a) is also an adjective, but it means related to words; it can also describe someone who is able to speak and communicate using words. Verbiage (c) is a noun meaning excessive words or wordiness rather than an adjective meaning wordy; it can also (more rarely) mean verbal style. Verbatim (d) is an adverb or adjective meaning exactly word for word.

2. C: The word "to" is a preposition indicating relationship or direction, used to connect verbs (e.g., "going to see"), verbs and objects (e.g., "talk to them"), pronouns (e.g., "from me to you"), nouns (e.g., "comparing apples to oranges"), etc. The word "too" can be an adverb used to modify adjectives (e.g., "too much," "too hard") or to mean "also" as it is here. The other choices use one (a), (b) or both (d) of these incorrectly.

3. B: "Sight" refers as a noun to something one sees (a sight) or to one's vision (eyesight), and as a verb to seeing something (e.g., "he was sighted nearby"). To state, reference, or quote something is to cite it, not site (a) it. A mechanism on a gun for aiming is a sight, not a cite (c). A location is a work or job site, not sight (d).

4. C: When referring to artistic expression (not only traditional art but also music, journalism, etc.), *medium* is singular and *media* is plural. Thus (a) should be *medium* and (d) should be *media*. The term in sentence (b) should be *median*, not *medium*, referring to the cost in the middle when all costs are arranged in order.

5. C: The verb to *saunter* means to stroll or walk with a leisurely, unhurried gait. To slink (a) means to walk or move in either a fearful or ashamed way; or a slow, winding, curving, graceful, and/or sexy way. To race (b) means to run or move speedily or hurriedly, which is the opposite of saunter. To gallop (d) also means to run, race, or hurry, with slightly jumping steps.

6. C: *Tailor* means to adapt or customize something for a particular person. Traditionally this refers to sewing clothes (a), but this does not fit the context. It does not simply mean to teach (b) and while change (d) is usually part of tailoring, it is not merely changing the instruction but customizing it for each student.

7. D: *Tantamount* (used with "to") means the same as or the equivalent of; *tant* in French and *tanto* in Italian mean as much as, i.e., to amount to as much as, e.g., "His deed was tantamount to a crime." A similar-sounding but different word meaning most important (a) is *paramount*. Because choice (d) is correct, choices (b) and (c) are incorrect.

8. C: The title (a) gives the topic but not the main idea. The first sentence of the first paragraph (b) introduces the topic but does not state a main idea. The last sentence of the last paragraph (d) gives a summary statement rather than the main idea. The main point of the article is about discovering gifted students and learning how to teach to their needs, as the last sentence of the first paragraph states.

9. A: The third paragraph lists several ways teachers can tailor education to gifted students. The first way is listed in the first sentence, followed by other ways for the entire paragraph. There is no topic sentence, leading into the topic for the paragraph. The details support the main idea rather than providing a counterargument (b). This is not comparison and contrast (c); the various teaching suggestions are simply listed rather than compared against each other. It is not narrative (d) as it is not retelling events but offering suggestions.

10. D: This selection offers an explanation of several ways to teach. These ways are not compared or contrasted against each other (a). There is no "effect" of these methods given, so it is not cause and effect (b). A classification essay (c) groups similar ideas together. This selection does not divide different teaching styles into different paragraphs for discussion, but puts them all in one paragraph.

11. B: The first sentence that opens the first paragraph is most like an introductory statement, as is often the case in informational text. The title (a) gives the topic but is not a statement that introduces the subject. The final sentence of the first paragraph (c) gives the main idea after the subject has already been introduced. The final sentence of the final paragraph (d) gives a summary statement.

12. D: According to the second paragraph, a gifted child may become a troublemaker if he/she is not being mentally stimulated. Being late to class (a) is something a gifted child may do, not a reason for being a troublemaker. Perhaps the work is too easy (b), and thus the child is not mentally stimulated, but this is not clearly stated. Like being late, failing to finish homework (c) is something a gifted child may do, not the cause of troublemaking.

13. C: Tiered learning (a) divides instruction into different levels. Differentiated instruction (b) also divides instruction into various levels. Challenging activities and worksheets (d) are likely for students to work on alone. Only student grouping (c) specifically notes that students are working together and bouncing ideas off each other.

14. B: The first paragraph states that approximately one in twenty students is enrolled in a gifted and talented program. One out of twenty is the same as five out of one hundred, or 5%.

15. D: While few would deny that teachers should remember that their students are still children when planning instruction, it is an opinion to say that this is "important," since facts are known or proven details. The legal age of students (a and c) or whether teachers study childhood development (b) have nothing to do with whether this statement is fact or opinion.

16. B: Paragraph 2 states that a common misconception is that gifted students excel in class. The selection also mentions that gifted students can be troublemakers (a), but this is not a misconception. Choices (c) and (d) are potential misconceptions but are not mentioned in the passage.

17. C: One technique mentioned in the third paragraph is to offer the most difficult level of instruction first, and then teach the other levels. Techniques of beginning with the easiest (a) or middle-of-the-road (b) are not mentioned, and "most engaging" (d) is not a level of instruction.

18. C: The passage does not mention using a different textbook to teach gifted students. Each of the other choices is a technique from the third paragraph.

19. D: Options (a) and (b) are mentioned in the last sentence of the first paragraph. Option (c) is mentioned in the first sentence of the first paragraph. The passage mentions that sometimes gifted students may not complete homework, but this is not described as a challenge the teacher must face.

20. A: The best way to determine the most effective method is to list the pros and cons of each, and how they compare with one another, so comparison and contrast is the preferred style. Cause and effect (b) would be better for showing whether a given teaching method is effective. Classification (c) could be used for discussion of each method without choosing a winner, and explanation (d) simply explains, as this passage already does.

21. B: A pie chart is best because it easily compares how many students benefit from the different types. A line graph (a) is good for showing progress rather than comparison. A Venn diagram (c) is for comparing items with overlap, such as when a person may like both chocolate and vanilla, or only one flavor. A Cartesian graph (d) is for graphing equations, not charting data.

22. A: As of the graph's date, both Arizona and New Mexico had 27 public postsecondary schools. The bars are different heights because New Mexico had fewer private schools: this graph stacks both values vertically for each state, differentiating public vs. private by bar color/shade. The number is displayed on each bar. Colorado has more public schools than Arizona or New Mexico, i.e., 29 vs. 27, not fewer (b). Arizona has fewer than Colorado and the same as New Mexico (c). Utah has one-third as many private institutions as Colorado (four vs. 12), not public (d).

23. B: Colorado has 12 private schools, three times the four that Utah has. New Mexico has nine, which is more than half the 16 in Arizona (a). Fifty percent more than Colorado's 12 would be 18 (12 + 6), but Arizona has 16 (c). Utah has four, while New Mexico has nine; four is not more than half of nine (d).

24. D: All four states have more public institutions than private institutions. The viewer can see this by looking at not only the numbers shown on each bar, but also the size of each color/shade on each bar: all four states have much bigger bars for public institutions than they do for private ones. None of these states has more private schools (a), (b), and choice (c) is the opposite of the correct answer (d).

25. D: Utah has the smallest total number of schools, i.e., 14 (10 + 4). The viewer can determine this not only by looking at the numbers, but just by looking at the heights of the bars. Because the other three states all have taller bars than Utah—both in total and for public and private schools separately—they all have more postsecondary schools than Utah.

26. B: New Mexico has 27 public institutions and nine private; nine is one third of 27. Colorado (a) has 29 public and 12 private schools. Utah (c) has 10 public and four private schools. Arizona (d) has 27 public and 16 private schools. None of these states' private school numbers will divide evenly into their public-school numbers by three, except for New Mexico's.

27. C: This is a fact because it objectively identifies how many inches Michelle is taller than Howie. "A whole lot taller" (a) is an opinion. While it is a fact that many girls are taller than boys at age 13, not all girls are; hence "like any girl aged 13" (b) is an opinion. Saying what someone else feels (d) is both an opinion and an assumption. If the sentence read, "Michelle says she is uncomfortable being taller than Howie," and she had indeed said so, that would be a fact.

28. C: The verb in option (a) should be plural "are" to agree with subject "shores," not singular to agree with modifier "Hawaii." Because both subjects "Harriet" and "sister" in option (b) are singular and so is the construction "Neither... nor," the verb should be singular "is," not plural "are." The verb is correctly plural "are" to agree with subject "people" in option (c), not with singular noun "Nation" in the modifying prepositional phrase. The verb should be singular "has" in option (d) to agree with subject "one," not with modifying plural noun "islands."

29. A: Both verbs in this sentence, "walk" and "hold," agree with their third-person plural subjects: "Stephen" and "sister" are two subjects, requiring a plural verb; plural subject "they" also does. In the second clause of choice (b), verb "gets" is singular, agreeing with "face"; but in the first clause, singular "she" requires "becomes," not "become." Because "family" is treated as a single unit in choice (c), the verb should be "leaves," not "leave." The two subjects "background" and "experience in choice (d) require plural verb "fit," not "fits."

30. A: The words "...had disappeared" is in the past perfect tense. "Had found" (b) is also past perfect, but does not match the present tense verb "is." "Is going" (c) uses the present progressive (continuous) tense to represent the simple future tense (e.g., "will install"). "Appreciated" (d) is in the simple past tense and "will be missing" is the future progressive or continuous participle of the verb.

31. C: Sentence (a) has its verb in the present perfect tense. Sentence (b) has the verb in the past perfect tense. Sentence (c) has the verb "wants" in the present tense (the infinitive "to participate" modifies "wants"). Sentence (d) has its verb in the simple past tense.

32. B: Choice (a) uses the present tense ("specializes"); choice (b) uses the future tense ("will... acquire"), which is the correct answer; choice (c) uses the present perfect tense ("has worked"); and choice (d) uses the past perfect tense ("had... been").

33. A: "We have delayed" is an example of the present perfect verb tense. "We had planned" (b) is an example of the past perfect verb tense. "We have ask" (c) is an incorrect form of the present perfect; it should be "we have asked." "We are ending" (d) is an example of the present progressive (continuous) tense.

34. D: Regular verbs, not all verbs (c), take the *-d* or *-ed* ending in the simple past tense, e.g., "walk" becomes "walked," "study" becomes "studied." The present perfect tense also takes this ending, but not for all verbs (a), only regular verbs (e.g., "have walked," "have studied"); irregular verbs differ (e.g., "speak," "spoke," and "have spoken"; "do," "did," and "have done"; and "go" "went, and "have gone"). The past perfect ("had" instead of "have") follows the same rule as present perfect: only regular verbs take *-d* or *-ed* endings, not irregular verbs (b).

35. D: This humorous quotation (used in *Pogo* by Walt Kelly, parodying Admiral Perry's "We have met the enemy and they are ours") shows disagreement between antecedent "enemy" and objective pronoun "us." Pronoun "you" agrees with antecedent "person" (a). Regardless of sequence, plural pronoun "They" agrees with plural noun "people" (b). Possessive plural pronoun "their" agrees with plural antecedent "Students" (c).

36. A: "Their" is plural, agreeing with antecedent "members," and because the plural is gender-neutral, there is no gender disagreement. However, the other choices all disagree in gender between pronoun and antecedent: her self-portrait portrayed her, not him (b); Mr. Davis wanted to supervise everything himself, not herself (c); and Susie asked her brother to give her a ride home, not him (d).

37. B: The second-person pronoun "you" has the same form in both subjective (e.g., "you are") and objective ("is you" here) uses. The other choices do not agree with antecedent "one" because these are all used objectively (e.g., "They like her [a], him [c], and me [d]"), not subjectively (e.g., "Her is the one," "Him is the one," or "Me is the one"). Therefore, to agree in this sentence, they would be "she," "he," and "I."

38. B: When indicating possession, ordinary nouns (e.g., "the girl's") and proper nouns (names, like "Mary's") require the *-'s* ending; however, possessive pronouns (like "hers") have the *-s* ending, but without an apostrophe. Option (a) incorrectly adds an apostrophe to the possessive pronoun, option (c) gets both possessives wrong, and option (d) incorrectly omits the apostrophe from the possessive proper noun.

39. D: The relative pronoun "which" should be used for nonrestrictive (or nonessential or nondefining) clauses, i.e., they add information that is supplemental but not essential or required. "Who" (a) is used to indicate persons, not things. "That" (b) should be used for restrictive (essential or defining) clauses providing essential (necessary) information (e.g., "things that matter"). "What" (c) should never be substituted for "that," a mistake some people make. That the advice helped is not essential to know which advice (d).

40. A: Demonstrative pronouns and adjectives indicate number and location. "This" is singular and indicates nouns nearby; "that," also singular, indicates nouns farther away. ("These" and "those" are their plurals.) Choice (b) incorrectly indicates both dogs are right here, while choice (c) incorrectly indicates both are over there. Choice (d) reverses the correct use of both words.

41. C: Although comparatives are commonly formed by adding *-er*, and superlatives by adding *-est*, to adjectives, a general rule with longer (most with two syllables and all with three or more) words is not to add these endings as they become unwieldy, and modify them with "more" and "most" respectively. Hence options (a) and (d) are incorrect. Also, comparatives can only compare two, i.e., one to another, whereas superlatives compare one to plural others. Hence option (b) is also incorrect for this sentence.

42. B: The author deliberately used word choice to emphasize the concept of increasingly odd occurrences, create humor, and make Alice's comment more memorable, thus he invoked poetic license to use an ungrammatical construction, not indicating poor writing in this instance (c). Normally, the rule is to add comparative *-er* endings (a) only to words with one syllable (and occasionally with two syllables, e.g., "angry/angrier, happy/happier"), but precede longer (most with two and three syllables or more) words with "more." Another way Carroll emphasized the unusual word choice was by repeating it, which is not excessive (d).

43. D: This is the only choice that is a complete sentence because it includes a subject ("He") and predicate ("ran"), and also expresses a complete thought. Choice (a) has three prepositional phrases, but no subject and no verb. Choice (b) has two verbs, but no subject. Choice (c) is essentially the same as choice (b), except it omits one preposition ("up").

44. C: This choice is a dependent clause, without accompanying the required independent clause. Choices (b) and (d) show ways of completing the sentence by adding an independent clause ("chaos occurred"). Choice (a) has only the independent clause without the modifying dependent clause, but it is nevertheless a complete sentence because it includes a subject and a verb, and expresses a complete thought.

45. A: This is a run-on sentence because it combines two independent clauses without any punctuation or conjunction between them. Some ways to correct it include rearranging wording (b and d) and placing a semicolon between the clauses (c).

46. D: This version is divided correctly by a comma plus the conjunction "but." Version (a) includes the conjunction, but is still akin to a run-on sentence by omitting punctuation before it. Version (b) incorrectly places the comma after the conjunction. Version (c) incorrectly uses a semicolon before and a comma after the conjunction, which is reserved for conjunctive adverbs like "however" or "nevertheless," not conjunctions like "but" or "and."

47. C: When listing a series of several units when any unit(s) includes internal commas (cities and states in this case), separate the units with semicolons to differentiate them from the unit parts that are separated by commas within each unit. The sentence makes no sense with all commas (a) or transposing commas and semicolons (b), and no punctuation between city and state (d) is nonstandard as well as less clear.

48. B: The first three clauses of this sentence combine to make a full, independent statement. The final clause, "you can count on that," is also independent. Thus, a semicolon is placed before the final clause to separate the two independent components.

49. A: Two independent clauses should be separated by a semicolon, and the second independent clause should not have its first word capitalized (unless, of course, that word is a proper noun or title). Hence option (b) is correctly punctuated but incorrectly capitalized. Because this sentence is short, the comma in option (c) is an acceptable alternative to a semicolon, but it is still incorrectly capitalized. Option (d) is a run-on sentence.

50. C: The names of government entities (e.g., Supreme Court) and of major government documents (e.g., the Constitution), like other names or proper nouns, should be capitalized. However, adjectives derived from those names (e.g., constitutional) should not be capitalized. Choice (a) breaks both rules, choice (b) breaks the first rule, and choice (c) is correct. Choice (d) capitalizes "Supreme" but not "court," but both are parts of the name and should both be capitalized.

51. C: Standard capitalization includes capitalizing the first letters of all words of the name of a government agency like the FTC. Thus option (d) is incorrect. However, the adjective "federal" and noun "regulations" are not names (i.e., they are regular nouns, not proper nouns) and generally not capitalized (a). The same applies to option (b): adverb "federally," adjective "mandated," and noun "reporters" should all have lower-case initials.

52. C: The correct spelling is "sheriff." When used as a title it is capitalized ("Sheriff Jones") but when used as a common noun it is lowercased ("the sheriff"). Only choice C both spells and capitalizes the word correctly.

53. A: This is the correct spelling of all words. "A lot" is a phrase consisting of the indefinite article "a" plus the noun "lot"; together, they mean much or many. "Allot," however, is a verb meaning to allow, allocate, or apportion, as with funds. Thus choice (b) incorrectly substitutes the verb for the noun phrase. Choice (c) incorrectly runs the article and noun together into one word, a common misspelling today. Choice (d) not only makes the same error as (c), but additionally misspells the verb, omitting an L.

54. B: The spelling "aide" signifies the job position of a helper or assistant; the spelling "aid" signifies help or assistance as a noun, and to help or assist as a verb. Therefore, option (a) should be spelled "aid," option (b) is correct, option (c) should be spelled "aid," and option (d) should be spelled "aide."

55. A: Since the underlined digit is in the hundreds place, its value is 4×100 or 400. The digit in the one's place has a value of 4×1 or 4. To determine how many times greater 400 is than 4, divide 400 by 4. So 400 is 100 times greater than 4.

56. C: The place value of a digit depends on its location in relation to the decimal point. The places to the left of the decimal are ones, tens, then hundreds, respectively. The places to the right of the decimal are tenths, hundredths, and thousandths, respectively. Since the digit 9 is in the first position to the right of the decimal point, its place value is tenths.

57. A: The place value of a digit depends on its location in relation to the decimal point. The places to the left of the decimal are ones, tens, then hundreds, respectively. To round a number to a certain place value, look at the digit to the immediate right. If the digit to the right is 5 or more, round up by adding one followed by a zero. If the digit is less than five, round down by keeping the same digit followed by a zero. For this problem, the digit in the hundreds place is 2. The digit to its immediate right is 4. Since 4 is less than 5, round down. So, 49,249 rounded to the nearest hundred is 49,200.

58. B: Since one meter equals 100 centimeters, the conversion factor is 100. Since a meter is longer than a centimeter, we multiply by the conversion factor. So, 6 meters equal 6×100 or 600 centimeters.

59. D: Since one kilogram equals 1,000 grams, the conversion factor is 1,000. Since a gram is less than a kilogram, we divide by the conversion factor. So, 58.6 grams equal $58.6 \div 1000$ or 0.0586 kilograms.

60. A: The height of the building equals the product of the number of stories and the height of a story. Since each story is approximately 12 feet high, this building is approximately 6×12 or 72 feet high.

61. D: The area of a square is found by the equation $A = s^2$ where A represents the area and s represents the length of the sides. The side length is approximately equal to 13 cm, so the area of this square is found by $A = (13)^2 = 169$ cm².

62. C: Since the digits in both the ones and tens places are zeros for each addend, the sum is found by adding the digits in the hundreds place ($2 + 3 + 4 + 5 = 14$). Then, zeros are placed in the ones place and tens place, and the sum is 1,400.

63. A: The sum is found by adding the ones column ($6 + 5 + 5 + 3 = 19$) and carrying the 1 to the tens column. Then add the tens column ($1 + 8 + 5 + 9 + 1 = 24$) and carry the 2 to the hundreds column. Then add the hundreds column ($2 + 6 + 4 + 2 + 6 = 20$) and carry the 2 to the thousands column. The sum is 2,049.

64. D: To find the difference between 1,250 and 449, we need to borrow 1 from the tens column. Subtract 1 from the 5 and add 10 to the 0 in the ones column to find that $1,250 - 449 = 801$.

65. C: TJ's remaining balance is equal to the difference between $3,281 and $425. So $3,281 - $425 = $2,856.

66. D: The total cost of the food is the sum of the individual food items. The total equals $2(\$3) + 3(\$2) + 6(\$2)$ or $24.

67. B: The number of nonfiction books is equal to the total number of books minus the number of reference books and fiction books. The number of nonfiction books is equal to $1,243 - (703 + 123) = 1,243 - 826 = 417$ books.

68. B: The factor 201 can be written as $200 + 1$, so the product of $724 \times 201 = 724 \times 200 + 724 \times 1 = 144,800 + 724 = 145,524$.

69. C: Since multiplication is commutative, the factors can be multiplied in any order. The factors can be rewritten as 4 × 3 × 2 × 5 × 1, which is equal to 12 × 10 or 120.

70. B: Since both the dividend and the divisor end in two zeros, those zeros can be cancelled from both. Now we have 360 divided by 9. Since 36 ÷ 9 = 4, 360 ÷ 9 = 40.

71. A: To divide 29,400 by 245, the first step is to divide 294 by 245. Since 245 × 1 = 245, the divisor 245 goes into 294 one time. Then place the 245 under the 294 in the dividend and subtract: 294 − 245 = 49. Now bring down the 0 and determine how many times 245 goes into 490. Since 245 × 2 = 490, the divisor 245 goes into 490 two times. Then place the 490 under the 490 and subtract to get zero. Add a zero in the ones place in the quotient. This means that 29,400 ÷ 245 = 120.

72. A: The amount of money Marcus earns is the product of the hourly rate, the number of hours worked each week, and the number of weeks worked. The amount earned equals $8 × 20 × 12, which is $1,920.

73. D: To find the number of miles per hour over the speed limit, divide the fine by the cost for each mile over the speed limit: 882 ÷ 49 = 18 mph over.

74. C: The decimal 0.2 is read *two tenths*. We can write this as the fraction $\frac{2}{10}$, which is reduced to $\frac{1}{5}$.

75. A: To divide a fraction by a fraction, multiply the dividend by the reciprocal of the divisor: $\frac{3}{4} \div \frac{3}{8} = \frac{3}{4} \times \frac{8}{3} = 2$.

76. C: The cost of the gasoline is equal to the product of the number of gallons and the price per gallon. The cost equals 20.7 × $2.30 or $47.61.

77. A: The new account balance is equal to the original balance minus the sum of the purchases. The new balance equals $1,507.23 − ($36.07 + $120.00 + $490.09), which simplifies to $1,507.23 − $646.16, which is $861.07.

78. B: If 70% of adults are in favor of the new community center, this means that 100% − 70% = 30% are NOT in favor. So, we need to find: what is 30% of 25,000? Let *n* represent *what*, and replace the *of* with a multiplication symbol and the *is* with an equal sign. But first, we need to convert the 30% to a decimal. Remove the percent sign and move the decimal point two places to the left. Then we have $n = 0.30 \times 25{,}000 = 7{,}500$. This means that 7,500 were not in favor of building a new community center.

79. A: The question we need to ask is, "What is 4% of $16,000?" Let *n* represent *what*, and replace the *of* with a multiplication symbol and the *is* with an equal sign. But first, we need to convert the 4% to a decimal. Remove the percent sign and move the decimal point two places to the left. Then we have $n = 0.04 \times 16{,}000 = 640$. This means that Mr. Franklin's commission is $640.

80. D: To convert a decimal to a percent, move the decimal point two places to the right and add the percent symbol. Thus 2.07 equals 207%.

81. B: To convert a decimal to a fraction, move the decimal point one place to the right, place the number over 10, and reduce the fraction if applicable. So, 0.1 equals $\frac{1}{10}$.

82. C: A video engages the visual sense for images and movement rather than only for print, and the auditory sense as well as verbal processing; text only engages the visual for print and verbal processing. Research finds that the more sensory modalities are accessed (a), the better students learn. Videos are more interesting to many students (b) than print. Also, students with reading difficulties can access information more easily by looking at and listening to video (d). However, without time to pause, rewind, and replay, students cannot analyze or review videos as they can print materials (c).

83. B: Young children are less likely to connect pictures with letters and words when these are presented separately, in either sequence (a) or (c). Even presenting them simultaneously can confuse young students if the two stimuli are separated (d): they are more likely to view them as representing two different objects or concepts instead of the same one. Presenting images together with print (b) helps young students connect these to understand that printed words represent real things.

84. D: An educational film (a) would not support reading without accompanying text. A dictionary entry (b) gives the spellings, pronunciations, parts of speech, definitions, etymology, and examples in sentences of words, not national or historical information. Photos of locations (c) in Puerto Rico, like films, inform about the country but do not support reading without additional text. An encyclopedia (d) will provide extensive information about the history of Puerto Rico, as well as other aspects.

85. A: A dictionary provides not only definitions to expand ELL students' English-language vocabulary, plus spelling, pronunciation, parts of speech, and correct usage in sentence context, but also word origins (e.g., Latin > Old French > Middle English) to inform their learning about cognates to facilitate developing English vocabulary. A text glossary (b) only defines vocabulary specific to that text. An encyclopedia (c) gives comprehensive information about varied subjects but does not focus on words as a dictionary does. A grammar guide (d) helps students write correct sentences, not learn about shared word origins.

86. C: Skimming text (a) is a strategy to use before students read text, not during or after reading. Teachers monitor student understanding, and students monitor their own understanding (b) during and after reading but not before reading. Reviewing or summarizing text (d) can only come after or during reading, not before. However, teachers can activate students' prior knowledge (c) before, during, and after they read to relate the text to it.

87. D: This is an example of the strategy of identifying what the comprehension difficulty is, i.e., its content. Example (a) is of the strategy of looking ahead in text for a resolution to the difficulty. Example (b) is of the strategy of looking back through text for an answer. Example (c) is of the strategy of restating the difficult part in the student's own words.

88. B: Phonological skills include recognizing which letters represent which sounds as a reading prerequisite. Being unable to do this likely indicates difficulty with phonological skills. Skipping words (a) may indicate difficulty with visual processing, as in dyslexia or other problems. Sounding out words indicates phonological skills; being unable to remember them (c), e.g., sounding out the same word every time it appears, indicates difficulty with retention. By mid-year, 1st-graders should be able to read at least 100 common words: this does not indicate difficulty (d).

89. A: The student's goal level is determined individually. For instance, if a 9th-grade student reads at the 6th-grade level, the teacher might select text at the 7th-grade level as the student's goal level for monitoring progress. Teachers should select text at the student's grade level (b) for screening student reading fluency rather than for monitoring progress. They should select text at the student's instructional level (c), i.e., 90 percent student success with text, for diagnostic assessment. At the student's independent level (d) is text the student can easily read with 95–100 percent accuracy.

90. C: It is important to help students understand that the writing process is recursive, i.e., that good writers often plan, draft, and revise repeatedly and cyclically to improve their work as much as possible. As such, it is less accurately described as finite (a) than ongoing (although assignments requiring submission for grading impose artificial limits). By definition, this process is not linear (b) but circular. Though motivation to write spontaneously is an asset, the actual writing process is typically not spontaneous (d), involving planning, drafting, revising, repeating, and proofreading.

91. B: Students can make the best use of spell-check and grammar-check features in word processing programs when they are proofreading their work for grammar, spelling, punctuation, capitalization, typing, and other mechanical errors. These features can help them correct those errors. The planning stage (a) involves determining purpose for writing, audience, focus, topic, main idea, etc. (and researching when applicable). Drafting (d) involves composing without correcting mechanics. Revision (c) involves editing content, not correcting mechanics.

92. A: RAFT stands for role, audience, format, topic. Role is that of the writer: students consider who they are or from whose perspective they will write (e.g., rock star, president, animal, etc.). Audience refers to who the students will be writing for (e.g., themselves, parents, politician, corporation, etc.). Format is how the students will present their writing (e.g., newspaper article, journal entry, love letter, scientific report, etc.). And topic is what the subject of the students' writing will be.

93. D: The topic is "Our school," and the more specific focus within this topic is trying to be more environmentally responsible. Hence choices (a) and (b) are both incorrect because both topic and focus are included, and choice (c) incorrectly reverses the correct identification of topic and focus.

94. C: The teacher will direct the student to consult a grammar guide, which will give not only definitions, but also examples of each sentence type as models for the student to follow in writing. A desk dictionary (a) gives word spellings, pronunciations, parts of speech, meaning definitions, origins, and examples in context, but not sentence structures. An encyclopedia (b) gives thorough information on content topics rather than focusing on grammar. A library database (d) compiles numerous information sources, unnecessary and excessive for this student's need.

95. D: In a K–12 comprehensive writing assessment system, the measures used to evaluate student writing should be valid and reliable for their purposes (a); explicitly connected to writing goals (b); made up of multiple, varied types of data sources (c)—e.g., student reading data, progress-monitoring formative assessments, achievement-testing summative assessments, student-centered portfolios of writing samples showing student goals and progress—and should inform instructional decisions about areas where students may need further support.

96. D: Reading assessments (a) are necessary components of a comprehensive writing assessment system because writing depends on reading, but they will not show yearlong individual student writing progress. Formative assessments (b) will each show student progress at a given time during the year, not throughout it. Summative assessments (c) will show what the student can achieve by the end of the year. Teachers can best review yearlong individual writing progress through student writing goals and samples collected in student writing portfolios (d), aligned with instruction.

97. B: A student could apply math to choice (a) most for an algebra class, or any other situation wherein some numbers are known but one is not. For an English class, a student could apply math most to determine what scores are needed to raise a "B" grade to an "A." A student could apply math to choice (c) most for planning attendance at a school play, assembly, or other event using the auditorium space; and to choice (d) for planning to furnish refreshments, seating, forms/paper, pens, etc. at a PTA meeting.

98. B: If the student does not understand how multiplication works, working problems together (a) or going over multiplication facts (d) will not help. While coins could be used for multiplication demonstrations, showing that a nickel is worth five times a penny does not help the student understand how to multiply.

99. A: Question (a) is good for meeting the standard of applying mathematics to real life. It is also a good way of introducing a new concept before the students understand it. Students will not be ready for questions on converting percentages to decimals (b), comparing percentages and fractions (c), or discussing why some percentages include decimals (d).

100. B: Finding and circling like items is a good assessment skill for kindergarten students. Choices (a), (c), and (d) are appropriate for assessing math skills in typical 3rd-grade students.

NYSTCE Practice Test #4

Questions 1–18 are based on the passage below:

Improving Student Fluency

Frederick Douglass famously stated, "Once you learn to read, you will be forever free." One of a teacher's most important tasks is to ensure that his or her students experience this freedom. Due to learning challenges, moving between schools, family trauma, and a host of other reasons, many children struggle with reading throughout their school years and are in imminent danger of failing classes, dropping out of school, or struggling in other areas of life. Poor fluency is one of the greatest handicaps a person can have, affecting every class, everyday life, the chance at higher education, and future careers. Teachers should be aware of practical steps they can take to help their students develop good reading strategies and become confident readers.

Several strategies can be used to help students improve fluency. Simply reading aloud to students as they follow along can help them with word recognition and comprehension. Having students recurrently read particular texts aloud is another way to familiarize them with vocabulary and build confidence, as well as elucidating problem areas. Working on phonemic awareness is a third approach that can help repair a precarious reading foundation. Finally, some students simply need more time. They may process slowly and just need practice with a patient listener.

At times the problem is not with reading ability but with attention. For many children, both those with attention deficit disorders and those without, sitting still and paying attention are difficult. What may seem to be a struggle with reading ability may be a struggle with focus instead. Teachers can employ strategies to help students, such as a quiet corner with fewer distractions or a time of day that is better (often early in the school day or after recess).

Lastly, it is important to remember that children can be easily overwhelmed. Teachers may notice that students are no longer retaining information toward the end of class, or are reverting to previous, less mature reading strategies when faced with unfamiliar material. Teachers can guide students to use better strategies or drop back to a simpler level until students are ready to try again. Through paying attention to student cues, exploring various strategies, and moving at a gentle pace, teachers can foster fluency in their classes.

1. From the context in the second sentence of the final paragraph, which is the correct definition of the word *reverting*?
   a. Leaping forward
   b. Moving steadily
   c. Remaining in a rut
   d. Turning backward

2. Which of the following words is an antonym for the adjective *imminent*, as seen in the third sentence of the first paragraph?

   a. Distant
   b. Looming
   c. Unknown
   d. Impending

3. Of these choices, which is most synonymous with the word *recurrently*, as seen in the third sentence of the second paragraph?

   a. Slowly
   b. Carefully
   c. Repeatedly
   d. Once

4. From the context in the fourth sentence of the second paragraph, which is the correct definition of *precarious*?

   a. Insecure
   b. Strong
   c. Injured
   d. Broken

5. The word *elucidating*, in the third sentence of the second paragraph, is synonymous with which of the following descriptions?

   a. Adding details to or expanding upon something
   b. Making clear or shedding light on something
   c. Lessening or relieving a tightness in something
   d. Making a test or assessment on something

6. Which text element in this passage best expresses its main idea?

   a. The title of the article
   b. The first sentence of the first paragraph
   c. The last sentence of the first paragraph
   d. The first sentence of the second paragraph

7. Which of the following is the clearest topic sentence?

   a. The first sentence of the first paragraph
   b. The last sentence of the first paragraph
   c. The first sentence of the second paragraph
   d. The last sentence of the last paragraph

8. Of these paragraphs, which begins with more of a transitional sentence than a topic sentence?

   a. Paragraph 1
   b. Paragraph 2
   c. Paragraph 3
   d. Paragraph 4

9. Where is/are any overall summary statements found in this text?
   a. The entire last paragraph
   b. The last sentence of the last paragraph
   c. The last sentence of each paragraph
   d. There are no overall summary statements

10. Which of the following strategies does the passage NOT recommend for improving fluency?
    a. Students reading passages recurrently
    b. Working on phonemic awareness
    c. Teachers reading aloud
    d. Timing student readings to improve speed

11. Which of the following can affect fluency, according to the selection?
    a. Improper nutrition
    b. Lack of sleep
    c. Family trauma
    d. Teachers who don't understand a student's unique learning needs

12. How many reading strategies are suggested in the second paragraph?
    a. Two
    b. Three
    c. Four
    d. Five

13. If a student has no learning difficulties with reading but is still struggling, this could indicate difficulty with _____, according to the article.
    a. Understanding
    b. Motivation
    c. Confidence
    d. Attention

14. The content of this piece may be characterized as problem-solution. Which choice most accurately represents this content in the first two paragraphs?
    a. The first paragraph focuses on problems; the second paragraph focuses on solutions.
    b. The first paragraph focuses on solutions; the second paragraph focuses on problems.
    c. Both paragraphs focus on problems; solutions are later in the selection.
    d. Both paragraphs describe problems and then their solutions.

15. According to the information given, when is it likely that students may stop retaining information?
    a. After learning something new
    b. After working in groups
    c. At the last part of the class
    d. When they are moving between schools

16. Which of the following strategies may help students focus better?
   a. Taking more time and going slowly
   b. Finding the best time of day to work
   c. Working on phonemic awareness
   d. Having the teacher read aloud while students follow along

17. What is the author's purpose in this article?
   a. To inform
   b. To persuade
   c. To entertain
   d. To narrate

18. Is the following sentence from the first paragraph fact or opinion? "Poor fluency is one of the greatest handicaps a person can have, affecting every class, everyday life, the chance at higher education, and future careers."
   a. Fact, because these effects have been documented
   b. Opinion, because not all students are interested in higher education
   c. Fact, because there is no question that reading affects every part of life
   d. Opinion, because ranking handicaps is subjective

Answer the following questions based on the graphic below.

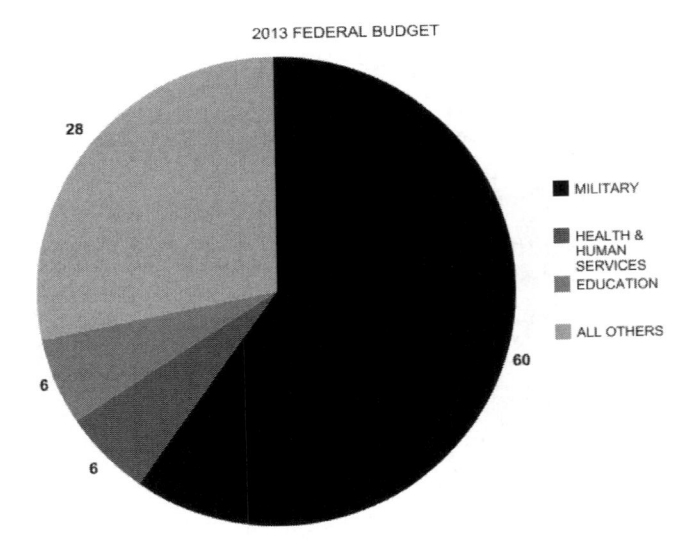

2013 FEDERAL BUDGET

- Military: 60
- Health & Human Services: 28
- Education: 6
- All Others: 6

NOTE: Numbers represent percentages, rounded.

19. According to this graph, the 2013 federal budget allotted the most money to which department and/or program types?
   a. Department of Health and Human Services (HHS)
   b. Military departments and programs
   c. The US Department of Education (ED)
   d. All other departments and programs

20. How much of the budget was allocated for military spending compared to health and human services and education spending combined?
    a. Three times as much
    b. Four times as much
    c. Five times as much
    d. Six times as much

21. What proportion of the entire federal budget was proposed for military spending?
    a. More than half
    b. Exactly one-half
    c. Less than a half
    d. Over two-thirds

22. Relative to military spending, how much of the budget was allocated for spending on education?
    a. One-quarter of military spending
    b. One-eighth of military spending
    c. One-sixth of military spending
    d. One-tenth of military spending

23. If the budget designated $1.6 billion for education, how much would be allotted to health and human services?
    a. $0.8 billion
    b. $1.6 billion
    c. $3.2 billion
    d. $16 billion

24. Which statement related to the pie chart is an example of a fact rather than an opinion?
    a. "The federal government proposed spending far too much of the budget on the military."
    b. "More of the budget was allocated for military spending than all other areas combined."
    c. "The government should spend more money on health and human services than it has."
    d. "The US Department of Education deserves a larger proportion of the federal budget."

25. Which of these sentences shows standard subject-verb agreement?
    a. "They are University of Georgia graduates."
    b. "He and she is graduated from UGA."
    c. "I are a University of Georgia graduate."
    d. "We was graduated from the U. of Ga."

26. In which of the following versions do the verbs agree with their subjects?
    a. She walk and I sits.
    b. She walk and I sit.
    c. She walks and I sit.
    d. She walks and I sits.

27. **The present tense of a verb is used in which of these choices?**
    a. He was awakened by sudden loud noise.
    b. He awakens at the same time every day.
    c. He has undergone a spiritual awakening.
    d. He will awaken everyone in the morning.

28. **Which of the following uses the past tense of the verb "to be"?**
    a. David was the only one to volunteer.
    b. David is the only one who volunteered.
    c. David will be the only one volunteering.
    d. David has been the only one to volunteer.

29. **Which of these sentences uses the future tense of a verb?**
    a. The secretary is forwarding all of your messages to his office.
    b. The secretary has forwarded all your messages to his office.
    c. The secretary forwards each of your messages to his office.
    d. The secretary will forward all your messages to his office.

30. **Of the following, which choice uses the past perfect tense?**
    a. I am wondering when they will get moving on this project.
    b. I have been wondering about this for several months now.
    c. I had contacted them several times before, with no results.
    d. I will continue my periodic contacts until I see some action.

31. **Which of these sentences incorporates the future perfect verb tense?**
    a. We will tell you when we are finished with the work.
    b. We will have finished all the work before we tell you.
    c. When we finish all of the work, we will be telling you.
    d. We have always told you after, not before we finish.

32. **Among the following, which choice uses the past progressive (past continuous) tense of a verb?**
    a. The authorities are conducting a crime investigation.
    b. He was walking home from work during the incident.
    c. He had been walking daily for years with no incident.
    d. He will still be walking, but taking safety precautions.

33. **Which of the following uses a verb in the present progressive (present continuous) tense?**
    a. I will be talking with you as soon as I finish work.
    b. I had been planning to talk with you later today.
    c. I have been planning to talk with you after lunch.
    d. I am working, so I cannot talk with you until later.

34. **Of the following, which is a regular verb?**
    a. To freeze
    b. To speak
    c. To listen
    d. To sing

35. **What is true about verb endings that regular verbs take according to verb tense?**
    a. Regular verbs take -ed endings in the simple past tense.
    b. Regular verbs take -en endings in present perfect tense.
    c. Regular verbs take -en endings in the past perfect tense.
    d. Regular verbs take -s or -es endings in present tense.

36. **In which of these examples does the pronoun agree with its antecedent?**
    a. While Leon and Carla cleaned, both of him found some valuable items.
    b. After Jo and I presented to the committee, we received their approval.
    c. Her supervisor heard all of her reasons, but they did not believe them.
    d. Though Jay and I went to see her in the hospital, she were not allowed.

37. **Pronoun-antecedent agreement is found in which of the following?**
    a. Laura found the task harder than he had expected it to be.
    b. Stewart brought the gift to his wife that he had promised.
    c. Bob feared the worst, but she received a pleasant surprise.
    d. Each member of the coed baseball team knew their position.

38. **The antecedent and pronoun agree in which of these sentences?**
    a. All of us contributed to our eventual success.
    b. I told Sheila that she should do that yourself.
    c. Larry, in order to get a grade, he must study.
    d. That family worked together for our results.

39. **"_____ car is that parked on our lawn?" Which of the following correctly completes this sentence?**
    a. Who
    b. Who's
    c. Whom
    d. Whose

40. **Of the following, what choice uses a relative pronoun(s) most appropriately?**
    a. Give the recognition for hard work to the person that deserves it.
    b. The house that we saw months ago is the one that we are buying.
    c. Of all their toys, the twins' favorites are those which I gave them.
    d. Even at a young age, he was grateful for everything which he had.

41. **Which of the following uses demonstrative pronouns with the most accuracy?**
    a. "Do you see that woman over there? That is my fiancée."
    b. "Do you see this woman right here? That is my fiancée."
    c. "Do you see that woman over there? This is my fiancée."
    d. "Do you see whom I am introducing? That is my fiancée."

42. **In describing how you should walk, which choice uses the correct modifier?**
    a. You need to walk quicker to keep up with the rest.
    b. You need to walk quickest to keep up with others.
    c. You must walk more quickly to keep up with them.
    d. You must walk most quickly to keep up with them.

43. Of the following, which choice demonstrates accurate comparative word use?
   a. "If you missed 8 problems or less, you won't need the extra credit."
   b. "With Internet access they buy less newspapers."
   c. "This job has better work but pays fewer money."
   d. "Use this line if you have 20 items or fewer."

44. Among these choices, which one represents a grammatically complete sentence?
   a. Although she protested loudly and long against the changes in policy.
   b. The implementation of the policy changes by the steering committee.
   c. The committee implemented the policy changes despite her protests.
   d. In spite of all her protests, the policy implementations by committee.

45. Which of the following choices is a sentence fragment?
   a. I have noticed it every time we are together.
   b. When we were together, I had noticed it.
   c. All of the times we were together, you did it.
   d. All of the times that we have been together.

46. Which version of these statements forms a run-on sentence?
   a. Hurry it up, Desmond and catch him he is getting away!
   b. Hurry up, Desmond, and catch him. He is getting away!
   c. Hurry up, Desmond! And catch him. He's getting away!
   d. Hurry up, Desmond, and catch him; he is getting away!

47. Of the following choices, which both avoids a run-on sentence and uses correct punctuation?
   a. I knew right away it was you as soon as you spoke, I recognized your voice.
   b. I knew right away it was you as soon as you spoke I recognized your voice.
   c. I knew right away it was you, as soon as you spoke I recognized your voice.
   d. I knew right away it was you; as soon as you spoke, I recognized your voice.

48. Which of these sentences is punctuated correctly?
   a. I wonder if you might come visit him with me?
   b. Will you come along with me to visit with him?
   c. Will you come along with me when I visit him.
   d. Will you say to her, "Come with me to visit him?"

49. Which version of this sentence uses all words correctly?
   a. "I could tell he was here because I could hear his footsteps."
   b. "I could tell he was hear because I could here his footsteps."
   c. "I could tell he was here because I could here his footsteps."
   d. "I could tell he was hear because I could hear his footsteps."

50. "One church would not allow the wedding to ____ the ____ for the bride's choice of floral decorations." Which words will correctly complete the blanks in this sentence?
   a. altar; alter
   b. alter; altar
   c. altar; altar
   d. alter; alter

51. Which of the following is capitalized correctly?
   a. The US Capitol is one of the largest capitol buildings in the nation.
   b. The US capitol is one of the largest capitol buildings in the nation.
   c. The US Capitol is one of the largest Capitol buildings in the nation.
   d. The US Capitol is one of the largest Capitol Buildings in the nation.

52. Which of the following sentences employs correct spelling?
   a. The milk was beginning to sour, but she was too poor to pore it out and buy a new jug.
   b. The milk was beginning to sour, but she was too pore to pour it out and buy a new jug.
   c. The milk was beginning to sour, but she was too poor to pour it out and buy a new jug.
   d. The milk was beginning to sour, but she was too pour to pore it out and buy a new jug.

53. Of these versions, which one shows correct capitalization?
   a. A Freudian Slip
   b. A freudian slip
   c. A Freudian slip
   d. A freudian Slip

54. In the context of its sentence, where is the word with a common sound in all choices spelled correctly?
   a. She checked her phone discretely, trying not to attract attention.
   b. Though the events occurred simultaneously, they were discreet rather than linked.
   c. When he was asked to come in secret, he was discrete enough to use the back door.
   d. The purchases were similar but discrete, made at separate times and locations.

55. How many times greater is the underlined digit than the digit in the one's place in 55,555?
   a. 100
   b. 500
   c. 5,000
   d. 1,000

56. What is 53,497 rounded to the nearest ten?
   a. 53,400
   b. 53,500
   c. 53,490
   d. 53,590

57. What is 18,753 rounded to the nearest hundred?
   a. 18,800
   b. 800
   c. 19,000
   d. 18,000

58. How many feet are in 7 yards?
   a. 14
   b. 42
   c. 84
   d. 21

59. How many pounds are equivalent to 32 ounces?
   a. 16
   b. 8
   c. 2
   d. 4

60. A triangle has side lengths of 19.7 cm, 20.4 cm, and 10.2 cm. Round each length to the nearest ten centimeters and estimate the perimeter of the triangle.
   a. 60 cm
   b. 50 cm
   c. 55 cm
   d. 65 cm

61. A mountain climber climbs through rough terrain. She climbs 480 feet, 610 feet, 295 feet and 303 feet over a period of 4 days. Estimate the distance she climbs over the four-day period to the nearest hundred feet.
   a. 1,500 feet
   b. 1,600 feet
   c. 1,700 feet
   d. 1,800 feet

62. Melissa receives the Master of Music Scholarship for $2,500 and the New Talent Scholarship for $4,500. What is the total amount of scholarship money she received?
   a. $6,000
   b. $2,000
   c. $7,000
   d. $8,000

63. Ms. Henderson shops for new clothing for her young son. She buys two pairs of pants at $24.99 each, and three shirts at $17.99 each. How much does Ms. Henderson spend on her son's clothing?
   a. $102.95
   b. $103.95
   c. $103.96
   d. $102.95

64. Find $501 - 379$.
   a. 132
   b. 122
   c. 111
   d. 101

65. Angel borrows $325,890 to purchase a new house. If he sells it for $427,980, what is his profit?
   a. $202,190
   b. $102,190
   c. $102,090
   d. $101,090

66. Ms. Elliott makes a down payment of $36,550 on her new house. She mortgages the remaining cost of $156,750. If the interest paid over her 20-year loan is $293,562, what is the total cost of her house, including interest?
   a. $486,862
   b. $486,863
   c. $486,872
   d. $487,862

67. Haley's violin instructor insists that she practice a minimum of 3.5 hours per week. If she practices 45 minutes on both Sunday and Monday, 25 minutes on both Tuesday and Wednesday, how many minutes does she have left to practice this week?
   a. 70
   b. 85
   c. 75
   d. 80

68. What is 525×275?
   a. 142,385
   b. 143,375
   c. 144,375
   d. 143,385

69. Find $5,622 \times 2,300$.
   a. 2,811,000
   b. 12,930,600
   c. 16,930,000
   d. 28,110,000

70. Find the quotient of 72 and 8.
   a. 576
   b. 80
   c. 9
   d. 64

71. What is the remainder when 3,245 is divided by 25?
   a. 18
   b. 20
   c. 22
   d. 24

72. Madison travels 672 miles in her car on 14 gallons of gas. How many miles per gallons did she get with her car?
   a. 46 mpg
   b. 48 mpg
   c. 44 mpg
   d. 42 mpg

73. Ms. Taylor purchases 6 chairs at $89 each. What is her total purchase?
    a. $536
    b. $524
    c. $534
    d. $526

74. What of the following decimals is equivalent to 1.25%?
    a. 0.000125
    b. 0.00125
    c. 0.0125
    d. 0.125

75. What is the product of $\frac{2}{6} \times \frac{3}{4} \times \frac{7}{8}$?
    a. $\frac{7}{16}$
    b. $\frac{7}{8}$
    c. $\frac{7}{12}$
    d. $\frac{7}{32}$

76. Catherine buys a bag of grapes for $9.36. If the bag weighs 7.2 pounds, what is the cost of a pound of grapes?
    a. $1.29
    b. $1.28
    c. $1.30
    d. $1.31

77. If Ms. Frisk divides $37.50 evenly among her 6 children, how much money does each child receive?
    a. $6.15
    b. $5.95
    c. $6.25
    d. $6.05

78. Ms. Watson paid $120,000 for her house several years ago. If the market value of her house is now 140% of the original price, what is the current value of her house?
    a. $857,000
    b. $168,000
    c. $85,700
    d. $680,000

79. If a television with a list price of $1,850 is on sale for 30% off, what is the discount?
    a. $450
    b. $555
    c. $45
    d. $55.50

80. How is the fraction $\frac{3}{8}$ entered as a decimal into a calculator?
   a. 0.374
   b. 0.295
   c. 0.386
   d. 0.375

81. What is 0.020% written as decimal?
   a. 0.002
   b. 0.02
   c. 0.0002
   d. 2

82. Which of Howard Gardner's multiple intelligences would most enable a student to identify rock types for a geology or earth science class?
   a. Kinesthetic intelligence
   b. Naturalist intelligence
   c. Logical-mathematical intelligence
   d. Spatial intelligence

83. Rob was the first among childhood friends to be able to tell identical twins Dave and Jeff apart by noticing a tiny scar that only Jeff had above his eyebrow. Which of Gardner's multiple intelligences does Rob's ability exemplify?
   a. Spatial intelligence
   b. Bodily-kinesthetic
   c. Interpersonal
   d. Intrapersonal

84. ELL student Maria can read and write many academic English words, but is not sure how to pronounce many of them as she has never heard them read aloud or spoken. What is the most accessible and practical resource for her to obtain this information?
   a. A special ELL pronouncing dictionary
   b. A standard English online dictionary
   c. Asking her teachers to say the words
   d. An encyclopedia of very high quality

85. Among the following, which is not a valid reason for using multimedia instructional materials?
   a. It addresses a variety of learning preferences within one student.
   b. It addresses a variety of learning preferences among all students.
   c. It relieves students with linguistic and/or quantitative difficulties.
   d. It relieves teachers of making decisions related to learning styles.

86. Teachers can provide instruction to help students improve how they monitor their own reading comprehension. To inform this instruction, which of these applies?
    a. Students need to use comprehension strategies and know what they do or do not understand.
    b. Students only need to know what they do not understand.
    c. Students having comprehension strategies need not know what they do or do not understand.
    d. Students only need to know what they do understand.

87. As a reading comprehension aid, which type of graphic organizer would help students differentiate between fiction and nonfiction text structures?
    a. Venn diagram
    b. Storyboard
    c. Story map
    d. T-Chart

88. Instructing students in summarizing the texts they have read will help them with which of these?
    a. Identifying main ideas, not with generating new main ideas
    b. Identifying and generating main ideas, not connecting them
    c. Remembering what they have read, including all the details
    d. Remembering only the most important information in texts

89. At the end of a unit on reading and understanding fiction, a teacher assesses class progress and finds that, although they have mastered other elements like setting, plot, and characters, most of the students are unclear about the element of problem-solution, even though the teacher devoted a full lesson to each element. The teacher plans another lesson to address this deficit. What should the teacher best use this lesson to do?
    a. Re-teach the entire unit in a summary form, treating all of the elements equally
    b. Re-teach the entire unit in summary, with more emphasis on problem-solution
    c. Re-teach the problem-solution lesson, including its role as an element of fiction
    d. Re-teach problem-solution, including its role in fiction, using a different method

90. In the process of writing, which activity would a student perform during the revision stages?
    a. Writing a whole piece without interrupting for corrections
    b. Reorganizing paragraph sequence, adding and removing parts
    c. Writing a new version that has a different focus or content
    d. Correcting all mistakes in grammar, mechanics, and typing

91. A student developing a focus statement for a composition writes this sentence: "The Galápagos Islands have many unique animal species." Which of the following analyzes this statement correctly?
    a. "The Galápagos Islands" is the topic of the statement; the rest is the focus.
    b. "The Galápagos Islands" is the focus of the statement; the rest is the topic.
    c. The entire sentence is the topic of the statement; it does not have a focus.
    d. The entire sentence is the focus of the statement; it does not have a topic.

92. Which feature of writing is most instrumental in determining the others?
   a. The punctuation
   b. The focus of a piece
   c. The selection of words
   d. The lengths of sentences

93. High school students have an assignment to write research papers. In which technological resource will they find the most complete and current information for research?
   a. In online dictionaries
   b. In an online database
   c. In online grammar books
   d. In an online encyclopedia

94. Reading assessment is a necessary component of a comprehensive system for writing assessment in K–12 education because of the relationship of reading and writing. Which of these statements is most accurate about this relationship?
   a. Reading instruction alone aids writing development.
   b. Writing instruction alone aids reading development.
   c. Reading and writing, albeit related, are independent.
   d. Reading and writing skills utilize disparate processes.

95. Teachers at a school use standardized, curriculum-based measures as formative assessments for monitoring student writing progress. When are these administered?
   a. Before writing instruction has commenced
   b. During regular writing instruction routines
   c. After the writing instruction has concluded
   d. In between the units of writing instruction

96. A student has a recipe that yields two dozen cookies as written. She wants to bake a total of six dozen cookies. To increase the amounts of all ingredients but maintain the same ratio, she sets up a proportion. For example, she determines that if the original recipe requires 1 cup of flour for two dozen cookies, then she will need 3 cups of flour to make six dozen. What kind of math is she using?
   a. Algebra
   b. Calculus
   c. Geometry
   d. Arithmetic

97. In trigonometry, students must find numbers in _____ and enter them as corresponding points on _____.
   a. Graphs; charts
   b. Charts; tables
   c. Tables; graphs
   d. Graphs; tables

98. In the equation, 741 __ 3 = 247. Which symbol correctly fills in the blank?
   a. +
   b. -
   c. ÷
   d. ×

99. In the operation: 88 ÷ 11 = 8, which of the following terms applies to 11?
   a. Remainder
   b. Quotient
   c. Dividend
   d. Divisor

100. Which of these math assessment tasks would be the most appropriate for 3rd -grade students?
   a. Completing a sequence like 1, __, 3, __, 5, __, 7
   b. Circling seven like items out of a total 12 in a picture
   c. Completing a series like 941, 952, __, 974, __
   d. Counting and writing numbers of pictured items

Answer Key and Explanations for Test #4

1. D: The key context clue in this sentence is "less mature." More mature reading strategies are signs of student reading progress, while less mature ones indicate lower levels of development. The word *revert* literally means "to turn back" in Latin, i.e., to return—not to leap forward (a) or stay the same (c). To move steadily (b) does not indicate in which direction; *revert* indicates movement backward, not forward, upward, downward, inward, outward, or sideways, but backward and only backward.

2. A: *Imminent* describes something that is about to happen or approaching soon; distant (a) is an antonym, meaning the opposite. Looming (b) and impending (d) are synonyms for imminent. Some people may confuse *imminent* with "eminent," which means famous or important; unknown (c) is an antonym for eminent, not for imminent.

3. C: *Recurrent* refers to something that occurs over and over. This is the opposite of "once" (d) and unrelated to being slow (a) or careful (b).

4. A: *Precarious* means insecure or likely to fail. This is the opposite of "strong" (b). "Injured" (c) and "broken" (d) may seem to fit the context, but the definition is different.

5. B: To *elucidate* comes from the word lucid, meaning clear, bright, or shining, which derives from the Latin *lux* meaning light; it means to shed light on something or make it clear (b), i.e., explain or clarify. To add details or expand upon (a) is to elaborate. Although it has a syllable sounding like "loose," elucidate does not mean to loosen, i.e., reduce or relieve tightness (c). To make a test or assessment (d) is to evaluate.

6. C: The title of this article (a) states the article's topic, but does not make any statement that could be the main idea. The first sentence (b) is a good introduction and topic sentence, but does not state the main idea—it merely lays the foundation for the main idea. The first sentence of the second paragraph (d) gives a topic sentence for that paragraph, supporting the main idea but not stating it. Only the last sentence of the first paragraph gives the main idea that teachers need to develop strategies for improving fluency.

7. C: The first sentence of the second paragraph clearly states what the paragraph will be about. The first sentence of the first paragraph (a) introduces the idea of reading but it is not clear what the paragraph will be about. The last sentence of the first paragraph (b) states the main idea. The last sentence of the last paragraph (d) sums the selection, repeating the main idea.

8. C: Paragraph 1 (a) begins with a topic sentence, followed by an explanation. Paragraph 2 (b) also opens with a topic sentence, followed by details elaborating on it. Paragraph 4 (d) begins with a transitional word, but the focus is on the topic of the current paragraph. However, the first sentence of paragraph 3 (c) refers back to the previous one "At times the problem is not with reading ability," so it is a transitional sentence.

9. B: The final sentence of the final paragraph sums up the main points of the previous paragraphs. The entire last paragraph (a) is not a summary because it introduces new information. The final sentences of each paragraph (c) are not overall summaries. Paragraphs 1 and 3 summarize those paragraphs. Paragraph 2 does not end with a summary. It is not true that there are no overall summary statements (d) because the final sentence of the final paragraph is one.

10. D: The strategies mentioned in (a), (b), and (c) are all from the second paragraph of the selection. The fourth strategy from this paragraph is giving more time, not timing the students' reading to improve speed.

11. C: The only one of the choices that is mentioned in the selection is family trauma, in the third sentence of the first paragraph.

12. C: The third paragraph lists four reading strategies: teacher read-aloud, student repetitive read-aloud, phonemic awareness, and taking time. We can see the number without counting because the next-to-last strategy is listed as "third" and the next as "finally," so it must be the fourth.

13. D: The text says in its third paragraph that some students struggle with attention rather than reading ability. The other three potential problems are not mentioned in the text.

14. A: The first paragraph introduces the problem of poor fluency and states that teachers must take steps to address it, but does not offer any solutions. The second paragraph does not mention any of the specific problems, but only focuses on solutions. Choice (b) has this sequence backwards. This piece does not have only problems in the first two paragraphs (c), nor does it include both problems and solutions within these paragraphs (d).

15. C: The fourth paragraph states that students may no longer be retaining information toward the end of class. Choices (a) and (b) are not mentioned in the selection. Moving between schools (d) is mentioned in the first paragraph as a potential factor in poor fluency, not retaining information.

16. B: All of the choices are all strategies for improving fluency, but the only one in this list that is specifically linked to helping students focus is finding a time of day that is most helpful.

17. A: The author's purpose is often most obvious in the main idea and summary statement. The main idea states that "teachers should be aware of practical steps they can take to help their students develop good reading strategies and become confident readers." The summary repeats the idea that "teachers can foster fluency in their classes." This is not a persuasive essay (b) because the article does not make an argument that can be countered (i.e., that teachers cannot take steps to improve fluency) or make any reference to an opposing viewpoint. This article is not for entertainment (c) because it is a serious topic recommending action. It is not to narrate (d) because it does not retell events but gives practical advice. Rather, it informs the reader, giving knowledge needed to take action.

18. D: The statement that poor fluency is "one of the greatest handicaps a person can have" is an opinion because it is not quantifiable. It is impossible to rank all handicaps objectively and state that poor fluency is among the most significant. The fact that not all students are interested in higher education (b) does not affect whether this argument is fact or opinion. Choices (a) and (c) incorrectly state this sentence as fact. While effects may have been documented and reading may affect every part of life, this does not change the fact that listing poor fluency as one of the greatest handicaps is an opinion.

19. B: This graph shows that 60 percent of the federal budget was allotted for military departments and programs. It shows six percent allotted for health and human services (a), six percent for education (c), and 28 percent for all other departments and programs combined (d).

20. C: The amount designated for health and human services and education spending combined is 12 percent (6 + 6). The amount for military spending is 60 percent, which is five times as much (5 ×

12 = 60). Therefore, options (a) and (b) are both lower amounts than the correct answer, and (d) is higher.

21. A: The proportion of the entire budget proposed for military spending was 60 percent, i.e., more than half (50 percent). Therefore, choice (b) is incorrect; choice (c) would have to be 49 percent or less to be correct; and choice (d) would have to be more than 66.7 percent (rounded), i.e., more than two-thirds, to be correct.

22. D: The amount allocated for military spending was 60 percent, and the amount allocated for education was six percent, i.e., one-tenth as much. One-quarter of 60 percent (a) would be 15 percent. One-eighth of 60 percent (b) would be 7.5 percent. One-sixth of 60 percent (c) would be 10 percent.

23. B: The pie chart shows that six percent of the budget was allocated for education, and six percent was allocated for health and human services, so the amounts were equal. If $1.6 billion was allotted for education, then health and human services would also receive $1.6 billion.

24. B: This is the only statement of fact, which can be verified by comparing the numbers and pie wedge sizes shown. The other choices are all statements of opinion because (1) they cannot be proven, and (2) they can vary from one individual to another. Clues to opinions here include "far too much" (a), "should spend more" (c), and "deserves a larger proportion" (d).

25. A: The subject "They" in this sentence is plural, so the verb "are" agrees with it. Sentence (b) has two subjects ("He and she"), so the verb should be "are," not "is." Sentence (c) has singular subject "I" and thus should have singular verb "is," not "are." The subject of choice (d) is plural "We," requiring plural verb "were," not singular "was."

26. C: The third person singular takes an -s ending in the present tense only, but the first-person singular does not gain any additional ending in the present tense. Hence option (a) has incorrect verb forms for both subjects, option (b) has the incorrect verb form for the third person singular subject only, option (c) has correct verb forms for both subjects, and option (d) has the incorrect verb form for the first-person singular subject only.

27. B: This is the only sentence using the present tense, "awakens." Choice (a) uses the past participle, "awakened," in the passive voice; choice (c) uses the progressive participle "awakening" as a gerund—i.e., a verb participle used as a noun—while the sentence's actual verb is "has undergone" in the present perfect tense. Choice (d) uses the future tense of the transitive verb, "will awaken (everyone)."

28. A: Because the question specifies the verb "to be," the tense of the verb "to volunteer" is immaterial here. "David was" is past tense. "David is" is present tense (b). "David will be" is future tense (c). "David has been" is present perfect tense (d).

29. D: The future tense of the verb "to forward" is "will forward." "Is forwarding" (a) is the present progressive (present continuous) tense. "Has forwarded" (b) is the present perfect tense. "Forwards" (c) is the (simple) present tense.

30. C: Sentence (a) uses the present progressive "am wondering" and future "will get moving." Sentence (b) uses the present perfect "have been wondering." Sentence (c) uses the past perfect "had contacted" and hence is the correct answer choice. Sentence (d) uses the future "will continue" and present "I see." ("Until" puts the meaning of this dependent clause in the future, but the form of "to see" is nevertheless in present tense grammatically.)

31. B: "Will have finished" is the future perfect tense of the verb "to finish." In the same sentence, "tell" is the present tense of "to tell" (despite "before" placing it in the future, the verb tense is still present). "Will tell you" is simple future tense, and "are finished" is present tense (a). "Finish" is present tense; "will be telling you" is future progressive (continuous) tense (c). "Have always told" is present perfect tense, while "finish" is simple present tense (d), the same as in (c).

32. B: "Was walking" is the past progressive (continuous) tense of "to walk." "Are conducting" (a) is the present progressive tense of "to conduct." "Had been walking" (c) is the past perfect progressive tense of "to walk." "Will... be walking" (d) is the future progressive tense of "to walk." "Taking" is the progressive participle of "to take," and by implication, part of the future progressive included with "walking" as also taking the auxiliary "will be."

33. D: The present progressive tense of "to work," with a first-person singular subject, is "I am working." "I will be talking" (a) is the future progressive tense of "to talk." "I had been planning" (b) is the past perfect progressive tense of "to plan." "I have been planning" (c) is the present perfect progressive tense of "to plan." (All other verbs are in the present, infinitive, or uninflected form.)

34. C: "To listen" is a regular verb: it is conjugated in present, past, present perfect, and past perfect as "listen," "listened," "have listened," "had listened" in the first and second persons, singular number; "listens" in third person singular; and "listen" in plural, with the other forms the same. Options (a) and (b) are irregular verbs conjugated as (a) "freeze," "froze," and "frozen"; and (b) "speak," "spoke," and "spoken." Option (d) is also irregular, conjugated as "sing," "sang," and "sung."

35. A: Regular verbs, e.g., "to walk," take *-ed* endings to denote past tense, e.g., "I walked," "we walked," "you walked," "he walked," "she walked," "they walked," "it walked." Only irregular, not regular, verbs take *-en* endings in the present perfect (b) and past perfect (c) tenses, e.g., "to speak": "have spoken," "has spoken," "had spoken." Regular verbs take *-s* or *-es* ends in present tense, but only in third person singular (e.g., "he," "she," or "it walks"), not always (d).

36. B: The first-person plural pronoun "we" agrees with the two subjects, "Jo and I." The two subjects "Leon and Carla" (a) require the third person plural object pronoun "them," not the third person singular object pronoun "him." The singular subject "supervisor" (c) requires "he" or "she," not plural "they." To agree both with the two subjects "Jay and I" as the antecedent, and also with the plural verb "were" which agrees with the subjects (d), the pronoun must be "we," not "she."

37. B: The third person singular masculine pronoun "he" agrees with subject "Stewart." However, "he" does not agree with subject "Laura" in choice (a), and "she" disagrees with subject "Bob" in choice (c). In choice (d), "member" is singular, so the pronoun should be either "his or her"; if this seems awkward, the subject can be changed to plural "All members," and the plural "their" [positions] will agree with this.

38. A: The object pronoun "us" (object of preposition "of" modifying subject "All") establishes that the subject is in the first-person plural, so "our," the possessive form of the pronoun (used as an adjective modifying object noun "success"), agrees. In choice (b), the third person singular subject of the dependent clause, "she", requires the reflexive pronoun "herself," not second-person "yourself." In choice (c), "Larry" is being addressed, so the pronoun must be second-person "you," not third-person "he," to agree. The first-person plural possessive "our" (d) disagrees with third-person subject "family"; it should be "its" or "their" results.

39. D: The possessive form is required to modify "car." "Who" (a) is not the possessive, but the subjective form of "who." "Who's" (b) is not a possessive, but a contraction of "who is." "Whom" (c) is not possessive, but is the objective form of "who." Possessive regular nouns and proper nouns take -'s (e.g., "the child's toy," "Sonny's car"), but possessive pronouns (e.g., "mine," "ours," "yours," "his," "hers, "theirs"), adjectives (e.g., "my," "our," "your," "his," "her," "their"), and interrogative possessive pronouns and adjectives (e.g., "whose") do not.

40. B: "That" is better restrictively, i.e., to introduce essential information: we would not know what specific house without "that we saw" and "that we are buying." "Which" is better non-restrictively or nonessentially, e.g., "the house that we saw months ago, which we liked, is the one that we are buying." Hence the twins' favorite toys are not those "which," but "that I gave them" (c), because this essential information identifies their favorites. Similarly, option (d) should read "...for everything that he had." "Who" more appropriately refers to a person than "that" (a).

41. A: When using demonstrative pronouns, choose "that" to indicate somebody "over there." To indicate somebody "right here" (b), use "this" instead. This choice first uses the correct "this," but then inconsistently switches to "That" in the second sentence. Choice (c) is also inconsistent, using "that" correctly in the first sentence, but "This" incorrectly in the second. In choice (d), "I am introducing" implies she is right here, so "That" in the second sentence is incorrect.

42. C: Inferring from sentence context, how you should walk is compared to how you are walking, hence the comparative is needed, not the superlative (b), (d). To make an adverb comparative, precede it with "more," e.g., "more quickly" (c). For superlative, precede it with "most"; however, this is inaccurate here as only two things are compared. (It could apply if the sentence ended "to finish ahead of them all"—comparing to how they walk.) Do not use the comparative adjective "quicker" (a) or superlative adjective "quickest" (b) for degrees of adverbs.

43. D: When comparing quantities, the word "fewer" is used with objects that can be counted individually, e.g., exam questions or grocery items, so option (a) is incorrect. The word "less" is used with amounts or things that cannot be counted separately, like time, money, music, air, water, etc. (e.g., "you drank less water than he did"); therefore, option (b) is incorrect because newspapers can be counted. "Fewer dollars" would be acceptable, but "fewer money" (c) is incorrect: whereas dollar is a count noun, money is a mass noun.

44. C: This choice is a grammatically complete sentence with a subject ("committee"), verb ("implemented"), and the expression of a complete thought. Choice (a) is a sentence fragment, consisting of a dependent clause without the necessary independent clause. Choice (b) has a subject ("implementation") but no verb, hence another fragment. Choice (d) is also a sentence fragment lacking a verb.

45. D: This is a sentence fragment because it is a dependent clause without an independent clause, which it should modify adverbially by identifying when—but no stand-alone clause stating a complete thought with a subject and verb exists for it to modify. Such an independent clause exists in option (a): "I have noticed it." In option (b): "I had noticed it." In option (c): "You did it." These three are all complete sentences, each with one independent and one dependent clause.

46. A: Despite some punctuation (a correct comma before "Desmond" and a correct exclamation point at the end), this is still a run-on sentence because the two independent clauses are not separated by any punctuation or conjunction before "he is getting away." The other choices are all alternatives for correcting a run-on sentence.

47. D: Choice (a) places one comma correctly, but omits needed punctuation between "...it was you" and "as soon as you spoke." Choice (b) is a run-on sentence with no internal punctuation where it is needed. Choice (c) incorrectly uses a comma after the first "you" instead of a semicolon, a colon, or a period. Choice (d) correctly uses a semicolon after the first independent clause, and a comma between the dependent clause and the (second) independent clause it modifies.

48. B: This is correctly punctuated with a question mark. However, an indirect question or statement containing a question (a) requires a period, e.g., "I wonder if you might come visit him with me." It could also be rewritten as separate introductory statement and question ("I wonder: Might you come visit him with me?"). Statements take periods; questions take question marks (c). For questions inside quotations, put the question mark inside the quotation marks (e.g., Ask her, "Will you come with me?") For questions outside quotations (d), put the question mark outside the quotation marks.

49. A: This sentence correctly uses "here" as the adverb indicating place, and also correctly uses "hear" as the verb meaning to sense through the ears and other auditory mechanisms, i.e., via audition or hearing. These words sound the same but have different meanings and parts of speech. The other choices misuse either both (b) or one (c), (d) of these words.

50. B: Altar is a noun naming a raised structure for conducting religious ceremonies; alter is a verb meaning to change something. Choice (a) reverses the order of the correct choices for filling in the blanks. Choice (c) identifies the first word incorrectly and the second word correctly. Choice (d) identifies the first word correctly, but the second word incorrectly.

51. A: When used as a proper noun, "capitol" should be capitalized, so (b) is incorrect. When used as a common noun, "capitol" or "capitol building" should not be capitalized, so (c) and (d) are incorrect.

52. C: *Pour* means to cause a liquid to flow into a container, *poor* means lacking money, and *pore* means to be absorbed in studying something. Option (a) uses only *poor* correctly, option (b) uses only *pour* correctly, and option (d) uses neither word correctly.

53. C: "Freudian" is an adjective derived from a proper noun (the name Freud), so it is capitalized, making options (b) and (d) incorrect. However, the ordinary noun that "Freudian" modifies, "slip," is not a proper name and thus is not capitalized, so options (a) and (d) are also incorrect.

54. D: "Discrete" means separate or isolated, and is spelled correctly here as indicated by the sentence context "at separate times and locations." "Discreet" means careful, prudent, tactful, or unobtrusive, particularly regarding something confidential, private, or delicate. Hence choices (a) and (c) should be "discreet," not "discrete." From context, choice (b) should be "discrete," not "discreet," as it refers to separate events, not confidential ones.

55. D: Since the underlined digit is in the thousands place, its value is 5×1000 or 5,000. The digit in the ones place has a value of 5×1 or 5. To determine how many times greater 5,000 is than 5, divide 5,000 by 5. So, 5,000 is 1,000 times greater than 5.

56. B: The place value of a digit depends on its location in relation to the decimal point. The places to the left of the decimal are ones, tens, then hundreds, respectively. To round a number to a certain place value, look at the digit to the immediate right. If the digit to the right is 5 or more, round up by adding one. If the digit is less than five, round down by keeping the same digit. For this problem, the digit in the tens place is 9. The digit to its immediate right is 7. Since 7 is greater than 5, round up to find that 53,497 rounded to the nearest ten is 53,500.

57. A: The place value of a digit depends on its location in relation to the decimal point. The places to the left of the decimal are ones, tens, then hundreds, respectively. To round a number to a certain place value, look at the digit to the immediate right. If the digit to the right is 5 or more, round up by adding one. If the digit is less than five, round down by keeping the same digit. For this problem, the digit in the hundreds place is 7. The digit to its immediate right is 5. Since 5 is equal to 5, round up. Thus 18,753 rounded to the nearest hundred is 18,800.

58. D: Since a yard equals 3 feet, the conversion factor is 3. Since a yard is longer than a foot, we multiply by the conversion factor. So, 7 yards equal 7×3 or 21 feet.

59. C: Since a pound equals 16 ounces, the conversion factor is 16. Since an ounce is less than a pound, we divide by the conversion factor. Thus 32 ounces equal $32 \div 16$ or 2 pounds.

60. B: The side lengths rounded to the nearest ten centimeters are 20 cm, 20 cm, and 10 cm. Then the estimated perimeter is the sum found by adding $20 + 20 + 10 = 50$. The perimeter is about 50 cm.

61. C: A quick estimation of the number of feet the mountain climber climbs is found by rounding each day's climb to the nearest hundred feet and finding the sum: $500 + 600 + 300 + 300 = 1,700$ feet.

62. C: The total amount of scholarship money is equal to the sum of the scholarships received. The total equals $\$2,500 + \$4,500 = \$7,000$.

63. B: The total amount that Ms. Henderson spends on the clothing is equal to the sum of the individual pieces of clothing. The total equals $\$24.99 + \$24.99 + \$17.99 + \$17.99 + \$17.99 = \$103.95$.

64. B: To find the difference between 501 and 379, we need to borrow 1 from the tens column of 501. Since there is a zero there, we need to borrow one from the hundreds column, making the tens column a ten. Then we can borrow one from the tens column, leaving a four in the hundreds place, a nine in the tens place and eleven in the ones column. We subtract from right to left: $11 - 9 = 2$, $9 - 7 = 2$, and $4 - 3 = 1$, so $501 - 379 = 122$.

65. C: Angel's profit is equal to the sell price minus his purchase price. The profit equals $\$427,980 - \$325,890 = \$102,090$.

66. A: The total cost of her house is equal to the sum of the down payment, the amount mortgaged, and the interest. The total cost equals $\$36,550 + \$156,750 + \$293,562$ or $\$486,862$.

67. A: We first convert the number of hours to minutes: $3.5 \times 60 = 210$ minutes. The number of minutes Haley has left to practice equal the number required minus the sum of the minutes she's already practiced. The number of minutes she has left equals $210 - (45 + 45 + 25 + 25) = 210 - 140 = 70$ minutes.

68. C: The factor 275 can be written as $200 + 70 + 5$. So, the product of $525 \times 275 = 525 \times 200 + 525 \times 70 + 525 \times 5 = 105,000 + 36,750 + 2,625 = 144,375$.

69. B: The factor 2,300 can be rewritten as $2,000 + 300$. So $5,622 \times 2,300 = 5,622 \times 2,000 + 5,622 \times 300 = 11,244,000 + 1,686,600 = 12,930,600$.

70. C: The quotient is the result when 72 is divided by 8. Since $72 \div 8 = 9$, the quotient is 9. Answer choices (a), (b), and (d) are the results of multiplying, adding, and subtracting, respectively.

71. B: To divide 3,245 by 25, the first step is to divide 32 by 25. Since 25 × 1 = 25, the divisor 25 goes into 32 one time. Then place the 25 under the 32 in the dividend and subtract: 32 − 25 = 7. Now bring down the 4 and determine how many times 25 goes into 74. Since 25 × 2 = 50, the divisor 25 goes into 74 two times. Then place the 50 under the 74 and subtract to get 24. Now bring down the 5 and determine how many times 25 goes into 245. Since 25 × 9 = 225, the divisor 25 goes into 245 nine times. Finally, place the 225 under the 245 and subtract to get 20. The remainder is 20.

72. B: The number of miles per gallon is determined by dividing the number of miles traveled by the number of gallons of gas. The amount equals 672 ÷ 14 or 48 miles per gallon.

73. C: The total cost is the product of the number of chairs and the cost per chair: 6 × $89 = $534.

74. C: To convert a percent to a decimal, remove the percent symbol and move the decimal point two places to the left. Thus 1.25% is equivalent to 0.0125.

75. D: When multiplying fractions, first try to cancel factors in the numerators with factors in the denominators. Then multiply the numerators and multiply the denominators: $\frac{2}{6} \times \frac{3}{4} \times \frac{7}{8} = \frac{1}{3} \times \frac{3}{4} \times \frac{7}{8} = \frac{1}{1} \times \frac{1}{4} \times \frac{7}{8} = \frac{7}{32}$.

76. C: The cost per pound is equal to the cost of the bag divided by the number of pounds of grapes. The cost per pound equals $9.36 ÷ 7.2 or $1.30.

77. C: The amount of money each child received is equal to the original amount divided by the number of children: $37.50 ÷ 6 = $6.25.

78. B: This question is basically asking, "What is 140% of $120,000?" Let n represent *what*, and replace the *of* with a multiplication symbol and the *is* with an equal sign. But first, we need to convert the 140% to a decimal. Remove the percent sign and move the decimal point two places to the left. Then we have $n = 1.40 \times 120,000 = 168,000$. This means that Ms. Watson's house has a current value of $168,000.

79. B: The discount is 30% of $1850. The question we need to ask is, "What is 30% of $1,850?" Let n represent *what*, and replace the *of* with a multiplication symbol and the *is* with an equal sign. But first, we need to convert the 30% to a decimal. Remove the percent sign and move the decimal point two places to the left. Then we have $n = 0.30 \times 1,850 = 555$. The discount is $555.

80. D: To convert a fraction to a decimal, divide the numerator of the fraction by the denominator: 3 ÷ 8 = 0.375.

81. C: To convert a percent to a decimal, remove the percent symbol, and move the decimal point two places to the left. So, 0.020% equals 0.00020, or 0.0002.

82. B: According to Gardner, naturalist intelligence is the ability to identify similarities, differences, and patterns in nature, natural life forms, and natural objects, e.g., rock types, mountain types, and animal and plant species. Kinesthetic, i.e., bodily-kinesthetic intelligence (a), is the ability for skillfully using one's body in controlled movements, e.g., sports, dance, etc. Logical-mathematical intelligence (c) is the ability for logical reasoning, e.g., in math problems, proofs, or scientific hypotheses. Spatial intelligence (d) is the ability to observe, reproduce, and discriminate among objects visually, and imagine and mentally manipulate visual images.

83. A: Gardner's spatial intelligence includes the ability to discriminate fine differences between and among things that are otherwise very similar. Gardner defines bodily-kinesthetic (b) intelligence as ability in using one's body (e.g., dance, sports). Interpersonal (c) intelligence identifies ability for observing subtleties in other people's moods, emotions, motivations, thoughts, etc., not physical characteristics. Intrapersonal (d) intelligence involves self-knowledge of one's own moods, emotions, motivations, thoughts, etc.

84. B: Standard English dictionaries provide word pronunciations, including syllable stresses and phonetic spellings of vowel and consonant sounds. While the latter are also according to English phonetic rules, online dictionaries add the helpful feature of sound files, so users can hear recorded spoken word pronunciations, making a special dictionary for ELLs (a) unnecessary. This feature is also more efficient and practicable than asking teachers (c). Encyclopedias (d) offer information on many subjects rather than specific dictionary information.

85. D: When teachers use multimedia instructional materials, one or more included media types will satisfy different learning preferences—both within any individual student (a) and among the predominant learning styles of all students (b). Including media beyond those addressing only linguistic and/or quantitative modes of learning also helps students having difficulties in these areas (c). However, the research literature finds that selecting media for different learning styles requires teachers to make a variety of decisions (d).

86. A: Instruction in comprehension monitoring teaches students to realize what they do understand (a), what they do not understand (b), and to learn and apply appropriate strategies for solving comprehension problems (c). They need these three kinds of knowledge, not just one of them, to monitor their comprehension most effectively.

87. C: A story map helps students identify text elements to chart text structure. This in turn helps them differentiate fiction vs. nonfiction, which have different text structures (e.g., nonfiction uses main idea and supporting details as elements; fiction uses setting, characters, plot, problems and solutions, etc.). A Venn diagram (a) helps students compare and contrast. A storyboard (b) helps students sequence text events and points. A T-Chart (d) helps students chart cause-and-effect, comparison-contrast, etc.

88. D: Instructing students in summarizing texts they have read helps them with identifying main ideas in text, generating new main ideas themselves (a), and making connections between or among main ideas (b). The purpose of summarizing text is not to remember all the details (c) but to identify the most important information, differentiate it from unnecessary information, rule out the latter, and remember the former (d).

89. D: Re-teaching a summary of the entire unit (a), (b) is unnecessary: students have mastered most of it. Treating all elements equally (a) will not address the deficient element. Emphasizing it more (b) is better, but re-teaching the entire unit is still unnecessary (b). Re-teaching the unclear element specifically, including its role within the unit (c), is better, but not as good as re-teaching while also trying a different instructional method (d): because equal lesson time was given, the previous method may have been ineffective with this class for this element.

90. B: The stages of revision or editing are the parts of the writing process for reorganizing, adding, and/or removing content. Writing uninterrupted by corrections (a) is part of the drafting stages, specifically the first or rough draft. Writing a new version (c) is also part of drafting, specifically an intermediate rather than first draft. Correcting all grammatical, mechanical, and typing errors (d) is part of the proofreading stage(s).

91. A: An easy formula for developing a focus statement is topic + focus = focus statement. The topic is what the student will write about, i.e., the subject of the composition; the focus directs what the student will write about that topic, i.e., the point s/he will make, or the position or perspective s/he will take. Hence option (b) reverses these definitions. Because the sentence contains both topic and focus, options (c) and (d) are both incorrect.

92. B: The focus of a piece of writing determines a writer's decisions about other features including punctuation (a), word choice (c), sentence lengths (d), etc. Good writers also reciprocally use these and other features to support and reinforce the focus of their work, but not to determine that focus—which they have determined before writing.

93. B: Among the online resources given, only a database will give students access to the most complete, current information for conducting research into the topics of their papers. Dictionaries (a) give only information on words, not other content. Grammar books (c) focus on grammatical rules but no other topics. Encyclopedias (d) are good resources for students in lower grades to begin learning how to research writing, but high school students can use the more specific, more frequently updated information offered by databases.

94. C: Even though reading and writing are interrelated, and skills in each can support development in the other, reading instruction alone does not aid writing development (a), nor does writing instruction alone aid reading development (b). Reading and writing skills utilize similar processes (d), but they require students to apply their knowledge differently. They are independent (c), evidenced by the fact that some students may read well but write poorly, or read poorly but write well.

95. B: Formative assessment focuses on assessment for learning, and as such is administered within the context of teaching, as a part of teachers' regular writing instruction routines—not before (a) or after (c) writing instruction, or in between units (d), but periodically during each unit, using multiple probes.

96. A: She is using algebra to determine an unknown value. In setting up the proportion, she would write:

$$\frac{1 \text{ cup of flour}}{Y \text{ cups of flour}} = \frac{2 \text{ dozen cookies}}{6 \text{ dozen cookies}}$$

This means 1 cup of flour is to two dozen cookies as Y cups of flour is to six dozen cookies—and then multiply: $Y \times 2 = 1 \times 6$, i.e., $2Y = 6$. Then divide: $6 \div 2 = 3$, so $Y = 3$. She does not need calculus (b) to get this answer. She would use geometry (c) to calculate something like area rather than find Y. Arithmetic alone (d) would not help set up the proportion or find the unknown quantity.

97. C: In trigonometry, students find numbers in tables provided, and then plot points corresponding to those numbers and connect those points to form line graphs representing various functions (e.g., sine, cosine, secant, tangent).

98. C: The only way to arrive at the number following the equals symbol is by division. Addition (a) would yield 744. Subtraction (b) would yield 738. Multiplication (d) would yield 2,223.

99. D: In division, the dividend (c) is the number to be divided—in this example, 88. The divisor (d) is the number by which the dividend is divided—in this example, 11. The quotient (b) is the result of the division operation—in this example, 8. The remainder (a) is the quantity left over by an uneven division; there is no remainder in this example. (Example: 88 ÷ 10 = 8.8; the remainder is 8.)

100. C: Completing the series given requires first subtracting 941 from 952 to get 11, then adding 11 to 952 to get 963, and then also adding 11 to 974 to get 985; identifying and completing a sequence ascending by 11s is appropriate for assessing typical 3rd-grade students. Choices (a), (b), and (d) are appropriate for assessing math skills in typical kindergarten students.

NYSTCE Practice Test #5

Answer questions 1–18 based on the passage below:

Making Real-World Connections

Many teachers are all too familiar with the question, "But how will we use this in real life?" While the question may be asked more in math classes, and the answer may be less intuitive than in other classes (classes such as language or computer programming have more obvious real-world applications), teachers of any class should take frequent opportunity to make real-world connections. It is important for teachers to explain why learning matters to students, connecting student knowledge to the real world so they will remain engaged and be empowered to use their knowledge.

Answering the infamous question with "because it's part of the curriculum" abets students in their inclination to tune out what they see as meaningless instruction. Likewise, giving a perfunctory response is unlikely to inspire students to pay attention and work hard. While it may seem like a waste of precious classroom time, discussing real-life applications is an integral part of teaching.

It is helpful to begin a lesson with this application to capture the interest of students. Even the most impassive student may become excited when he realizes how this knowledge could affect him or her personally. There are several steps a teacher can take to integrate this into the lesson. First, he or she should research before class and come prepared with examples and/or visual aids to demonstrate. Second, the teacher should encourage students to think of their own examples before giving an explanation. The more students invest in their own learning, the more they will learn and the better they will retain. Third, the teacher can guide discussion, adding his or her prepared examples and making sure the whole class is making the connection. In some cases, a fourth step can be assigning research projects, allowing students to explore more in-depth connections between the subject material and the real world.

Of course, some subjects are more difficult to connect than others. A student struggling with geometric proofs may grumble at what he or she sees as an egregious waste of time. A teacher can point out that these are training logical thinking that can be employed in a variety of careers such as law.

1. As used in the first sentence of the second paragraph, what is the meaning of the word *abets*?
   a. Supports
   b. Gambles on
   c. Discourages
   d. Interferes with

2. Which of the following words can be used as an antonym for the word *egregious*, as seen in the second sentence of the final paragraph?
   a. Deplorable
   b. Concealed
   c. Inordinate
   d. Notorious

3. Of these choices, which one is most synonymous with the term *impassive*, as seen in the second sentence of the third paragraph?
   a. Active
   b. Deadlocked
   c. Assertive
   d. Unfeeling

4. Which of the following is an antonym for the word *perfunctory*, as used in the second sentence of the second paragraph?
   a. Dilatory
   b. Apathetic
   c. Thorough
   d. Debatable

5. Which part of this text best defines its main idea?
   a. The first sentence
   b. The second sentence
   c. The third sentence
   d. The final sentence

6. What is most accurate about this piece regarding overall main idea and overall summary sentence?
   a. The piece has a main idea but is missing a summary sentence.
   b. The main idea and summary sentence are distinctly different.
   c. The summary sentence repeats the main idea.
   d. The piece has a summary sentence but is missing a main idea.

7. Where in this article is an introductory statement?
   a. There isn't one
   b. The first sentence
   c. The title
   d. The final paragraph

8. In this article, where can a summary statement of its content be found?
   a. At the very end of it
   b. At the beginning
   c. In the title
   d. It has no such statement

9. Which of the following best restates the main idea of the text?
    a. Some classes have more real-world connections than others.
    b. Teachers should bring examples and visual aids to help students understand what they are learning.
    c. Teachers should make real-world connections with what students are learning.
    d. Some learning may have indirect connections that are still useful.

10. According to the text, what is the first step a teacher can do to integrate real-world applications into their lessons?
    a. Begin the lesson with the application
    b. Encourage impassive students to be excited about real-world connections
    c. Research prior to class and prepare examples and visual aids
    d. Encourage students to think of their own examples before sharing his/her own

11. Which of the following examples is given of a subject that can be more difficult to connect to the real world?
    a. Language
    b. Geometric proofs
    c. Computer programming
    d. Early elementary mathematics

12. What two benefits do all students receive from integrating real-world connections, according to the article?
    a. Being interested in learning, preparing for a law career
    b. Preparing examples of connections, finding visual aids
    c. Choosing subjects with clear connections, preparing for future careers
    d. Staying engaged with the lesson, being empowered to use their knowledge

13. According to the article, why is giving a short answer and redirecting back to the lesson an insufficient response to the question, "How will we use this in real life?"?
    a. Students cannot focus on the lesson until they know the application.
    b. They are unlikely to pay attention and work hard if they do not know why.
    c. They need to see a visual aid before they can understand.
    d. They need to make a connection to a future career such as law or they won't have the correct focus in class.

14. According to the selection, what is the final, optional step a teacher should take in implementing real-world connections?
    a. Bringing visual aids
    b. Asking students to think of their own connections
    c. Assigning research projects
    d. Showing how even unlikely subjects can have a career connection

15. What type of article is this?
    a. Comparison and contrast
    b. Process
    c. Cause and effect
    d. Entertainment

16. What is the author's tone?
    a. Ambiguous
    b. Indifferent
    c. Angry
    d. None of the above

17. What is the best time during the lesson to make real-world connections, according to the article?
    a. At the beginning
    b. After introducing the topic but before students lose interest
    c. At the end
    d. In the homework assignment

18. Which of the following organizational principles is most applicable to this piece?
    a. Chronological order
    b. Spatial order
    c. Climactic order
    d. Topical order

Answer the following three questions based on the graphic below.

Alice's 4th-grade teacher assesses her oral reading fluency at the beginning of the school year and again monthly. Her 5th-grade teacher conducts the same assessment at the beginning of the following school year. Answer the following questions based on the graphic below.

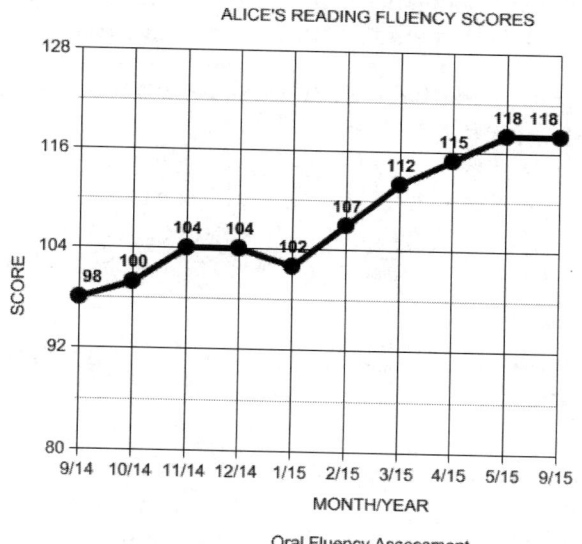

ALICE'S READING FLUENCY SCORES

Month/Year	Score (WCPM)
9/14	98
10/14	100
11/14	104
12/14	104
1/15	102
2/15	107
3/15	112
4/15	115
5/15	118
9/15	118

Oral Fluency Assessment

NOTE: Score equals words correct per minute (WCPM).

19. Oral reading fluency goals are 114 WCPM by the end of 3rd grade, 118 WCPM by the end of 4th grade, and 128 WCPM by the end of 5th grade. How do Alice's scores relate to these goals?
   a. Alice's reading fluency was on the 3rd-grade level at the beginning of the 4th grade.
   b. Alice's reading fluency was below 4th- and 3rd-grade levels beginning 4th grade.
   c. Alice's reading fluency was below the goal for her grade at the end of the 4th grade.
   d. Alice's reading fluency had reached the 5th-grade goal by the end of the 4th grade.

20. What overall trend in Alice's assessment scores does this graph indicate?
   a. Ascending
   b. Descending
   c. Stable overall
   d. Unstable overall

21. When did Alice get a lower score on the reading fluency assessment than in the prior month?
   a. September 2014
   b. December 2014
   c. January 2015
   d. March 2015

22. What do the graph and the information above it show about Alice's oral reading fluency from the end of 4th grade to the beginning of 5th grade?
   a. Alice lost some gains in fluency over the summer, as is common.
   b. Alice improved her fluency over the summer, maybe by reading.
   c. Alice improved since the 5th-grade assessment had harder text.
   d. Alice maintained her oral reading fluency level over the summer.

23. By how many points did Alice's reading score change from September 2014 to September 2015?
   a. 30 points
   b. 15 points
   c. 20 points
   d. 10 points

24. Which of the following is an opinion rather than a fact?
   a. "My kitten is three months old."
   b. "I love my kitten so very much."
   c. "My kitten is yellow and white."
   d. "I have the best kitten there is."

25. All subject-verb agreement is standard in which of these sentences?
   a. Sheri says that she and her husband are volunteering to help.
   b. Sheri says either she or her husband are volunteering to help.
   c. Sheri says not only she but also her husband are volunteering.
   d. Sheri says she always volunteers, and her husband have also.

26. In which of these sentences do the subject and verb agree?
   a. Some of the flowers in that vase is wilted.
   b. Some of the people are opposing the law.
   c. Some of the state funding have been used.
   d. Some of the apple pies was already eaten.

27. Of the following sentences, which one shows correct subject-verb agreement?
   a. He and they disagrees on that issue.
   b. She and the rest of us agrees on this.
   c. Only you and she is in disagreement.
   d. You and I agree regarding this issue.

28. Which of the following sentences uses the future progressive (future continuous) verb tense?
   a. We all attend this convention each year.
   b. We will attend the convention together.
   c. We will all be attending the convention.
   d. We will have attended it five years now.

29. In which of these choices is the past perfect verb tense found?
   a. I am hearing of that for the first time today.
   b. I have never heard of that before in my life.
   c. I had never heard of that before yesterday.
   d. I will now have heard of that the next time.

30. Which of the following sentences uses the past tense?
   a. We hoped for the best while we prepared for the worst.
   b. We always hope for the best and prepare for the worst.
   c. We will just hope for the best but prepare for the worst.
   d. We have hoped for the best and prepared for the worst.

31. What choice conjugates the verb in the present perfect tense?
   a. I had given him his birthday gift the day before the party.
   b. I have given him his gift before his birthday for years now.
   c. I give him his present early so he can enjoy it individually.
   d. I will have given him his gift early for eight years this year.

32. Which of the following includes a verb in the present progressive tense?
   a. Their youngest child was awaiting school all year.
   b. Their youngest child has been anticipating school.
   c. Their youngest child will be entering school soon.
   d. Their youngest child is beginning school this year.

33. Among the following, which sentence uses the verb in the present tense?
   a. You were the best friend to her among all friends.
   b. You are being the best friend to her of all friends.
   c. You are the best friend to her among her friends.
   d. You will always be the best among all her friends.

34. Of these choices, which one conjugates the verb in the future tense?
   a. Vanessa helps people with that.
   b. Vanessa will help you with that.
   c. Vanessa will be helping you now.
   d. Vanessa is helping only with that.

35. The future perfect verb tense appears in which of these choices?
   a. His next birthday will also be our 20th friendship anniversary.
   b. By his next birthday, we will have been friends for 20 years.
   c. On his next birthday, we will be friends for a whole 20 years.
   d. His next birthday will commemorate our 20-year friendship.

36. In which of the following are all of the verb tense endings consistent?
   a. We had two tables until Sandra brought two more.
   b. We have two tables until Sandra brought two more.
   c. We had two tables until Sandra brings another two.
   d. We have two tables, but Sandra had brought more.

37. The pronoun agrees with its antecedent in which of these choices?
   a. The persons who should know are me.
   b. The person who should know is they.
   c. The person who should know this is I.
   d. The persons who should know are he.

38. Correct pronoun-antecedent agreement is demonstrated in which sentence?
   a. Sheila would like you to accompany her.
   b. Sheila does not want to go all by himself.
   c. Sheila needs somebody to support them.
   d. Sheila wants you to come along with she.

39. In which of these sentences does the pronoun agree with its antecedent?
   a. She has designated himself as driver.
   b. Mr. Jones identified themself as the driver.
   c. The designated driver today are you.
   d. The designated driver tonight is you.

40. Which version of the sentence below is correct?
   a. I remember the man that sold me this car.
   b. I remember the man which sold me a car.
   c. I remember the man who sold me that car.
   d. I remember the man whom sold me a car.

41. The correct sentence is which of the following?
   a. I want that color I am holding, not that one you have there.
   b. I want this color I am holding, not this one you have there.
   c. I want that color I am holding, not this one you have there.
   d. I want this color I am holding, not that one you have there.

42. **Of the following, which is the correct superlative form of the adjective "thorough?"**
    a. Thorougher
    b. Most thorough
    c. Thoroughest
    d. More thorough

43. **Which of these would be correct in formal written English?**
    a. "This car must go more faster for it to win."
    b. *Mo' Better Blues*
    c. "I am the bestest plumber anyone can find."
    d. "Our next meeting needs to be far quieter."

44. **Which of the examples below is a complete sentence?**
    a. In all these years I have never witnessed.
    b. In all of the years that I have known him.
    c. I have never witnessed anything like that.
    d. In all the years knowing him I have never.

45. **Of the following sentences, which is/are divided correctly?**
    a. I am so sorry; I know you loved him so much, and you must miss him dearly.
    b. I am so sorry, I know you loved him so much and you must miss him dearly.
    c. I am so sorry, I know. You loved him so much; and you must miss him dearly.
    d. I am so sorry. I know you loved him, so much and you must miss him, dearly.

46. **In which of the following versions is all of the punctuation correct?**
    a. "What, he queried, am I supposed to think?"
    b. What, he queried, am I supposed to think?
    c. "What," he queried, "am I supposed to think?"
    d. "What," he queried, am I supposed to think?"

47. **What version of the sentence below is written correctly?**
    a. She is sick. She needs help, we will go help her now.
    b. She is sick, she needs help. We will go help her now.
    c. She is sick. she needs help. we will go help her now.
    d. She is sick. She needs help. We will go help her now.

48. **Which version of the sentence below correctly uses all words included?**
    a. They will except every application submitted by the deadline.
    b. They will accept all applications accept those submitted late.
    c. They will except all applications accept the ones that are late.
    d. They will accept all applications except those submitted late.

49. **Of these choices, which uses the correct verb?**
    a. "Why didn't we forego that appetizer?"
    b. "Did you order the forgoing appetizer?"
    c. "Does an appetizer forego the entrée?"
    d. "May we have salad after dinner rather than foregoing it?"

50. Among the following, which version of this sentence spells all words correctly?
   a. It's surprising how many people confuse its spelling.
   b. Its surprising how many people confuse it's spelling.
   c. It's surprising how many people confuse it's spelling.
   d. Its surprising how many people confuse its spelling.

51. Which of these sentences is correct and has not confused one word with another?
   a. "He maintained duel identities in different towns."
   b. "They founded the organization for dual purposes."
   c. "The parents gave the twins duel homework desks."
   d. "Aaron Burr shot Alexander Hamilton during a dual."

52. Which of the following uses correct capitalization?
   a. We stopped at the Carnegie museum of art.
   b. We arrived at the Museum just in time.
   c. We were excited to see the Carnegie Museum's new exhibit.
   d. Our favorite museum was the carnegie.

53. Among the following, which sentence uses correct capitalization?
   a. All of the Mothers in our PTA are active volunteers.
   b. We invited her, but Mother did not want to attend.
   c. Their beloved Mother passed away a few years ago.
   d. Star Mary Martin was Larry "JR" Hagman's Mother.

54. In which version of this sentence are all word meanings and spellings correct?
   a. The sneak peak had peaked my interest; the trailer has made my curiosity peek.
   b. The sneak peek had piqued my interest; the trailer has made my curiosity peak.
   c. The sneak pique had peeked my interest; the trailer has made my curiosity peak.
   d. The sneak peek had peaked my interest; the trailer has make my curiosity pique.

55. In which place value is the digit 3 in 457.3?
   a. Ones
   b. Hundreds
   c. Tens
   d. Tenths

56. What is 6,709 rounded to the nearest ten?
   a. 6,700
   b. 6,710
   c. 7,000
   d. 6,810

57. What is 2,077 rounded to the nearest thousand?
   a. 2,080
   b. 2
   c. 2,100
   d. 2,000

58. How many feet are in 2 miles?
   a. 5,150
   b. 11,640
   c. 10,560
   d. 5,700

59. The length of a rectangular room is 11.8 meters and the width is 7.9 meters. Which of the following is the best estimate for the perimeter of the room to the nearest whole meter?
   a. 46 m
   b. 20 m
   c. 96 m
   d. 40 m

60. A rectangle has a length of 1299 cm and a width of 725 cm. Round each length to the nearest hundred centimeters and estimate the area of the rectangle.
   a. 910,000 cm²
   b. 1,040,000 cm²
   c. 840,000 cm²
   d. 960,000 cm²

61. Franklin has $234 in his checking account. He deposits checks in the amounts of $52, $121, and $32. How much money does he have in his checking account after the deposits?
   a. $439
   b. $440
   c. $429
   d. $539

62. A fruit vendor has 52 mangoes, 88 kiwis, 48 pineapples, and 45 papayas. How many pieces of fruit does the vendor have?
   a. 221
   b. 243
   c. 231
   d. 233

63. Mr. Otto has $1,252 in his checking account. He pays his monthly rent in the amount of $650. How much money does he have left in his checking account?
   a. $501
   b. $601
   c. $602
   d. $702

64. What is $400,000 - 382,789$?
   a. 7,211
   b. 17,211
   c. 17,221
   d. 17,321

65. Marcie has $860 in her checking account. She deposits her paycheck of $525. Then she pays the following bills: rent $495, cell phone $55, and car insurance $110. What is the new balance of her checking account?

   a. $715
   b. $720
   c. $725
   d. $730

66. Mr. Carlson has $540 in his checking account and then deposits a check for $762. Then he purchases gasoline for $50 and groceries for $132 using checks. What is the new balance in his checking account?

   a. $1,125
   b. $1,220
   c. $1,120
   d. $1,116

67. What is $2 \times 5 \times 0 \times 1 \times 3$?

   a. 1
   b. 30
   c. 0
   d. 10

68. A case of canned corn has 2 layers. Each layer contains 4 rows of 6 cans. How many cans of corn does one case contain?

   a. 12
   b. 20
   c. 36
   d. 48

69. What is the remainder when 64 is divided by 7?

   a. 9
   b. 3
   c. 2
   d. 1

70. A supplier is shipping 6,720 pineapples. If the pineapples are divided evenly between 280 crates, how many pineapples are in each crate?

   a. 24
   b. 22
   c. 26
   d. 34

71. If 24 pineapples are packed in a crate, how many pineapples are in 535 crates?

   a. 12,740
   b. 10,840
   c. 12,840
   d. 12,820

72. Mr. Beauchamp travels 265 miles in 5 hours. What is his average rate of travel in miles per hour?
   a. 52 mph
   b. 53 mph
   c. 54 mph
   d. 55 mph

73. Patsy buys $7\frac{1}{3}$ yards of material at a cost of $12 a yard. What is the cost of the material?
   a. $88.00
   b. $84.33
   c. $66.00
   d. $86.33

74. What percent is equivalent to $\frac{4}{5}$?
   a. 85%
   b. 60%
   c. 65%
   d. 80%

75. Lola went shopping for some new clothes. She bought a dress for $68.99, a new jacket for $79.00, and three pairs of shoes for $45.49 each. What was the total cost?
   a. $264.44
   b. $238.97
   c. $193.48
   d. $284.46

76. Ms. Schwartz works as a teacher's aide for 6.5 hours a day. If she earns $8.50 per hour, how much does Ms. Schwartz earn in 45 days?
   a. $1,486.25
   b. $2,396.25
   c. $2,476.15
   d. $2,486.25

77. The label on a t-shirt reads 85% cotton. If the remainder is polyester, what percent of the t-shirt is polyester?
   a. 15%
   b. 85%
   c. 25%
   d. 5%

78. Frannie missed 3 out of 15 quiz questions. What percent of quiz questions did she miss?
   a. 25%
   b. 5%
   c. 20%
   d. 5%

79. If McKenna eats $\frac{2}{3}$ of a chicken club sub, what percent of the sub did she eat?
    a. 0.333%
    b. 70%
    c. 6.7%
    d. $66\frac{2}{3}\%$

80. Convert 0.45 to a fraction.
    a. $\frac{9}{10}$
    b. $\frac{3}{5}$
    c. $\frac{9}{20}$
    d. $\frac{4}{9}$

81. Convert 72.5% to a fraction.
    a. $\frac{27}{40}$
    b. $\frac{29}{40}$
    c. $\frac{29}{50}$
    d. $\frac{27}{50}$

82. A teacher has several ELL students whose families recently immigrated to the US. They had little or no formal education in their native countries and helped their parents by doing physical and manual labor. They are unfamiliar with reading for instruction or enjoyment. Which strategy should the teacher use?
    a. Explain to them why reading will be so important in their lives.
    b. Replace all reading with hands-on learning similar to their lives.
    c. Give them reading about things familiar to them from their lives.
    d. Let them choose whichever reading they can relate to their lives.

83. A teacher's assistant works with students under the teacher's guidance. Which of the following learning materials or topics would be most amenable to the assistant's use of drilling instruction?
    a. The Dolch list of sight words
    b. The spelling of regular words
    c. Conjugations of regular verbs
    d. Tenses of each irregular verb

84. One feature of dictionaries is syllabication, i.e., divisions of each word into its syllables. What is true about this feature?
    a. Students cannot recognize word origins more readily by using this feature.
    b. Students may not need this feature when using word processing software.
    c. Students use this feature primarily to identify which syllables are stressed.
    d. Students primarily use this feature to find correct pronunciation of vowels.

85. Which of the following is the best example of multimedia instructional materials to support reading?
   a. Books that incorporate many illustrations
   b. "Books on Tape" reading aloud recording
   c. Following in text as teacher reads it aloud
   d. Interactive, audiovisual, touchscreen text

86. What is most accurate about the instructional strategy of asking questions of students about their reading?
   a. Students can more readily relate learning to existing knowledge.
   b. Students must know their purposes for reading to answer them.
   c. It distracts the attention of students from what they must learn.
   d. It makes students more passive by directing the ways they read.

87. Research finds explicit instruction best for teaching reading comprehension strategies. Which is the proper sequence for a teacher to implement these explicit instruction steps?
   a. Modeling, direct explanation, application, guided practice
   b. Guided practice, application, modeling, direct explanation
   c. Direct explanation, modeling, guided practice, application
   d. Application, guided practice, direct explanation, modeling

88. Curriculum-based measurement (CBM) is a prominent research-based method for monitoring K–12 student reading progress. In one technique, teachers assess 4th- or 5th-graders using passages with every seventh word missing, and three choices to fill each blank with only one choice making sense. Students read and fill in blanks for three minutes, and the number they get correct is their score. Which type of CBM is this?
   a. Word identification fluency
   b. Passage reading fluency
   c. Letter-sound fluency
   d. CBM maze fluency

89. In terms of supporting a teacher's assessment design, which of the following should a teacher do that best reflects the relationship of gathering student progress monitoring information to writing tests?
   a. Write the tests according to the lesson plan objectives and activities.
   b. Write the tests as informed by progress monitoring and lesson plans.
   c. Write the tests first, and then write lesson plans aligned to those tests.
   d. Write the tests before monitoring progress to see what the tests taught.

90. What is true about the proofreading stage of student writing and computer word processing software spell-check and grammar-check features?
   a. Students will get the best results by always proofreading immediately after finishing the latest draft.
   b. Students using MS Word can always right-click and select "Add to dictionary" to delete red markups.
   c. Students cannot rely on word processors to correct for parallel structure or subject-verb agreement.
   d. Students should expect software programs to detect and replace homonyms when used incorrectly.

91. Writing features such as organizational structure, elaborative details, and sentence types most affect which aspect of a written piece?
   a. Main idea
   b. Flow
   c. Difficulty
   d. Mood

92. Principles of effective writing instruction include allotting enough time for systematic writing opportunities and teaching discourse knowledge (e.g., text structure, linguistic features). Among additional principles, which is most related to using writing to improve reading comprehension?
   a. Differentiation among tiers
   b. Explicit strategy instruction
   c. Cross-curricular integration
   d. Authentic writing activities

93. Researchers find that proper progress monitoring improves communication of student progress and raises teachers' expectations of students' performance. What else have they found?
   a. It enables students to learn better, but not faster.
   b. It decreases referrals to special education testing.
   c. It primarily only satisfies accountability mandates.
   d. It has no effect on instructional teacher decisions.

94. In which application of geometry to everyday situations would a student need to use pi?
   a. Calculating the area of the circular music room in the school
   b. Calculating the area of a rectangular classroom in the school
   c. Calculating the water volume of the swimming pool (rectangular prism) in school
   d. Calculating the distance for walking from home to the school

95. A student is struggling to understand counting by tens. Which of the following would be most helpful?
   a. Giving the child a chart of multiples of 10 in bright colors
   b. Separating a pile of pennies into stacks of 10 to count
   c. Showing the child that two nickels make 10 cents
   d. Having the child take an online quiz to test counting by tens

96. A student is calculating the cost of a vacation. She is researching the cost of gas, lodging, meals, and state park entrance fees and adding everything to find the total cost. What kind of math is she using?
   a. Algebra
   b. Calculus
   c. Geometry
   d. Arithmetic

97. Which of the following problems illustrate the importance of memorizing multiplication tables in elementary school?
   a. Jen bought six books at $7 each. How much did she pay?
   b. Lucy purchased four books: $4, $12, $8, and $7. How much did she pay?
   c. Ben walked 2 miles to school, 0.5 miles to the soccer field, and then 1.8 miles home. How far did he walk altogether?
   d. Mark paid $28 for pizza and Liz paid him back $13 for her share. How much did Mark's portion cost?

98. In algebra, students must use known _____ to find unknown _____.
   a. Constants; multiplicands
   b. Variables; constants
   c. Variables; letters
   d. Constants; variables

99. Which instructional resources are typically most useful for teaching early math concepts to the youngest students?
   a. Hands-on materials
   b. Computer programs
   c. Mathematical charts
   d. Mathematical graphs

100. According to experts, the greatest deficiencies in tools for monitoring student progress in mathematics exist at which educational levels?
   a. High school grades
   b. Middle school grades
   c. Elementary school grades
   d. Preschool and primary grades

Answer Key and Explanations for Test #5

1. A: To *abet* is a transitive verb (it takes an object) meaning to support, help, or facilitate, typically relative to a crime or other wrongdoing. Despite containing the syllable "bet," it does not mean gambling on the misdeed (b). Because another synonym of abetting is encouraging, discouraging (c) is an antonym. Similarly, interfering with the misdeed (d) is the opposite of facilitating it.

2. B: *Egregious* is an adjective meaning outstandingly bad, blatant, flagrant, or extreme. Synonyms include deplorable (a), i.e., shameful or unfortunate; inordinate (c), i.e., excessive; and notorious (d), i.e., infamous. Concealed (b), meaning hidden, is the only word given that can be used as an antonym for something standing out as very obvious or overt.

3. D: *Impassive* is an adjective meaning unfeeling, emotionless, not suffering, or serene and calm. Active (a) is an antonym of passive, not of impassive. Deadlocked (b) can be synonymous with "at an impasse," which is a different term from impassive. Assertive (c) can be an antonym of passive, but not of impassive.

4. C: *Perfunctory* means routine, hasty, or superficial as opposed to thorough (c). It can also mean indifferent, unenthusiastic, or apathetic (b), which is a synonym rather than an antonym. Dilatory (a) means late, slow, or delaying and is an antonym of punctual, rather than of perfunctory. Debatable (d) is an antonym of peremptory, not of perfunctory.

5. C: The third sentence, which is the final sentence in the first paragraph, defines the main idea of the text. The first sentence (a) only provides the topic, not the main idea. The second sentence (b) provides supporting details, building up to the main idea. The last sentence (d) also provides supporting facts rather than summing up the main idea.

6. A: The main idea can be found in the last sentence of the first paragraph. However, the passage does not have a summary sentence. The final paragraph adds new information rather than summarizing what has already been written. Since a summary sentence does not exist, options (b), (c), and (d) cannot be true.

7. B: The first sentence introduces the topic. The title (c) is not an introductory statement because it only names the general topic. The final paragraph (d) adds new information rather than introducing the article.

8. D: Some informational texts include summary statements and some do not. This article is one of the latter. The final (a) paragraph adds new information rather than summarizing. The beginning (b) introduces the piece rather than summarizing it. The title (c) identifies the subject matter of the article.

9. C: This is the most accurate restatement of the main idea. Choices (a), (b), and (d) are mentioned in the article but are supporting details rather than the main idea.

10. C: In the third paragraph, the text identifies three steps for integrating real-world connections with student learning. The first step is to research before class and bring examples and visual aids to share with students. Choices (a) and (b) are not part of the three steps, but are mentioned before the steps. Choice (d) is step two.

11. B: The last paragraph states that some subjects, such as geometric proofs, are more difficult to connect to the real world. Language (a) and computer programming (c) are mentioned in the first paragraph as subjects that connect more obviously. Early elementary mathematics (d) is not mentioned in this article.

12. D: According to the first paragraph, students are benefited by remaining engaged and being empowered to use their knowledge. The paragraph mentions being interested in learning (a), and likewise gives the example of geometric proofs contributing to prep for law studies, but this would not apply to all students. Preparing examples of connections and finding visual aids (b) is a task for the teacher, not a benefit for the students. Choosing subjects with clear connections (c) is not mentioned in the article.

13. B: The second paragraph states that teachers should not give a perfunctory response because students will be unlikely to pay attention and work hard. The article does not state that they will be unable to focus until they know the connection (a). Visual aids (c) are mentioned in the third paragraph, but are discussed as optional ("examples AND/OR visual aids") rather than vital to student understanding. Making a career connection (d) is discussed in the last paragraph but is not the reason to avoid giving a short answer.

14. C: Based on the information in the third paragraph, teachers have three steps to follow, with an optional fourth step of assigning research projects. Bringing visual aids (a) is an optional part of the first step. Asking students to think of their own connections (b) is the third step. Showing a career connection with unlikely subjects is discussed in the final paragraph and is not part of the listed steps.

15. B: This is a process, or how-to, essay. The author describes the process of integrating real-world connections in student learning. It is not comparison and contrast (a) because it does not compare results of integrating with results of failure to integrate. It is not cause and effect (c) because it does not show specific results of integrating. It is not entertainment (d) because it is a serious essay.

16. D: The author is writing in a serious, calm tone, expressing the importance of real-world connections and giving practical advice. The tone is not ambiguous (a) because the author is very clear on this importance. The tone is not indifferent (b) because the author seems to care about the subject, stressing its importance. The tone is not angry (c), but merely informative and gently urging the reader to act.

17. A: The third paragraph states that the connection should be made at the beginning of the lesson to capture the interest of the students, so choices (b), (c), and (d) cannot be true.

18. D: This piece does not present information in chronological order or order of occurrence (a). It does not follow spatial order (b), moving from point to point by physical proximity. It does not organize information in order of importance (climactic order). It presents information in topical order, i.e., subtopics naturally emerge from the topic (d).

19. B: At the beginning of 4th grade, Alice's score was 98 WCPM; the question identifies the goal for the end of 3rd grade as 114 WCPM, so her first 4th-grade score was not on the 3rd-grade level (a), but below the fluency goals for the ends of both 3rd and 4th grades (b). However, by the end of 4th grade, Alice's score exactly matched the goal rather than being below it (c). But her score of 118 had not reached the end of 5th-grade goal of 128 (d).

20. A: This graph indicates an overall ascending trend, as Alice's scores go up every month except for one small dip in January. Her scores do not go down overall (b). Her scores are not stable overall (c) because they go up significantly over the year rather than staying flat or relatively similar.

However, they are not unstable overall (d) either, as they do not fluctuate up and down inconsistently from month to month.

21. C: Alice received a score of 102 WCPM in January 2015, whereas her December 2014 score was 104 WCPM (as her November 2014 score was also). Her score in September 2014 (a) is the first score on the graph, so there is no prior month's score for comparison. Her score in December 2014 (b) was the same as her score in the prior month. Her score in March 2015 (d) was five points higher, not lower, than her February 2015 score.

22. D: Alice maintained her oral reading fluency rate over the summer because her scores in May and September 2015 are identical. Though it is common for students to lose some gains over the summer (a), in this case the graph does not show that. Though students who read copiously over the summer may improve (b), the graph does not show this either. The information above the graph says both teachers gave Alice the same assessment, not that the 5th-grade assessment in September used harder text (c).

23. C: Alice's score was 98 in September 2014, and 118 in September 2015. This is a difference of 20 points (and also shows improvement from below the goal for the end of 3rd grade to meeting the goal for the end of 4th grade). Option (a) is 10 points more than this difference, option (b) is five points less, and option (d) is 10 points less than the actual difference.

24. D: This is an opinion because "best ever" is a value judgment that cannot be proven or disproven. Option (a) is a fact, stating age which can be verified. Option (b) is a fact because the emotion of love is expressed by the person feeling it, so it is true for him/her. If it were stated by someone else without citing or quoting that person, it would be a supposition, hence an opinion. Option (c) is a fact, stating colors that can be seen.

25. A: The two subjects "she" and "husband" in the dependent clause require the plural auxiliary verb "are." In choice (b), the "either… or" construction dictates singular "is," not plural "are." In choice (c), the "not only… but also" construction, like "either… or," demands singular "is," not "are." In choice (d), "husband," the subject of the second independent clause (following "and"), is singular, requiring "has" rather than plural "have."

26. B: In this sentence, "Some" refers to the plural noun "people," so the plural auxiliary verb "are" agrees with it. ("Opposing" is the progressive participle and can go with any tense of the auxiliary verb "to be.") The same applies in option (a): "flowers" are plural, so the verb should be "are," not "is." However, in option (c), "funding" is a mass noun, so "some" is singular, requiring "has," not "have" (c). Plural "pies" (d) requires "were," not "was."

27. D: The two subjects "You" and "I" require the plural form of the verb "agree." The subjects "He" and "they" (a) likewise need "disagree," not singular "disagrees." "She" and "the rest of us" (b) also need the plural "agree," not singular "agrees." As "you" and "she" (c) also require a plural verb, it should be "are," not singular "is."

28. C: "Will… be" (future) plus "attending" (progressive/continuous) combine to form the future progressive tense. Choice (a) is in the present tense, choice (b) is in the simple future tense, and choice (d) is in the future perfect tense.

29. C: "Had… heard" is in the past perfect tense, one step before the present perfect, "have… heard" (b). Choice (a) is in the present progressive (present continuous) tense, "am… hearing." "Will… have heard" (d) is in the future perfect tense.

30. A: This version is in the past tense ("hoped," "prepared"). Version (b) is in the present tense ("hope," "prepare"). Version (c) is in the future tense ("will... hope... prepare"). Version (d) is in the present perfect tense ("have hoped... prepared").

31. B: The present perfect tense of the verb "to give" is "(I) have given." (In the third person singular, it would be "[s/he] has given.") Choice (a) uses the past perfect tense, "had given." Choice (c) uses the present tense, "give." Choice (d) uses the future perfect tense, "will have given."

32. D: The present progressive tense of the verb "to begin" is "is beginning" (or, with a plural or second-person subject, "are beginning"). "Was awaiting" (a) is the past progressive tense of "to await." "Has been anticipating" (b) is the present perfect progressive tense of "to anticipate." "Will be entering" (c) is the future progressive tense of "to enter."

33. C: Second person "you" (singular or plural) takes "are" as the present tense of "to be." "Were" (a) is the past tense of the verb (with a first- or third-person singular subject, it would be "was"). "Are being" (b) is in the present progressive (present continuous) tense. "Will... be" (d) is in the future tense.

34. B: The future tense of "to help" is "will help." "Helps" (a) is the present tense (third person singular; for first and second person, singular or plural, it is "help"). "Will be helping" (c) is the future progressive (aka future continuous) tense, not the simple future tense. "Is helping" (d) is the present progressive (aka present continuous) tense.

35. B: "We will have been" is the future perfect tense of the verb "to be." "(His next birthday) will... be" (a) is the simple future tense of this verb, as is "(We) will be" (c) also. "Will commemorate" (d) is the simple future tense of the verb "to commemorate." Only option (b) is future perfect rather than simple future.

36. A: "We had" is past tense, and so is "Sandra brought." However, "We have" (b) is present tense, but "Sandra brought" is past tense; "We have... until" cannot be followed by "brought." Conversely, past tense "We had" (c) cannot be followed by "until Sandra brings," present tense. Version (a) would correct this; or "We have... until Sandra brings" (or "We will have...") would. "We have" (d) requires "but Sandra will bring," "but Sandra is bringing," or must be "We had had" (or "had") to agree with "Sandra had brought."

37. C: Though some people accustomed to incorrectly saying "It's me" think it sounds unnatural, "I" is the correct first-person pronoun to agree with the singular antecedent "person." Plural "persons" and plural verb "are" require "we," not "me" (a). Singular antecedent "person" and singular verb "is" take the third-person singular "he" or "she," not plural "they" (b). Plural "persons" and "are" (d) need "they," not singular "he."

38. A: The third-person singular feminine pronoun "her" renames the subject, i.e., the proper noun "Sheila." The reflexive pronoun "himself" (b) disagrees with "Sheila" in gender. The plural object pronoun "them" (c) also disagrees, but in number. "She" (d) is a subject pronoun, but should be the object pronoun "her" as it is the object of the preposition "with."

39. D: The subject is "driver," and the second-person singular pronoun "you" agrees with it. In choice (a), the third-person singular feminine pronoun "She" is the subject, but the reflexive pronoun renaming it is incorrectly the masculine "himself" instead of "herself." Conversely, "Mr. Jones" (b) is a singular masculine proper noun, so the reflexive pronoun should be "himself," not "themself." Although "You are" is correct, the subject in options (c) and (d) is not "you" but "driver"; so "are" is incorrect, but "is" (d) agrees.

40. C: "Who" refers to people, whereas the relative pronouns "that" (a) and "which" (b) refer to things. "Whom" (d) only refers to people as objects (e.g., "the man whom I met," "the man with whom I spoke"), not subjects. In this sentence, the relative pronoun "who" introduces and is the subject of the restrictive relative clause (a type of dependent/subordinate clause) identifying the man.

41. D: Use the demonstrative pronoun "this" to indicate something right here, and the demonstrative pronoun "that" to indicate something over there. Hence only option (d) is correct; option (a) gets the first usage wrong, option (b) gets the second usage wrong, and option (c) gets both wrong by switching them.

42. B: Although some two-syllable adjectives have their comparatives and superlatives formed by adding -er and -est endings (e.g., "gentle," "gentler," "gentlest"; "narrow," "narrower," "narrowest"; and "busy," "busier," "busiest"), the comparatives and superlatives of most other adjectives with two syllables (and all adjectives with three or more syllables) are formed by preceding them with "more" and "most," as with "thorough." The correct superlative is choice (b). The correct comparative is choice (d).

43. D: This sentence uses the correct comparative form of "quiet," i.e., "quieter." Sentence (a) incorrectly duplicates the comparative by adding both "more" and -er to "fast"; comparatives use only one or the other, and "more fast" is not standard whereas "faster" is. Writer/producer/director Spike Lee's 1990 title (b) deliberately uses a culturally idiomatic expression, which is artistically acceptable but would be incorrect in formal written English. The superlative of "good" is "best"; redundantly adding another -est ending (c) is incorrect.

44. C: This has a subject and a verb, and expresses a complete thought. Example (a) has a subject and verb, but does not express a complete thought: the construction needs a direct object to modify the verb "witnessed." Example (b) is neither a complete sentence nor expresses a complete thought; it is a dependent clause with no independent clause. Adding example (c), a complete sentence by itself, to example (b) would make another complete sentence. Example (d) has a subject and verb, but not a complete thought: "I have never" needs another verb to complete it.

45. A: The semicolon correctly divides the first independent clause from the second, and the comma correctly precedes the conjunction "and" before the third independent clause. The single comma in choice (b) creates a comma splice, aka a run-on sentence. All three punctuation marks are placed incorrectly in choice (c): the comma contradicts the meaning; the period interrupts "I know you loved him"; and when a conjunction like "and" connects independent clauses, it is preceded by a comma, not a semicolon. Both commas are incorrectly placed in choice (d).

46. C: This is a quotation interrupted by the non-quoted description "he queried." Only the quoted parts are enclosed in quotation marks. Version (a) fails to close the quotation marks after "What," incorrectly including "he queried" in the quotation. Version (b) lacks all necessary quotation marks. Version (d) fails to open new quotation marks before "am."

47. D: The initial letter of the first word of every new sentence is always capitalized in standard, formal written English. Option (c) fails to capitalize both words beginning the second and third sentences. Options (a) and (b) incorrectly use commas, creating run-on sentences.

48. D: Many people confuse the spellings of these words that sound alike. "Accept" means to receive or take, consent, agree, accede, confirm, undertake, believe, admit, or reconcile in other senses; whereas "except" means but, save, or excluding as a preposition as it is used here, or as a verb ("to except," "excepting") with the same meaning. The other choices use one (a), (b) or both (c) of these words incorrectly.

49. C: The verb "forego" means to precede or go before something, whereas the verb "forgo" means to do without something. Thus option (a) should be "forgo," option (b) should be "foregoing," option (c) is correct, and option (d) should be "forgoing."

50. A: "It's" is a contraction of "it is," and therefore it indicates a gender-neutral subject pronoun plus a third-person singular present tense verb. In contrast, "its" is the possessive form of the gender-neutral third-person singular pronoun "it." Attaching a -'s to the end of a word is only used with nouns and proper nouns, not pronouns. Choice (b) wrongly transposes both words, choice (c) gets the second one wrong, and choice (d) gets the first one wrong.

51. B: Although they sound alike, "dual" and "duel" have different meanings. "Dual" refers to two and means twofold, double, or binary. "Duel" refers to a fight or contest, typically between two individuals, as in the famous historical gun duel between Burr and Hamilton (d); the song "Dueling Banjos" used in the movie *Deliverance*, wherein two musicians exchanged musical riffs (which eventually became a duet, a related word); or the expression "a duel of wits." Therefore, choices (a) and (c) should be dual, choice (b) is correct, and choice (d) should be duel.

52. C: "Museum" should be capitalized when part of a title, such as Carnegie Museum of Art, and lowercase when used as a common noun ("the museum"). Choice (c) correctly capitalizes the title. Choices (a) and (d) fail to capitalize a proper noun, and choice (b) incorrectly capitalizes a common noun.

53. B: When a kinship or family name like "Mother" replaces a proper name (or precedes one, e.g., Aunt Mary), it is capitalized. However, it is not capitalized when it does not refer to a specific person (a), (c). It is also not capitalized when it follows the personal name, and/or when it is used with possessive pronouns or possessive nouns (d).

54. B: "Peek" means a small look or glance as a noun, and to take a small look as a verb. "Peak" means the top, highest point, or tip as a noun, and to reach its greatest height as an intransitive verb. "Pique" means to whet, stimulate, arouse, or annoy as a verb, and ill temper or humor (e.g., "a fit of pique") as a noun. The other choices incorrectly use all three (a) or two (c), (d). Additionally, choices (a) and (d) not only misspell "pique," but also incorrectly use "peak" as a transitive verb.

55. D: The place value of a digit depends on its location in relation to the decimal point. The places to the left of the decimal are ones, tens, then hundreds, respectively. The places to the right of the decimal are tenths, hundredths, and thousandths, respectively. Since the digit 3 is in the first position after the decimal point, its place value is tenths.

56. B: The place value of a digit depends on its location in relation to the decimal point. The places to the left of the decimal are ones, tens, then hundreds, respectively. To round a number to a certain place value, you look at the digit to the immediate right. If the digit to the right is 5 or more, round up by adding one. If the digit is less than five, round down by keeping the same digit. For this problem, the digit in the tens place is 0. The digit to its immediate right is 9. Since 9 is greater than 5, round up. So, 6,709 rounded to the nearest ten is 6,710.

57. D: The place value of a digit depends on its location in relation to the decimal point. The places to the left of the decimal are ones, tens, then hundreds, respectively. To round a number to a certain place value, look at the digit to the immediate right. If the digit to the right is 5 or more, round up by adding one. If the digit is less than five, round down by keeping the same digit. For this problem, the digit in the thousands place is 2. The digit to its immediate right is 0. Since 0 is less than 5, round down. So, 2,077 rounded to the nearest thousand is 2,000.

58. C: Since 1 mile equals 5,280 feet, the conversion factor is 5,280. Since a mile is longer than a foot, we multiply by the conversion factor, so 2 miles equal $2 \times 5,280$ or 10,560 feet.

59. D: The perimeter of a rectangle is equal to the sum of twice the length and twice the width. The length is approximately 12 meters, and the width is approximately 8 meters, so $2(12) + 2(8) = 40$ m.

60. A: The length rounded to the nearest hundred centimeters is 1,300 cm. The width rounded to the nearest hundred centimeters is 700 cm. The area of the rectangle is the product of the length and the width or $1300 \times 700 = 910,000$ cm².

61. A: The amount of money in Franklin's checking account is the sum of the original amount and the deposits. The total amount is equal to $234 + 52 + 121 + 32$ or \$439.

62. D: The number of pieces of fruit that the vendor has is equal to the sum of the numbers of individual types of fruit. The number equals $52 + 88 + 48 + 45$ or 233 pieces of fruit.

63. C: The amount left in Mr. Otto's checking account is the difference between the current amount in his checking account and his rent. The amount equals $1,252 - \$650$ or \$602.

64. B: To find the difference between 400,000 and 382,789, we need to borrow. A shortcut is to subtract 1 from 400,000 replacing it with 399,999 and add the 1 back after:

$$400,000 - 382,789 = 400,000 - 1 - 382,789 + 1$$
$$= 399,999 - 382,789 + 1$$
$$= 17,210 + 1$$
$$= 17,211$$

$$\begin{array}{r} 399999 \\ - 382789 \\ \hline 17210 \end{array}$$

65. C: The new balance of Marcie's checking account is determined by adding deposits and subtracting the sum of her bills. After her deposit of \$525, her account balance is \$1,385. Her bills total \$660. The new balance of her account is equal to $\$1,385 - \$660$ or \$725.

66. C: When Mr. Carlson deposits the \$762, his new checking account balance is \$1,302. After he purchases gasoline, his balance is at \$1,252. After he purchases groceries, his balance is at \$1,120.

67. C: Multiplication is commutative, which means that the factors may be arranged in any order. Since one of the factors is 0, the product is 0.

68. D: The number of cans in a case is equal to the product of the number of cans in a layer and the number of layers. Each layer contains 4 rows of 6 cans or 24 cans. The case contains two layers, so it has a total of 2×24 or 48 cans.

69. D: Since 7 is not a factor of 64, there is a remainder when 64 is divided by 7. Since $7 \times 9 = 63$, and $64 - 63 = 1$, the remainder is 1.

70. A: The number of pineapples in each crate is equal to the total number of pineapples divided by the number of crates. The number of pineapples equals $6,720 \div 280 = 24$ crates.

71. C: The number of pineapples packed in 535 crates is equal to the product of the numbers of pineapples per crate and the number of crates. The amount equals 535×24 or 12,840 pineapples.

72. B: Mr. Beauchamp's average rate of travel is equal to the distance traveled divided by the time of travel. The rate of travel equals 265 ÷ 5 or 53 miles per hour.

73. A: The cost of the material equals $7\frac{1}{3} \times \$12$. Convert the mixed number to an improper fraction and then multiply: $\frac{22}{3} \times \$12 = \$88$.

74. D: To convert a fraction to a percent, divide the numerator by the denominator. Then move the decimal two places to the right and add the percent symbol. Then $\frac{4}{5} = 0.8 = 80\%$.

75. D: The total cost is the sum of the individual items. The total cost equals $\$68.99 + \$79.00 + 3(\$45.49)$, which is $\$284.46$.

76. D: The amount earned is the product of the pay rate, the number of hours per day, and the number of days. The amount earned equals $\$8.50 \times 6.5 \times 45$ or $\$2,486.25$.

77. A: The t-shirt consists only of cotton and polyester. If 85% is cotton, then the polyester is 100% − 85% or 15% of the t-shirt.

78. C: This question is basically asking, "What percent of 15 is 3?" Let n represent *what percent*, and replace the *of* with a multiplication symbol and the *is* with an equal sign. Then we have $n \times 15 = 3$. To solve this equation, divide both sides by 15. Then $n = 3 \div 15 = 0.2$. This is in decimal form. To convert a decimal to a percent, move the decimal point two places to the right and add the percent symbol. The decimal 0.2 is 20%.

79. D: To convert a fraction to a percent, divide the numerator of the fraction by the denominator. Then move the decimal point two places to the right and add the percent sign. Since $2 \div 3 = 0.666666\ldots$, we write the percent as $66.6666\ldots$ or $66\frac{2}{3}\%$.

80. C: To covert this decimal to a fraction, move the decimal two places to the right, and place the number over one hundred. Thus 0.45 is represented by the fraction $\frac{45}{100}$, which reduces to $\frac{9}{20}$.

81. B: To convert a percent to a fraction, remove the percent symbol and place the number over 100. Thus 72.5% equals $\frac{72.5}{100}$. To remove the decimal from the numerator, multiply both the numerator and the denominator by 10. Thus $\frac{72.5}{100}$ equals $\frac{725}{1000}$. Now reduce the fraction to find that 72.5% equals $\frac{29}{40}$.

82. C: Simply hearing about the value of reading (a) is never as effective as direct personal experience with reading and its value. While hands-on learning is vital, reading cannot be replaced (b). Though giving students choices is generally effective, the students described currently lack knowledge and experience with English-language texts for selecting their own reading (d). Thus, the best choice is to provide them texts about things familiar to them from their background experiences—e.g., well-digging, childcare, farming, food preparation, handcrafts, etc. (c).

83. A: The Dolch sight word list contains words with irregular spellings. Because these lack letter-sound (phonic) relationships, students must simply memorize them, supported by drilling. Regular word spellings (b) follow phonics rules, and students learn to read better through decoding by sounding them out. Regular verb conjugations (c) follow grammatical rules students can learn and apply to multiple verbs. Though irregular verbs do not follow these rules, drilling is unnecessary for each verb (d) because many can be classified into groups with patterns (e.g., "freeze," "froze," "frozen"; "speak," "spoke," "spoken"; "swim," "swam," "swum"; "drink," "drank," "drunk," etc.).

84. B: Students can use dictionary syllabication to recognize word origins more readily, as many individual syllables are more recognizable as similar to the roots and affixes they derived from in Greek, Latin, etc. than whole words, whose syllables come from different word sources. One common use of this feature historically has been determining correct word hyphenation, but word processing software, with word-wrap, justification, etc. makes hyphenating words unnecessary (b). Syllabication does not show which syllables are stressed (c), but accents and diacritical marks do. Phonetic spellings, not syllabication, show pronunciation (d).

85. D: Books with illustrations (a) combine verbal and nonlinguistic visual media only. "Books on Tape" represent auditory media only. Following in the text as the teacher reads it aloud (c) combines mainly verbal and auditory, and some visual stimuli. Electronic text including audio, visual, touchscreen, and interactive features (d) combines verbal, visual, auditory, and tactile media, plus more active reader participation and immediate feedback.

86. A: Asking questions about reading for students to answer not only helps them monitor their own comprehension, but also helps them relate what they learn to what they already know, gives them a purpose for reading (b), focuses their attention on what they should learn (c), and promotes active student thinking while reading (d).

87. C: First, the teacher should explain directly to students how a specific strategy will aid their reading comprehension, and when they should use different strategies. Second, the teacher should demonstrate for students how to apply each strategy as modeling. A good way to model is think-alouds while reading the same text students are reading. Third, the teacher should help students learn when and how to apply strategies during guided practice. Fourth, the teacher should support students in practicing each strategy until they can independently apply it.

88. D: Word identification fluency (a) is a CBM approach used to monitor grade 1 reading progress: students read grade-level text passages aloud for one minute. Passage reading fluency (b) is a CBM assessment best for monitoring reading progress in grades 2–3: students read aloud for one minute, and testers count the number of correctly read words. Letter-sound fluency (c) is one CBM assessment for monitoring reading-related progress in kindergarten: presented with randomly sequenced uppercase and lowercase letters, children say their corresponding sounds for one minute. CBM maze fluency (d), described in the question, is recommended for grades 4–5.

89. B: Although tests should be aligned with lesson plan objectives and activities to test what the students actually learned and did (a), this alone is insufficient: monitoring student progress in lessons to date will additionally inform teachers what and how to test. Writing lesson plans based on previously written tests (c) does not allow teachers to inform either planning or assessment with progress monitoring information. Tests should be informed by progress monitoring, and are more for evaluating what students have learned and need to learn than for teaching them (d).

90. C: Students, like other writers, can often proofread better by allowing some time (as permitted) after finishing the latest draft (a). "Add to dictionary" in MS Word will remove red zigzag underlines, but students should not always do this (b): these marks are wrong when Word cannot recognize certain words, but other times they correctly identify misspellings. Students must correct for parallel structure, as such programs cannot, and these only identify some instances of subject-verb disagreement, but not many others (c). Software programs also routinely miss incorrect homonyms, or replace misspellings with wrong homonyms (d).

91. B: Organizational structure, details, and sentence types in a passage play a role in each of these categories, but primarily affect flow of thought. Organizational structure may refer one of several models, including cause and effect, compare and contrast, or a thesis model, where a problem is addressed with various reasons over the course of several paragraphs. Details may be used to reinforce points in an argument or add flavor to text, and switching between sentence types affects the speed of information processing on the part of the reader. Each of these factors contributes in controlling the flow of a passage from one idea to another. Main idea is not usually dictated by these factors, but may instead have an influence on the structure the writer chooses. Complex sentence types and details can change the difficulty of a passage and mood of a passage, such as by using flowery language or informational examples, but the organization and use of different types of sentences has the most effect on the flow of a passage.

92. C: Effective writing instruction not only teaches writing for its own sake, but also uses writing to improve reading comprehension and learning across the curriculum. It differentiates instruction via multiple tiers (a), which addresses individual student differences; teaches writing strategies explicitly (b), which enables students to understand and apply them; and provides authentic activities (d) and strategies to enhance student self-efficacy for writing, which increases student motivation to write.

93. B: Researchers have found that correct progress monitoring enables accelerated student learning (a), decreases referrals to evaluation for special education (b), satisfies accountability mandates by documenting student progress—not only and/or primarily (c), but along with these and other benefits—and enables teachers to make better instructional decisions (d).

94. A: The geometric formula for calculating a circle's area is $A = \pi r^2$ where A = area and r = radius. π is a number whose decimal places extend indefinitely without resolution to a whole number; abbreviated, it equals approximately 3.14159. Calculating a rectangle's area (b) uses the formula $A = L \times W$ (length times width). Calculating water volume (c) uses the formula Cubic feet = Base × Width × Average depth. Calculating distance (d) uses a variant of the Pythagorean theorem wherein distance equals a right triangle's hypotenuse.

95. B: The most helpful tool for teaching counting by tens is the pile of pennies that the child can both see and handle, watching how groups of ten are made. A chart of multiples of ten (a) would be helpful for memorizing facts but not for learning how counting works. Showing that two nickels make 10 cents (c) is unrelated to counting by tens. An online quiz (d) can help to test knowledge but not help acquire it.

96. D: The math used is simple addition, which is arithmetic. Algebra (a) could be used to solve for missing information or calculate miles per gallon, etc. Calculus is not needed (b) to get this answer. The student would use geometry (c) to calculate something like area.

97. A: If a student has memorized that 6 × 7 = 42, this is a simple problem. If not, the student will have to add six 7s. Choices (b) and (c) use addition, and choice (d) uses subtraction.

98. D: In algebra problems, students use given values called *constants* to solve for unknowns, called *variables*. Multiplicands (a) are numbers that are multiplied by others in math problems (not necessarily algebra). The variables are typically represented by letters (c), but this is not what they are called. Choice (b) reverses the correct answers.

99. A: Young children need concrete objects they can see, touch, and manipulate to learn abstract concepts as their thinking is typically not yet abstract in nature. Though computer programs (b) can help teachers with instruction and children with learning of math concepts, even the most advanced interactive programs and touchscreen technology still involve two-dimensional images, whereas real objects are three-dimensional, concrete, and familiar. Charts (c) and graphs (d) are more abstract, useful for older students but inappropriate for young children.

100. A: As of 2008, researchers had observed that some curriculum-based measurement (CBM) resources for monitoring progress with basic math computation in grades 1–6 were available, only one publisher provided such measures for grades 7–8, and no such measures were offered specifically for grades 9–12. Experts attribute this deficiency to lack of consensus about general outcome measures in high school math. Some researchers have recently been developing Pre-Algebra and Algebra 1 progress-monitoring instruments, but there remains a dearth of tools for monitoring progress in more advanced high school math courses.

How to Overcome Test Anxiety

Just the thought of taking a test is enough to make most people a little nervous. A test is an important event that can have a long-term impact on your future, so it's important to take it seriously and it's natural to feel anxious about performing well. But just because anxiety is normal, that doesn't mean that it's helpful in test taking, or that you should simply accept it as part of your life. Anxiety can have a variety of effects. These effects can be mild, like making you feel slightly nervous, or severe, like blocking your ability to focus or remember even a simple detail.

If you experience test anxiety—whether severe or mild—it's important to know how to beat it. To discover this, first you need to understand what causes test anxiety.

Causes of Test Anxiety

While we often think of anxiety as an uncontrollable emotional state, it can actually be caused by simple, practical things. One of the most common causes of test anxiety is that a person does not feel adequately prepared for their test. This feeling can be the result of many different issues such as poor study habits or lack of organization, but the most common culprit is time management. Starting to study too late, failing to organize your study time to cover all of the material, or being distracted while you study will mean that you're not well prepared for the test. This may lead to cramming the night before, which will cause you to be physically and mentally exhausted for the test. Poor time management also contributes to feelings of stress, fear, and hopelessness as you realize you are not well prepared but don't know what to do about it.

Other times, test anxiety is not related to your preparation for the test but comes from unresolved fear. This may be a past failure on a test, or poor performance on tests in general. It may come from comparing yourself to others who seem to be performing better or from the stress of living up to expectations. Anxiety may be driven by fears of the future—how failure on this test would affect your educational and career goals. These fears are often completely irrational, but they can still negatively impact your test performance.

> **Review Video: 3 Reasons You Have Test Anxiety**
> Visit mometrix.com/academy and enter code: 428468

Elements of Test Anxiety

As mentioned earlier, test anxiety is considered to be an emotional state, but it has physical and mental components as well. Sometimes you may not even realize that you are suffering from test anxiety until you notice the physical symptoms. These can include trembling hands, rapid heartbeat, sweating, nausea, and tense muscles. Extreme anxiety may lead to fainting or vomiting. Obviously, any of these symptoms can have a negative impact on testing. It is important to recognize them as soon as they begin to occur so that you can address the problem before it damages your performance.

> **Review Video: 3 Ways to Tell You Have Test Anxiety**
> Visit mometrix.com/academy and enter code: 927847

The mental components of test anxiety include trouble focusing and inability to remember learned information. During a test, your mind is on high alert, which can help you recall information and stay focused for an extended period of time. However, anxiety interferes with your mind's natural processes, causing you to blank out, even on the questions you know well. The strain of testing during anxiety makes it difficult to stay focused, especially on a test that may take several hours. Extreme anxiety can take a huge mental toll, making it difficult not only to recall test information but even to understand the test questions or pull your thoughts together.

> **Review Video: How Test Anxiety Affects Memory**
> Visit mometrix.com/academy and enter code: 609003

Effects of Test Anxiety

Test anxiety is like a disease—if left untreated, it will get progressively worse. Anxiety leads to poor performance, and this reinforces the feelings of fear and failure, which in turn lead to poor performances on subsequent tests. It can grow from a mild nervousness to a crippling condition. If allowed to progress, test anxiety can have a big impact on your schooling, and consequently on your future.

Test anxiety can spread to other parts of your life. Anxiety on tests can become anxiety in any stressful situation, and blanking on a test can turn into panicking in a job situation. But fortunately, you don't have to let anxiety rule your testing and determine your grades. There are a number of relatively simple steps you can take to move past anxiety and function normally on a test and in the rest of life.

> **Review Video: How Test Anxiety Impacts Your Grades**
> Visit mometrix.com/academy and enter code: 939819

Physical Steps for Beating Test Anxiety

While test anxiety is a serious problem, the good news is that it can be overcome. It doesn't have to control your ability to think and remember information. While it may take time, you can begin taking steps today to beat anxiety.

Just as your first hint that you may be struggling with anxiety comes from the physical symptoms, the first step to treating it is also physical. Rest is crucial for having a clear, strong mind. If you are tired, it is much easier to give in to anxiety. But if you establish good sleep habits, your body and mind will be ready to perform optimally, without the strain of exhaustion. Additionally, sleeping well helps you to retain information better, so you're more likely to recall the answers when you see the test questions.

Getting good sleep means more than going to bed on time. It's important to allow your brain time to relax. Take study breaks from time to time so it doesn't get overworked, and don't study right before bed. Take time to rest your mind before trying to rest your body, or you may find it difficult to fall asleep.

> **Review Video: The Importance of Sleep for Your Brain**
> Visit mometrix.com/academy and enter code: 319338

Along with sleep, other aspects of physical health are important in preparing for a test. Good nutrition is vital for good brain function. Sugary foods and drinks may give a burst of energy but this burst is followed by a crash, both physically and emotionally. Instead, fuel your body with protein and vitamin-rich foods.

Also, drink plenty of water. Dehydration can lead to headaches and exhaustion, especially if your brain is already under stress from the rigors of the test. Particularly if your test is a long one, drink water during the breaks. And if possible, take an energy-boosting snack to eat between sections.

> **Review Video: How Diet Can Affect your Mood**
> Visit mometrix.com/academy and enter code: 624317

Along with sleep and diet, a third important part of physical health is exercise. Maintaining a steady workout schedule is helpful, but even taking 5-minute study breaks to walk can help get your blood pumping faster and clear your head. Exercise also releases endorphins, which contribute to a positive feeling and can help combat test anxiety.

When you nurture your physical health, you are also contributing to your mental health. If your body is healthy, your mind is much more likely to be healthy as well. So take time to rest, nourish your body with healthy food and water, and get moving as much as possible. Taking these physical steps will make you stronger and more able to take the mental steps necessary to overcome test anxiety.

> **Review Video: How to Stay Healthy and Prevent Test Anxiety**
> Visit mometrix.com/academy and enter code: 877894

Mental Steps for Beating Test Anxiety

Working on the mental side of test anxiety can be more challenging, but as with the physical side, there are clear steps you can take to overcome it. As mentioned earlier, test anxiety often stems from lack of preparation, so the obvious solution is to prepare for the test. Effective studying may be the most important weapon you have for beating test anxiety, but you can and should employ several other mental tools to combat fear.

First, boost your confidence by reminding yourself of past success—tests or projects that you aced. If you're putting as much effort into preparing for this test as you did for those, there's no reason you should expect to fail here. Work hard to prepare; then trust your preparation.

Second, surround yourself with encouraging people. It can be helpful to find a study group, but be sure that the people you're around will encourage a positive attitude. If you spend time with others who are anxious or cynical, this will only contribute to your own anxiety. Look for others who are motivated to study hard from a desire to succeed, not from a fear of failure.

Third, reward yourself. A test is physically and mentally tiring, even without anxiety, and it can be helpful to have something to look forward to. Plan an activity following the test, regardless of the outcome, such as going to a movie or getting ice cream.

When you are taking the test, if you find yourself beginning to feel anxious, remind yourself that you know the material. Visualize successfully completing the test. Then take a few deep, relaxing breaths and return to it. Work through the questions carefully but with confidence, knowing that you are capable of succeeding.

Developing a healthy mental approach to test taking will also aid in other areas of life. Test anxiety affects more than just the actual test—it can be damaging to your mental health and even contribute to depression. It's important to beat test anxiety before it becomes a problem for more than testing.

> **Review Video: Test Anxiety and Depression**
> Visit mometrix.com/academy and enter code: 904704

Study Strategy

Being prepared for the test is necessary to combat anxiety, but what does being prepared look like? You may study for hours on end and still not feel prepared. What you need is a strategy for test prep. The next few pages outline our recommended steps to help you plan out and conquer the challenge of preparation.

STEP 1: SCOPE OUT THE TEST

Learn everything you can about the format (multiple choice, essay, etc.) and what will be on the test. Gather any study materials, course outlines, or sample exams that may be available. Not only will this help you to prepare, but knowing what to expect can help to alleviate test anxiety.

STEP 2: MAP OUT THE MATERIAL

Look through the textbook or study guide and make note of how many chapters or sections it has. Then divide these over the time you have. For example, if a book has 15 chapters and you have five days to study, you need to cover three chapters each day. Even better, if you have the time, leave an extra day at the end for overall review after you have gone through the material in depth.

If time is limited, you may need to prioritize the material. Look through it and make note of which sections you think you already have a good grasp on, and which need review. While you are studying, skim quickly through the familiar sections and take more time on the challenging parts. Write out your plan so you don't get lost as you go. Having a written plan also helps you feel more in control of the study, so anxiety is less likely to arise from feeling overwhelmed at the amount to cover.

STEP 3: GATHER YOUR TOOLS

Decide what study method works best for you. Do you prefer to highlight in the book as you study and then go back over the highlighted portions? Or do you type out notes of the important information? Or is it helpful to make flashcards that you can carry with you? Assemble the pens, index cards, highlighters, post-it notes, and any other materials you may need so you won't be distracted by getting up to find things while you study.

If you're having a hard time retaining the information or organizing your notes, experiment with different methods. For example, try color-coding by subject with colored pens, highlighters, or post-it notes. If you learn better by hearing, try recording yourself reading your notes so you can listen while in the car, working out, or simply sitting at your desk. Ask a friend to quiz you from your flashcards, or try teaching someone the material to solidify it in your mind.

STEP 4: CREATE YOUR ENVIRONMENT

It's important to avoid distractions while you study. This includes both the obvious distractions like visitors and the subtle distractions like an uncomfortable chair (or a too-comfortable couch that makes you want to fall asleep). Set up the best study environment possible: good lighting and a comfortable work area. If background music helps you focus, you may want to turn it on, but otherwise keep the room quiet. If you are using a computer to take notes, be sure you don't have any other windows open, especially applications like social media, games, or anything else that could distract you. Silence your phone and turn off notifications. Be sure to keep water close by so you stay hydrated while you study (but avoid unhealthy drinks and snacks).

Also, take into account the best time of day to study. Are you freshest first thing in the morning? Try to set aside some time then to work through the material. Is your mind clearer in the afternoon or evening? Schedule your study session then. Another method is to study at the same time of day that you will take the test, so that your brain gets used to working on the material at that time and will be ready to focus at test time.

Step 5: Study!

Once you have done all the study preparation, it's time to settle into the actual studying. Sit down, take a few moments to settle your mind so you can focus, and begin to follow your study plan. Don't give in to distractions or let yourself procrastinate. This is your time to prepare so you'll be ready to fearlessly approach the test. Make the most of the time and stay focused.

Of course, you don't want to burn out. If you study too long you may find that you're not retaining the information very well. Take regular study breaks. For example, taking five minutes out of every hour to walk briskly, breathing deeply and swinging your arms, can help your mind stay fresh.

As you get to the end of each chapter or section, it's a good idea to do a quick review. Remind yourself of what you learned and work on any difficult parts. When you feel that you've mastered the material, move on to the next part. At the end of your study session, briefly skim through your notes again.

But while review is helpful, cramming last minute is NOT. If at all possible, work ahead so that you won't need to fit all your study into the last day. Cramming overloads your brain with more information than it can process and retain, and your tired mind may struggle to recall even previously learned information when it is overwhelmed with last-minute study. Also, the urgent nature of cramming and the stress placed on your brain contribute to anxiety. You'll be more likely to go to the test feeling unprepared and having trouble thinking clearly.

So don't cram, and don't stay up late before the test, even just to review your notes at a leisurely pace. Your brain needs rest more than it needs to go over the information again. In fact, plan to finish your studies by noon or early afternoon the day before the test. Give your brain the rest of the day to relax or focus on other things, and get a good night's sleep. Then you will be fresh for the test and better able to recall what you've studied.

Step 6: Take a Practice Test

Many courses offer sample tests, either online or in the study materials. This is an excellent resource to check whether you have mastered the material, as well as to prepare for the test format and environment.

Check the test format ahead of time: the number of questions, the type (multiple choice, free response, etc.), and the time limit. Then create a plan for working through them. For example, if you have 30 minutes to take a 60-question test, your limit is 30 seconds per question. Spend less time on the questions you know well so that you can take more time on the difficult ones.

If you have time to take several practice tests, take the first one open book, with no time limit. Work through the questions at your own pace and make sure you fully understand them. Gradually work up to taking a test under test conditions: sit at a desk with all study materials put away and set a timer. Pace yourself to make sure you finish the test with time to spare and go back to check your answers if you have time.

After each test, check your answers. On the questions you missed, be sure you understand why you missed them. Did you misread the question (tests can use tricky wording)? Did you forget the information? Or was it something you hadn't learned? Go back and study any shaky areas that the practice tests reveal.

Taking these tests not only helps with your grade, but also aids in combating test anxiety. If you're already used to the test conditions, you're less likely to worry about it, and working through tests until you're scoring well gives you a confidence boost. Go through the practice tests until you feel comfortable, and then you can go into the test knowing that you're ready for it.

Test Tips

On test day, you should be confident, knowing that you've prepared well and are ready to answer the questions. But aside from preparation, there are several test day strategies you can employ to maximize your performance.

First, as stated before, get a good night's sleep the night before the test (and for several nights before that, if possible). Go into the test with a fresh, alert mind rather than staying up late to study.

Try not to change too much about your normal routine on the day of the test. It's important to eat a nutritious breakfast, but if you normally don't eat breakfast at all, consider eating just a protein bar. If you're a coffee drinker, go ahead and have your normal coffee. Just make sure you time it so that the caffeine doesn't wear off right in the middle of your test. Avoid sugary beverages, and drink enough water to stay hydrated but not so much that you need a restroom break 10 minutes into the test. If your test isn't first thing in the morning, consider going for a walk or doing a light workout before the test to get your blood flowing.

Allow yourself enough time to get ready, and leave for the test with plenty of time to spare so you won't have the anxiety of scrambling to arrive in time. Another reason to be early is to select a good seat. It's helpful to sit away from doors and windows, which can be distracting. Find a good seat, get out your supplies, and settle your mind before the test begins.

When the test begins, start by going over the instructions carefully, even if you already know what to expect. Make sure you avoid any careless mistakes by following the directions.

Then begin working through the questions, pacing yourself as you've practiced. If you're not sure on an answer, don't spend too much time on it, and don't let it shake your confidence. Either skip it and come back later, or eliminate as many wrong answers as possible and guess among the remaining ones. Don't dwell on these questions as you continue—put them out of your mind and focus on what lies ahead.

Be sure to read all of the answer choices, even if you're sure the first one is the right answer. Sometimes you'll find a better one if you keep reading. But don't second-guess yourself if you do immediately know the answer. Your gut instinct is usually right. Don't let test anxiety rob you of the information you know.

If you have time at the end of the test (and if the test format allows), go back and review your answers. Be cautious about changing any, since your first instinct tends to be correct, but make sure you didn't misread any of the questions or accidentally mark the wrong answer choice. Look over any you skipped and make an educated guess.

At the end, leave the test feeling confident. You've done your best, so don't waste time worrying about your performance or wishing you could change anything. Instead, celebrate the successful completion of this test. And finally, use this test to learn how to deal with anxiety even better next time.

> **Review Video: 5 Tips to Beat Test Anxiety**
> Visit mometrix.com/academy and enter code: 570656

Important Qualification

Not all anxiety is created equal. If your test anxiety is causing major issues in your life beyond the classroom or testing center, or if you are experiencing troubling physical symptoms related to your anxiety, it may be a sign of a serious physiological or psychological condition. If this sounds like your situation, we strongly encourage you to seek professional help.

How to Overcome Your Fear of Math

The word *math* is enough to strike fear into most hearts. How many of us have memories of sitting through confusing lectures, wrestling over mind-numbing homework, or taking tests that still seem incomprehensible even after hours of study? Years after graduation, many still shudder at these memories.

The fact is, math is not just a classroom subject. It has real-world implications that you face every day, whether you realize it or not. This may be balancing your monthly budget, deciding how many supplies to buy for a project, or simply splitting a meal check with friends. The idea of daily confrontations with math can be so paralyzing that some develop a condition known as *math anxiety*.

But you do NOT need to be paralyzed by this anxiety! In fact, while you may have thought all your life that you're not good at math, or that your brain isn't wired to understand it, the truth is that you may have been conditioned to think this way. From your earliest school days, the way you were taught affected the way you viewed different subjects. And the way math has been taught has changed.

Several decades ago, there was a shift in American math classrooms. The focus changed from traditional problem-solving to a conceptual view of topics, de-emphasizing the importance of learning the basics and building on them. The solid foundation necessary for math progression and confidence was undermined. Math became more of a vague concept than a concrete idea. Today, it is common to think of math, not as a straightforward system, but as a mysterious, complicated method that can't be fully understood unless you're a genius.

This is why you may still have nightmares about being called on to answer a difficult problem in front of the class. Math anxiety is a very real, though unnecessary, fear.

Math anxiety may begin with a single class period. Let's say you missed a day in 6th grade math and never quite understood the concept that was taught while you were gone. Since math is cumulative, with each new concept building on past ones, this could very well affect the rest of your math career. Without that one day's knowledge, it will be difficult to understand any other concepts that link to it. Rather than realizing that you're just missing one key piece, you may begin to believe that you're simply not capable of understanding math.

This belief can change the way you approach other classes, career options, and everyday life experiences, if you become anxious at the thought that math might be required. A student who loves science may choose a different path of study upon realizing that multiple math classes will be required for a degree. An aspiring medical student may hesitate at the thought of going through the necessary math classes. For some this anxiety escalates into a more extreme state known as *math phobia*.

Math anxiety is challenging to address because it is rooted deeply and may come from a variety of causes: an embarrassing moment in class, a teacher who did not explain concepts well and contributed to a shaky foundation, or a failed test that contributed to the belief of math failure.

These causes add up over time, encouraged by society's popular view that math is hard and unpleasant. Eventually a person comes to firmly believe that he or she is simply bad at math. This belief makes it difficult to grasp new concepts or even remember old ones. Homework and test grades begin to slip, which only confirms the belief. The poor performance is not due to lack of ability but is caused by math anxiety.

Math anxiety is an emotional issue, not a lack of intelligence. But when it becomes deeply rooted, it can become more than just an emotional problem. Physical symptoms appear. Blood pressure may rise and heartbeat may quicken at the sight of a math problem – or even the thought of math! This fear leads to a mental block. When someone with math anxiety is asked to perform a calculation, even a basic problem can seem overwhelming and impossible. The emotional and physical response to the thought of math prevents the brain from working through it logically.

The more this happens, the more a person's confidence drops, and the more math anxiety is generated. This vicious cycle must be broken!

The first step in breaking the cycle is to go back to very beginning and make sure you really understand the basics of how math works and why it works. It is not enough to memorize rules for multiplication and division. If you don't know WHY these rules work, your foundation will be shaky and you will be at risk of developing a phobia. Understanding mathematical concepts not only promotes confidence and security, but allows you to build on this understanding for new concepts. Additionally, you can solve unfamiliar problems using familiar concepts and processes.

Why is it that students in other countries regularly outperform American students in math? The answer likely boils down to a couple of things: the foundation of mathematical conceptual understanding and societal perception. While students in the US are not expected to *like* or *get* math, in many other nations, students are expected not only to understand math but also to excel at it.

Changing the American view of math that leads to math anxiety is a monumental task. It requires changing the training of teachers nationwide, from kindergarten through high school, so that they learn to teach the *why* behind math and to combat the wrong math views that students may develop. It also involves changing the stigma associated with math, so that it is no longer viewed as unpleasant and incomprehensible. While these are necessary changes, they are challenging and will take time. But in the meantime, math anxiety is not irreversible—it can be faced and defeated, one person at a time.

False Beliefs

One reason math anxiety has taken such hold is that several false beliefs have been created and shared until they became widely accepted. Some of these unhelpful beliefs include the following:

There is only one way to solve a math problem. In the same way that you can choose from different driving routes and still arrive at the same house, you can solve a math problem using different methods and still find the correct answer. A person who understands the reasoning behind math calculations may be able to look at an unfamiliar concept and find the right answer, just by applying logic to the knowledge they already have. This approach may be different than what is taught in the classroom, but it is still valid. Unfortunately, even many teachers view math as a subject where the best course of action is to memorize the rule or process for each problem rather than as a place for students to exercise logic and creativity in finding a solution.

Many people don't have a mind for math. A person who has struggled due to poor teaching or math anxiety may falsely believe that he or she doesn't have the mental capacity to grasp mathematical concepts. Most of the time, this is false. Many people find that when they are relieved of their math anxiety, they have more than enough brainpower to understand math.

Men are naturally better at math than women. Even though research has shown this to be false, many young women still avoid math careers and classes because of their belief that their math abilities are inferior. Many girls have come to believe that math is a male skill and have given up trying to understand or enjoy it.

Counting aids are bad. Something like counting on your fingers or drawing out a problem to visualize it may be frowned on as childish or a crutch, but these devices can help you get a tangible understanding of a problem or a concept.

Sadly, many students buy into these ideologies at an early age. A young girl who enjoys math class may be conditioned to think that she doesn't actually have the brain for it because math is for boys, and may turn her energies to other pursuits, permanently closing the door on a wide range of opportunities. A child who finds the right answer but doesn't follow the teacher's method may believe that he is doing it wrong and isn't good at math. A student who never had a problem with math before may have a poor teacher and become confused, yet believe that the problem is because she doesn't have a mathematical mind.

Students who have bought into these erroneous beliefs quickly begin to add their own anxieties, adapting them to their own personal situations:

I'll never use this in real life. A huge number of people wrongly believe that math is irrelevant outside the classroom. By adopting this mindset, they are handicapping themselves for a life in a mathematical world, as well as limiting their career choices. When they are inevitably faced with real-world math, they are conditioning themselves to respond with anxiety.

I'm not quick enough. While timed tests and quizzes, or even simply comparing yourself with other students in the class, can lead to this belief, speed is not an indicator of skill level. A person can work very slowly yet understand at a deep level.

If I can understand it, it's too easy. People with a low view of their own abilities tend to think that if they are able to grasp a concept, it must be simple. They cannot accept the idea that they are capable of understanding math. This belief will make it harder to learn, no matter how intelligent they are.

I just can't learn this. An overwhelming number of people think this, from young children to adults, and much of the time it is simply not true. But this mindset can turn into a self-fulfilling prophecy that keeps you from exercising and growing your math ability.

The good news is, each of these myths can be debunked. For most people, they are based on emotion and psychology, NOT on actual ability! It will take time, effort, and the desire to change, but change is possible. Even if you have spent years thinking that you don't have the capability to understand math, it is not too late to uncover your true ability and find relief from the anxiety that surrounds math.

Math Strategies

It is important to have a plan of attack to combat math anxiety. There are many useful strategies for pinpointing the fears or myths and eradicating them:

Go back to the basics. For most people, math anxiety stems from a poor foundation. You may think that you have a complete understanding of addition and subtraction, or even decimals and percentages, but make absolutely sure. Learning math is different from learning other subjects. For example, when you learn history, you study various time periods and places and events. It may be important to memorize dates or find out about the lives of famous people. When you move from US history to world history, there will be some overlap, but a large amount of the information will be new. Mathematical concepts, on the other hand, are very closely linked and highly dependent on each other. It's like climbing a ladder – if a rung is missing from your understanding, it may be difficult or impossible for you to climb any higher, no matter how hard you try. So go back and make sure your math foundation is strong. This may mean taking a remedial math course, going to a tutor to work through the shaky concepts, or just going through your old homework to make sure you really understand it.

Speak the language. Math has a large vocabulary of terms and phrases unique to working problems. Sometimes these are completely new terms, and sometimes they are common words, but are used differently in a math setting. If you can't speak the language, it will be very difficult to get a thorough understanding of the concepts. It's common for students to think that they don't understand math when they simply don't understand the vocabulary. The good news is that this is fairly easy to fix. Brushing up on any terms you aren't quite sure of can help bring the rest of the concepts into focus.

Check your anxiety level. When you think about math, do you feel nervous or uncomfortable? Do you struggle with feelings of inadequacy, even on concepts that you know you've already learned? It's important to understand your specific math anxieties, and what triggers them. When you catch yourself falling back on a false belief, mentally replace it with the truth. Don't let yourself believe that you can't learn, or that struggling with a concept means you'll never understand it. Instead, remind yourself of how much you've already learned and dwell on that past success. Visualize grasping the new concept, linking it to your old knowledge, and moving on to the next challenge. Also, learn how to manage anxiety when it arises. There are many techniques for coping with the irrational fears that rise to the surface when you enter the math classroom. This may include controlled breathing, replacing negative thoughts with positive ones, or visualizing success. Anxiety interferes with your ability to concentrate and absorb information, which in turn contributes to greater anxiety. If you can learn how to regain control of your thinking, you will be better able to pay attention, make progress, and succeed!

Don't go it alone. Like any deeply ingrained belief, math anxiety is not easy to eradicate. And there is no need for you to wrestle through it on your own. It will take time, and many people find that speaking with a counselor or psychiatrist helps. They can help you develop strategies for responding to anxiety and overcoming old ideas. Additionally, it can be very helpful to take a short course or seek out a math tutor to help you find and fix the missing rungs on your ladder and make sure that you're ready to progress to the next level. You can also find a number of math aids online: courses that will teach you mental devices for figuring out problems, how to get the most out of your math classes, etc.

Check your math attitude. No matter how much you want to learn and overcome your anxiety, you'll have trouble if you still have a negative attitude toward math. If you think it's too hard, or just have general feelings of dread about math, it will be hard to learn and to break through the anxiety. Work on cultivating a positive math attitude. Remind yourself that math is not just a hurdle to be cleared, but a valuable asset. When you view math with a positive attitude, you'll be much more likely to understand and even enjoy it. This is something you must do for yourself. You may find it helpful to visit with a counselor. Your tutor, friends, and family may cheer you on in your endeavors. But your greatest asset is yourself. You are inside your own mind – tell yourself what you need to hear. Relive past victories. Remind yourself that you are capable of understanding math. Root out any false beliefs that linger and replace them with positive truths. Even if it doesn't feel true at first, it will begin to affect your thinking and pave the way for a positive, anxiety-free mindset.

Aside from these general strategies, there are a number of specific practical things you can do to begin your journey toward overcoming math anxiety. Something as simple as learning a new note-taking strategy can change the way you approach math and give you more confidence and understanding. New study techniques can also make a huge difference.

Math anxiety leads to bad habits. If it causes you to be afraid of answering a question in class, you may gravitate toward the back row. You may be embarrassed to ask for help. And you may procrastinate on assignments, which leads to rushing through them at the last moment when it's too late to get a better understanding. It's important to identify your negative behaviors and replace them with positive ones:

Prepare ahead of time. Read the lesson before you go to class. Being exposed to the topics that will be covered in class ahead of time, even if you don't understand them perfectly, is extremely helpful in increasing what you retain from the lecture. Do your homework and, if you're still shaky, go over some extra problems. The key to a solid understanding of math is practice.

Sit front and center. When you can easily see and hear, you'll understand more, and you'll avoid the distractions of other students if no one is in front of you. Plus, you're more likely to be sitting with students who are positive and engaged, rather than others with math anxiety. Let their positive math attitude rub off on you.

Ask questions in class and out. If you don't understand something, just ask. If you need a more in-depth explanation, the teacher may need to work with you outside of class, but often it's a simple concept you don't quite understand, and a single question may clear it up. If you wait, you may not be able to follow the rest of the day's lesson. For extra help, most professors have office hours outside of class when you can go over concepts one-on-one to clear up any uncertainties. Additionally, there may be a *math lab* or study session you can attend for homework help. Take advantage of this.

Review. Even if you feel that you've fully mastered a concept, review it periodically to reinforce it. Going over an old lesson has several benefits: solidifying your understanding, giving you a confidence boost, and even giving some new insights into material that you're currently learning! Don't let yourself get rusty. That can lead to problems with learning later concepts.

Teaching Tips

While the math student's mindset is the most crucial to overcoming math anxiety, it is also important for others to adjust their math attitudes. Teachers and parents have an enormous influence on how students relate to math. They can either contribute to math confidence or math anxiety.

As a parent or teacher, it is very important to convey a positive math attitude. Retelling horror stories of your own bad experience with math will contribute to a new generation of math anxiety. Even if you don't share your experiences, others will be able to sense your fears and may begin to believe them.

Even a careless comment can have a big impact, so watch for phrases like *He's not good at math* or *I never liked math*. You are a crucial role model, and your children or students will unconsciously adopt your mindset. Give them a positive example to follow. Rather than teaching them to fear the math world before they even know it, teach them about all its potential and excitement.

Work to present math as an integral, beautiful, and understandable part of life. Encourage creativity in solving problems. Watch for false beliefs and dispel them. Cross the lines between subjects: integrate history, English, and music with math. Show students how math is used every day, and how the entire world is based on mathematical principles, from the pull of gravity to the shape of seashells. Instead of letting students see math as a necessary evil, direct them to view it as an imaginative, beautiful art form – an art form that they are capable of mastering and using.

Don't give too narrow a view of math. It is more than just numbers. Yes, working problems and learning formulas is a large part of classroom math. But don't let the teaching stop there. Teach students about the everyday implications of math. Show them how nature works according to the laws of mathematics, and take them outside to make discoveries of their own. Expose them to math-related careers by inviting visiting speakers, asking students to do research and presentations, and learning students' interests and aptitudes on a personal level.

Demonstrate the importance of math. Many people see math as nothing more than a required stepping stone to their degree, a nuisance with no real usefulness. Teach students that algebra is used every day in managing their bank accounts, in following recipes, and in scheduling the day's events. Show them how learning to do geometric proofs helps them to develop logical thinking, an invaluable life skill. Let them see that math surrounds them and is integrally linked to their daily lives: that weather predictions are based on math, that math was used to design cars and other machines, etc. Most of all, give them the tools to use math to enrich their lives.

Make math as tangible as possible. Use visual aids and objects that can be touched. It is much easier to grasp a concept when you can hold it in your hands and manipulate it, rather than just listening to the lecture. Encourage math outside of the classroom. The real world is full of measuring, counting, and calculating, so let students participate in this. Keep your eyes open for numbers and patterns to discuss. Talk about how scores are calculated in sports games and how far apart plants are placed in a garden row for maximum growth. Build the mindset that math is a normal and interesting part of daily life.

Finally, find math resources that help to build a positive math attitude. There are a number of books that show math as fascinating and exciting while teaching important concepts, for example: *The Math Curse; A Wrinkle in Time; The Phantom Tollbooth;* and *Fractals, Googols and Other Mathematical Tales*. You can also find a number of online resources: math puzzles and games, videos that show math in nature, and communities of math enthusiasts. On a local level, students can compete in a variety of math competitions with other schools or join a math club.

The student who experiences math as exciting and interesting is unlikely to suffer from math anxiety. Going through life without this handicap is an immense advantage and opens many doors that others have closed through their fear.

Self-Check

Whether you suffer from math anxiety or not, chances are that you have been exposed to some of the false beliefs mentioned above. Now is the time to check yourself for any errors you may have accepted. Do you think you're not wired for math? Or that you don't need to understand it since you're not planning on a math career? Do you think math is just too difficult for the average person?

Find the errors you've taken to heart and replace them with positive thinking. Are you capable of learning math? Yes! Can you control your anxiety? Yes! These errors will resurface from time to time, so be watchful. Don't let others with math anxiety influence you or sway your confidence. If you're having trouble with a concept, find help. Don't let it discourage you!

Create a plan of attack for defeating math anxiety and sharpening your skills. Do some research and decide if it would help you to take a class, get a tutor, or find some online resources to fine-tune your knowledge. Make the effort to get good nutrition, hydration, and sleep so that you are operating at full capacity. Remind yourself daily that you are skilled and that anxiety does not control you. Your mind is capable of so much more than you know. Give it the tools it needs to grow and thrive.

Tell Us Your Story

We at Mometrix would like to extend our heartfelt thanks to you for letting us be a part of your journey. It is an honor to serve people from all walks of life, people like you, who are committed to building the best future they can for themselves.

We know that each person's situation is unique. But we also know that, whether you are a young student or a mother of four, you care about working to make your own life and the lives of those around you better.

That's why we want to hear your story.

We want to know why you're taking this test. We want to know about the trials you've gone through to get here. And we want to know about the successes you've experienced after taking and passing your test.

In addition to your story, which can be an inspiration both to us and to others, we value your feedback. We want to know both what you loved about our book and what you think we can improve on.

The team at Mometrix would be absolutely thrilled to hear from you! So please, send us an email at tellusyourstory@mometrix.com or visit us at mometrix.com/tellusyourstory.php and let's stay in touch.

Additional Bonus Material

Due to our efforts to try to keep this book to a manageable length, we've created a link that will give you access to all of your additional bonus material.

> Please visit http://www.mometrix.com/bonus948/nystceatas to access the information.